FOCUS

ON COLLEGE AND CAREER SUCCESS

FOCUS

ON COLLEGE AND CAREER SUCCESS

Second Edition

Steve Staley
Colorado Technical University

Constance Staley
University of Colorado, Colorado Springs

Australia • Brazil • Mexico • Singapore • United Kingdom • United States

CENGAGE
Learning·

FOCUS on College and Career Success,
Second Edition
Steve Staley and Constance Staley

Senior Product Manager: Shani Fisher

Content Developer: Damaris Curran Herlihy

Content Coordinator: Rebecca Donahue

Market Development Manager: Josh Adams

Marketing Director: Jennifer Levanduski

Senior Media Developer: Amy Gibbons

Senior Content Project Manager: Jessica Rasile

Production Manager: Elena Montillo

Senior Art Director: Pam Galbreath

Rights Acquisition Specialist:
Shalice Shah-Caldwell

Manufacturing Planner: Sandee Milewski

Production Service/Compositor: MPS Limited

Cover Designer: Lisa Delgado

Cover Image: © Radius Images / Alamy;
© Yuri Arcurs/Shutterstock.com; © kurhan/
Shutterstock.com; © Lane Oatey/Blue jean
Images/Corbis; © BlueMoon Stock / Alamy

For product information and technology assistance, contact us at
Cengage Learning Customer & Sales Support, 1-800-354-9706

For permission to use material from this text or product,
submit all requests online at **www.cengage.com/permissions**
Further permissions questions can be emailed to
permissionrequest@cengage.com

Library of Congress Control Number: 2013949206

ISBN-13: 978-1-4354-6237-3

ISBN-10: 1-4354-6237-8

Cengage Learning
20 Channel Center Street
Boston, MA 02210
USA

Cengage Learning is a leading provider of customized learning solutions with office locations around the globe, including Singapore, the United Kingdom, Australia, Mexico, Brazil and Japan. Locate your local office at **international.cengage.com/region.**

Cengage Learning products are represented in Canada by Nelson Education, Ltd.

For your course and learning solutions, visit **www.cengage.com.**

Purchase any of our products at your local college store or at our preferred online store **www.cengagebrain.com.**

Instructors: Please visit **login.cengage.com** and log in to access instructor-specific resources.

Printed in the United States of America
2 3 4 5 6 7 17 16 15 14

Brief Contents

Contents

chapter 1 — Getting the Right Start 1

chapter 2 — Building Dreams, Setting Goals 29

chapter 3 — Learning Styles and Studying 49

chapter 4 — Managing Your Time, Energy, and Money 81

Acknowledgments

It's been said that "Achievement is a *we* thing, not a *me* thing, always the product of many heads and hands." There are so many people to thank that this acknowledgements section could be as long as a chapter of *FOCUS*! However, here we'll at least mention those who have contributed the most, including all the students over the last thirty-five-plus years who have taught us more than we've ever taught them.

Family Let us start at the center of our lives. Our daughters, Shannon and Stephanie, help bring some much-needed balance to our lives. And aside from being the most adorable children on the planet, our grandtwins, Aidan and Ailie, have been a living learning laboratory for us. As children mastering one new thing after another, they truly have taught us about of the pure joy of learning. And to our beautiful mothers, Elizabeth and Evelyn, who lovingly alternated between urging us to "slow down and relax" and "hurry up and finish," heartfelt thanks to both of you for all your motherly love.

Reviewers The list of reviewers who have contributed their insights and expertise to *FOCUS on College and Career Success* is long. Our heartfelt thanks to the reviewers who helped inform the second edition revisions: Trish Elley, Colorado Technical University; Karen Ernst, Colorado Technical University; Maryann Errico, Georgia Perimeter College; Mel Ervi, Lamar University; Deborah Horant, Colorado Technical University; La-Dana Jenkins, Borough of Manhattan Community College; Nohra Levy, Miami Dade College; Irene Moksha, SWFC- Southwest Florida College; Robin Ouzts, Thomas Universtiy; Chris Schnupp, St. Paul; Bernard Stancati, Colorado Technical University; Marci Twombly, Colorado Technical University; Ruth Williams, Southwest Florida College.

We'd be remiss to ignore the valuable input gained from reviewers of the previous edition of *FOCUS on College and Career Success* that helped shape this book: Craig Baranovic, Remington College; Virginia Ann Berent, Gallipolis Career College; James Booker, Remington College; Jennifer Cooper, The Art Institute of Pittsburgh Online Division; Angelina Dale, Goodwin College; Annette Davis, Madison College; Mominka Fileva, Davenport University; Andrea Goldstein, South University; Evelyn Hyde, Brown Mackie College-Salina; Laura Ristrom Goodman, Pima Medical Institute; Kevin Kelly, Andover College; Forrest Marston, Sanford Brown Institute Tampa; Gurmeet Mohem, Heald College; Kelley Montford, Colorado Technical University; Katrina Neckuty-Fodness, Globe University; Debra Olsen, Madison Area Technical College; Vickie Saling, Heald College; John Smith, Corinthian Colleges, Inc; Kristen Smith, Hallmark College; Camilla Swain-LeDoux, Ivy Tech Community College, Evansville; Cynthia Vessel, Northwestern College; Pamela Walker, Northwestern College; Pamela White, Springfield Technical Community College.

The Cengage Team No book, of course, gets very far without a publisher, and *FOCUS* has had the best publishing team imaginable: the dynamic, highly people-skilled Annie Todd, Product Director; the best-in-the industry, innovative, energetic Shani Fisher, Senior Product Manager; the meticulous and multitalented Damaris Curran Herlihy, Content Developer; true professionals who combed pages and probably did more than we'll ever know, Jessica Rasille, Content Project Manager, and Ed Dionne, Project Manager at MPS Limited; Content Coordinator, Rebecca Donahue, for her work on all the outstanding supplements to *FOCUS*; and the obviously talented Art Director, Pam Galbreath. We'd like to especially thank Larry Harwood, the master photographer who took photos of the *FOCUS* cast on the University of Colorado at Colorado Springs campus. And heartfelt thanks to Annie Mitchell and Sean Wakely, who believed in this project from the very start at Wadsworth; Sylvia Shepherd, whose creative vision shaped much of the first *FOCUS* book, and Lauren Larsen, whose wit and wisdom formed the basis for several of the original early chapters.

Other Contributors   We'd also particularly like to thank the "*FOCUS* All-Stars," as we call them, who modeled for the photo shoots and starred in the "Inside the *FOCUS* Studio" videos. They followed artistic direction like pros, and they make this book unique. We'd also like to thank our colleagues at CTU and UCCS who have helped us develop many of the ideas in this book, whether they know it or not—all the Academic and Career Success faculty and the Freshman Seminar faculty past and present. We also can't go without thanking the many authors who granted us permission to use their work and three essential scholars who allowed us to use, apply, and extend their instruments throughout the book: Neil Fleming, Brian French, and John Bransford. And thanks to our brilliant CTU faculty colleague Karen Ernst for helping us update the Instructor's Manual. In addition, special thanks to Aren Moore, who worked with us to create the "props" for each chapter's opening case study, and the dynamic, groundbreaking, multimedia *FOCUS*points for each chapter. And finally, we'd like to thank Matt McClain, the comedy writer who brought his innovative humor to the learning process through podcast summaries of the chapters and television scripts for the website TV shows. He took the "big ideas" from *FOCUS* chapters and made them memorable to students by using their own best loved media.

Above all, *FOCUS* has taught both of us truly to focus. Writing a book takes the same kind of endurance and determination that it takes to get a college degree. Our empathy level for our students has, if anything, increased—and we are thankful for all we've learned while writing. It has been a cathartic experience to see what has filled each computer screen as we've tapped, tapped, tapped away, reviewed each other's work, and made decisions on the final product. Ultimately, what we have chosen to put into each chapter has told us a great deal about who we are what we know (and don't), and what we value. There's no doubt: we are better teachers for having written this book. May all our readers grow through their *FOCUS* experience, too.

Meet the Cast

Chapter 1: Dexter Lewis / Branden

Larry Harwood Photography.

Hometown: Colorado Springs, Colorado

Major: Communication

Lessons Learned: Branden knows some of the problems challenging his character, Dexter Lewis, and is learning the importance of facing those problems head on.

Toughest First-Year Class: Economics, because of the challenge of the course, his fear of the subject, and not studying the material enough.

Advice to New Students: "Don't bury your head in the sand and don't procrastinate. Whether it's dealing with how to pay for college, studying, scheduling your time or anything else – putting things off until the last minute or hoping that 'they will just work themselves out' is a recipe for disaster. The little bit of time it takes to organize, to make a phone call, to talk to a professor, or to budget for your college expenses will pay off BIG TIME, giving you greater peace of mind when it counts and greatly aiding in your college success and overall experience."

Free Time: Groups and activities on campus, playing video games with friends, playing ultimate Frisbee or volleyball outside the dorms, or going out to the movies.

Helpful Study Apps: "I couldn't survive without my cell phone calendar. I schedule everything."

Chapter 2: Sylvia Sanchez / Alycia

© Larry Harwood Photography. Property of Cengage Learning.

Hometown: I've lived all over Colorado. I consider the whole state to be my hometown!

Major: Nursing with a minor in psychology

Lessons Learned: Alycia is still learning lessons about college. She keeps growing and discovering new things about herself and has made lifelong friends. She plans to remember college as the best years of her life!

Toughest First-Year Class: Anatomy ... It was hard to study *all* the time.

Advice to New Students: "Listen to your heart; it will lead you to the right place. Take every opportunity that comes to you because college is about finding out who you are and what you want from life."

Chapter 3: Tammy Ko / Jessica

© Larry Harwood Photography. Property of Cengage Learning.

Hometown: Manitou Springs, Colorado

Major: Marketing

Lessons Learned: Juggling a part-time job while in school, Jessica loved meeting new people, but she regretted not talking to other students about which instructors and courses to take toward her marketing major. In order to succeed, she says, you've "gotta give it all you've got!"

Toughest First-Year Class: Microeconomics because it wasn't like high school courses that just required memorizing a lot of facts.

Advice to New Students: "Talk to other students to learn about the best instructors, and make sure you are studying something that you are interested in."

Chapter 4: Derek Johnson / Derrick

© Larry Harwood Photography. Property of Cengage Learning.

Hometown: Colorado Springs, Colorado

Major: Communications/Recording Arts

Lessons Learned: Even though he's not married and has no children, Derrick and his case study character have much in common—too much to do and too little time! Derrick felt his biggest mistake in college was not asking enough questions in class. He knows now he should ask for clarity on content or assignments he doesn't understand.

Toughest First-Year Class: English because he and his instructor had differing opinions, but he communicated through the tough spots and earned an "A."

Advice to New Students: "Surround yourself with positive people. As the saying goes, 'You are the company you keep.' I've seen many of my friends drop out because the people they called friends were holding them back from their full potential."

Free Time: composing music and producing films

Chapter 5: Desiree Moore / Regina

Hometown: Colorado Springs, Colorado

Major: MA Communication

Lessons Learned: Organization, time management, study groups, and note cards

Toughest First-Year Course: Psychology because in this class I had to be very organized to keep my notes in order. There were only two exams in this class during the entire semester. I did not organize my notes or my time very well.

Advice to New Students: "Get to know your professors, ask questions, and have a study buddy."

Free Time: In my free time, I work out at the gym. I also spend quality time with my son.

Chapter 6: Dario Jones / Orlando

Hometown: Fountain, Colorado

Major: MA, Communication

Lessons Learned: Start strong, work hard, and finish strong

Toughest First-Year Course: Math 099

Advice to New Students: "Get to know your instructors and fellow classmates. Ask questions in class when you're not sure about something."

Free Time: What free time? To relax, I listen to jazz or classical music, or I'll channel surf until I find something interesting to watch.

Chapter 7: Rachel White / Shannon

Hometown: Denver, Colorado

Major: Philosophy

Lessons Learned: Go to class!

Toughest First-Year Course: Intro to Geography (it might have been easier if I'd gone to class).

Advice to New Students: "Balance fun and schoolwork, so you don't get burned out on either one!"

Free Time: Acting and improv

©Larry Harwood Photography. Property of Cengage Learning.

Chapter 8: Katie Alexander / Christina

Hometown: Colorado Springs, Colorado. Because she went to college in her hometown, Christina really enjoyed the opportunity college provided to meet new people.

Major: Nursing

Lessons Learned: Spending her free time with her friends watching movies, going bowling or dancing, and just hanging out, Christina found that like her *FOCUS* Challenge Case character, she, too, would make up excuses to get out of studying and doing her homework. She quickly learned the importance of reading and taking notes. "As weird as it may sound, reading cuts your end study time by more than half. Reading the material ahead of time helps you understand everything so much better."

Advice to New Students: "Stay motivated. College is going to *fly* by! If you stay motivated and get good grades, it really will be over before you know it."

© Larry Harwood Photography. Property of Cengage Learning.

Chapter 9: Kevin Baxter / Dave

Hometown: St. Paul, Minnesota

Background: Portraying a student returning to school after fifteen-plus years in the working world, Dave is currently a professor of chemistry at University of Colorado at Colorado Springs.

College Memories: Dave remembers how much he liked the different social environment college provided after graduating from high school.

Toughest First-Year Course: English Composition because writing wasn't exactly his forte.

Advice to New Students: "Study hard, and use your time wisely."

Free Time: Woodworking, hiking, and climbing

© Larry Harwood Photography. Property of Cengage Learning.

Chapter 10: Serena Jackson / Queen

Hometown: Denver, Colorado

Major: Nursing

Toughest First-Year Course: Biology, because the way the class was taught in college (lecture-based) was very different than the way classes were taught in high school. She had to learn on her own what material was most important to study.

Lessons Learned: Queen wishes she had gone to more study groups and devoted more of her time to subjects that she struggled with in order to be more successful. She also would have asked for help from professors since she now realizes they are fully ready to help a student become better in their class.

Advice to New Students: "Make the most out of your college years. Make new friends because they could be great resources in the future. Also, if your professor tells you to read something, make sure you read the entire thing and you are able to teach it back to them because that will help your grade."

Free Time: Hanging out with friends, participating in club events, and volunteering

Helpful Study Apps: Quizlet, Learnsmart, and Study Blue help Queen study for upcoming quizzes and exams.

© Larry Harwood Photography. Property of Cengage Learning.

Chapter 11: Ethan Cole / Josh

Hometown: Fort Morgan, Colorado

Major: Sociology

Lessons Learned: Like his *FOCUS* Challenge Case character, Josh noticed that he, too, didn't always push himself to reach his potential. But he learned through his first-year seminar course that he is responsible for himself and that instructors aren't like high school teachers. They will let you fail a class if you don't do what you need to. It's up to you.

Advice to New Students: "Not only did getting involved on campus help me have more fun in school, but it has also helped me academically. It has taught me how to manage my time and has made it so much easier for me to participate with confidence in class. Just make sure you get what you need to do done, and you will enjoy your college experience so much more."

Free Time: "Free time? What's that?! I'm too busy to have free time!" (But he secretly admits he snowboards, plays guitar, draws, and spends time with friends.)

Chapter 12: Anthony Lopez / Luis

© Larry Harwood Photography. Property of Cengage Learning.

Hometown: Aguascalientes, Mexico

Major: Spanish with an emphasis on secondary education

Lessons Learned: Luis is extremely involved on campus and within his community—he is President of the Association of Future Teachers, sings with his church choir, plays intramural soccer, and works for the Air Force on weekends. Luis thinks one mistake he made in his first term was that he procrastinated with homework because his new freedom let him think he could have fun first and study later, but he quickly learned he was wrong.

Advice to New Students: "Be smart and be involved, but always do your homework first. If you are involved on campus, you will meet people that will help make your college experience easier and more fun."

MEET THE AUTHOR: Steve Staley

Used by permission of Steve Staley.

Hometowns: Watford City, North Dakota, for his first five years; then Seattle, Washington, through high school graduation.

Background: Steve has taught at the U.S. Air Force Academy and Colorado Technical University after earning a B.S. in International Relations, an M.A. in National Security and Strategic Studies, and an M.A. and Ph.D. in English Language and Literature.

College Memories: Steve loved both the sciences and the humanities and had a hard time deciding which direction to choose. Most important memories? Great friends and rewarding activities, including singing in his college chorale.

Advice to New Students: "During hard times, remember that 'Attitude is Everything'! Look for what you can learn from each experience, and keep thinking about how to apply your college experiences to your future career success."

Free Time: Reading, fly fishing, traveling, family time, and working with other faculty on helping students be the best they can be during their college years.

MEET THE AUTHOR: Constance Staley

© Larry Harwood Photography. Property of Cengage Learning.

Hometown: Pittsburgh, Pennsylvania (although she never actually lived there. Instead, she lived all over the world and went to ten schools in twelve years.)

Background: Connie has taught at the University of Colorado at Colorado Springs for more than 35 years after getting a bachelor's degree in education, a master's degree in linguistics, and a Ph.D. in communication.

College Memories: Connie remembers loving her public speaking class as a first-year student and having tons of friends, but being extremely homesick for her family.

Advice to New Students: "Earning a college degree is hard work, takes a long time, and requires a substantial investment of your time, energy, and resources. But it's the best investment you can make in your own future—one you'll never regret."

Free Time: Spending time with her husband, her two daughters, and her boy/girl grandtwins; relaxing at her cabin in the mountains; and traveling around the country to speak to other professors who also care about first-year students and their success.

Introduction to Students

Dear Reader,

This book is different. It won't coerce, coddle, caution, or coax you. Instead, it will give *you* the tools you need to coach yourself. Ultimately, this book is about you, your college career, and your career beyond college. It's about the future you will create for yourself.

FOCUS on College and Career Success stars a cast of our own students, several colleagues, and one of our daughters, like a stage play. One student "actor" is featured in each chapter's opening case study. All twelve cast members reappear throughout the book, so that you'll get to know them as you read. We've been teaching for a combined total of more than seventy years now and worked with thousands of students. Each case study is about a real student (with a fictitious name) that we've worked with or a mixture of several students. You may find you have some things in common with them. But whether you do or not, I hope they will make this book come to life for you.

We both love what we do, and we care deeply about students. We hope that comes through to you as a reader. You'll see that we've inserted some of our own personalities had a bit of fun at times, and tried to create a new kind of textbook for you. In our view, learning should be engaging, personal, memorable, challenging, and fun.

Most importantly, we know that these next few years hold the key to unlock much of what you want from your life. And from all our years of experience and research, we can tell you straightforwardly that what you read in this book works. It gets results. It can turn you into a better, faster learner. *Really?,* you ask. Really! The only thing you have to do is put all the words in this book into action. That's where the challenge comes in.

Becoming an educated person takes time, energy, resources, and focus. At times, it may mean shutting down the six windows you have open on your computer, and focusing all your attention to one thing in laser-like fashion. It may mean disciplining yourself to dig in and stick with something until you've nailed it. Can you do it? We're betting you can, or we wouldn't have written this book. Invest yourself fully in what you read here, and then decide to incorporate it into your life. If there's one secret to college success, that's it.

So, you're off! You're about to begin one of the most fascinating, liberating, challenging, and adventure-filled times of your life. We may not be able to meet each one of you personally, but we *can* wish you well, wherever you are. We hope this book helps you on your journey.

Steve Staley   *Constance Staley*

INFORMATION ABOUT YOU

Name _____

Student Number _____   Course/Section _____

Instructor _____

Gender _____   Age _____

> Although you may not have experienced life as a new college student for long, we're interested in how you expect to spend your time, what challenges you think you'll face, and your general views of what you think college will be like. Please answer thoughtfully.

Your Background

1. **Ethnic Identification (check all that apply):**

   ____ American Indian or Alaska Native   ____ Native Hawaiian or Other Pacific Islander   ____ Asian

   ____ Hispanic/Latino   ____ Black or African American   ____ White

   ____ Mixed Race (for example, one Caucasian parent and one Asian)   ____ Prefer not to answer

2. **Is English your first (native) language?**

   ____ yes   ____ no

3. **Did your parents graduate from college?**

   ____ yes, both   ____ yes, father only   ____ yes, mother only   ____ neither   ____ not sure

Your Previous School Experience

4. **If you are entering college soon after completing high school, on average, how many total hours per week did you spend studying outside of class in high school?**

   ____ 0–5   ____ 6–10   ____ 11–15   ____ 16–20   ____ 21–25
   ____ 26–30   ____ 31–35   ____ 36–40   ____ 40+   ____ I am a returning student and attended high school some time ago.

5. **What was your high school grade point average when you graduated?**

   ____ A+   ____ A   ____ A–   ____ B+   ____ B
   ____ B–   ____ C+   ____ C   ____ C–   ____ D or lower
   ____ I don't remember.   ____ I earned a GED.

6. **Did you go to college elsewhere before enrolling in this one?**

   ____ yes   ____ no   ____ I've attended more than one other college.

Information About This Semester/Quarter

7. How many credit hours are you taking this term?

____ 6 or fewer   ____ 7–11   ____ 12–14   ____ 15–16   ____ 17 or more

8. Where are you living this term?

____ with my immediate family   ____ with a relative other than my immediate family

____ on my own   ____ other (please explain)

Working While in College

9. In addition to going to college, do you expect to work for pay at a job (or jobs) this term?

____ yes   ____ no

10. If so, how many hours per week do you expect to work?

____ 1–10   ____ 11–20   ____ 21–30   ____ 31–40   ____ 40+

YOUR COLLEGE EXPECTATIONS
Your Reasons and Predictions

11. Why did you decide to go to college? (Check all that apply.)

____ because I want to build a better life for myself.   ____ because I want to build a better life for my family.

____ because I want to be well off financially in the future.   ____ because I need a college education to achieve my dreams.

____ because my friends were going to college.   ____ because my family encouraged me to go.

____ because it was expected of me.   ____ because I want to prepare for a *new* career.

____ because I want to continue learning.   ____ because the career I am pursuing requires a degree.

____ because I was unsure of what I might do instead.   ____ other (please explain) _____

12. How do you expect to learn best in college? (Check all that apply.)

____ by looking at charts, maps, graphs   ____ by looking at color-coded information   ____ by looking at symbols and graphics

____ by listening to instructors' lectures   ____ by listening to other students during in-class discussions   ____ by talking about course content with friends or family

____ by reading books   ____ by writing papers   ____ by taking notes

____ by going on field trips   ____ by engaging in activities   ____ by actually doing things

13. The following sets of opposite descriptive phrases are separated by five blank lines. Put an X on the line between the two that best represent your response, like this: For me, high school was easy _____:___X___:_____:_____:_____ hard

I expect my first term of college to:

challenge me academically	____:____:____:____:____	be easy
be very different from high school	____:____:____:____:____	be a lot like high school
be exciting	____:____:____:____:____	be dull
be interesting	____:____:____:____:____	be uninteresting
motivate me to continue	____:____:____:____:____	discourage me
be fun	____:____:____:____:____	be boring
help me feel a part of this school	____:____:____:____:____	make me feel like an outsider

14. How many total hours per week do you expect to study outside of class for your college courses?

____ 0–5	____ 6–10	____ 11–15	____ 16–20	____ 21–25
____ 26–30	____ 31–35	____ 36–40	____ 40+	

15. What do you expect your grade point average to be at the end of your first term of college?

____ A+	____ A	____ A−	____ B+	____ B
____ B−	____ C+	____ C	____ C−	____ D or lower

Your Strengths, Personality, and Interests

16. Please identify your *strengths*—personal characteristics that will contribute to your college success. (Check all that apply.)

____ a. I am good at building relationships.

____ b. I can usually convince others to follow my plan.

____ c. I like to win.

____ d. I work toward future goals.

____ e. I like to be productive and get things done.

____ f. I have a positive outlook on life.

____ g. I'm usually the person who gets things going.

____ h. I enjoy the challenge of learning new things.

____ i. I am focused.

____ j. I can usually look at a problem and figure out a plan of action.

____ k. I work to keep everyone happy.

____ l. I'm a take-charge kind of person.

____ m. I help other people develop their talents and skills.

____ n. I'm a very responsible person.

____ o. I can analyze a situation and see various ways things might work out.

____ p. I usually give tasks my best effort.

17. How confident are you in yourself in each of the following areas? (1 = very confident, 5 = not at all confident)

____ overall academic ability

____ mathematical skills

____ leadership ability

____ reading skills

____ public speaking skills

____ study skills

____ technology skills

____ physical well being

____ writing skills

____ social skills

____ emotional well being

____ teamwork skills

18. For each of the following pairs of descriptors, which set sounds most like you? (Please choose between the two options on each line and place a check mark by your choice.)

____ Extraverted and outgoing   or   ____ Introverted and quiet

____ Detail-oriented and practical   or   ____ Big-picture and future-oriented

____ Rational and truthful   or   ____ People-oriented and tactful

____ Organized and self-disciplined   or   ____ Spontaneous and flexible

19. *FOCUS* is about twelve different aspects of college life. Which are you most interested in applying to yourself in your academic work? (Check all that apply.)

____ Getting the right start

____ Building dreams, setting goals

____ Managing time, energy, and money

____ Learning online

____ Reading, writing, and presenting

____ Building relationships, valuing diversity

____ Learning styles and studying

____ Thinking critically and creatively

____ Engaging, listening, and note-taking in class

____ Developing memory, taking tests

____ Choosing a college major and career

____ Creating a future

Your Challenges

20. Of the twelve aspects of college life identified in the previous question, which do you expect to be most challenging to apply to yourself in your academic work? (Check all that apply.)

_____ Getting the right start

_____ Building dreams, setting goals

_____ Managing time, energy, and money

_____ Learning online

_____ Reading, writing, and presenting

_____ Building relationships, valuing diversity

_____ Learning styles and studying

_____ Thinking critically and creatively

_____ Engaging, listening, and note-taking in class

_____ Developing memory, taking tests

_____ Choosing a college major and career

_____ Creating a future

21. Which one of your current classes do you expect to find most challenging this term and why?

Which class? (course title _or_ department and course number) _____

Why? _____

Do you expect to succeed in this course? _____ yes _____ no _____ Perhaps (please explain): _____

22. Please mark your _top three areas of concern_ relating to your first term of college by placing 1, 2, and 3 next to the items you choose (with 1 representing your top concern).

_____ I might not fit in.

_____ I might have difficulty making friends.

_____ I might not be academically successful.

_____ My performance might disappoint my family.

_____ My personal life might interfere with my studies.

_____ My studies might interfere with my personal life.

_____ I might have financial difficulties.

_____ My job might interfere with my studies.

_____ My studies might interfere with my job.

_____ My social life might interfere with my studies.

_____ My studies might interfere with my social life.

_____ My instructors might not care about me as an individual.

_____ I might not finish my degree.

_____ I might not manage my time well.

_____ I might be bored in my classes.

_____ I might feel intimidated by my instructors.

_____ I might feel overwhelmed by all I have to do.

_____ other (please explain)_____

Your Future

23. How certain are you now of the following (1 = totally sure, 5 = totally unsure)?

_____ Finishing your degree or certificate

_____ Finishing your degree or certificate at this school

_____ Sticking with the major you've chosen

_____ Continuing on to work toward a bachelor's or advanced degree

24. What are you most looking forward to in college?

25. Describe the best outcomes you hope for at the end of this first semester/quarter. Do you expect to achieve them? Why or why not?

FOCUS

ON COLLEGE AND CAREER SUCCESS

Getting the Right Start

READINESS CHECK

How this chapter relates to YOU

1. When it comes to getting the right start in college, what are you most unsure about, if anything?

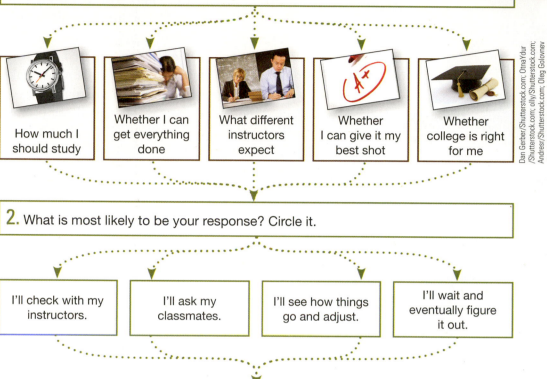

| How much I should study | Whether I can get everything done | What different instructors expect | Whether I can give it my best shot | Whether college is right for me |

2. What is most likely to be your response? Circle it.

| I'll check with my instructors. | I'll ask my classmates. | I'll see how things go and adjust. | I'll wait and eventually figure it out. |

3. What would you have to do to increase your likelihood of success? Will you do it this term?

Example: Find out now before it's too late. Yes!

How YOU will relate to this chapter

What are you most interested in learning about? Put check marks by those topics.

☐ Who goes to a career college and why

☐ What different types of degrees are available

☐ How to connect academic and career professionalism

☐ Why developmental courses are important

☐ How to master a syllabus

☐ Why college success courses work

● How motivated are you to learn more about getting the right start in college? (5 = high, 1 = low) ____

● How ready are you to read now? ____ (If something is in your way, take care of it if you can. Zero in and focus.)

● How long do you think it will take you to complete this chapter? If you start and stop, keep track of your overall time. ____ hour(s) ____ minutes

DEXTER LEWIS

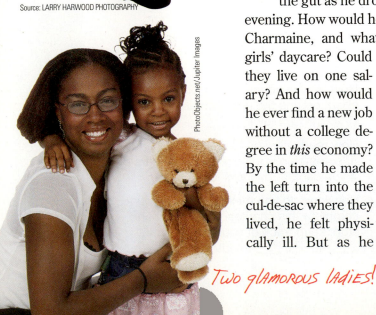

Source: LARRY HARWOOD PHOTOGRAPHY

Dexter Lewis was a solid, hard-working, good guy who impressed people. He impressed his high school teachers with his work ethic. He impressed the football recruiters who invited him to play big-time football in college. He even dropped out of college after a year to serve his country in Iraq. When he returned, he got married, had two kids, and did all the "right" things, like working his way up the ranks at a big box store to get a managerial job. Most of his days were frantically stressful, but at the end of the day, he usually felt pretty good about things. His boss always commented that Dexter was truly respected by the people who worked for him. They saw him as a true professional.

That's why it seemed so unfair when things suddenly took a nosedive. The announcement came at 10 A.M. on a Friday morning: the chain would close 300 stores nationally, and his was one of them. A wave of panic hit him in the gut as he drove home that evening. How would he tell his wife, Charmaine, and what about their girls' daycare? Could they live on one salary? And how would he ever find a new job without a college degree in *this* economy? By the time he made the left turn into the cul-de-sac where they lived, he felt physically ill. But as he approached the house, Dexter saw the girls playing in the front yard. He knew he'd have to put on a good face.

Amazingly, Charmaine was completely calm when he told her. *No problem,* she said. *We'll tighten our belts, and you'll get a college degree in management. You've got some good experience behind you, and we'll find a program with some online courses.* Although he'd been dreading the conversation all the way home, Charmaine seemed to have a ready-made solution. Come to think of it, Charmaine's ability to think through problems and arrive at good solutions was one of the things Dexter had always admired most about

PhotoObjects.net/Jupiter Images

Two glamorous ladies!

The Daily Times

SECTION 3

BUSINESS NEWS

LOCAL CHAIN CLOSES, 180 JOBS GO

By Arthur Snyder, Daily Times writer -GREAT BLUFFS, CO-- More local bad news, as another familiar chain closes its doors. Approximately 180 local employees are to be affected by the closures of all 14 state-wide locations, according to a statement released today. In an interview with Kevin Hoffman, Senior Vice President, he reports, "The marketplace is very difficult, given competition from web-based retailers, compounded by a number of other current factors, including high retail rent costs and lower- priced discounters. All stores reported losses throughout the last calendar year, which led to this latest decision.

Juanita Ramirez, a long-time employee, said this morning in an interview with The Daily News, "My husband was laid off last year, and my son has been looking for a job for six months with no luck. These are difficult times, and now that I'm going to be laid off, too, we're going to have to do something to survive. At the moment, however, I'm not sure what that's going to be." Others expressed similar concerns. "When are new businesses going to move to Great Bluffs? It's a good community with solid citizens and tourism potential."

See CHAIN, Page 8

© iStockphoto.com/RapidEye

her. Her "cooler head" prevailed, so he followed her advice and enrolled that week in an online course to earn a bachelor's degree in management.

As time went on, however, one nagging question bothered him: *was it a good solution?* At midnight on a Thursday, as he was posting to the class portal in Introduction to Managerial Practice, he put his finger on some of the things that were beginning to worry him. Was a management degree what he really wanted? Considering his family responsibilities, would a certificate or an associate's degree be better? Did he really need a bachelor's degree? And just because he had been a manager in a large chain store, was he stuck in the management field? He found it hard to stay focused, and frankly, he sometimes questioned how much he was learning. He didn't always find his online classmates' work to be all that professional. Some of them obviously didn't have any experience in management or even generally in life, and their class posts showed it. In fact, it seemed as if some of them were just getting a degree to get a degree because they couldn't find a job. But then in some ways that was true of him, too. Questions like these made it hard for him to keep his mind on his schoolwork.

Above all, Dexter wanted to be a solid, hard-working, good guy who impressed people, not only on the job but in college, too. He wanted to live up to other people's expectations of him—and his own expectations of himself. He just had some important questions to sort out first.

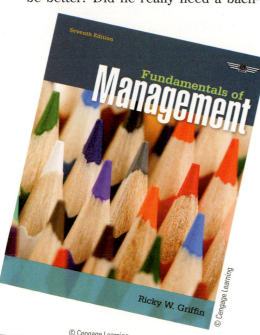

Seventh Edition

Fundamentals of Management

Ricky W. Griffin

Introduction to Managerial Pract
Class Syllabus

Class: BUS 1004 - Online
Instructor: Baker, David   **Office:** N304   **Ph:** 867-5308
Dates/Times: ONLINE

Course Objectives - to develop an understanding of:
- Management Theory
- Organizational Culture
- The Elements of Management
- Management versus Leadership
- Dispute Resolution

Class Structure and Grading:

Online Test #1
Online Test #2

100 points

GREAT BLUFFS TECHNICAL COLLEGE
Learn at your peak.™

GBTC

About GBTC   Academics   New Students   Campus Events   Press Releases   e-TC   Webmail

Search Site for Keywords   GO

http://www.gbtc.edu

🏠 HOME > ACADEMICS > ONLINE CLASSES

- About Online Classes
- Enrolling into Online Classes
- Preparing for Your Online Classes
- Starting Your Class
- Blackboard Vista Student Tutorial
- Online Tech Support
- Username & Password

e-TC   GREAT BLUFFS TECHNICAL COLLEGE

Courses for Fall 2014

Great Bluffs Technical College Blackboard Tutorial

Welcome to the Great Bluffs Technical College Blackboard Learning system.

To go through this tutorial, click on the arrows at the bottom of each page. The last page will gin to your the Vista login page so that you can lo gin to your class. You will not be able to login until the first day of your class, beginning at 8:00 a.m. Are you ready to go?

Let's get started!

1. What are some of the advantages of going back to college after a life-changing experience, like being laid off? What are some of the challenges?

2. In your experience, what are some of the main academic differences between high school and college? How did you read and study in high school, and how do you think that will change in college?

3. What are some of the similarities and differences between the academic professionalism required in college and the career professionalism required in the workplace?

4. Some students, like Dexter, drop out of college and then return some years later. What strengths might these returning college students bring with them—strengths that a student coming to college from high school might not have cultivated yet?

You're in College Now

academic having to do with education

Congratulations! You're in college. You've just started a new chapter of your life! As the saying goes, "The first step toward getting somewhere is to decide that you are not going to stay where you are." In choosing to go to college, that's what you've decided. You're *not* going to stay where you are. Your journey has begun. This chapter will launch you on your journey to professional career achievement by covering the basics. You may already know much of this information, but not everyone does. So, let's start at the beginning.

Why do people like Dexter Lewis go to a professional, career, or technical college? Generally, people go to college to improve their skills or gain completely new ones. Often, students are aiming at specific careers and choose the school and their academic majors in order to get a good start in that career. Many career and technical college students differ from traditional college students in ways like these: they attend school part-time, support themselves, work full-time, are single parents, waited to go on to college, or got their high school degrees in nonstandard ways. (In fact, if you don't yet have a high school diploma or **GED**, your college may be able to help you with that.)

GED stands for **g**eneral **e**duca-tion **d**evelopment; passing these tests is an alternative to earning a traditional high school diploma

© Larry Harwood Photography. Property of Cengage Learning.

> **Reason 1: Transitioning from High School to College.** If you just finished high school, you may see college as the obvious next step. Like Dexter when he graduated high school, you'll find college to be a very different game. Think

> **First say to yourself what you would be; and then do what you have to do.**
>
> *Epictetus, Greek philosopher, 55–135* A.D.

marketplace of ideas a place where many ideas are exchanged freely

of it this way: some students arrive at college, playing what they think is a decent game of checkers. But they quickly discover that their instructors expect them to play chess. They've been successful in high school, and to the inexperienced eye, college looks like the same game board. After all, school is school, right? Wrong! These new students quickly discover that college is a new game with different rules!

Other students you know may have gone off to college somewhere else. But you considered things like cost and convenience and chose a college in your own community, one that offered the convenience of online courses as well as personal support from faculty, advising, and financial aid. A career or technical college is a *real* college—a **marketplace of ideas**, where you can try out all kinds of new things. A career college that focuses on practical experience, on good teaching, and on *you,* can be a great place to be.

For some, a career or technical college can be a great place to test the waters. You may want to see if college is right for you at this point in your life. After you get into the rhythm of your classes, you may decide you've made a good decision. Or you may decide to wait until your life is less complicated or your head is in the right place. (That's okay, but your instructor hopes you'll decide to follow through and prove that you can be successful—and you can if you follow this book's advice!)

> **Reason 2: Going Back to School after a Break.** Perhaps you've tried college before and quit. But now you've decided to get back on the road to success. Maybe you're absolutely committed to making it this time, so you're more motivated. Something may have changed in your life, or you worked to save up for college for a while, or you've been a stay-at-home mom, or you have an employer now who will help foot your tuition bill.

One of the most interesting things about many colleges is the amazing mix of students from all walks of life. You're just as likely to be sitting beside a grandmother who's decided it's her turn now, a soldier who's just come back from overseas, or a businessman gaining credentials for a promotion. College classrooms like yours are rich learning environments because different types of people are gathered in one place to discuss the same ideas. Adult college students are practical, self-directed learners who want to build on their past experiences, apply what they learn to their everyday lives, and build the skills and attitudes that lead to professional success. Does that describe you?[1]

Joseph Pitz/iStockphoto.com

> "
> **The road to success is lined with many tempting parking spaces.**
>
> *Traditional proverb*

Understanding Where Your College "Fits"

There's no doubt about it: Where and why you choose to go to college are important decisions. Dexter Lewis chose to go to a career college. What type of college did you choose to attend? What's the "feel" of the campus itself? Each individual campus has a different culture. Finding the right fit is important, just like finding the right place to work or finding the right life partner.

Four-Year College or University Many colleges and universities offer a traditional college experience, one that includes student life, residence halls, sports events, student clubs, sorority or fraternity membership, and face-to-face collaboration with professors and peers. Four-year schools can be small, medium, or large, public or private. Major research universities provide particular advantages, like an opportunity to learn from leading experts, collaborate with professors on research, and interact with graduate students; they also tend to give you expanded opportunities in choosing a major—including unusual majors like Genetics, Immunology, Demography, Folklore, and Lesbian/Gay/Bisexual and Transgender Studies.[2] But with these opportunities come major responsibilities. Your professors will expect you to adhere to rigorous standards; demonstrate a mature work ethic; and read, write, and think at a high level. If you want to be successful, you'll find that every recommendation in this book is essential.

Community College Some students want to earn an associate's degree or certificate for a particular degree, test the waters to see if college is right for them, or save money on their first year or two of college. Perhaps they plan to attend school part-time, support themselves, work full-time, are single parents, are waited to go to college, are returning to college to retool, or got their high school degrees in nonstandard ways.[3] Typically, community colleges provide smaller classes, specialized degrees, faster career preparation, specific certificate programs, more hands-on classes, and more flexible schedules. More than 8 million college students in America choose to go to community colleges.[4] They can be great places to launch your college education if you want the convenience of going to college right in your own community and if any of the descriptors above fit you.

Career or Technical College If you want special preparation for a specific career, or you're an older adult who wants to change careers, you may have chosen a career or technical college. Sometimes these schools are called "click" institutions, rather than "brick" institutions, because they emphasize technology and don't have large, sprawling campuses with dozens of buildings. If you have specific career goals and want hands-on training, job placement, and a quick jumpstart to a career, a career or technical college might fit.[5]

No matter which type of institution you have chosen to attend, you have made a pact—with the institution itself, with the people who are supporting you, and with yourself. As this chapter's title suggests, start strong and keep going. Although Steven Spielberg, self-made billionaire in the film industry and winner of the Academy Award for his films *Schindler's List* and *Lincoln*, didn't complete the college degree he started, he went back to college more than thirty years later—after he had already achieved world fame. He felt the need to finish the college degree he had started and keep the promise he had made to himself, "I wanted to accomplish this for many years as a 'thank you' to my parents for giving me the opportunity for an education and a career, and as a personal note for my own family—and young people everywhere—about the importance of achieving their college education goals," he said. "But I hope they get there quicker than I did. Completing the requirements for my degree 33 years after finishing my principal education marks my longest 'post-production schedule.'"[6]

EXERCISE 1.1

We'd Like to Get to Know You ...

Take a few minutes to finish the following statements. Think about what each sentence says about you. Use your responses to introduce yourself to the class, or form pairs, talk over your responses together, and use your partner's answers to introduce him or her to the class.

1. I'm happiest when _____.
2. If I had an extra $100, I'd _____.
3. The thing I'm most proud of is _____.
4. Once people get to know me, they're probably surprised to find I'm _____.
5. I've been known to consume large quantities of _____.
6. I'd rather be _____ than _____.
7. My best quality is _____.
8. My worst quality is _____.
9. The academic skill I'd most like to develop is _____.
10. One thing I'd like to figure out about myself is _____.

People go to a college like yours at a particular point in their lives for a variety of reasons. As you discuss this exercise in class, explore these additional questions: What is your background and why are you here?

Earning a Degree or Certificate

If you're in college to earn a degree, you may consider whether you'd be better aiming for a four-year bachelor's degree or a two-year associate's degree. An associate's degree will prepare you to go one of two ways in a relatively short amount of time: (1) into a career or (2) on to further education. If you want a career-oriented associate's degree, in two years you can train for one of the fastest-growing jobs in the economy by taking approximately twenty classes. The best jobs for the future requiring a two-year degree include becoming a nurse, environmental technician, paralegal, fashion designer, dental hygienist, occupational therapist, or radiologic technologist.[7] If you prefer hands-on coursework and a career like one of these is your goal, a career college is exactly the right place for you. (It's also quite possible that you couldn't prepare for some of these specific degrees in a four-year program.)

Instead of a career-oriented associate's degree, you may want to earn a fairly general two-year degree to apply toward a bachelor's degree when you continue your schooling later on. Part of the coursework you'll complete to get an associate's degree will consist of core requirements or general education courses, like writing and speaking, that apply to any career field. If those are your plans, you'll leave your college with transferable courses when the time comes.[8]

Perhaps instead of a two-year associate's degree, you want to specialize even further and finish your coursework sooner, so instead you opt for a certificate. Certificates generally require fifteen to as many as fifty credits, and you'll most likely only take courses that apply specifically to the career field you're preparing for. You set your sights on a target and finish your certificate program in as little as one year, sometimes less.[9]

One of the biggest differences between an associate's degree and a certificate is that the courses you take for an associate's degree usually transfer to a four-year program and include core requirements, general courses like speaking, writing, and math.[10] That may not be true of certificate programs. So if you think you may want to earn a bachelor's degree at some point, choose an associate's degree. It's up to you. How soon do you need a job? What interests you? How hands-on do you want your course of study to be?[11]

Academic and Career Professionalism: What Instructors Will Expect from You

Imagine this: You've just landed a new job, and it's a good one, one you really wanted. How do you know what to do and how to act? What will your boss expect from you? Should you just show up whenever it's convenient, take on this job on top of others you already have, and start firing off casual e-mails and texts about business? ["what up with the johnson report i thought jules was gonna write that"] Probably not—at least not if you want to be successful. You'll want to display workplace professionalism by noting how professionalism is defined in your new organization, and then start doing those things right away. The same thing is true in college: If you want to be successful, you have to display academic professionalism. It's a theme you start now and carry with you into your career. How is academic professionalism defined? If you surveyed college instructors across the country, they'd give you advice like this:

1. **Don't just pile on.** College isn't just "one more thing" to add to the daily agenda of your life. You may have to give something up (like watching every single TV show you love every week) to give it all you've got. Some people hope they'll be able to just add college to an already-long list of obligations. But when they add one more thing, the entire stack crumbles. Something in your life will need adjusting to make room for coursework. You may have to reduce your hours at work for a while, or tell your aunt that you can't watch her kids on Thursday nights so she can go to class, because you have to go to class, too. Put college at the top of your list of obligations.

2. *Choose* **to go to class.** Let's face it: Life is complicated. It involves overlapping demands and making choices on a minute-by-minute basis. Your boss wants a piece of you, your kids (if you have any) want your attention while you try to study, your friend wants to go to the movies the night before your midterm exam, the bills keep mounting, and on and on. Some students choose to miss class to pick up a relative at the airport or shop with a friend who's in town, for example, and just skip class. Sometimes true emergencies in your personal life will interfere with your academic life. If you're ill, for example, call or e-mail your instructor beforehand, if for no other reason than

GOING PRO

BE NOTICEABLE

> **You never get a second chance to make a first impression.**
> ANONYMOUS

Start strong. Professionalism is more than just one or two things. Rather it's a collection of traits and attitudes that predominate in successful people. For example, a true professional will always start *strong*—a trait that leads to success not only in the classroom but in the workplace as well. When you show up for an advisor appointment, a first class, or a job interview, you want to create a positive first impression. This valuable truth goes far beyond just that first interaction, however. Each day on the job shows your professional colleagues who you are in small but important ways, and these interactions add up. For example, if you're late turning in your first project on the new job, and if you show up for work with unkempt hair, dirty fingernails, and body-odor problems, you start out in a hole—and it may be hard to dig your way out. When someone is late, we tend to think he'll be unreliable. When someone takes good care of the way she dresses, we tend to believe she'll also take good care of details on the job. Noticeable employees are those who dress thoughtfully, who cultivate habits of personal hygiene, who keep their work area neat, and whose work is always correct, organized, punctual, and professional—these are the people who end up on the "A-list."

to be courteous. But your instructors will expect you to plan nonemergencies around your already scheduled (and paid for!) classes. Many things in your life are important—it's true—but while you're in school, coming to class and doing your coursework are the right choices to make. Unfortunately, many college students sabotage themselves within the first few weeks of classes by skipping class (25 percent), turning in an assignment late (33 percent), or not turning an assignment in at all (24 percent). Don't allow yourself to become one of these statistics![12]

3. **Don't be an ostrich!** Some students fall prey to "the Ostrich Syndrome." If reading or homework assignments seem too hard or feel like busywork, they just don't do them. Instead, they bury their heads in the sand and pretend like nothing's at stake. Somehow they may even think that they can't get a bad grade if they don't turn in an assignment for the instructor to grade. It goes without saying (but here it is anyway) that "ostriching" is the opposite of academic professionalism. Always do your best work and submit it on time. If the assignment is due on October 1, it's due on October 1. Honest-to-goodness realism and continuous upkeep in your courses work wonders in college, just as they do in the workplace.

4. **Show respect.** One thing instructors dislike is getting a sense from students that school isn't a top priority. When you breeze in late or sneak out early, you're communicating that you don't value school, your instructor, and your classmates, whether you realize it or not. If you criticize a classmate or your instructor in public—even if you think it's constructive—that's

> **An ostrich with its head in the sand is just as blind to opportunity as to disaster.**
> *Anonymous*

Juniors Bildarchiv/Age Fotostock

© Larry Harwood Photography. Property of Cengage Learning.

disrespectful, too. And when you whip out your cell phone to see how many "likes" you have after your last Facebook post, or text your boyfriend about where to go for dinner, everyone knows where your head is. When you're in class, be in class. Dress like you're a serious student who's there to learn. Leave the muscle tanks and halter tops for truly informal occasions. You're not in college to score fashion points, draw attention to your tattoos, or define your personality with your baseball cap. That doesn't mean you can't be yourself, but it does mean that you should use good judgment. Always remember why you're there: to learn.

5. **Know the rules.** Your college has policies you need to know about up front. What constitutes cheating? How can you avoid plagiarism? Who should you talk to if you have a concern about your grade? Do instructors accept texts and cell phone calls? What kind of writing will they expect in e-mails? Even when it comes to everyday things—like weather cancellations—your college has policies and procedures to guide you.

6. **Take charge.** When it comes right down to it, who is responsible for your success? None other than you! Even though you may be afraid to speak up or not want to admit that you're fuzzy about something, your instructors will rely on *you* to let them know that. They aren't mind readers. Do what you need to do: get help, take advantage of instructors' office hours, or hire a tutor. Don't sit idly by while success drifts away.

7. **Invest enough time.** In high school you may have done well without trying very hard. A teacher may have forgiven a late assignment, provided opportunities for extra credit, or graded on a curve so that everyone passed. But college is different. In college, it's important to get ready for class beforehand by reading and doing assignments, and then jump in once you're there. Bring your books, notebook, and pen, and sit up straight, too, just like mom always used to say. College isn't a place to just slide by or wing it. It's a place to put your best foot forward. That may mean rewriting a paper three times or rereading a textbook chapter more than once. Academic professionalism requires you to invest as much time as it takes.

8. **Learn to work in groups.** Your instructors know the value of teamwork later in your career, so they'll expect you to work with your classmates in class, outside of class, or online. They may even think it's important enough to assign points for group projects in the course syllabus. Even though you may prefer to work alone, teamwork skills are highly valued in today's workplace, and you'll learn things from other students that you might not learn from your instructor.[13]

9. **Check your e-mail regularly.** Sure, you can talk to an instructor on the phone or text a classmate with a question about an assignment. But the primary

means of communication in college is e-mail. Most colleges will send all "official correspondence" (like bills) this way, and many professors will use campus e-mail to communicate with you. If you never check your school e-mail account, but instead only use your personal account, you'll miss important information. ("What? The instructor's sick today? I just drove 20 miles to get here!") Your campus IT department or an online helpsheet can tell you how to forward one e-mail account to the other so that you're always up to speed. Believe it or not, this one simple thing trips up more students than you would ever imagine!

10. **Engage!** Students who soak up all they can enjoy college most. When they're in class, they're tuned in. Sure, Professor Whoever may not be quite as entertaining as your favorite TV star, and going to class isn't as much fun as the latest box office smash hit. But college is about becoming an *educated* person, not an *entertained* one.

EXERCISE 1.2

Academic Professionalism Versus Career Professionalism

Both academic professionalism and career professionalism are key to your success. Are they the same thing—or are they different? Look at the ten suggestions for academic professionalism listed above, and retitle each bullet as the information pertains to the world of work. You should come to the conclusion that the same kinds of skills are required in these two contexts.

Academic Responsibilities: How to Help Yourself Succeed

Any time you start something new, there's a **learning curve** involved. The best thing to do is to admit it, decide what to do, and start climbing! Beyond conducting yourself as a professional student, what other things will help you succeed? Here are some additional responsibilities.

learning curve a measure of how long it takes you to learn something and how hard it is

> **If you don't know where you are going, you might wind up someplace else.**
>
> *Yogi Berra, major league baseball player and manager*

Develop a Degree Plan and Plan Your Coursework

In some ways, college is like a journey with parts of the itinerary planned for you. You can't just hitchhike wherever you like. It's more like a guided tour planned by experts in the areas you'd like to explore. You can choose to go left or right at particular moments, but much of the trip is planned in advance.[14] If you'd like to become a nurse, for example, your coursework will be prescribed for you. However, everyone appreciates the focused knowledge of nurses when they need one!

iStockphoto.com/Rhienna Cutler

Why Do I Have to Take This Class?

Here is a road map, or a sample degree plan, for Dexter, assuming he decides to get a general Associate of Arts Degree at his technical college. (The requirements at your college will be different from this example.)

GREAT BLUFFS TECHNICAL COLLEGE

DEGREE TRACKING WORKSHEET

NAME_____Dexter Lewis_____ E-MAIL ADDRESS_____dlewis@gbtc.edu_____

STUDENT NUMBER___123-45-6789___ PHONE_____555-9876_____

GENERAL STUDIES

Associate of Arts Degree

> Many colleges, yours included, use a worksheet or degree plan, like this one of Dexter's, to help you stay on course and track your progress as you earn your degree. Check with an advisor to see what aids like this your campus provides.

Program Course #	Course Title	Term (to be) Taken	Term Hours	Grade A = 4 B = 3 C = 2 D = 1 F = 0	Notes
ENGL 090	English Composition I	Fall 2013	3	?	
HIST 103	United States History I		3		
	Foreign Language		5		
GBTC 100	College Success		3		
SPE 115	Public Speaking	Fall 2013	3	?	
ENGL 102	English Composition II		3		
HIST 104	United States History II		3		
	Foreign Language (must be the same language)		5		
	Humanities		3		
PSC 205	United States Government		3		
	Literature		3		
	Visual and Performing Arts		3		
SOC 103	Introduction to Sociology		3		
	Mathematics		3		
	Humanities		3		
PSC 206	State and Local Government		3		
	Natural Science I		3–4		
	Natural Science II		3–4		
	Unrestricted Elective		3		
	Unrestricted Elective		3		

> In the "Notes" column, Dexter can keep track of his thoughts about each course and things to keep in mind when registering for the next term.

> The courses with department abbreviations and numbers listed are required for Dexter's degree plan. The open categories are places where he can choose from a list of possible courses. His advisor will help him know his options.

(Adapted from Austin Community College online degree plan website and Colorado Technical University catalog.)

To complete this activity, visit your academic advisor to get a degree plan for the degree or certificate program you're most interested in now. (You may change your mind later.) Fill it in with the help of your advisor, looking ahead to which courses you'll take, term by term. Use this degree plan as a working document as you progress through your program.

Sharpen Your FOCUS

TRY IT!

> **The simple act of paying attention can take you a long way.**
>
> —KEANU REEVES,
> AMERICAN ACTOR

Why do college students sometimes lose their focus? In each chapter, "Sharpen Your Focus" will examine one common reason. See if any of these apply to you.

Reason 1: They do the right things at the wrong times.

One reason many of us lose our FOCUS is because we aren't truly present. We don't pay attention. Perhaps we do the right things, but we do them at the wrong times. If you're a morning person, and math is your toughest course, study math in the mornings! The same goes for night owls. In order to be completely present for challenging tasks, ready to give all our attention, we must know ourselves and our own natural rhythms.

On the chart below, put a circle around your peak energy times. Now go back to the list of times, and put a checkmark by your regular study times. Do they match up? Are you studying when you're most effective? If not, can you rearrange things so that you are?

8 A.M. _____	4 P.M. _____
9 A.M. _____	5 P.M. _____
10 A.M. _____	6 P.M. _____
11 A.M. _____	7 P.M. _____
12 A.M. _____	8 P.M. _____
1 P.M. _____	9 P.M. _____
2 P.M. _____	10 P.M. _____
3 P.M. _____	11 P.M. _____

Some courses will count toward your major or area of **concentration**, and some will satisfy **core** requirements. Core requirements often make students wonder: "I'm never going to be another Stephen King. Why do I have to suffer through writing courses I'll never use?" The key words in that last sentence are *never use*. You'll speak and write and think and solve problems in any career. Even though you're in college to prepare for a career, becoming a more knowledgeable person in general should be a big part of your mission.

Most colleges will ask you to fill out a degree plan up front. You'll plan your coursework for each semester or quarter from now until you've finished. Not only do you end up taking the right courses, but you can watch your progress as you go.

concentration focused effort; specialization

core basic

Be Advised! Advising Mistakes Students Make

One of the most important relationships you'll have as a college student is the one you build with your academic advisor. On your campus, this person may be an advisor, a counselor, or a faculty member who can steer you toward courses you can handle and instructors you can learn best from. An advisor can keep you from taking classes that bog you down academically or unnecessary ones that take you extra time to earn your degree. Here's a list of advising mistakes students make, from real advisors who work with college students every day.

1. **Not using the campus advising office or your faculty advisor.** If you don't get regular advice from an advisor, counselor, or a designated faculty member who's serving as your advisor, your degree may take longer and cost more money. It's that simple. It's your college career, after all, and it's important that you and your advisor work as partners.

2. **Not planning ahead.** Some students walk into the advising office or e-mail an advisor and expect help right away, and sometimes that works. However, planning ahead is a better option. Planning ahead includes making an appointment, looking through the course offerings, making a list of questions to ask, and thinking in advance about which days you can attend classes based on your work schedule, how many classes you can take, and on which days of the week. And, if you're leaving your advisor a voice-mail, remember to include all of this important information. What's wrong with this message? "Hi, this is Tony. I have a question about my schedule. Please call me back, OK?" Tony who? And what's his phone number? Or how about an e-mail like this from hotchick13@email.com? "Do I need to take English 090? Please let me know." Exactly who is "hotchick13"?

3. **Procrastinating.** It's important not to put off advising appointments. To drop a class, you may need to meet a deadline. Or you may need help from an advisor to solve a problem with a faculty member, but by the time you get around to it, the instructor has already left campus for the summer. If you deal with problems right away, while they're small, they may be reversible. (And it's always a good idea to discuss dropping a class with the instructor first.)

4. **Skipping prerequisites.** Some students want to skip the required **prerequisites**. They think they can handle the work. They think prereqs are a waste of time and money when, actually, they're in place because hundreds of students before you have shown that these classes help you succeed. And in some cases, students who haven't taken a prereq are actually disenrolled from the course that requires it.

5. **Choosing the wrong major.** Sometimes students lock on to a major because someone else thinks it's a good idea or because a particular career field pays well, not because they enjoy the subject and are suited for it. Staying motivated is hard when you're not interested in something. Advisors can help you figure out which major is right for you.

6. **Taking too many credits or too few.** Some students are overly optimistic and think they can handle a heavier course load than the other factors in their lives will permit. Other students may underestimate the number of courses they should take, which increases the time it takes them to finish school. An advisor can help you stay on target.

7. **Ignoring problems.** If you run into difficulty and end up on academic probation, for example, an advisor or college official will work with you to get you back on track. But you must agree to that bargain and accept the help, possibly by signing a contract of steps you must take to reverse the situation.

8. **Being afraid to drop a course.** Sometimes, when you've tried everything (for example, tutoring, extra help sessions, and the campus learning center), but you're still not succeeding in a course, the best thing to do may be to drop the course by filling out a drop form (online or on paper) and submitting it. Then retake the course later. That option is better than just not going to class and assuming that by not coming, you've dropped the course. Colleges require deliberate action from you. It's always best to know your school's rules and talk with your instructor first. *And beware that dropping a course may affect your financial aid.*[15]

prerequisites courses that you need to take before advancing on to other ones

Make the Grade: Computing Your GPA

One of the most important things to learn as a new college student—and fast—is what grade point averages (**GPAs**) are and how they work. Your GPA is an indication of how well you're doing, and you keep track of it over time, term by term. Your academic record will follow you for the rest of your life! Some students don't realize how grade points add up. They end up on academic probation, even if they only have one failing grade. Let's say you're taking four courses this term, and you earn the following grades:

GPA an average of all your grades for a single semester or a running average across all your coursework

Course	Credits	Final Grade	Grade Point Value
English Composition	3 credits	C (2 points)	6
College Algebra	3 credits	F (0 points)	0
College Success	3 credits	B (3 points)	9
Public Speaking	3 credits	D (1 point)	3
TOTAL	**12 credits**		**18 grade points**

You may look at this record and think, *Not bad. I passed three of my four courses.* But divide that Grade Point Value column total (18) by the total number of credits (12), and you get 1.5.

$$\text{GPA} = \text{Grade Point Value} \div \text{Total Number of Credits}$$

At most schools, a 1.5 GPA puts you on academic probation, and eventually, you may be facing suspension. That can be a discouraging way to start, and digging yourself out of a GPA hole once you're there takes a very long time, like paying off credit card debt.

Not only is it important to keep track of your grades over the whole term, but it's also important to keep track of your grade in each course. If you stop going to your math class because it's too hard or because you don't like the teacher, your grade will suffer. If an assignment is worth 25 percent of your grade, and you don't turn it in, the highest grade you can possibly earn, even if you do everything else perfectly, is a 75 percent or "C." You may think, *but it's only one assignment.* It is only one assignment, but it counts as one-quarter of your grade. In college, everything counts. The typical grading scale in college is:

A = 90–100%   B = 80–89%   C = 70–79%
D = 60–69%   F = 59% and below

Thomas Sztanek/Photoservice/iStockphoto.com

> **Problems are only opportunities in work clothes.**
>
> *Henry J. Kaiser, American industrialist (1882–1967)*

Realize the Value of Developmental Courses

Many career and technical colleges have what's called an open-door admissions policy. That means that anyone who wants to get an education is invited in. You don't have to get a certain score on the SAT or ACT standardized national tests, and you don't have to have a particular GPA in high school to be admitted. That's a good thing. As a nation, we are opening the doors of education to everyone, and our society as a whole benefits in many ways. Education improves the quality of life.[16]

But when restrictions are removed, more variety is a natural result, right? Think of it this way: If every student at your college had to be over six feet tall to be admitted, then you and all your classmates would tower over the general public. But if anyone of any height could attend, you'd see a range from very short to very tall. Some people would need steps to reach high places, and others would have to duck under low ceilings. But variety presents challenges. Career and technical colleges are characterized by variety, and they've devised ways to make it work. Here's how.

developmental designed to develop or improve a skill

New students bring standardized test scores or take placement tests that help schools know where to *place* them. If you're "short" on some necessary skills for success, like reading, writing, or math, they'll place you in a **developmental** (also called *remedial*) class to help you catch up fast. Some students see these courses negatively, thinking they're a waste of time or money. Not so! Don't get discouraged if you're in one or more of these classes. They're insurance that you will grow into the skills you'll need.

If you're enrolled in a developmental class, you're in good company. In one study of thirty-five colleges that are all part of a proposal to increase student success, 37 percent of incoming students required one remedial course, 26 percent required two courses, and 22 percent required three courses—for a total of 85 percent. And note this piece of good news: In a related study, students who earned a C or better in a developmental course during their first semester were, from that point forward, more likely to stay in school and succeed than students who weren't required to take a developmental course in the first place![17] In another study, students who took a developmental writing course earned higher English grades in later courses and higher GPAs overall than students who did not.[18] If you're enrolled in a developmental class, perhaps you're beginning to see its value *now*. If you don't see the value yet, chances are you'll greatly appreciate what it did for you *later*.

EXIT **1A**

Careers
This Lane

Achievers
Merge Right

SOLUTIONS This EXIT
SUCCESS 10 Miles
MOTIVATION 25 Miles

rjmiz/iStockphoto.com

> **Your current safe boundaries were once unknown frontiers.**
> *Anonymous*

BOX 1.1 Analyzing a Syllabus

Take a look at this example syllabus to see what you think. What is this professor like? Do you get a sense of her standards and values from her syllabus? Will this be a challenging course? Take a close look at a syllabus from one of your current classes. Analyze it, just as this one has been analyzed, and make a list of things you learn about specific aspects of the syllabus that can help you be successful.

Some colleges have a syllabus template or standard format so that your syllabus for each class will look basically the same and contain similar kinds of information.

Pay attention to the course description. It's a summary of what you can expect.

You can buy the textbook from your college bookstore or order it online. But often textbooks are "customized" with portions inserted from different books or material that pertains to your own campus. You must buy those books from your campus bookstore. Even though textbooks cost money, they are a critical investment. Trying to get by without one puts you at a disadvantage right from the start.

The instructor has devoted a substantial portion of the syllabus to this topic, and she has spelled out her expectations in detail. Professional conduct must be important to him.

This syllabus actually continues on for several more pages and includes three other things: (1) a campus statement about academic honesty and plagiarism, (2) due dates for each assignment, and (3) specific information on how speeches will be graded.

Send the instructor an e-mail the first week of class, introducing yourself and discussing your thoughts about how this class will help you. Remember, however, that in college, you must use good grammar and correct spelling in ALL your writing, including e-mails.

GREAT BLUFFS TECHNICAL COLLEGE
COURSE SYLLABUS

Course ID: SPE 115
Term: Fall 2013
Instructor: Steve Staley
Office: Vail Hall 501

It's appropriate to ask the instructor what he prefers to be called: Steve, Dr. Staley, Professor Staley, and so on.

Course Title: Public Speaking
Credit Hours: 3
E-mail Address: steve.staley@gbtc.edu
Office Phone: 555–1234

Office Hours: MW 10:00–11:00 a.m., TR 2:00–3:00 p.m., by appointment only

Course Description: This course combines the theory of speech communication with oral performance skills. Emphasis is on researching, organizing, and preparing speeches and analyzing the needs and interests of your particular audience. Although this is primarily a performance class, you will also build your writing and researching skills.

Prerequisites/Co-Requisites: ENG 090, REA 090

Course Textbook: *Public Speaking: Concepts and Skills for a Diverse Society,* 2013. Cengage Learning.

Professional Conduct in Class: Students are responsible for knowing and abiding by the "Standards of Conduct" listed in the 2013–2014 GBTC Catalog (beginning on page 10). Your cell phone or pager should be turned off, set to vibrate only, or left at home. Eating, sleeping, social discussions, or doing reading or homework for other classes are distracting behaviors and communicate indifference and disrespect for this learning environment and subject matter. Children should not be brought to class. Getting up and coming in and out during class (unless you are sick, of course) is distracting to your classmates. These activities are unacceptable in academic environments and qualify as examples of inappropriate conduct in class, which may result in your academic withdrawal from the class.

Online Course Management System (CMS): e-CC (pronounced EASY). All students have access to the materials posted on the CMS website through the Internet from a campus computer lab or from home.

Attendance: If you must miss a class for an emergency, you must still submit assigned work by the due date. Please provide documentation to indicate that the absence was due to a situation beyond your control. There are no excused absences without documentation. In order to receive credit for attendance, you must attend the ENTIRE class period. IF YOU MISS A CLASS, IT IS YOUR RESPONSIBILITY TO CONTACT A CLASSMATE FOR NOTES AND ASSIGNMENTS. NO MAKEUP WORK IS ALLOWED.

Grading: Assignments must be turned in on time and speeches must be presented on schedule. Grades for makeup speeches are automatically reduced by 20 percent. Only one makeup day will be scheduled for speeches missed due to emergencies! THERE ARE NO MAKEUP EXAMS OR WRITTEN ASSIGNMENTS.

Americans with Disabilities Act (ADA): Any student eligible for academic accommodations because of a learning or physical disability should speak with the instructor during the first week of class and contact the Office of Support Services.

Speeches: You will be required to give a minimum of five speeches.
- SP 1: Informative 5 mins. (+ or −1 min.) (1 visual aid) Prep and speaking outline required.
- SP 2: Career (Impromptu) Speaking on the spot!
- SP 3: Ceremonial 3 mins. (+ or −1 min.) (1 quote) Prep and speaking outline required.
- SP 4: Persuasive 7 mins. (+ or −1 min.) (2 visual aids and 2 sources) Prep and speaking outline required. You must have a partner for the opposition.
- SP 5: Public Speaking Outside the Box 10 mins. (+ or −2 mins.) (Poster, flyer, 2 visual aids) Presented in TV studio.

Source: Steve Staley, Colorado Technical University.

Master the Syllabus

You'll get a syllabus (or course schedule) for most all of the college classes you'll take. If the syllabi (plural of syllabus) for your courses are available online, check them often to keep up with any changes in the schedule or new assignments. If you have a hard copy, keep it handy and refer to it often. Think of a syllabus as:

> a preview of what to expect during every class

> a road map for where the course will take you

> a contract between you and your instructor

> a summary of all the assignments and how much they count toward your grade

> a tool that lists reading and homework to help you prepare for class

> evidence of an instructor's standards, grading system, and values

Avoid the PCP Syndrome: Use Campus Resources

The convenience of a career college can also be a drawback. If you're going to college in your own community, it's easy to develop a drive-through mentality. You show up for classes and then hightail it for work or home right away. Some experts describe this phenomenon as the "PCP Syndrome: Parking Lot, Class, Parking Lot." What's wrong with that? you ask. When you've finished grocery shopping, you get back in your car and go home, right? You don't cruise the aisles and hang around.

But going to college is very different from shopping for groceries. Your campus has many things available for you to take advantage of: student clubs, special presentations, musical events, and learning resource centers, for example. You may never find out about these "free samples" if you're not there. You won't make new friends or get to know your instructors, two practices that are essential to your success.[19] The danger is that when the going gets rough, which can happen during exam time, you may be tempted to retreat to what you're most familiar with—your life before college—and abandon your efforts. Whatever the problem, there's a place to go for help on campus. Even if your campus doesn't have every possible kind of support center right there, your advisors or instructors can always direct you to services off campus.

Remember that "HELP" is not a four-letter word. Getting help when you need it isn't a stigma; it's smart. Take this example: In 1979, Diana Nyad achieved the record for open-water swimming a distance of 102.5 miles. But it took fifty-one other people to help her reach her goal (guides to check winds and currents, divers to look for sharks, and NASA nutrition experts to keep her from losing more than the twenty-nine pounds she lost during that one swim).[20] Your campus has all kinds of resources available for the taking, but you must take them. They won't come to you. Here are some of the FAQs new college students often ask:

> **How can I meet other students?** Take advantage of favorite gathering spots on campus. If you're finding it hard to meet people, could it be because you're not around? To meet people, it helps to be where they are.

> **What if I need help with a challenging course?** Many campuses have support centers: a science learning center or a math learning center, for example. Or particular courses may offer what's called supplemental instruction, extra help beyond class sessions with basic course materials or homework assignments.

You may be able to work with a tutor, too—a student who's extra-good at math, for example. Check out whatever options are available to you, and use them, rather than struggle on your own if you're not getting results.

> **I'm thinking of dropping a class. How do I do it?** The Office of the Registrar or Office of Admissions and Records is where to go. They also help with things like transferring credits and getting transcripts if you've attended college somewhere before or plan to transfer. Think through the results of dropping a class, however. Will doing so change your financial aid status, for example?

> **What if I need a counselor?** College is a time of change. Your relationships may be affected or you may suffer from symptoms of stress. If your campus has a counseling center and you need to use its services, do so. And if you find yourself in the middle of a real crisis, call the campus hotline for immediate help.

> **How can I find out if I have a learning disability?** Check to see whether your campus has a learning center or a special office that helps with learning disabilities. You can work with a specialist there who can help. If you've been diagnosed with a learning disability before, bring your documentation to that office for their records and let your instructors know. They can help, too.

> **What if I have a technology crisis?** Your campus probably has a computer help desk, where techies can often solve what sounds like a complicated problem, with simple advice. Also, use the campus computer labs. They may have better computers than yours at home, and you can make good use of blocks of time between classes.

> **Are health services available to students?** Many campuses have a student health center where you can find a range of free or inexpensive services—everything from flu shots to strep throat tests to birth control advice if you're sexually active.

> **What do I want to be when I grow up?** Thinking ahead to a career when you finish college is sometimes hard when so much is going on at the moment. What do you like to do? What people skills do you have? Visit your campus's career center. Experts there can help you discover a major and career that will work for you.

> **Is child care available?** Many campuses have inexpensive child care available. Being able to drop off a child in the morning right on campus and pick him up after your classes are over can be a real help.

> **Where can I buy my books?** Textbooks are a big investment

©iStockphoto.com/walik

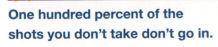

One hundred percent of the shots you don't take don't go in.

Wayne Gretzky, called the greatest ice hockey player of all time

these days, and it's important to buy the right editions for your classes. Should you buy them from your campus bookstore or order online? Buying books online may save you money, although you'll have to wait for shipment. The bookstore is a much quicker option, and it's a good idea to find out where it is, no matter where you buy your books. You'll most likely need it for other school supplies. Renting your books or buying an e-book that you can read online may be an option, too.

> **Where can I get other pieces of information I may need?** Try your campus website, the school bulletin or catalog, the student handbook, or the school newspaper.

> **What if I need the help of Campus Security?** If you feel unsafe walking to your car late at night or you need information about parking permits on campus, check with the Campus Security or Public Safety Office. They're there for your protection.

EXERCISE 1.4

Top Ten Resources Your Campus Offers

Make a list of ten resources your campus offers that can help you succeed in your coursework. For example, does your campus have a health center, a day care center, or a learning center? Visit each location, and identify specific ways you will use each office or service.

	Name of office/service	Contact information	How will I use this resource?
1.			
2.			
3.			
4.			
5.			
6.			
7.			
8.			
9.			
10.			

What's the bottom line? Get to know your campus and its full range of offerings—and take advantage of everything that's in place to help you be as academically successful as possible.

Toughing It Out: What College Takes

What does it mean to succeed? Actually, success is difficult to define, and different people define success differently. Right now in college, you may think of success in terms of the money you'll make after you finish. But is success just about money? Is it about fame? Status? According to motivational author Robert Collier, "Success is the sum of small efforts, repeated day in and day out." Perhaps to you, success is somewhere off in the distant future, and it happens more or less suddenly, like winning the lottery.

Actually, your professional success begins right now. You should be the one to define what success will look like in your life, but generally, success is *setting out to do something that means something to you, and then being fully engaged while doing it.* It's that simple. And it applies to your college experience as well. It starts now.

In order to understand your own definition of success in college, first you need to ask yourself why you're here. Why *did* you come—or return—to college, anyway? Do you want to develop into a more interesting, well-rounded, educated human being? Are you working toward a degree that leads to a specific career? Do you have children and want an education in order to give them a better life? This book will provide you with an honest look at what that takes, including plenty of opportunities to ask yourself questions about these things. It will also offer you tools you can use throughout your college courses and in your life beyond college.

Some students think going to college is like any other financial transaction: buying a gallon of milk, for example. You pay the cashier the money, and the milk now belongs to you. They think if they pay tuition, the college credits should be theirs. Not so. There's much more to it than that. A college education requires more than a financial commitment. It requires you to invest your ability, your intellect, your drive, your effort—and yourself. College has to do with more than the brain matter found between your ears.

The Good News and the Bad News (Benefits and Obstacles)

What's the good news about going to college? The benefits are wide-reaching and long-lasting. Think about how this list applies to you.

1. **Higher earning potential.** College increases your potential to earn money. It's that simple. On average, people with associate's degrees earn 20 to 30 percent more than those with a high school diploma only. Experts say that one-third of new job growth from 2008 until 2018 will require some education after high school.[21] And there's some evidence that jobs requiring certificates or associate's degrees will grow at an even faster rate than jobs requiring a four-year degree.[22] Sixty percent of jobs right now are held by people with post–high school education or training.[23]

2. **Lower unemployment rates.** College decreases your risk of unemployment. This is especially helpful when the economy takes a downturn. According to

one recent major study, getting an associate's or bachelor's degree is a better investment today than the stock market, gold, or housing.[24]

3. **Wisdom.** College gives you opportunities to gain understanding about many things—politics, people, and current affairs to name a few. Beyond theories, facts, and dates, well-educated people know how to think critically, contribute to society, and manage their lives.

4. **Insight.** College students have the opportunity to understand themselves better as they learn different ways of doing things.

5. **Lifelong learning.** According to research, getting a college degree—even for a career that doesn't require one—leads to a happier, healthier life.[25] College students are prepared to become lifelong learners. It's not just about grades. It's about becoming the best student-learner you can be—inside or outside of the classroom. This one benefit will stay with you through the rest of your life.

What's the bad news? What obstacles may stand in your path? Dexter Lewis is still struggling with important questions about being in college. Will he be successful? It depends, doesn't it? Here's some evidence on what "it" consists of.

Some experts say that fewer than half of college students reach their educational goals.[26] But who goes, who finishes later, and who transfers to another school are hard things to track. The risk factors for dropping out of college include working more than thirty hours per week, going to school part-time, being a single parent or having children at home, and being a first-generation college student.[27] It's true that going to college is "A Whole 'Nother World," as one major report's title says. Juggling a job, family, friends, transportation, tuition, and all the things that are impacted by the energy and effort it takes to go to college can be overwhelming. If you're a first-generation college student, you may not have a role model at home who can help you, because your parents didn't go to col-

lege. (That's why it's important to make connections with your classmates, instructors, and advisors who can guide you.)[28] Even though college may be more challenging for first-generation students, you can still be highly successful. Perhaps the most famous current example is Michelle Obama, who went from first-generation college student to First Lady.[29]

The important thing to keep in mind as you think about risk factors is that they alone cannot determine your ultimate level of success. Don't throw in the towel now if you had a child at age sixteen or are working

> " Always bear in mind that your own resolution to succeed is more important than any one thing.
>
> *Abraham Lincoln, 16th President of the United States (1809–1875)*

iStockphoto/Luis Pedrosa

ONLINE TechKnow

As you begin your college career, you'll find opportunities to take whole courses, or parts of courses, online. In fact, many schools now have an online component for every course you'll take. What should you know as you consider and enroll in these online courses? Here are some useful tips:

- Pay close attention to your school's CMS, or Course Management System—the online system your school uses to deliver and manage your course materials. Learn how to use everything your online course offers, like discussion boards, chat rooms, online assignments, and other course resources.

- Create a VPN (Virtual Private Network) account to access library data bases from home. Your library will help you set up and use that connection.

- Turn to your school's IT help desk when you have questions or when things don't work the way you think they should.

- Use this self-evaluation checklist as you prepare for online learning:

Rarely – 1   Sometimes – 2

Most of the Time – 3 All of the Time – 4

A. I am able to easily access the Internet as needed for my studies.

B. I am willing to communicate actively with my classmates and instructors electronically.

C. I am willing to set aside an amount of time each week to effectively engage in online study.

D. I believe that online learning can be as effective as traditional classroom learning.

E. When it comes to learning and studying, I am a selfdirected person.

F. I am able to manage my study time effectively and easily complete online assignments on time.

G. I am the one responsible for my learning—even when I work online without a teacher in my presence.

Be especially aware of those questions where you answered "Rarely." Ask for help and look for ways to improve in those areas yourself. For example, if you answered "Rarely" to question 2, look for ways to build learning communities, form online study groups, or join in when you're assigned virtual group projects.[30]

Improve Your Grade
Online Flashcards
Glossary

---

thirty-five hours per week. These factors are presented merely as information to assist you on your journey. They are simply *predictors*—not *determiners*. Your effort, attitude, and willingness to get any help you need to succeed are all vital. Only you can determine your outcomes in life, and that includes college.

predictors something that indicates something in the future may happen

> I am only one,
> But still I am one.
> I cannot do everything,
> But still I can do something;
> And because I cannot do everything
> I will not refuse to do the something that I can do.
>
> *Edward Everett Hale, American author (1822–1909)*

This Course Has a Proven Track Record

If you're reading this book, there's a good chance you're enrolled in a first-year seminar course, called something like First-Year Seminar, First-Year Experience, College Success, Learning Community, or any of a host of other names. These courses are designed to introduce you to college life, familiarize you with your own campus, and help you improve your academic skills. Do they work? According to experts, the answer is yes! Of course, you have to keep your part of the bargain, but in general, college students who complete first-year seminars are much more successful. Take a look at the results of one major study in Figure 1.1.

Students who completed a college success course were more likely to stay in school, succeed academically, and transfer to universities. And students who completed a college success course and also needed to take developmental courses in one to three subject areas were even more likely to achieve these results! That's what this course is about: your success. Your instructor and your classmates are rooting for you. Now it's up to you!

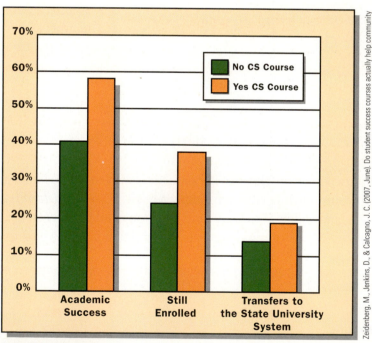

Zeidenberg, M., Jenkins, D., & Calcagno, J. C. (2007, June). Do student success courses actually help community college students succeed? Reprinted by permission of Teachers College, Columbia University and Data Trend #31. Florida Department of Education.

FIGURE 1.1

Outcomes of College Students Completing a College Success Course and Those Who Did Not (1999–2000 through 2003–2004)

BOX **1.2**

Generation 1: First in the Family?

Did both your parents graduate from college? If not, you are a "first-generation college student." Quite an impressive title, isn't it? Being first at something has some definite pros. You're a trailblazer, a pioneer, someone to be looked up to. "Imagine, our son Dion with a college degree! Isn't that something?" But along with pros come potential challenges. Who will you go to for advice? Will your family understand what it takes? Will they support your efforts? At moments when your confidence is shaken, you may wonder: Can a first-generation student be successful? The answer? Of course! (Your author is a first-generation college graduate!) In the end, your success is up to you. As you begin your college career, take these suggestions to heart:

1. **Communicate with your family.** Research shows that the *quality* and *quantity* of communication about college that you engage in with your family is key to your success. Although they can't empathize because they haven't "been there and done that," they can listen and encourage you. Talk to them openly about your college experience.[31]

2. **Keep your stress level in check.** If your family puts extra pressure on you to perform, your stress level may increase dramatically. But stress isn't the best motivator. This is something you want to do, so hone in and hunker down. Pay particular attention to your instructors, keep track of due dates, and focus. All you can do is your best. Think of it this way: you're "demystifying" college. You may just inspire Mom or Dad or your little brother to go to college one day too.[32]

3. **Get going.** Remember this: when the going gets tough, the tough get going. Sometimes first-generation students are tempted to drop out, scale back (from four classes to three, for example), avoid assessment (thinking, oddly, "If I don't turn my paper in, I can't get a bad grade on it"), or lower their own expectations ("I was hoping for a 4.0 GPA, but maybe a 2.0 will do"). Although sometimes these options may be the right ones, sabotaging your own efforts is never a good idea. Keep your eye on the prize—that degree you'll be the first one to earn in your family.[33]

4. **Find a true mentor.** Look for a particular professor or advisor to serve as a mentor—someone you can go to for advice and support. Just knowing that someone cares can be a powerful motivator. Ask this person to help you through rough patches or go to her to get recharged when your "academic batteries" are low.

5. **Get involved.** College may feel like a "foreign" culture to you. You may have conflicting emotions: excitement, confusion, and anxiety. You may not understand what instructors expect, how to fit in, or how to get it all done. But you won't learn these things if you aren't around. If you breeze in for your classes and bolt afterward, it will be harder to adjust to your new role. Ease into the campus culture and take full advantage of what it means to be in college. Make friends and feel the beat of campus life.[34]

If you follow this advice, you *can* be successful! If you're a first-generation college student, dog-ear or bookmark this page, and refer back to it whenever you need to.

Ryan McVay/Photodisc/Getty Images

> **Though no one can go back and make a brand new start, anyone can start from now and make a brand-new ending.**
>
> *Carl Bard*

How Do I Want to Be Different When I'm Done?

One thing is sure: College will change you. Most every high-intensity experience full of opportunities does. Take advantage, meet new people, and stretch yourself. You may notice that as a result of your college experience, your old relationships may "fit" differently. Your romantic partner may brag about you or secretly envy you. Your family may praise your efforts or hardly notice. But you will. If you finish what you've begun, you will watch yourself become a more sophisticated, more knowledgeable, more confident person. You can't help but be. Ask yourself now, at the beginning of your college experience, just how you'd like to change, and make it happen.

BOX 1.3

How to Read a Case Study

Each chapter of *FOCUS* will begin with a case study about a real student, marked as **STEP 1** and portrayed by a member of the FOCUS cast. (You'll see the cast members in photos throughout the book—and will perhaps almost feel you know them all by the end.) As you read the case, you may think: *Hmmm . . . this is an interesting story, but what does it have to do with me?* Make the most out of these case studies by following these suggestions:

- **Make a connection.** Although you may be a different age, gender, or ethnicity, look at the issues beneath the surface. Actually, you may have some things in common with the case study character, or you may know someone else who does. Are you tempted to make some of the mistakes Dexter is making? Is your best buddy worried about similar issues? Did your sister, who was in college before you, struggle with her writing class, as Dexter does?

- **Get engaged.** The case studies are designed to be a fully interactive and visual experience for you. You can gain a complete picture of the case study students by reading their story *and* looking closely at the photos and visual examples. Learn even more about the students by looking at sample e-mails, notes, text messages, Facebook profiles, and other key visual examples of their lives.

- **Think critically.** Imagine yourself in a conversation with the case study students. What advice would you give them? How would you help them solve their problems? Becoming an active reader and critical thinker will help you build skills that will contribute to your success as a college student.

- **Prepare to learn.** The case study will preview all the topics you'll read about in the chapter. The chapters will provide you with strategies to deal with these challenges. Make sure you read each case thoroughly, watch for things you will learn in the chapter, and then answer the Reaction questions listed in **STEP 2**.

If you follow them through the book, these featured students will lead you into a rich, "FOCUSed" learning experience!

Write Your Own Case Study

Everyone has a story. This is your opportunity to tell yours! Start by flipping through FOCUS and skimming the other Challenge cases. Perhaps your biggest challenge will be something like those facing Katie Alexander or Derek Johnson, or maybe your particular challenge doesn't appear in this book. (If you expect everything to be "smooth sailing" for you, you may prefer to write about a friend or relative beginning college, and that's acceptable too.) This exercise will allow you to personalize what you will learn in this class and identify possible issues that may interfere with your success in college early on. Here are the steps you will follow:

1. First, write your CHALLENGE story. Your instructor will give you specific guidelines, but in general, write a two-page case study that highlights your previous learning experiences, your expectations for college, key pieces of your life outside of college that may interfere with your success, and the top challenges you are facing right now in college. You should write your story in the third person, and you may give yourself a fictional (but real-sounding) name. You may write, for example, "It was her first day of college, and the temperature outside had reached a record high. She rushed into the building from the parking lot so that the air conditioning would start cooling her down right away. But she had more than the temperature on her car thermometer on her mind. She was nervous. No one from her family had ever gone to college, and suddenly she felt pressure to impress them"—or whatever was true for you.

2. Choose personalized images to surround your story—a photo of you, other photos of people in the story, images that relate to the case, whatever you wish—and place them around the story. (Go to an online site that has free images you can choose from or download photos from your Facebook page, if you have one.) Your case should look something like one of the ones in FOCUS. You may use whatever e-tool you wish to create your case (PowerPoint or Word, for example), but your instructor may want you to turn in a paper copy. This part of the assignment should be two (facing) pages.

3. Write three to five REACTION questions to go along with your case. Start by thinking about issues where you need the most advice, and build your questions around those. You may want to ask your reader, "What's the primary challenge facing this new student? Describe it in your own words." or "Why is this issue (whatever it is) something that could interfere with college success?" Your instructor may ask you to answer these questions yourself or swap your case with a classmate and answer his or her questions. At the end of this course, you will look back at your beginning case study (CHALLENGE→REACTION) and write about the INSIGHT→ACTION learning that has taken place for you along the way.

At the beginning of this chapter, Dexter Lewis faced a series of challenges as a new college student. Now after learning from this chapter, would you respond differently to any of the questions you answered about the "FOCUS Challenge Case"? Using what you learned in the chapter, write a paragraph ending Dexter's case study. What are some of the possible outcomes for Dexter?

step

4 ACTION Your Plans for Change

1. Identify one new thing you learned in reading this chapter. Why did you select the one you've selected? How will it affect what you do in your college classes?

2. Why are you going to college? How do you see your college experience impacting your future?

3. How do you want college to change you? Why?

chapter 2

Building Dreams, Setting Goals

READINESS CHECK

How this chapter relates to **YOU**

1. When it comes to dreams, goals, and your own future, what are you most unsure about, if anything?

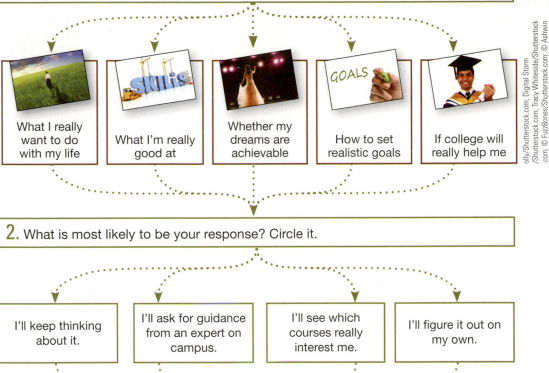

What I really want to do with my life

What I'm really good at

Whether my dreams are achievable

How to set realistic goals

If college will really help me

2. What is most likely to be your response? Circle it.

I'll keep thinking about it.

I'll ask for guidance from an expert on campus.

I'll see which courses really interest me.

I'll figure it out on my own.

3. What would you have to do to increase your likelihood of success? Will you do it this term?

Example: Start working with an advisor or career counselor now! Yes!

How **YOU** will relate to this chapter

What are you most interested in learning about? Put check marks by those topics.

☐ How this book will help you learn

☐ What motivates you

☐ How your attitude can sabotage you

☐ Why you should distinguish between dreams and goals

☐ How to develop goals that work

• How motivated are you to learn more about getting the right start in college (5 = high, 1 = low)? ___

• How ready are you to read now? ____ (If something is in your way, take care of it if you can, zero in and focus.)

• How long do you think it will take you to complete this chapter? If you start and stop, keep track of your overall time. ____ hour(s) ____ minutes

Sylvia Sanchez

Her own apartment—finally! As Sylvia opened the new package of turquoise sheets for her bed, she felt excited but at the same time, amazingly calm. Frankly, she couldn't believe her parents had agreed to it. But their response to the idea had been, "Sure, if you're willing to pay your own rent, we'll find plenty of uses for your room." So Sylvia had been counting off the days all summer, and frankly, it felt good to be on her own. No younger brothers and sisters squawking, no parents breathing down her neck, no grandparents living right next door, and no lame boyfriend thinking he could just hang around all the time. A fresh start—that's what she wanted. She stopped to check her cell phone—four new texts, probably all from him. And all those pictures of her he had posted on Facebook this morning! She wanted to write back and tell him to get over it, but she thought she'd better wait awhile for that. *Let's just see what college has to offer. That's smarter*, she admitted. Her three best friends, and now roommates, hadn't arrived yet, so naturally Sylvia claimed the best bedroom. *They'd probably have done the same thing*, she reassured herself. *They should have gotten here earlier.*

Sylvia had always been smart—not brilliant, but smart enough to know how to play the game. She was always rushing around, doing a hundred things at once. Focusing wasn't her strong point, and multitasking didn't always get her the best grades, but truthfully, she'd never even cracked a book back in high school and still passed all her classes. She had always done her homework (that is, when she did any) in front of the TV while she played with the dog, texted her friends, and checked her Facebook page. College, she imagined, would be a slightly harder version of high school. And though she'd graduated four years ago and worked to support herself ever since, living at home to save money, she was ready to go back to school. It couldn't be as hard as her parents had warned. She remembered their threats when she brought home a bad grade in high school: *You just wait until you start college!* How

© Larry Harwood Photography. Property of Cengage Learning

Source: Google, Inc.

Andy Dean Photography/Shutterstock.com

Mom & Dad - last summer

would they know? They'd never even been to college themselves. If all that propaganda from parents and high school teachers were really true, no one would go to college! *How hard can it possibly be?* she asked herself. Her parents said they'd help financially when they could, but she wasn't expecting much. "And we're not paying for anything below a B!" her father had insisted. She just had to keep her grades up enough to hold onto her financial aid, and if she could manage to impress her parents, that wouldn't hurt, either. Her track record in school had never been all that great, but just maybe she could change that in college.

Of her four new college courses, Sylvia was least worried about her college success class. *Automatic A*, she predicted. *Everyone knows how to study. It's just common sense*, she thought to herself. But whether studying enough to "live up to her potential" was on her agenda was another thing. The thought of writing an essay every week for her English Composition class brought on major dread; in fact, she wasn't all that excited about any of her classes. There might be other, more compelling pursuits that took up her time in college, like meeting interesting people and finishing her demo CD.

The one thing Sylvia knew for sure was that she desperately wanted to make it in the music industry, and her parents desperately wanted her to major in business. "How many people actually become famous musicians?" they would ask. Her Dad grilled her regularly on the subject. "There are all kinds of possible careers if you earn a business degree, but how many people actually make it as musicians—even if they're good? What are the odds? College is the way to go, and a certificate in business makes sense." Your mother

and I never had the chance; don't blow this opportunity!" "Yeah, whatever . . ." was her usual retort.

But all Sylvia really wanted in life was to be behind a microphone in front of an audience. And the bigger the audience, the better. Someday—she just knew it—she'd sign a recording contract with a major record label. All her friends told her how good she was. They'd even encouraged her to try out for a TV singing competition. Imagine—fame and fortune. *Sylvia Sanchez, recording artist* . . . even her name had the right ring to it and eventually, everyone would recognize it. They'd download her top hits, and she'd have the clothes, hair, make-up, and money she'd always wanted.

As she stood at the foot of the bed, admiring her new sheets, Sylvia caught a glimpse of herself in the mirror on the wall. "Looking good!" she whispered. Was she referring to how her new bedroom was shaping up or how she'd made the right decision on what to wear?

Suddenly, Sylvia heard laughter in the hallway and realized it was her new roommates. They had hung out together back in high school, but how would she like actually living with them? Would they start getting on one another's nerves? Deep down, Sylvia realized, she really did want to be successful in college. But she also wanted to live her own life and do her own thing. Still, she rationalized, *If this whole college thing doesn't work out, I'll move back home, pick up where I left off, get back my old job at the restaurant close to home, and wait for the future I really want.*

SDV 101: Academic
Focus on College S

CHECK IT OUT!

"Excellence is achieved by the mastery of fundamentals"
Vince Lombardi

In this requi

- Empower yourself
- ...te School resourc

SHAKIRA
SALE EL SOL

Classified Ads

JOBS in BUSINESS!

ACME Business Professionals, Inc. is a rising company in North America that employs a wide range of business professionals. Currently seeking professionals ready to launch a career in business (marketing, finance, and sales).

JOB TITLE: Sales Associate, Midwestern Region
RESPONSIBILITIES:
- Assess current status of all existing business
- Provide current level of service or improve service to all clients
- Formulate plan to develop all new business opportunities
- Work with local interns to develop future staffing
- Select and train new associates
- Develop regional hiring/training opportunities
- Expand regional potential

SALARY: commensurate with experience and qualifications Acme Business Professionals, Inc. is known for its commitment to quality, diversity, and exceptional service.

TO APPLY: Send a current resume, along with a cover letter, to our Human Resources Department at Dana.Horner@acmepro.com.

A distributor of office and computer products is in "URGENT" need of individuals to fill-up the following positions:

ACCOUNTING / AUDITING STAFF (2)
- Male / Female, not more than 30 years old
- BS in Accountancy graduate
- At least 6 months experience in related field
- Extensive knowledge on merchandise inventory and general accounting functions
- With good analytical skills

TECHNICAL ASSISTANT

© Cengage Learning

Course Schedule
Main Campus
FALL SEMESTER

Instructor

Student: Sanchez,

Course ID	Course T
PSYCH 100	INTRO TO
ENGL 130	ENGLISH
UNIV 101	COLLEGE
PHIL 102	PHIL
Credi	

Work Schedule Week # 46

Fernando's Hideaway, South Loca

	Sunday	Monday	Tuesday	Wedensday	Thursday	Friday	Satur
Abel, Nora	8-5	2-CL			8-5	9-6	8-5
Collins, Becky	2-CL		9-6	2-CL		2-CL	9-6
Sanchez, Sylvia		8-5	2-CL		9-6	8-5	10-
Harper, Alex			9-6	8-5	10-7	2-CL	9-6
Monahan, Zoe		10-7		2-CL		8-5	

1. Is Sylvia sufficiently motivated to succeed in college? Why or why not?

2. Describe Sylvia's beliefs about her intelligence. Does she think college is mostly about effort or about ability? Is Sylvia a *learner* or a *performer*?

3. Is Sylvia's vision of becoming a famous singer a goal or a dream? Why?

4. Identify three things that show focus and might help Sylvia make good life management choices.

5. Are any elements of Sylvia's situation similar to your own college experience thus far?

Who Are You? And What Do You Want?

Imagine this voicemail greeting: "Hi. At the tone, please answer two of life's most important questions. Who are you? And what do you want?" Beep. Can you answer these questions right now? How much do you really know about yourself and what you want from this life of yours?

Don't worry. These aren't trick questions and there are no wrong answers. But there are some answers that are more right for you than others. College is a great time to think about who you are and what you want. In addition to learning about biology or history or business, college will be a time to learn about yourself: your motivation, values, dreams, and goals. You may make some of the most important choices of your life. Which major will you choose? Which career will you aim for? From this point on, it's up to you. Have you ever heard this phrase with 10 two-letter words: "If it is to be, it is up to me"? It's true.

Think about it: a college education is one of the best investments you can make. Once you've earned a college degree, it's yours forever. Someone can steal your car or walk away with your cell phone, but once you've earned a college degree, no one can ever take it from you. Your choice to go to college will pay off in many ways. So even if you aren't sure exactly how you want to spend the rest of your life right now, you can't go wrong by investing in your future.

This book starts with the big picture: managing your life. Notice the phrase is "managing your life"—not *controlling* your life. Let's face it: Many things in life are beyond our control. But you can manage your life

PhotostoGo.com

PhotoObjects.net/Jupiter Images

> **What is important is to keep learning, to enjoy challenge, and to tolerate ambiguity. In the end there are no certain answers.**
>
> *Martina Horner, former President of Radcliffe College*

by making smart choices, setting goals you can work toward, paying attention to your time and energy, and motivating yourself. As the title of this book states boldly, it's about focus.

For many of us, focusing is a challenge. We work too many hours, crowd our lives with obligations, and rush from one thing to the next. We think we're good at **multitasking**. We can surf the Internet, listen to our favorite music, watch a DVD, and read this chapter—all at the same time, right? But think about Gandhi's wise words applied to today's lifestyle: "There is more to life than increasing its speed." The truth is that over the long haul, the more time we spend multitasking, the less we're able to focus when we need to. Of course, it's not hard to multitask when you're doing simple things, like petting your dog and watching TV. But when you add in something that's academically challenging, you won't get much done, and chances are that it won't get done well. Recent research indicates that multitasking hurts your brain's ability to learn, and that what you learn while you're distracted by other things is harder to use and recall.[1] In fact, even though technology gives you quick access and new abilities, according to one study, when you're distracted by e-mail or phone calls, your IQ drops by 10 points.[2] Technology's stimulation gives your brain a squirt of dopamine, which can actually be addictive. And being constantly connected, research shows, can cause brain fatigue.[3] Or, here's another way to think about it. Remember those summer days when the temperature outside is above 100 degrees, and everyone's air conditioners are maxed out? The city may experience a brownout from the energy overload. Many experts say that multitasking causes a brownout in your brain; there's just not enough power to go around. The truth is your stress level can skyrocket when you "fragment" your attention in dozens of directions at the same time, and "rebooting" after you've interrupted yourself to bounce out to something else can take from seconds to hours.[4] Let's be honest: multitasking and learning don't mix very well. Succeeding in college requires you to know when to focus on just one urgent, important thing—and then to do it.

If you read this book carefully and follow its advice, it will help you become the best student you can possibly be. It will give you practical tools to help you manage your life. It will take you into your next level of education, into professional success in your career—or both. And most of all, it will encourage you to become a true learner. That is this book's challenge to you as you begin your college experience.

multitasking doing many different things at once

Spending Time "in the System"

Spending time "in the system"? No, being in college isn't like being in jail—far from it. "The system" is the approach used in this book to help you learn: the Challenge → Reaction → Insight → Action system. It is based on the work of Dr. John Bransford and his colleagues, who together wrote an influential book called *How People Learn.*

Bransford believes learning is a chain reaction that might look something like this:

FIGURE 2.1

CRIA System: How People Learn

Source: Based on J. Bransford, et al. (2000). *How People Learn: Brain, Mind, Experience, and School.* Washington, DC: National Academy Press.

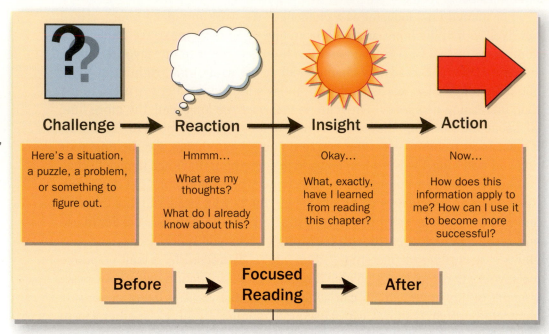

This Challenge → Reaction → Insight → Action learning chain reaction is integrated into *FOCUS* to help you learn. Each chapter takes you through "the system" by walking you through four steps:

STEP 1: Challenge. Whenever you're learning something new, the best place to start is by identifying what you think you already know. For example, each chapter's "Readiness Check" will ask you how this chapter will relate to you and how you'll relate to it. Then you'll continue by reading a case study about a new college student who's facing problems related to the topics in the chapter. Research shows that people generally learn more from examples of things going wrong than they can from examples of things going right. The challenges are real ones many students face. Perhaps you (or a classmate you know) are facing similar issues yourself. Read the case studies carefully and think about solutions that would help these students—before you read the chapter's content. Every chapter begins with a challenge as the first step of the learning chain reaction.

STEP 2: Reaction. After you read the case study, you are asked for your reaction by answering a few questions about it. What is the student in the case study doing wrong or right? What should the student do differently? Your instructor may ask you to discuss your reaction in class or answer the questions in writing. This step of the learning process shows you how much you already know—before you begin reading. It also shows you what you don't know and what you can learn by reading. The goal of this book is help you become a **deep learner**, as opposed to someone who skims the surface and simply rushes on to the next assignment and the next course. It will ask you to pause, **take stock**, focus, and think.

deep learner someone who learns everything they can about a topic

take stock evaluate your progress

Surround yourself with people who take their work seriously, but not themselves, those who work hard and play hard.

Colin Powell, former U.S. Secretary of State

STEP 3: Insight. At the end of each chapter, you'll be asked to revisit some of the questions you were asked in the chapter's opening Step 2: Reaction. Rethinking your responses to the Challenge case will help you gauge how much you've learned. For example, Sylvia Sanchez dreamed of becoming a famous singer, a dream that could have become reality if things fell into place for her. But after reading about it in the chapter, you might decide that you really hadn't thought about it very deeply and there's more to it than you originally thought. The difference between Step 2 (your immediate reaction) and Step 3 (the new insights you've gained from reading) demonstrate that you've learned! After reading the chapter and discussing it in class, you'll know some research on the subject, the chapter's suggestions, examples you can apply, and your instructor's thoughts about how the case study student handled the challenges. You'll also gain some insights about yourself, if you face any of these issues, too.

STEP 4: Action. The final step in this learning chain reaction is about action. What have you learned that will change how you face similar challenges? Learning takes place when it relates to you personally, and insights have no impact unless they lead to change. The bottom line is: You must use your insights to take action. Think of this comparison. One day you feel tired, you notice that your clothes are tight, and you are suddenly aware that you're out of shape. You realize that you must eat healthier food and exercise more. But if you don't take action, it won't happen. To become real, new knowledge must lead to personal insights that result in action. What you learned by reading relates to you, and you must use it!

If you follow the system built into this book and use it as you read all your textbooks, the learning chain reaction will become automatic for you.

How Do You "Spend" Your Time?[5]

Add up the cost of going to college for an entire term: tuition for one semester/trimester/quarter, the total esti-mated cost of all the gas you will use to get to and from class for the term, books and supplies, a computer you may have bought, and child care or any other expenses related to your going to school. Put down everything you can think of. Divide that grand total by the number of hours you are in school (number of weeks class is in session multiplied by the number of hours you are scheduled to be in class). For example, if you are taking two 3-hour classes for a 16-week semester, the number you will divide your grand total by 96 (= 6 hours × 16 weeks). Com-pleting this exercise will show you how much money each class session costs you—and the cost of missing class! Compare your "hourly rate" with that of your classmates and discuss the results as a group.

How Motivated *Are* You and *How* Are You Motivated?

Academic Intrinsic Motivation Self-Assessment

How intrinsically motivated are you? Read each of the following statements and circle the number beside each statement that most accurately represents your views about yourself.

	Completely Not True	Somewhat Not True	Neutral	Somewhat True	Completely True
1. I have academic goals.	1	2	3	4	5
2. I am confident I can complete my degree.	1	2	3	4	5
3. I determine my career goals.	1	2	3	4	5
4. I enjoy solving challenging, difficult problems.	1	2	3	4	5
5. I work on an assignment until I understand it.	1	2	3	4	5
6. I am confident I will finish a degree or certificate.	1	2	3	4	5
7. I determine the quality of my academic work.	1	2	3	4	5
8. I am pursuing college because I value education.	1	2	3	4	5
9. I feel good knowing that I determine how my academic career develops.	1	2	3	4	5
10. I have high standards for academic work.	1	2	3	4	5
11. Staying in college is my decision.	1	2	3	4	5
12. I study because I like to learn new things.	1	2	3	4	5
13. I enjoy doing outside readings in connection to my future coursework.	1	2	3	4	5

	Completely Not True	Somewhat Not True	Neutral	Somewhat True	Completely True
14. I am intrigued by the different topics introduced in my courses.	1	2	3	4	5
15. I study because I am curious.	1	2	3	4	5
16. I look forward to going to class.	1	2	3	4	5
17. I am excited to take more courses within my major.	1	2	3	4	5
18. I enjoy learning more within my field of study.	1	2	3	4	5
19. I like to find answers to questions about material I am learning.	1	2	3	4	5
20. I enjoy studying.	1	2	3	4	5
21. I have pictured myself in a career after college.	1	2	3	4	5
22. I am excited about the job opportunities I will have later.	1	2	3	4	5
23. I have pictured myself being successful in my chosen career.	1	2	3	4	5
24. I believe I will make a substantial contribution to my chosen profession.	1	2	3	4	5
25. I feel good knowing I will be a member of the professional community in my area of study.	1	2	3	4	5

Total each column, then add your scores across.   _____ + _____ + _____ + _____ + _____ =

_____ **OVERALL SCORE**

Continue reading to find out what your overall score means.

French, B. F., & Oakes, W. (2003). Measuring academic intrinsic motivation in the first year of college: Reliability and validity evidence for a new instrument. *Journal of the First Year Experience 15(1)*, 83–102.

When it comes to getting a college education, where does motivation come into the picture? In general, motivation is your desire to put forth effort, even when the going gets rough. The word *motivation* comes from Medieval Latin, *motivus*, meaning "moving." What moves you to learn? There are many ways to define motivation, and different people are motivated by different things.

How motivated would you be to learn something difficult, like a new language, one you'd never studied before? Let's say that you were offered a chance to learn Finnish, a challenging language that is not related to English. For example, in Finnish *Kiitoksia oikein paljon* means "thank you very much." Finnish would be a challenge to learn. To determine your level of motivation, it would help to know your attitude toward Finland and Finnish people, whether you needed to learn Finnish for some reason, how you felt about learning it, whether you thought you could learn it successfully, whether you were rewarded in some way for learning it, and just how stimulating you found the learning process to be.[6] In other words, your motivation depends on many factors, right?

You'd probably be more motivated to learn Finnish if these sorts of things were part of the picture: (1) you were going to visit relatives in Finland and were excited about it; (2) you'd always been good at learning foreign languages and you expected to learn this one easily; (3) your boss was planning to transfer you to Helsinki as part of a big promotion; or (4) you enjoyed your Finnish language class, thought the instructor was a gifted teacher, and found the other students to be as motivated as you were. So, whose job is it to motivate you? Your instructor's? This book's? Yours? Can anyone else besides you motivate you? This book will ask you: how motivated *are* you to succeed in college? And *how* are you motivated?

extrinsically outside yourself

intrinsically inside yourself

To assess your own motivation, it's important to understand the difference between *extrinsic* and *intrinsic* motivation. People who are **extrinsically**, or externally, motivated learn in order to get a grade, earn credits, or complete a requirement, for example. They are motivated by things outside themselves. You could be motivated to learn Finnish to earn three credits or to get an A. People who are **intrinsically**, or internally, motivated learn because they're curious, fascinated, or challenged, or because they truly want to master a subject. They are motivated from within. You could be motivated to learn Finnish for the challenge, because you're curious about it, or because you find it fascinating. Let's be realistic, however. Extrinsic motivation is real and important. You need to earn college credits, and you'd rather get A's than F's. But how intrinsically motivated you are in college will have a great deal to do with just how successful you are. The motivation to become truly educated must come from within you.

FIGURE 2.2

Extrinsic versus Intrinsic Motivation

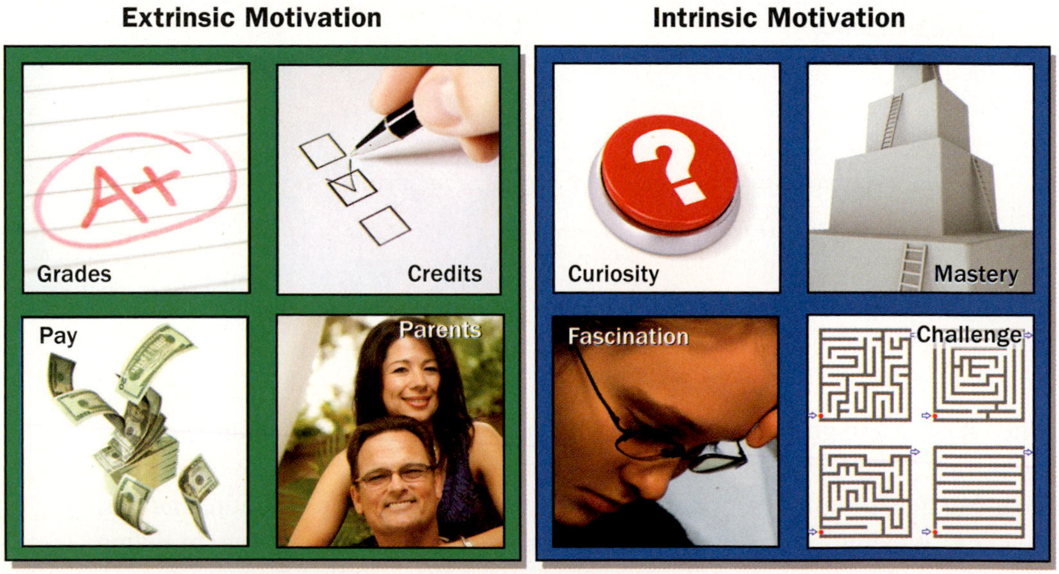

Extrinsic Motivation

Intrinsic Motivation

Grades — Credits — Pay — Parents — Curiosity — Mastery — Fascination — Challenge

(clockwise from top left): Christopher Hall/Shutterstock.com; Yari/Shutterstock.com; Palto/Shutterstock.com; Pling/Shutterstock.com; Vasilius/Shutterstock.com; Yuri Arcurs /Shutterstock.com; Andy Dean Photography/Shutterstock.com; Scott Maxwell/LuMaxArt/Shutterstock.com.

You completed the Academic Intrinsic Motivation Scale (AIMS) in Exercise 2.2, which is designed to measure your intrinsic, or internal, motivation to succeed in college in terms of these four C-Factors:

1. **Curiosity.** Do you want to learn new things? Are you truly interested in what you're learning? Are you curious? Do you ask questions?

2. **Control.** Do you think working hard in your academic courses will pay off? Do you believe you can control how successful you'll be?

3. **Career Outlook.** Are you goal oriented? Are you future oriented? Can you imagine yourself using what you learn in college to help you get a job you want and build a successful professional career?

4. **Challenge.** Does your college coursework challenge you? It is important that the level of challenge is right for you. Too much challenge can cause you to become frustrated and give up. Not enough challenge can cause you to lose interest.[7]

Think about it this way: If your overall score on the AIMS was 100–125, you're intrinsically motivated at a high level. If you scored between 75 and 99, you're intrinsically motivated at a moderate level, but increasing your intrinsic motivation may help you achieve more. If you scored below 75, a lack of intrinsic motivation could interfere with your college success. If you're intrinsically motivated, you'll use all the learning tools offered to you in *FOCUS*.

Because FOCUS works to build connections between academic success in college and professional success in your career field, we'll concentrate most here on the third C-Factor—"Career Outlook"—throughout the text and at the end of each chapter. These two features will help you focus on the connections between college success and career success:

Going Pro: What does it take to go from amateur to professional—whether in athletics or the career you're heading toward? Here we'll examine some of the habits, attitudes, and approaches that will strengthen your performance and lead to success both in school and in your career—as you find yourself "Going Pro"!

What's In YOUR Briefcase?: As you head toward college and career success, it'll pay to have in your "briefcase," your "professional toolkit," techniques that will prove useful both in school and on the job. In this feature, we'll provide some useful answers to the important question, "What's In YOUR Briefcase?"

EXERCISE **2.3**

The Ideal Student

Create your own personal top-ten list of the characteristics (attitudes and actions) of an ideal student. Bring your completed list to your next class session so that all students can read their lists and create a master list that everyone can agree on. Put your initials next to each of the ten items on the master list that you promise to do throughout the term. Your personal top-ten list, which your instructor may discuss with you individually at a later time, will become your own list of goals for the course.

Give Yourself an Attitude Adjustment

There's a difference of opinion on the subject of **attitude**. Some people say attitude is not all that important. Attitude-schmattitude, they say. Others say, "Attitude is everything!"—implying that *attitude* is more important than **aptitude**. What do you think?

attitude state of mind or mental position

aptitude natural ability

© Larry Harwood Photography. Property of Cengage Learning.

> ❝ You must motivate yourself EVERY DAY! ❞
>
> *Matthew Stasior, motivational speaker*

In research studies conducted by Rick Snyder at the University of Kansas, students who scored high on a measure of hope got higher grades. Snyder explained that students with high hopes set themselves higher goals and know how to work hard to attain them.

Quick quiz. How many times a day do you catch yourself saying "Whatever . . . ," and rolling your eyes? Whatever-ness—an attitude of boredom and impatience—takes a lot less effort than staying positive. Whether you realize it or not, whatevers chip away at your motivation, and they can cause you to give up on your dreams and goals. When it comes to your college education and your professional success, one good thing you can do for yourself is to delete the word *whatever* from your vocabulary. Your education and your career are much too important for whatevers—and so are you.

Five Ways to Adjust Your Attitude

The good thing about attitude is that you can change it yourself. As you think about benefits of fine-tuning your attitude, keep these five recommendations in mind:

1. **Know that you always have choices.** Regardless of circumstances—your income, your background, or your academic experiences—you always have a choice, even if it's limited to how you choose to view your current situation.

2. **Take responsibility for your own outcomes.** Coach Vince Lombardi used to have his players look in a mirror before every game and ask themselves, "Am I looking at the person who is helping me win or the one who is holding me back?" Blaming others simply diminishes your own power to work toward **constructive responses** to challenges.

constructive responses
statements or actions that promote improvement

3. **Turn down your negativity meter.** "Can't" and "won't" are two of the biggest obstacles to a healthy attitude. Also pay attention to how you describe things. Is the cup half empty or half full? State things in the positive rather than the negative (for example, "stay healthy" rather than "don't get sick"). Paying attention to positive role models whose traits you admire is also a great way to boost your outlook.

4. **Turn learning points into turning points.** Have you ever watched someone do something so badly that you've said to yourself, "I'm never going to do that! I'm going to do it differently!"? You can also choose to learn from your own mistakes and setbacks. They all offer some sort of lesson, even if it takes a bit of distance from the event to see what you can learn.

5. **Acknowledge your blessings.** Taking time at the end of each day to recognize and feel gratitude for the blessings in your life—no matter how large or small—is a great way to develop a positive attitude.

Statements That Ought to Be Outlawed in College . . . and Why

Because words reflect attitudes (and help shape them), listen for statements like these escaping from your mouth. They can negatively affect your attitude and therefore your learning:

- **"I thought college classes would be more interesting than they are."** Interesting is in the mind of the beholder.

- **"I didn't learn a thing in that class."** Actively search for what you can take away from a class, even if it didn't quite meet your expectations.

- **"The textbook is really dull. Why bother reading it?"** Reading may not be your favorite pastime, but you may learn more from a textbook than you can predict.

- **"The professor is soooo-o-o boring."** In college and on the job, we interact with all types of personalities, so begin to appreciate differences in communication styles.

- **"Why do I have to take this required course? What's the point?"** The point is to broaden your horizons, expand your skills as a critical thinker, and become a lifelong scholar.

Care enough to give yourself every opportunity to do your best. And, yes, every class, every situation in life, is an opportunity. You're worth it.[8]

Ability versus Effort: What's More Important?

Both in school and on the job, successful people have several things in common: They love learning, seek challenges, value effort, and persevere even when things become difficult.[9] They demonstrate both ability and effort. These two things are the basic requirements for success. College and career are about both.

Think about some of the possible combinations of ability and effort. If you have high ability and exert great effort, you'll most likely succeed. If you have high ability and exert little effort, and still succeed, you've just proven how smart you must be! But if you have high ability and exert little effort and fail, you can

>
>
> **Ability is what you're capable of doing. Motivation determines what you do. Attitude determines how well you do it.**
>
> *Lou Holtz, former collge football coach and ESPN sports analyst*

Theories of Intelligence Scale

What is intelligence? Are people born with a certain amount? Or can it be cultivated through learning? Using the following scale, write in the number that corresponds to your opinion in the space next to each statement. There are no right or wrong answers.

1	2	3	4	5	6
Strongly Agree	**Mostly Agree**	**Agree**	**Disagree**	**Mostly Disagree**	**Strongly Disagree**

_____ 1. You have a certain amount of intelligence, and you can't really do much to change it.

_____ 2. You can learn new things, but you can't really change your basic intelligence.

_____ 3. You can always substantially change how intelligent you are.

_____ 4. No matter how much intelligence you have, you can always change it quite a bit.

self-handicapping hurting your own chances to succeed

performers someone who is driven to appear smart

learners someone who is driven to learn, even by making mistakes

always claim you didn't have the time to invest or you didn't care, right? You can always say that you could have done well if you'd tried harder: "I could have written those Harry Potter books; I'm a great writer." If you had really tried for that kind of success, you wouldn't have been able to say that. That's a dangerous strategy, one that's called "**self-handicapping**."[10] Some college students consciously or unconsciously apply this strategy. They exert little effort, perhaps because they have no confidence in themselves or because they fear failure, and then they rationalize when they don't do well.

Research shows that what you believe about your own intelligence—your *mindset*—can make a difference in how successful you'll be in college. At first glance, this statement seems absurd. After all, you're either smart or you're not, right? Wrong.

The scaled questions demonstrate that there are two basic ways to define intelligence. Some of us are **performers**, who agree with statements 1 and 2, while others of us are **learners**, who agree more with statements 3 and 4. *Performers* believe that intelligence is a fixed trait that cannot be changed. From the moment you're born, you have a certain amount of intelligence that belongs to you, and that's that. *Learners*, on the other hand, believe you can grow your intelligence if you capitalize on opportunities to learn. Whenever you tackle a tough challenge, you learn from it. The more you learn, the more intelligent you can become. Understanding which view of intelligence you believe in will make a difference in how you approach your college classes, and how successful you'll be.

Students who are taught the value of a learning mindset over a performance mindset can actually achieve more than students who don't.[11] In one study, college students' views of intelligence predicted the goals students valued in college. *Performers* were more likely to want to give up in challenging situations; learners wanted to try harder.[12] In one study that measured the electrical activity in college students' brains as they performed a difficult task, brain activity showed that *performers* cared most about whether their answers were right or wrong, whereas *learners* were interested in follow-up information they could learn from.[13] Yet another study showed that *learners* are more likely to buckle down academically, even when they feel depressed.[14] It's clear: Believing you're a *learner* provides advantages in motivation, achievement, enjoyment, and commitment.

Regardless of what you believe about your precise intelligence level, the fact is this: *Intelligence can be cultivated through learning.* And people's theories about their intelligence levels can be shifted.

ONLINE TechKnow

As you think about how you'll complete your online coursework, keep these pointers in mind:

- **Be detailed in setting your goals.** Include what you will achieve, where (at home or in a lab on campus), and when (Thursday afternoon from 5–7 p.m. after I get off work). For example, "I will do online research for my next assignment for two hours every weeknight with no interruptions until the due date."

- **Make sure your goals are realistic.** Don't say you'll work in the evening for two hours on online homework, two hours on tasks from your job, two hours on answering e-mails, and spend two hours with your family. There's not enough time in the evening to do all that—so prioritize and cut back in your goals

- **State your goals positively.** It's better to say, "I will work on my online assignments for one hour before checking my e-mails," than "I won't check e-mail until I complete my online studies."

- **Approach your goals with a positive attitude.** Respond to online assignments with spirit, enjoyment, and enthusiasm. You'll be much more productive and proud of what you accomplish.[15]

Improve Your Grade
Online Flashcards
Glossary

What Drives You? Values, Dreams, and Goals

EXERCISE 2.5

Core Values Self-Assessment

What are your core values? What's most important to you—deep down inside? Review the following list and check off the items that you value. Don't spend too much time thinking about each one; just go with your initial gut reaction. For each item, ask yourself, "Is this something that's important to me?"

_____ Health	_____ Physical Appearance	_____ Financial wealth
_____ Fitness/Physical strength	_____ Independence	_____ Commitment
_____ Loyalty	_____ Honesty	_____ Compassion
_____ Academic achievement	_____ Children	_____ Leisure time
_____ Success	_____ Leadership	_____ Balance
_____ Happiness	_____ Family	_____ Friendship
_____ Social life	_____ Marriage/Partnership	_____ Recognition
_____ Athletics	_____ Spirituality	_____ Status
_____ Creativity	_____ Variety	_____ Wisdom
_____ Meaningful work	_____ Challenge	_____ Time spent alone
_____ Adventure	_____ Personal growth	_____ Other (list here)

Now review all of the items you checked off, and circle the five that are most important to you at this point in your life. Then rank them by putting a number next to each of the five circled values, with number one as your top priority. Finally, take stock. Is this the person you want to be? Is there anything about your values that you would like to change? If so, what's keeping you from making this change?

Before tackling the big questions about what you want to create with your life, it's important to first take a close look in the mirror. Who are you? What makes you tick? What do you **value**? What are your **goals**? Where will your **dreams** take you?

value something you think is important

goals something you make specific plans to achieve

dreams something you wish for

> **You have to learn the rules of the game. And then you have to play better than anyone else.**
>
> ALBERT EINSTEIN

earn the rules of the game. In college and throughout your professional life you'll be learning what's sometimes called "The Hidden Curriculum." These are things everyone knows, more or less, but never learned formally. For example, most people know that it's not polite to tell off-color jokes to people you've just met or smack your gum while giving a speech. In the same way, the "grapevine" or informal network on the job is important to understand. To be successful, you must be tuned in. Observe your colleagues and supervisors. How do they act, how do they talk, what are their values and boundaries, what lines do they just not cross? When you have questions about these things, talk about them with people who seem to be "in the know." Understand the culture of the organization you work for. What does it value? Who holds the power? Where do you fit in, and what can you contribute? Watch, learn, listen—and become a successful career professional. Remember, you're "Going Pro"!

Values at the Core

What do you value in life? By taking time to examine your personal values, managing your life will become easier and make more sense. Values can be things you can't exactly see or touch, like love or respect, or things that are visible and real, like family or money. Understanding how they motivate you isn't as simple as it might seem. Values can change as you go through life. For example, if you're single now, you may value the freedom to meet a variety of potential romantic partners. Later, however, you may want a committed relationship because you want stability in your life. For this reason, it's important to look at your values from time to time and rethink them.

Another complicating factor is that values can conflict with one another. Suppose that you value honesty and kindness, and you are at a party and a friend asks you what you think of her new hair color. You honestly think it's hideous, but telling her so would hurt her feelings, thus violating your value of being kind. How do you respond? That would depend on which value is a higher priority for you. You have to make an on-the-spot decision about which value to use. Once you define and prioritize your values, however, they can help you make everyday choices as well as big decisions, like which major to pursue in college. For example, if academic achievement is one of your top values, the next time you have the urge to do something else instead of go to class, consider what that choice says about your value system. And if career success is one of your highest values, and yet you don't feel like going in to work some Monday morning, the same question is relevant. There is a great inner satisfaction that comes from living a life tied to core values.

> **You are never given a wish without the power to make it come true. You may have to work for it, however.**
>
> *Richard Bach, from* Illusions

Patrik Giardino/Corbis

Dreams versus Goals

Do you agree or disagree with this statement: "I can be anything I want to be"? You've probably heard this statement frequently. Your family and teachers all want you to have positive self-esteem, and certainly there are many career options available today. But is it true? Can you be *anything* you want to be? What's the difference between a dream and a goal?

As a student, you may dream of being a famous doctor or a famous athlete or just plain famous. That's the beauty of dreams—you can imagine yourself doing anything. When you're dreaming, you don't even have to play by the rules of reality. Dreams are fantasy-based—*you* in a perfect world. But when it's time to come back to reality, you discover that there are rules, after all. You may have dreamed of becoming a top-earning NBA player or a top fashion model when you were a child, but you have grown up to be the same height as Uncle Al or Aunt Sue—and that's not tall enough.

Dreams alone are not enough when it comes to creating your future. As professional life coach Diana Robinson says, "A dream is a goal without legs." And without legs, that goal is going nowhere. Dreaming is the first step to creating the future you want, but making dreams come true requires planning and hard work. Sylvia Sanchez wanted to become a famous singer because she likes music, and people always told her she was good. As she continues through college, however, she will come to understand herself better. The music industry might be challenging to break into, but that doesn't mean she should abandon her dream. She must find a realistic way to help her turn her dreams into goals. Just dreaming isn't enough. Dreams are exciting; you can let your imagination run wild. Goals are real; you must work out how to actually achieve your dreams.

Goal setting is an important part of the life management skills this book will help you develop. Your goals may not seem at all clear to you right now, but the important thing is to learn that there's a right way and a wrong way to set your goals. The best way to ensure that the goals you set will serve you well is to make sure you *FOCUS*. Here's a brief overview of what that means.

Flying Colours Ltd/Digital Vision/Getty Images

F   Fit. Your goal must fit your values, your character, and who you are as a person. Goals that conflict with any of these things will not only be difficult to accomplish, but they just won't work. If your goal is to become a writer for a travel magazine because you love adventure, but flying in planes terrifies you, you're in trouble.

O   Ownership. Own your goal: See it, taste it, want it! It must be your goal, not someone else's goal for you. Ask yourself: Does the thought of achieving this goal get me fired up? Do I genuinely own this goal or do I feel I ought to have this goal because it sounds good or makes someone else happy?

C   Concreteness. For any goal to be effective, it must be real. In other words, you must be able to describe your goal in detail: "To run a mile in less than six minutes by March 4th" is much more concrete than "to eventually run faster." The more concrete, the better.

U   Usefulness. Goals must be useful. They must serve a purpose, and that purpose should be tied to your long-term vision of the person you want to become. For example, if you want to work for an international hotel some day, it would be useful to begin studying a foreign language now.

S   Stretch. In the business world, people talk about stretch goals. These are goals that require employees to stretch beyond their usual limits to achieve something more challenging. Goals must be based in reality, but also offer you a chance to grow beyond the person you currently are.

Your goals should include both short- and long-term goals. Once your long-term goals are set (though they may shift over time as *you* shift over time), you will then want to set some short-term goals, which act as in-between steps to achieving your long-term goals.

Long-Term Goals What do I want to accomplish . . .	Short-Term Goals What do I want to accomplish . . .
In my lifetime?	This year?
In the next twenty years?	This month?
In the next ten years?	This week?
In the next three to five years?	Today?

> **This constant, unproductive preoccupation with all the things we have to do is the single largest consumer of time and energy.**
>
> —KERRY GLEESON,
> TIME MANAGEMENT EXPERT

Reason 2: They're immobilized by worry.

It's easy to feel overwhelmed when you think about the big picture—school assignments, work demands, financial struggles and relationship ups and downs. The "big picture" is a gigantic puzzle that looms so large that it's hard to focus on any one individual piece. How much time do you spend worrying about how much is on your plate—as opposed to removing things one at a time in a systematic way? Sometimes the biggest enemy of focus is worry. Our ability to concentrate is hijacked by anxiety, pure and simple.

TRY It!

List the three items you worry about getting done most, and for each one, list three suggestions you should follow to improve your focus and your life.

1. _____
   a.
   b.
   c.
2. _____
   a.
   b.
   c.
3. _____
   a.
   b.
   c.

What's In **YOUR** Briefcase?

KNOW THYSELF

Expectations. They play a big role in our lives. Some expectations may come from your early family years: "Our Gabe is going to be a doctor. We've known it since we watched him play with his toy doctor's kit as a little kid." The story has been repeated so many times that it's now turned into a long-term expectation.

But here's an important question: What do *you* want to do with your life? Although others may have communicated expectations over the years, figuring this out for yourself is one of the most important questions you begin to answer in college. Many college students change their majors at least once, just as many adults change their careers.

Use college as an opportunity to truly get to know yourself. Pay attention to which disciplines fascinate you as a learner. Make decisions for the right reasons. A career that pays well but holds no real appeal for you may result in major dissatisfaction later on. Project some alternative futures for yourself based on various career possibilities. Imagine yourself wearing different career "hats." As a French Pulitzer Prize–winning author once said, "Be faithful to that which exists nowhere but in yourself." And set your own course.

Are there particular expectations related to getting an education that others have for you? How well do they align with your own dreams and goals? If there's disagreement, how do you plan to handle it?

_____
_____
_____

At the beginning of this chapter, Sylvia Sanchez faced a series of challenges as a new college student. Now after learning from this chapter, would you respond differently to any of the questions you answered about the "FOCUS Challenge Case"? Using what you learned in the chapter, write a paragraph ending to Sylvia's case study. What are some of the possible outcomes for her?

1. Identify one new thing you learned in reading this chapter. Why did you select the one you've selected? How will it affect what you do in your college classes?

2. Do you have some of the same questions Sylvia does about your own level of motivation to achieve in college? How could you increase your motivation? How important might that be?

3. How do your own goals and dreams differ? How do you plan to turn your dreams into goals?

chapter 3 Learning Styles and Studying

READINESS CHECK

How this chapter relates to **YOU**

1. When it comes to learning and studying in college, what are you most unsure about, if anything?

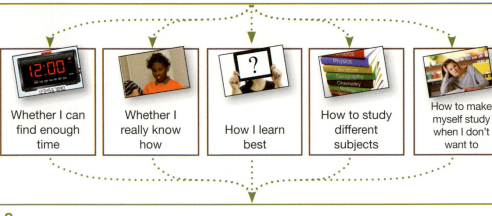

| Whether I can find enough time | Whether I really know how | How I learn best | How to study different subjects | How to make myself study when I don't want to |

2. What is most likely to be your response? Circle it.

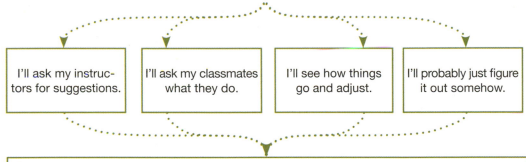

| I'll ask my instructors for suggestions. | I'll ask my classmates what they do. | I'll see how things go and adjust. | I'll probably just figure it out somehow. |

3. What would you have to do to increase your likelihood of success? Will you do it this term?

Example: Read this book. Yes!

How **YOU** will relate to this chapter

What are you most interested in learning about? Put check marks next to those topics.

☐ How learning changes your brain

☐ How people are intelligent in different ways

☐ How you learn through your senses

☐ How your personality type can affect your learning style

☐ What metacognition is and how it can help you

☐ How to apply your learning style to your study style

☐ How to become an intentional learner and make a master study plan

● How motivated are you to learn more about getting the right start in college? (5 = high, 1 = low) ____

● How ready are you to read now? ____ (If something is in your way, take care of it if you can, zero in and focus.)

● How long do you think it will take you to complete this chapter? If you start and stop, keep track of your overall time. ____ hour(s) ____ minutes

49

Antun Hirsman/Shutterstock.com; Pattie Steib/Shutterstock.com; DmitriMaruta /Shutterstock.com; balein/Shutterstock.com; Simone van den Berg/Shutterstock.com

© Larry Harwood Photography. Property of Cengage Learning.

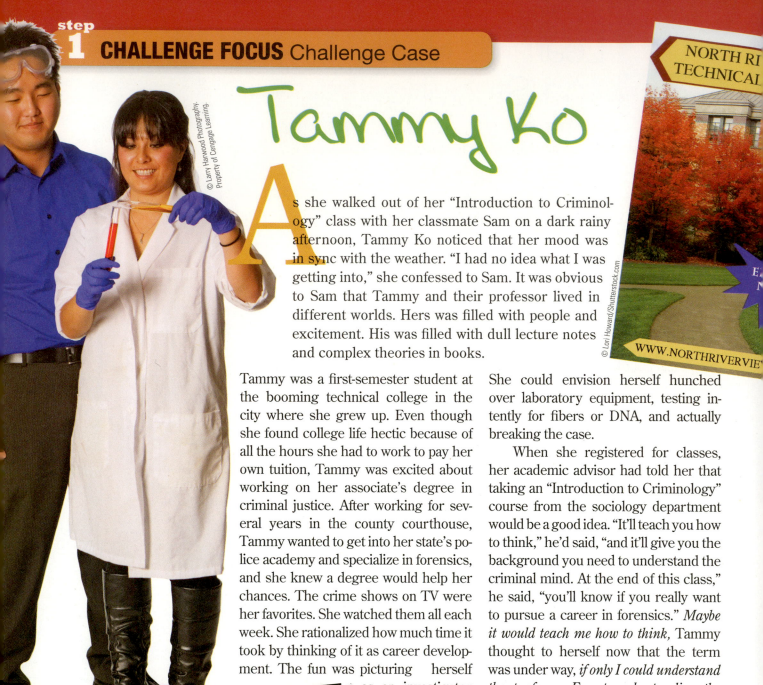

Tammy Ko

**NORTH RI
TECHNICAL**

WWW.NORTHRIVERVIE

As she walked out of her "Introduction to Criminology" class with her classmate Sam on a dark rainy afternoon, Tammy Ko noticed that her mood was in sync with the weather. "I had no idea what I was getting into," she confessed to Sam. It was obvious to Sam that Tammy and their professor lived in different worlds. Hers was filled with people and excitement. His was filled with dull lecture notes and complex theories in books.

Tammy was a first-semester student at the booming technical college in the city where she grew up. Even though she found college life hectic because of all the hours she had to work to pay her own tuition, Tammy was excited about working on her associate's degree in criminal justice. After working for several years in the county courthouse, Tammy wanted to get into her state's police academy and specialize in forensics, and she knew a degree would help her chances. The crime shows on TV were her favorites. She watched them all each week. She rationalized how much time it took by thinking of it as career development. The fun was picturing herself as an investigator solving headline cases: "Man Slain, Found in City Park" or "Modern Day 'Jack the Ripper' Terrorizes Las Vegas."

She could envision herself hunched over laboratory equipment, testing intently for fibers or DNA, and actually breaking the case.

When she registered for classes, her academic advisor had told her that taking an "Introduction to Criminology" course from the sociology department would be a good idea. "It'll teach you how to think," he'd said, "and it'll give you the background you need to understand the criminal mind. At the end of this class," he said, "you'll know if you really want to pursue a career in forensics." *Maybe it would teach me how to think,* Tammy thought to herself now that the term was under way, *if only I could understand the professor. Forget understanding the criminal mind—I'd just like a glimpse into his!* Most of the time, Sam agreed with her just to keep the peace, although he always aced everything.

Professor Caldwell was quiet and reserved, and he seemed a bit out of touch. He dressed as if he hadn't bought

Program Description
Criminology

Although we think of criminology as a relatively new discipline, the foundations of criminology can be traced back over two centuries. Criminology is the "scientific study of the causes of crime and delinquency, crime control policies, institutions designed to control crime, and media depictions of crime, criminals, and victims." Criminology draws from many other disciplines, including: psychology, sociology, political science, economics, and others.

Criminology is a rapidly growing field of study, and has many possible career options, including: Federal Agent, Counselor, Drug Enforcement Agent, Probation Officer, Forensic Specialist, Victim Services Specialist, Litigation Manager, etc.

Course Work

First Year	Second Year
CRIM 103 – Introduction to Criminology	CRIM 315 – Advanced Criminology
CRIM 105 – Research Methods for Social Science	CRIM 318 – Juvenile Delinquency
ENGL 130 – Scientific Writing	CRIM 320 – Capital Punishment
CHEM 106 – General Chemistry I	PHIL 300 – Ethical Dilemmas in Criminal Justice
CHEM 108 – General Chemistry II	CRIM 350 – The Correctional System
MATH 135 – Calculus I	CRIM 360 – The Judicial System
MATH 136 – Calculus II	PSYC 310 – Abnormal Psychology
Elective – 3 credits	Electives – 6 credits

ELECTIVES
- CSI: Fact or Fantasy?
- Interview and Interrogation Techniques
- Professionalism and Ethics
- Investigation of Injury and Death
- Crime Scene & Crime Lab
- Psychosociology of Criminology

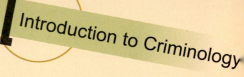
a new piece of clothing in as many years as he'd been teaching. In class, he was very articulate, knowledgeable, and organized, with his handouts neatly piled on the desk, and he covered each day's material methodically, point by point. Tammy wished he'd leave his notes occasionally to explore other interesting things. Tammy had always preferred teachers who created exciting things to do in class over teachers who went completely by the book. Tammy's biggest complaint about Professor Caldwell was that he only talked about *theories* of criminology. When was he ever going to get to the hands-on part of the course? She couldn't help thinking,

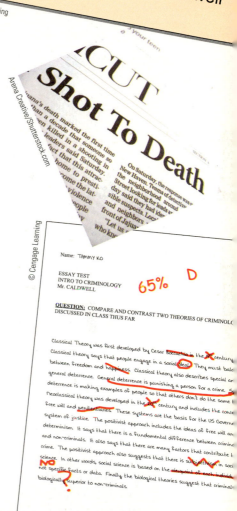

Michael J. Thompson/Shutterstock.com

When will we stop talking about theories and start working on real cases—like the ones on all those TV shows?

To make matters worse, learning from lectures was not Tammy's strong suit. In fact, she really didn't know how to study, and furthermore she just flat out didn't enjoy it. Honestly, she avoided studying as much as she could. Her social life was her top priority. She hadn't done well on the first exam because she'd had to resort to memorizing things that didn't make much sense to her, and her D grade showed it.

The entire exam consisted of one question: "Compare and contrast two theories of criminology discussed in class thus far." Tammy hated essay tests. She was at her best on tests with right or wrong answers, like true–false or multiple-choice questions. Making sense out of spoken words that go by very quickly during a lecture and trying to psych out professors' preferred answers on essay tests were challenges to her.

But her "Introduction to Criminology" class was far from hands-on. In fact, Tammy had noticed that many of her teachers preferred *talking* about things to *doing* things. They seemed to take more interest in theories than in the real world. Too bad, she thought. *The real world is where exciting things happen.* Although she hated to admit it, sometimes Tammy couldn't wait for college to be over so that she could begin her career in the real world.

A few of Tammy's friends had taken Mr. Caldwell's classes, too. Her friends' advice was "Just try and memorize the stuff; that's all you can do." Regardless of what they happened to be talking about, somehow the conversation always came around to Mr. Caldwell and how impossible it was to learn in his classes.

© Cengage Learning

NORTH RIVERVIEW POLICE
Requirements for Applicants

Prospective North Riverview Police Officers must meet all of the following minimum requirements. Requirements are determined by the City of North Riverview and the State Government.

QUICK CHECKLIST:

Be 19 years of age or older as outlined above.

Possess a high school diploma or GED.

Be a citizen of the United States.

Be free from convictions of disqualifying offenses.

Be personally examined by a State licensed physician.

Be personally examined by a State licensed psychologist.

Be subject to a thorough background investigation.

Successfully complete a basic police training course given at a commissioned, certified school.

CANDIDATES MUST HAVE A WORKING KNOWLEDGE OF:

• the laws controlling, and the procedures, practices, and techniques necessary to

1. Do you have anything in common with Tammy? If so, how are you managing the situation so that you can be successful?

2. Is Tammy smart? If so, in what ways? What is she particularly good at?

3. What sensory modality does Tammy prefer for taking in information? Does she learn best by viewing information through charts and graphs, for example, or by talking and listening, by reading and writing, or by actually doing things?

4. Tammy says straightforwardly that she doesn't know how to study and dislikes doing it. In your view, what specifically should she do to succeed, not only in this class but in college?

Go to the Head of the Class: Learning and the Brain

EXERCISE 3.1

What Is Learning?

The following statements represent common student views on learning. Think about each statement, and mark it true or false based on your honest opinion.

_____ 1. Learning is often hard work and really not all that enjoyable.

_____ 2. Memorization and learning are basically the same thing.

_____ 3. The learning done in school is often gone in a few weeks or months.

_____ 4. In college, most learning takes place in class.

_____ 5. Learning is usually the result of listening to an instructor lecture or reading a textbook.

_____ 6. The best way to learn is by working alone.

_____ 7. Most students know intuitively how they learn best.

_____ 8. Teachers control what students learn.

_____ 9. Learning only deals with subjects taught in school.

_____10. The learning pace is controlled by the slowest learner in the class.

You probably noticed that many of these statements attempt to put learning in a negative light. How many did you mark true? This chapter will help you understand more about learning as a process and about yourself as a learner. As you read, your goal should be to use the insights you gain to become a better learner.

In one of his most famous plays, Shakespeare wrote, "O this learning. What a thing it is!" He was right. The fact that human beings can learn throughout their lives is an amazing characteristic. We learn language, numbers, and concepts right from the very start, and we keep learning until we draw our last breaths. But how do we do it, and more specific to this chapter, how do we learn at our best? In this chapter, you'll learn a great deal about yourself and your learning preferences, and you'll discover new ways to study so that you can learn more productively and efficiently, both in college and throughout your career. That kind of knowledge can definitely give you an advantage!

Let's start our exploration of the learning process close to home—in our own heads. What's going on up there, anyway? While your hands are busy manipulating test tubes in chemistry lab or your eyes are watching your psychology instructor's PowerPoint presentation, what's your brain up to? The answer? Plenty.

Use It or Lose It

The human brain consists of a complex web of connections between neurons or nerve cells. This web grows in complexity as it incorporates new knowledge. But if the connections are not reinforced frequently, you lose them. As you learn new things, you work to hardwire these connections, making them less likely to deteriorate. When your instructors repeat portions of the previous week's lecture or assign homework so you can practice material covered in class, they're helping you to form connections in your brain by using and reusing them—or, in other words, helping you to learn. Repetition is vital to learning. You must use and reuse information in order to hardwire it.

American humorist Will Rogers once said, "You know, you've got to exercise your *brain* just like your muscles." He was right. Giving your brain the exercise it needs—now and in your years after college—will help you form connections between neurons that, if you keep using them, will last a lifetime. From a biological point of view, that's what being a lifelong learner means. The age-old advice "use it or lose it" is true when it comes to learning.

Ask Questions and Hardwire Your Connections

Your instructors have been studying their disciplines for years, perhaps decades. They have developed extensive hardwired connections between their brain neurons. They are *experts*.

By contrast, you are a *novice*, or newcomer, to whatever discipline you're studying. You've not yet developed the brain wiring that your instructors have developed. That can lead to a potential problem. Sometimes instructors are so familiar with what they already know from years of traveling the same pathways in their brains that what you're learning for the first time seems obvious to them. Without even realizing it, they can expect what is familiar to them to be obvious to you. Think of how challenging it is when you try to teach something that you understand thoroughly to another person who doesn't, like teaching someone who has never used a computer before how to upload an assignment.

Because you're a novice, you may not understand everything your instructors say. Ask questions, check, clarify, probe, and persist until you do understand. Sometimes your confusion is not due to a lack of knowledge, but a lack of the *correct* knowledge. For example, you may study for a test by doing only one thing—reading and rereading the textbook. Actually, it's important to be familiar with many different ways to study and then choose the ones that work best for you.

Think of it this way. Some of the brain wiring you brought with you to college is positive and useful, and some actually hurts more than it helps. When you learn, you not only add new connections, but you rewire some old connections. While you're in college, you're under construction![1]

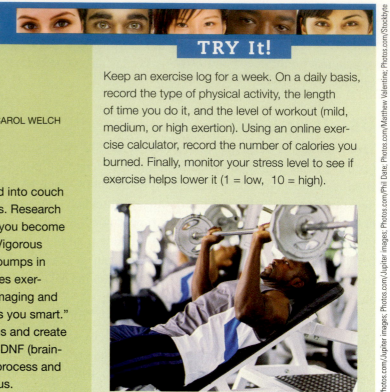

> ❝ **Movement is a medicine for creating change in a person's physical, emotional, and mental states.** ❞
>
> —CAROL WELCH

Reason 3: They prefer to veg out.

Some people lose their focus because they've turned into couch potatoes. Their brains become as soft as their bodies. Research shows that just twenty minutes of exercise can help you become calm and focused for as long as twenty-four hours. Vigorous exercise helps you get rid of excess adrenaline and pumps in endorphins that block pain and anxiety.[2] Not only does exercise help you burn off cheeseburgers, recent brain-imaging and neurochemical studies indicate that "sweating makes you smart." Physical exercise helps reinforce existing connections and create new ones between brain wiring via a protein called BDNF (brain-derived neurotrophic factor). Brain wiring helps you process and store information, thus sharpening your ability to focus.

TRY It!

Keep an exercise log for a week. On a daily basis, record the type of physical activity, the length of time you do it, and the level of workout (mild, medium, or high exertion). Using an online exercise calculator, record the number of calories you burned. Finally, monitor your stress level to see if exercise helps lower it (1 = low, 10 = high).

Stockbyte/Photos.com

	Sunday	Monday	Tuesday	Wednesday	Thursday	Friday	Saturday	TOTAL
Activity								
Time								
Exertion Level								
Calories Burned								
Overall stress level for the day (1 = low; 10 = high)								

Take Charge and Create the Best Conditions for Learning

Throughout this discussion, we've been talking about processes inside your brain. *Your* brain, not anyone else's. The bottom line is this: Learning must be *internally initiated*—by you. It can only be *externally encouraged*—by someone else. You're in charge of your own learning. Learning actually changes your brain.

Let's look at food as an analogy: If learning is a process that is as biological as digestion, then no one can learn for you, in the same way that no one can eat for you. The food in the refrigerator doesn't do you a bit of good unless you walk over, open the door, remove it, and start eating. It's there for the taking, but you must make that happen. To carry the analogy further, you eat on a daily basis, right? "No thanks, I ate last week" is a silly statement. Learning does for your brain what food does for your body. Nourish yourself!

Brain researchers tell us the best state for learning has many dimensions. Let's look at some of the most important ones.

When we come to know something, we have performed an act that is as biological as when we digest something.

Henry Plotkin, Darwin Machines and the Nature of Knowledge (1994)

Colin Anderson/Blend Images/Corbis

1. **You're intrinsically motivated (from within yourself) to learn material that is appropriately challenging.**

   > **Examine where your motivation to learn comes from.** Are you *internally* motivated because you're curious about the subject and want to learn about it or *externally* motivated to get an A or avoid an F? Can you generate your own internal motivation? This book has built-in reminders to boost your intrinsic motivation. Use them to your advantage as a learner.

   > **Adjust the level of challenge yourself.** If you're too challenged in a class, you become nervous. Make sure you're keeping up with the workload and that you've completed the **prerequisites**. In many classes, you must know the fundamentals before tackling more advanced concepts. If you're not challenged enough, you can become bored and tune out. Your instructor will provide one level of challenge for everyone in the class. But it's up to you to fine-tune that challenge for yourself. Get extra help if you aren't quite up to the task, or bump up the challenge a notch or two if you're ahead of the game so that you're continually motivated to learn.

   prerequisite something that must be completed before something else

2. **You're appropriately stressed, but generally relaxed.**

   > **Assess your stress.** According to researchers, you learn best in a state of *relaxed alertness,* a state of high challenge and low threat.[3] Although relaxed alertness may sound impossible, it can be achieved. No stress at all is what you'd find in a no-brainer course. Some stress is useful; it helps you learn. Stress can heighten your alertness and help you focus. How stressed are you—and why—when you get to class? Are you overstressed because you've rushed from your last class, you're late because you missed your bus, or because you haven't done the reading and hope you won't be called on? Prepare for class so that you're ready to jump in. Or instead of too much stress, are you understressed because you don't value the course material? Consider how the information can be useful to you—perhaps in ways you've never even thought of. Here's the vital question to ask yourself: How much stress do I need in order to trigger my best effort?

> **Pay attention to your overall physical state.** Are you taking care of your physical needs so that you can stay alert, keep up with the lecture, and participate in the discussion?

3. **You're curious about what you're learning, and you look forward to learning it.**

> **Get ready to learn by looking back and by looking ahead.** When you're about to cross the street, you must look both ways, right? Keep that image in mind because that's what you should do before each class. What did class consist of last time? Can you predict what it will consist of next time?

> **Focus on substance, not style.** Part of Tammy's bias against Mr. Caldwell focused on his appearance. Despite society's obsession with attractiveness, grooming, and fashion, a student's job is to ask, "What can I learn from this person?" Deciding an instructor isn't worth paying attention to because he doesn't dress well or because his hair style is outdated is just an excuse not to learn.

4. **You search for personal meaning and patterns.**

> **Ask yourself: What's in it for me?** Why is knowing this important? How can I use this information in the future? Instead of dismissing material that appears unrelated to your life, try figuring out how it *could* relate. You may be surprised!

> **Think about how courses relate to one another.** How does this new knowledge relate to things you're learning in other courses? Does sociology have anything to do with history? Psychology with economics?

It is not the answer that enlightens, but the question.

Eugene Ionesco, Romanian and French playwright (1909–1994)

© Larry Harwood Photography. Property of Cengage Learning.

5. **Your emotions are involved, not just your mind.**

> **Evaluate your attitudes and feelings.** Do you like the subject matter? Do you admire the teacher? Remember your high school teacher, Mr. Brown, whose class you just couldn't stand? Not every class will be your favorite. That's natural. But if a class turns you off as a learner, instead of allowing your emotions to take over, ask why and whether your feelings are in your best interest.

> **Make a deliberate decision to change negative feelings.** Fortunately, feelings can be changed. Hating a course or disliking a professor can only build resentment and threaten your success. It's possible to do a 180–degree turn and transform your negative emotions into positive energy.

6. **You realize that as a learner you use what you already know in constructing new knowledge.**[4]

> **Remember that passive learning is impossible.** When it comes to learning, you are the construction foreman, building on what you already know to construct new knowledge. You're not just memorizing facts someone else wants you to learn. You're a full partner in the learning process!

> **Remind yourself that constructing knowledge takes work.** No one ever built a house by simply sitting back or just hanging out.

> It is what we think we know already that often prevents us from learning.
>
> *Claude Bernard, French physiologist (1813–1878)*

Builders work hard, but in the end they have something to show for their efforts. In your college courses, identify what you already know, and blend new knowledge into the framework you've built in your mind. By constructing new knowledge, you are building yourself into a more sophisticated, more polished, and most certainly more educated person.

7. **You're given a degree of choice in terms of what you learn, how you do it, and feedback on how you're doing.**

   > **Make the most of the choices you're given.** College isn't a free-for-all in which you can take any classes you like toward earning a degree. However, which electives you choose will be up to you. Or in a particular course, if your instructor allows you to write a paper or shoot a video, choose the option that will be more motivating for you. When you receive an assignment, select a topic that fires you up. It's easier to generate energy to put toward choices you've made yourself.

   > **Use feedback to improve, and if feedback is not given, ask for it.** It's possible to get really good at doing something the wrong way. Take a golf swing or a swimming stroke, for example. Without someone intervening to give you feedback, it may be difficult to know how to improve. Your instructors will most likely write comments on your assignments to explain their grades. Evaluating your work is their job; it's what they must do to help you improve. Take their suggestions to heart and try them out.

All of us are already good learners in some situations. Let's say you're drawn to technology, for example. You're totally engrossed in computers and eagerly learn everything you can from books, classes, and online sources—and you sometimes totally lose yourself in a flow state as you're learning. No one has to force you to practice your technology skills or pick up an issue of *Wired* or *PC World*. You do it because you want to. In this case, you're self-motivated and therefore learning is easy. This chapter provides several different tools to help you understand your own personal profile as a learner so that you can try to learn at your best in *all* situations.

> The purpose of learning is growth, and our minds, unlike our bodies, can continue growing as long as we live.
>
> *Mortimer Adler, American philosopher, educator, and editor (1902–2001)*

Multiple Intelligences: *How Are You Smart?*

Multiple Intelligences Self-Assessment

Are people smart in different ways? How so? On each line, put check marks next to all the statements that best describe you.

Linguistic Intelligence: The capacity to use language to express what's on your mind and understand others ("word smart")

_____ I'm a good storyteller.

_____ I enjoy word games, puns, and tongue twisters.

_____ I'd rather listen to the radio than watch TV.

_____ I've recently written something I'm proud of.

_____ I can hear words in my head before I say or write them.

_____ When riding in the car, I sometimes pay more attention to words on billboards than I do to the scenery.

_____ In high school, I did better in English, history, or social studies than I did in math and science.

_____ I enjoy reading.

_____ TOTAL check marks

Logical-Mathematical Intelligence: The capacity to understand cause/effect relationships and to manipulate numbers ("number/reasoning smart")

_____ I can easily do math in my head.

_____ I enjoy brainteasers or puzzles.

_____ I like it when things can be counted or analyzed.

_____ I can easily find logical flaws in what others do or say.

_____ I think most things have rational explanations.

_____ Math and science were my favorite subjects in high school.

_____ I like to put things into categories.

_____ I'm interested in new scientific advances.

_____ TOTAL check marks

Spatial Intelligence: The capacity to represent the world visually or graphically ("picture smart")

_____ I like to take pictures of what I see around me.

_____ I'm sensitive to colors.

_____ My dreams at night are vivid.

_____ I like to doodle or draw.

_____ I'm good at navigating with a map.

_____ I can picture what something will look like before it's finished.

_____ In school, I preferred geometry to algebra.

_____ I often make my point by drawing a picture or diagram.

_____ TOTAL check marks

Bodily-Kinesthetic Intelligence: The capacity to use your whole body or parts of it to solve a problem, make something, or put on a production ("body smart")

_____ I regularly engage in sports or physical activities.

_____ I get fidgety (tap my foot, etc.) when asked to sit for long periods of time.

_____ I get some of my best ideas while I'm engaged in a physical activity.

_____ I need to practice a skill in order to learn it, rather than just reading or watching a video about it.

_____ I enjoy being a daredevil.

_____ I'm a well-coordinated person.

_____ I like to think through things while I'm doing something else like running or walking.

_____ I like to spend my free time outdoors.

_____ TOTAL check marks

Musical Intelligence: The capacity to think in music; hear patterns; and recognize, remember, and perhaps manipulate them ("music smart")

_____ I can tell when a musical note is flat or sharp.

_____ I play a musical instrument.

_____ I often hear music playing in my head.

_____ I can listen to a piece of music once or twice, and then sing it back accurately.

_____ I often sing or hum while working.

_____ I like music playing while I'm doing things.

_____ I'm good at keeping time to a piece of music.

_____ I consider music an important part of my life.

_____ TOTAL check marks

Interpersonal Intelligence: The capacity to understand other people ("people smart")

_____ I prefer group activities to solo activities.

_____ Others think of me as a leader.

_____ I enjoy the challenge of teaching others something I like to do.

_____ I like to get involved in social activities at school, church, or work.

_____ If I have a problem, I'm more likely to get help than tough it out alone.

_____ I feel comfortable in a crowd of people.

_____ I have several close friends.

_____ I'm the sort of person others come to for advice about their problems.

_____ TOTAL check marks

Intrapersonal Intelligence: The capacity to understand yourself, who you are, and what you can do ("self-smart")

_____ I like to spend time alone thinking about important questions in life.

_____ I have invested time in learning more about myself.

_____ I consider myself to be independent minded.

_____ I keep a journal of my inner thoughts.

_____ I'd rather spend a weekend alone than at a place with a lot of other people around.

_____ I've thought seriously about starting a business of my own.

_____ I'm realistic about my own strengths and weaknesses.

_____ I have goals for my life that I'm working on.

_____ TOTAL check marks

(Continued)

Naturalistic Intelligence: **The capacity to discriminate between living things and show sensitivity toward the natural world ("nature smart")**

_____ Environmental problems bother me.

_____ In school, I always enjoyed field trips to places in nature or away from class.

_____ I enjoy studying nature, plants, or animals.

_____ I've always done well on projects involving living systems.

_____ I enjoy pets.

_____ I notice signs of wildlife when I'm on a walk or hike.

_____ I can recognize types of plants, trees, rocks, birds, and so on.

_____ I enjoy learning about environmental issues.

_____ TOTAL check marks

Which intelligences have the most check marks? Write in the three intelligences in which you had the most number of check marks.

_____   _____   _____

Although this is an informal instrument, it can help you think about the concept of multiple intelligences, or MI. How are you smart?

Based on Armstrong, T. (1994). *Multiple intelligences in the classroom.* Alexandria, VA: Association for Supervision and Curriculum Development, pp. 18–20.

Have you ever noticed that people are smart in different ways? Consider the musical genius of Mozart, who published his first piano pieces at the age of five. Olympic Gold Medalist Lindsey Vonn started skiing when she was two years old. Not many of us are as musically gifted as Mozart or as physically gifted as Lindsey Vonn, but we all have strengths. You may earn top grades in math, and not-so-top grades in English, and your best friend's grades may be just the opposite.

According to Harvard psychologist Howard Gardner, people can be smart in the eight different categories you saw in Exercise 3.2. Most schools focus on particular types of intelligence, linguistic and logical-mathematical intelligence, reflecting the three R's: reading, writing, and 'rithmetic. But Gardner claims there are many different types of intelligence that can't be measured by traditional one-dimensional standardized IQ tests and represented by a three-digit number: 100 (average), 130 (gifted), or 150 (genius). Gardner defines intelligence as "the ability to find and solve problems and create products of value in one or more cultural settings."[5]

So instead of asking the traditional question "How smart are you?" a better question is "How are you smart?" The idea is to find out how, and then apply this understanding of yourself to your academic work in order to achieve your best results.

Use Intelligence-Oriented Study Techniques

Do you sometimes wonder why you can't remember things for exams? Some learning experts believe that memory is intelligence-specific. You may have a good memory for people's faces but a bad memory for their names. You may be able to remember the words of a country-western hit, but not the dance steps that go with it. The Theory of Multiple Intelligences may explain why.[6]

Examine your own behaviors in class. If your instructors use their linguistic intelligence to teach, as many do, and your intelligences lie elsewhere, do you get frustrated? Instead of zeroing in on the lecture, do you fidget (bodily-kinesthetic), doodle (spatial), or socialize (interpersonal)? You may need to translate the information into your own personal intelligences, just as you would if your instructor speaks French and you speak English. This strategy might have worked for Tammy Ko from the "FOCUS Challenge Case." Mr. Caldwell's most developed intelligence is linguistic, whereas Tammy's are bodily-kinesthetic (manipulating test tubes) and interpersonal (interacting with people). Tammy's learning problems are partially due to her inability to translate from one set of intelligences (his) to another (hers). Creating flash cards, for example, or talking over the lectures with Sam might have really helped her. Take a look at this chart of possible intelligence-oriented study options:

Linguistic --→	1. Rewrite your class notes. 2. Record yourself reading through your class notes, and play the recording as you study. 3. Read the textbook chapter aloud.
Logical Mathematical --→	1. Create hypothetical conceptual problems to solve. 2. Organize chapter or lecture notes into a logical flow. 3. Analyze how the textbook chapter is organized and why.
Spatial --→	1. Draw a map that demonstrates your thinking on course material. 2. Illustrate your notes by drawing diagrams and charts. 3. Mark up your textbook to show relationships among concepts.
Bodily–Kinesthetic --→	1. Study course material while engaged in physical activity. 2. Practice skills introduced in class or in the text. 3. Act out a scene based on chapter content.
Musical --→	1. Create musical memory devices by putting words into well-known melodies. 2. Listen to music while you're studying. 3. Sing or hum as you work.
Interpersonal --→	1. Discuss course material with your classmates. 2. Organize a study group that meets regularly. 3. Meet a classmate before or after class for coffee and class conversation.
Intrapersonal --→	1. Keep a journal to track your personal reactions to course material. 2. Study alone and engage in internal dialogue about course content. 3. Coach yourself on how to best study for a challenging class.
Naturalistic --→	1. Search for applications of course content in the natural world. 2. Study outside (if weather permits and you can resist distractions). 3. Go to a physical location that exemplifies course material (for example, a park for your geology course).

Develop Your Weaker Intelligences

It's important to cultivate your weaker intelligences. Why? Because life isn't geared to one kind of intelligence. It's complex. A photo journalist for *National Geographic,* for example, might need linguistic intelligence, spatial intelligence, interpersonal intelligence, and naturalistic intelligence. Being well-rounded, as the expression goes, is truly a good thing. Artist Pablo Picasso once said, "I am always doing that which I cannot do, in order that I may learn how to do it."

Use your multiple intelligences to multiply your success. Remember that no one is naturally intelligent in all eight areas. Each individual is a unique blend of intelligences. But the Theory of Multiple Intelligences claims that we all have the capacity to develop all of our eight intelligences further. That's good news!

How Do You Perceive and Process Information?

Style—we all have it, right? What's yours? Baggy jeans and a T-shirt? Sandals, even in the middle of winter? A signature hairdo that defies gravity? When it comes to appearance, you have your own style. You know it, and so does everyone who knows you.

perceive become aware of

> ❝ **Learning how to learn is life's most important skill.**
>
> *Tony Buzan, memory expert*

Holger Winkler/Cusp/Corbis

Think about how your mind works. For example, how do you decide what to wear in the morning? Do you turn on the radio or TV for the weather forecast? Stick your head out the front door? Ask someone else's opinion? Throw on whatever happens to be clean? We all have different styles, don't we?

So what's a learning style? A learning style is defined as your "characteristic and preferred ways of gathering, interpreting, organizing, recalling, and thinking about information."[7]

Here's one way of looking at things. The way you **perceive** information and the way you process it—your perceiving and processing preferences—are based in part on your senses. Which senses do you prefer to use to take in information—your eyes (visual-graphic or visual-words); your ears (aural); or all your senses, using your whole body (kinesthetic)? Which type of information sinks in best? Which type of information do you most trust to be accurate?

To further understand your preferred sensory channel, let's take this hypothetical example. Assume a rich relative you didn't even know leaves you some money, and you decide to use it to buy a new car. You must first answer many questions: What kind of car do you want to buy—an SUV, a sedan, a sports car, a van, or a truck? What are the differences between various makes and models? How do prices, comfort, and safety compare? Who provides the best warranty? Which car do consumers rate highest? How would you go about learning the answers to all these questions?

Marcela Barsse/iStockphoto.com

Visual. Some of us would **look**. We'd study charts and graphs comparing cars, mileage, fuel tank capacity, maintenance costs, and customer satisfaction. We learn through graphic representations that explain what could have been said in normal text format.

Johanna Goodyear /Dreamstime.com

Aural. Some of us would **listen.** We'd ask all our friends what kind of cars they drive and what they've heard about cars from other people. We'd pay attention as showroom salespeople describe the features of various cars. We learn through sounds by listening.

Nadezda Firsova /iStockphoto.com

Read/Write. Some of us would **read** or **write**. We'd buy a copy of *Consumer Reports* annual edition on automobiles, or copies of magazines such as *Car and Driver* or *Road and Track*, and write lists of each car's pros and cons. We learn through words by reading and writing.

Pascal Genest/iStockphoto.com

Kinesthetic. Some of us would want to **do it**. We'd go to the showroom and test-drive a few cars to physically try them out. We learn through experience when all our senses are activated.

What would you do? Eventually, as you're deciding which vehicle to buy, you might do all these things, and do them more than once. But learning style theory says we all have preferences for how we perceive and process information.

EXERCISE 3.3

VARK Learning Styles Assessment

Choose the answer that best explains your preference, and circle the letter. Please select more than one response if a single answer does not match your perception. *Leave blank any question that does not apply.*

1. You are helping someone who wants to go downtown, find your airport, or locate the bus station. You would:
   (a) draw or give her a map.
   (b) tell her the directions.
   (c) write down the directions (without a map).
   (d) go with her.

2. You are not sure whether a word should be spelled "dependent" or "dependant." You would:
   (a) see the word in your mind and choose by the way different versions look.
   (b) think about how each word sounds and choose one.
   (c) find it in a dictionary.
   (d) write both words on paper and choose one.

3. You are planning a group vacation. You want some feedback from your friends about your plans. You would:
   (a) use a map or website to show them the places.
   (b) phone, text, or e-mail them.
   (c) give them a copy of the printed itinerary.
   (d) describe some of the highlights.

4. You are going to cook something as a special treat for your family. You would:
   (a) look through the cookbook for ideas from the pictures.
   (b) ask friends for suggestions.
   (c) use a cookbook where you know there is a good recipe.
   (d) cook something you know without the need for instructions.

(Continued)

5. A group of tourists want to learn about the parks or wildlife reserves in your area. You would:
   (a) show them Internet pictures, photographs, or picture books.
   (b) talk about, or arrange a talk for them about, parks or wildlife reserves.
   (c) give them a book or pamphlets about the parks or wildlife reserves.
   (d) take them to a park or wildlife reserve and walk with them.

6. You are about to purchase a digital camera or cell phone. Other than price, what would most influence your decision?
   (a) Its attractive design that looks good
   (b) The salesperson telling me about its features
   (c) Reading the details about its features
   (d) Trying or testing it

7. Remember a time when you learned how to do something new. Try to avoid choosing a physical skill, like riding a bike. You learned best by:
   (a) diagrams and charts—visual clues.
   (b) listening to somebody explaining it and asking questions.
   (c) written instructions—for example, a manual or textbook.
   (d) watching a demonstration.

8. You have a problem with your heart. You would prefer that the doctor:
   (a) show you a diagram of what was wrong.
   (b) describe what was wrong.
   (c) give you a pamphlet to read about it.
   (d) use a plastic model of a heart to show what was wrong.

9. You want to learn a new software program, skill, or game on a computer. You would:
   (a) follow the diagrams in the book that came with it.
   (b) talk with people who know about the program.
   (c) read the written instructions that came with the program.
   (d) use the controls or keyboard and try things out.

10. You like websites that have:
    (a) interesting design and visual features.
    (b) audio channels where you can hear music, radio programs, or interviews.
    (c) interesting written descriptions, lists, and explanations.
    (d) things you can click on or try out.

11. Other than price, you would most be influenced in your decision to buy a new nonfiction book by:
    (a) a cover that looks appealing.
    (b) a friend talking about it and recommending it.
    (c) quickly reading parts of it.
    (d) its containing real-life stories, experiences, and examples.

12. You are using a book, CD, or website to learn how to take photos with your new digital camera. You would like to have:
    (a) diagrams showing the camera and what each part does.
    (b) a chance to ask questions and talk about the camera and its features.
    (c) clear written instructions with lists and bullet points about what to do.
    (d) many examples of good and poor photos and how to improve them.

13. You prefer a teacher or a presenter who uses:
    (a) diagrams, charts, or graphs.
    (b) question and answer, talk, group discussion, or guest speakers.
    (c) handouts, books, or readings.
    (d) demonstrations, models, field trips, role plays, or practical exercises.

14. You have finished a competition or test and would like some feedback. You would like to have feedback:
    (a) using graphs showing what you achieved.
    (b) from somebody who talks it through with you.
    (c) in a written format, describing your results.
    (d) using examples from what you have done.

15. You are going to choose food at a restaurant or cafe. You would:
    (a) look at what others are eating or look at pictures of each dish.
    (b) ask the server or friends to recommend choices.
    (c) choose from the written descriptions in the menu.
    (d) choose something that you have had there before.

16. You have to give an important speech at a conference or special occasion. You would:
    (a) make diagrams or create graphs to help explain things.
    (b) write a few key words and practice your speech over and over.
    (c) write out your speech and learn from reading it over several times.
    (d) gather many examples and stories to make the talk real and practical.

Source: N. Fleming. (2001–2011). VARK, a Guide to Learning Styles. Version 7.1. Available at http://www.vark-learn.com/english/page.asp?p=questionnaire. Adapted and used with permission from Neil Fleming.

Scoring the VARK

Let's tabulate your results.

Count your choices in each of the four VARK categories.	(a)	(b)	(c)	(d)
	Visual	Aural	Read/Write	Kinesthetic

Now that you've calculated your scores, do they match your perceptions of yourself as a learner? Could you have predicted them? The VARK's creators believe that you are best qualified to verify and interpret your own results.[8] Try the "just-in-time" VARK IT! suggestions that appear alongside as you read this book. They will help you apply your preferred VARK strategies and learn at your best.

Using Your Sensory Preferences

Knowing your preferences can help you in your academic coursework. If your highest score (by four or five points) is in one of the four VARK modalities, that particular learning modality is your preferred one.[9] If your scores are more or less even between several or all four modalities, these scores mean that you don't have a strong preference for any single modality. A lower score in a preference simply means that you are more comfortable using other styles. If your VARK results contain a zero in a particular learning modality, you may realize that you do indeed dislike this mode or find it unhelpful. You might want to reflect on why you don't like to use this learning modality. To learn more about your results and suggestions for applying them, see Figure 3.1 for your preferred modality.

Most college classes emphasize reading and writing; however, if your lowest score is in the read/write modality, don't assume you're academically doomed. VARK can help you discover alternative, more productive ways to learn the same course material. You may learn to adapt naturally to a particular instructor or discipline's preferences, using a visual modality in your economics class to interpret graphs and a kinesthetic modality in your chemistry lab to conduct experiments.

However, you may also find that you need to deliberately and strategically reroute your learning methods in some of your classes, and knowing your VARK preferences can help you do that. Learning to capitalize on your preferences and translate challenging course material into your preferred modality may serve you well. Remember these suggestions about the VARK, and try them out to see whether they improve your academic results.

1. **VARK preferences are not necessarily strengths.** However, VARK is an excellent vehicle to help you reflect on how you learn and begin to reinforce the productive strategies you're already using or select ones that might work better.

2. **If you have a strong preference for a particular modality, practice using it in many different ways.** (See Figure 3.1 later in this chapter.) Reinforce your learning by doing many things in that column.

3. **An estimated 60 percent of people are multimodal.** In a typical classroom of 30 students (based on VARK data):

    > 17 students would be multimodal,

    > 1 student would be visual,

    > 1 student would be aural,

    > 5 students would be read/write,

    > 6 students would be kinesthetic,

    and the teacher would most likely have a strong read/write preference![10]

4. **If you are multimodal, as most of us are, it may be necessary to use several of your modalities to boost your confidence in your learning.** Practice the suggestions for all of your preferred modalities.

5. **While in an ideal world, it would be good to try to strengthen lesser preferences, you may wish to save that goal for later in life.** Some experts suggest that college isn't the place to experiment. Grades count, and your continuing success will depend on how well you do. You may decide it's better to try to strengthen your current preferences now and

multimodal preferring to use more than one sense

ONLINE TechKnow

Have you ever thought about how you can use your VARK preferences for online coursework? Here are a few useful ideas.

- **If you're a visual learner,** capitalize on course material that comes to you as diagrams, charts, jpegs, and flowcharts—or better yet, take textual information and transform it into visual material to help you understand and remember it.

- **If you're an aural learner,** make the most of voiced-over lectures or narrated resources provided by the course—or find your own. Read the screen aloud as often as you can, and talk with others taking the same course.

- **If you're a read/write learner,** you'll be in your element for many online courses. But go beyond just reading the assigned online material by taking notes, making lists, and writing summaries of each lesson and activity.

- **If you're a kinesthetic learner,** the keyboard action will help, but also remember to get up and move around regularly—and connect your stretching or walking with what you've just learned online. Focus on the real-life examples provided in your online materials. You might also want to take advantage of gaming interfaces, drag and drop technology, interactive flash animations, simulations with 3D graphics, or virtual reality environments (e.g., http://secondlife.com/).

Improve Your Grade
Online Flashcards
Glossary

work on expanding your lesser preferences later. This book will give you an opportunity to practice your VARK learning preferences—whatever they are—in each chapter. Ultimately, learning at your best is up to you.

Gaining the insights provided in this chapter and acting on them have the potential to greatly affect your college success. Understand yourself, capitalize on your preferences, build on them, focus, and learn!

VARK It!

Aural: After you finish reading these five points about the VARK, try summarizing them aloud in your own words—until you can talk through all five.

What Role Does Your Personality Play?

One of the best things about college is having a chance to meet so many different types of people. At times you may find these differences intriguing. At other times, they may baffle you. Look around and listen to other students, and you'll start to notice. Have you heard students saying totally opposite things such as those listed here?

"There's no way I can study at home. It's way too noisy."

"There's no way I can study in the library. It's way too quiet."

"I'm so glad I've already decided on a major. Now I can go full steam ahead."

"I have no idea what to major in. I can think of six different majors I'd like to choose."

"My sociology instructor is great. She talks about all kinds of things in class, and her essay tests are actually fun!"

"My sociology instructor is so confusing. She talks about so many different things in class. How am I supposed to know what to study for her tests?"[11]

You're likely to run into all kinds of viewpoints and all types of people, but differences make life much more interesting! We're each unique. Perhaps your friends comment on your personality by saying, "She's really quiet," or "He's a 'party animal,'" or "He's incredibly logical," or "She trusts her gut feelings." What you may not know is how big a role your personality plays in how you prefer to learn.

The Myers-Briggs Type Indicator® (MBTI) is the most well-known personality assessment instrument in the world. Each year, approximately 2 million people worldwide get a look into their personalities, their career choices, their interaction with others, and their learning styles by completing it. If you are able to complete the full Myers-Briggs Type Indicator in the class for which you're using this textbook, or through your college counseling center or learning center, do so. You'll learn a great deal about yourself.

The Myers-Briggs Type Indicator shows you your preferences in four areas:

E or I **What energizes you and where do you direct energy?** Do you get energy from other people (Extravert) or do you go within yourself to find strength (Introvert)?

Each person is an exception to the rule.

Carl Jung, psychiatrist (1875–1961)

© Larry Harwood Photography. Property of Cengage Learning.

S or N How do you gather information and what kind of information do you trust? Do you trust your senses and factually based information (**S**ensor) or do you trust your gut feelings (i**N**tuition)?

T or F How do you make decisions, arrive at conclusions, and make judgments? Do you think things through logically (**T**hinker) or do you care about how others react and feel (**F**eeler)?

J or P How do you relate to the outer world? Do you prefer organization and structure (**J**udging) or do you like spontaneity and going with the flow (**P**erceiver)?

If you take the Myers-Briggs Type Indicator you should realize that it isn't about what you can do. It's about what you prefer to do. Here's an illustration. Write your name on the first line.

_____

_____

Now put the pen in your other hand, and try writing your name on the second line. What was different the second time around? For most people, the second try takes longer, is messier, probably feels strange, and requires more concentration. But could you do it? Yes. It's just that you prefer doing it the first way. The first way is easier and more natural; the second way makes a simple task seem like hard work! It's possible that you might have to try "writing with your other hand" in college—doing things that don't come naturally.

In the "FOCUS Challenge Case," Tammy was described as outgoing (**E**xtraverted) and hands-on (**S**ensing), whereas Mr. Caldwell was described as reserved (**I**ntroverted) and theoretical (i**N**tuitive). It's unlikely that Mr. Caldwell will change his teaching style, and even if he did, students in his class have a variety of learning styles. Whose style would he try to match? Both Tammy's personality and Mr. Caldwell's are similar to the most common types found in college classrooms. Although you couldn't be sure without looking at actual MBTI scores, you'd expect Tammy to be an ESFP. ESFP's are outgoing, like facts as opposed to theories, pay attention to the feelings of others, and prefer exploring options to following a structure. Based on the clues in the "Focus Challenge Case," you'd also expect Mr. Caldwell to be an INTJ—the opposite.

This chapter has covered learning from several different perspectives, and you now know more about yourself as a learner than you did before you read it. But you may be wondering: So how do Multiple Intelligences, VARK preferences, and personality traits (MBTI) work together to produce a unique learner? Although the three perspectives aren't intended to connect, let's look at this example to help you understand how each one would explain how people learn.

Let's say the person you sit by in your math class always asks you whether you want to join his study group. Based on what you've learned in this chapter, you'd be more likely to say yes if you:

1. **MI:** have *interpersonal* (or social) intelligence
2. **VARK:** are an *aural* learner who likes to discuss things
3. **MBTI:** are *extraverted* (you get energy from other people).

The three perspectives don't overlap; they're different. That's why this chapter presents all three. Each perspective explains how people learn in a different way.

Although simply knowing about these three perspectives is good, it's important to go further and act on that knowledge. As a single learner in a larger class, you will need to adjust to the teaching style of your instructor in ways such as the following:

> **Translate for maximum comfort.** The way to maximize your comfort as a learner is to find ways to translate from your instructor's preferences to yours. If you know that you prefer feeling over thinking, and your instructor's style is based on thinking, make the course material come alive by personalizing it. How does the topic relate to you, your lifestyle, your family, and your future choices?

> **Make strategic choices.** Although learning preferences can help explain your academic successes, it's also important not to use them to rationalize your nonsuccesses. An introvert could say, "I could have aced that assignment if the instructor had let me work alone! I hate group projects." Become the best learner you can be at what you're naturally good at. But also realize that you'll need to become more versatile over time. In the workforce, you will not always be able to choose what you do and how you do it. Actively choose your learning strategies rather than simply hoping for the best. Remember: No one can learn for you, just as no one can eat for you.

> **Take full advantage.** College will present you with an extensive menu of learning opportunities. You will also build on your learning as you move beyond your general, introductory classes into courses in your chosen major—and across and between classes. Don't fall victim to the temptation to make excuses as some students do ("I could have been more successful in college if . . . I hadn't had to work so many hours . . . I hadn't had a family to support . . . my instructors had been more supportive. . . ." If, if, if. College may well be the most concentrated and potentially powerful learning opportunity you'll ever have. Ultimately, learning at your best is up to you.

There's a crack in everything. That's how the light gets in.

Leonard Cohen

BOX 3.1

Learning Disability? Five Ways to Help Yourself

Perhaps you were diagnosed with Attention-Deficit/Hyperactivity Disorder (ADHD) or dyslexia as a young child. If you're beginning your college career with a learning disability (LD), you're not alone. In a college or university with an enrollment of 25,000 students, for example, approximately 550 of those students have learning disabilities.[12] By some estimates, two-thirds of students with diagnosed LDs continue on to college after high school.[13] Does a learning disability mean all the odds are against you? No, but there are some important steps you must take to help yourself. Successful college students with LDs recognize, understand, and accept these steps, and develop compensating strategies to offset their LDs.

1. If you've been previously diagnosed with a learning disability, bring a copy of your evaluation or Individualized Education Plan (IEP) with you to campus. Some schools require documentation in order to use the institution's support services.

2. If your school has a learning support office, use it. These services are free and can make all the difference in your success.

3. Learn more about your specific LD. Read about it. Visit credible websites. Understanding the ins and outs of what you're up against is important.

4. If you need special accommodations such as taking exams somewhere other than the classroom, schedule an appointment with your instructors early in the term to let them know. Having a learning disability doesn't mean you're required to do less work, but you'll get the support you need in order to do your best.

5. Remember that the advice in this book, which is helpful to all college students, can be even more useful to anyone with a learning disability. Time management strategies and study skills tailored to your specific LD are key.

Don't let fear of failure immobilize you. Instead, keep your eye on the goal and take charge of your own learning.[14]

Metacognition: Take Charge of How You Study

Do You Know How to Study?

To what extent do these ten statements apply to you? Write the number for each statement on the line preceeding it.

Never		Sometimes		Always
1	2	3	4	5

_____ 1. I keep going with things I have to learn rather than skipping over what I don't understand.

_____ 2. When I'm studying something difficult, I realize when I'm stuck and ask for help.

_____ 3. I make a study plan and stick to it in order to master class material.

_____ 4. I quiz myself as I'm studying to see what I understand and what I don't.

_____ 5. I talk through my problems, understanding things while I study.

_____ 6. After I study something, I think about how well it went.

_____ 7. I know when I learn best: morning, afternoon, or evening, for example.

_____ 8. I know how I study best: alone, with one other person, in a group, etc.

_____ 9. I know where I study best: at home, at the library, at my computer, etc.

_____ 10. I believe I'm in control of my own learning.

Now tally your scores on this informal instrument. If you scored between 40 and 50 total points, you have excellent metacognitive skills. If you scored between 30 and 40 points, your skills are probably average. However, note any items you rated down in the 1 to 2 range, and then continue reading this section of the chapter carefully.

Talk about needing to use a dictionary! What does the word *metacognition* mean? *Meta* is an ancient Greek prefix that is often used to mean *about*. For example, metacommunication is communicating *about* the way you communicate. ("I feel humiliated when you tease me in front of other people. Can you *not* do that?")

Because cognition means thinking and learning, metacognition is thinking about your thinking and learning about your learning. It's about identifying your learning goals, monitoring your progress, backing up or getting help when you're stuck, forging ahead when you're in the groove, and evaluating your results. Metacognition is about knowing yourself as a learner and about your ability (and motivation) to control your own learning. Some things are easy for you to learn; others are hard. What do you know about yourself as a learner, and do you use that awareness intentionally to learn at your best?[15]

These questions may seem simple, but how do you know:

1. When you've finished a reading assignment?

2. When your paper is ready to turn in?

3. When you've finished studying for an exam?

When you're eating a meal, you know when you're full, right? But when it comes to academic work, how do you know when you're done? Some students resort to

Dmitry Kalinovsky/Photos.com

answers like this to the question "How do you know when you're done?" Look at the range of students' answers:

> I just do.
> I trust in God.
> My eyelids get too heavy.
> I've been at it for a long time.
> My mom tells me to go to bed.
> I understand everything.
> I can write everything down without looking at the textbook or my notes.
> I've created a practice quiz for myself and get all the answers right.
> When my wife or girlfriend drills me and I know all the answers.
> When I can teach my husband everything I've learned.
> When I've highlighted, recopied my notes, made flash cards, written sample questions, tested myself, and so on.

You can see that their answers become increasingly reliable as you progress down the list.[16]

Metacognition is about having an "awareness of [your] own cognitive machinery and how the machinery works."[17] It's about knowing the limits of your own learning and memory capabilities, knowing how much you can accomplish within a certain amount of time, and knowing what learning strategies work for you.[18] Know your limits, but at the same time, stretch.

Apply Your Learning Style to Your Study Style

Now that you've gained some insight into how you prefer to learn, it's time to apply those preferences to how you study. Are you the kind of student who re-reads a textbook page five times without having the information sink in? Do you procrastinate when it comes to reading assignments for your classes? If so, through this chapter, you may have discovered why. Perhaps your linguistic intelligence is relatively low. Perhaps Read/Write is your least preferred VARK modality. Perhaps your off-the-charts extraverted personality enjoys the company of others, not a book.

Metacognition means thinking about your thinking and learning about your learning—taking charge of your own learning—and maybe that's exactly what you need to do. Early on, this chapter advised you about "Creating the Best Conditions for Learning." Monitoring how you study and how well it's working is at the top of the list. Use this chart as your guide, and note the results. You may just see an improvement!

	Everyday Study Strategies	Exam Preparation Study Strategies
VISUAL Marcela Barsse/iStockphoto.com	• Convert your lecture notes to a visual format. • Study the placement of items, colors, and shapes in your textbook. • Put complex concepts into flowcharts or graphs. • Redraw ideas you create from memory.	• Practice turning your visuals back into words. • Recall the pictures you made of the pages you studied. • Use diagrams to answer exam questions, if your instructor will allow it.
AURAL Johanna Goodyear /Dreamstime.com	• Read your notes aloud. • Explain your notes to another auditory learner. • Ask others to "hear" your understanding of the material. • Record your notes or listen to your instructors' podcasts. • Realize that your lecture notes may be incomplete. You may have become so involved in listening that you stopped writing. Fill your notes in later by talking with other students or getting material from the textbook.	• Practice by speaking your answers aloud. • Listen to your own voice as you answer questions. • Opt for an oral exam if allowed. • Imagine you are talking with the teacher as you answer questions.
READ/WRITE Nadezda Firsova/iStockphoto.com	• Write out your lecture notes again and again. • Read your notes (silently) again and again. • Put ideas and principles into different words. • Translate diagrams, graphs, etc., into text. • Rearrange words and "play" with wording. • Turn diagrams and charts into words.	• Write out potential exam answers. • Practice creating and taking exams. • Type out your answers to potential test questions. • Organize your notes into lists or bullets. • Write practice paragraphs, particularly beginnings and endings.
KINESTHETIC Pascal Genest/iStockphoto.com	• Recall experiments, field trips, etc. Remember the real things that happened. • Talk over your notes with another "K" person. • Use photos and pictures that make ideas come to life. • Go back to the lab, your manual, or your notes that include real examples. • Remember that your lecture notes will have gaps if topics weren't concrete or relevant for you. • Use case studies to help you learn abstract principles.	• Role-play the exam situation in your room (or the actual classroom). • Put plenty of examples into your answers. • Write practice answers and sample paragraphs. • Give yourself practice tests.

FIGURE 3.1

Visual, Aural, Read/Write, and Kinesthetic Learning Strategies

Becoming an Intentional Learner: Make a Master Study Plan

What's your favorite class this term? Or let's turn the question around: What's your least favorite class? Becoming an educated person may well require you to study things you wouldn't *choose* to study. Considering all you have to do, including your most and least favorite classes, what would making a master study plan look like? You've "been there, done that" all through your schooling, but do you *really* know how to study?

To begin, think about what you have to think about. What's your goal? Is it to finish your English essay by 10:00 p.m. so that you can start your algebra homework? Or is it to write the best essay you can possibly write? If you've allowed yourself one hour to read this chapter, but after an hour you're still not finished, you have three choices: keep reading, finish later, or give up entirely. What's in your best interest, honestly? See whether you find the following planning strategies helpful.

1. **Make sure you understand your assignments.** Understanding is critical to making a master plan. You can actually waste a great deal of time trying to read your instructor's mind after the fact: "Did she want us to *analyze* the play or *summarize* it?" When you leave class, make sure you're clear on what's been assigned.

2. **Schedule yourself to be three places at once.** Making a master plan requires you to think simultaneously about three different time zones:

   The past: Ask yourself what you already know. Is this a subject you've studied before? Have your study habits worked well for you in the past? How have you done your best work—in papers, on exams, on projects?

   The present: Ask yourself what you need to learn now. How interested are you in this material? How motivated are you to learn it? How much time will you devote to it?

   The future: Ask yourself how you'll go about learning it. Will you learn it using the strategies that work best for you? Which learning factors will you control? Will you do what you can to change what's not working?[19]

3. **Talk through your learning challenges.** There's good evidence that talking to yourself while you're studying is a good thing. Researchers find it helps you figure things out: *Okay, I understand the difference between a neurosis and a psychosis, but I'm not sure I can provide examples on my psychology test.* Once you've heard yourself admit that, you know where to focus your efforts next.[20] Or consider the possibility on "talking online" to other students worldwide at openstudy.com.

4. **Be a stickler.** Sticklers pay attention to details. They want to make sure everything is absolutely right. Have you ever thought about how important accuracy is? For example, if you were 99 instead of 100 percent accurate, that would mean that:

   > 500 airplanes in U.S. skies each day wouldn't be directed by air traffic controllers.[21] Disastrous!

   As you read and study, remember this example. Be thorough. Read the entire assignment. Pay attention to details. If you make a mistake, for example in solving a math problem, figure out exactly what went wrong so that you don't hold on to a bad academic habit. Rework the problem at least twice, write a few sentences describing the right way to solve it, and try another problem similar to it to see whether you really understand.[22] Accuracy counts!

5. **Take study breaks.** The human attention span is limited, and according to some researchers, it's shrinking, rather than expanding.[23] Plan to take brief scheduled breaks to stretch,

No one can become really educated without having pursued some study in which he took no interest.

T. S. Eliot, American-born poet (1888–1965)

© Larry Harwood Photography. Property of Cengage Learning.

GOING PRO

WORK HARD, WORK SMART

> **I'm a great believer in luck, and I find the harder I work the more I have of it.**
> THOMAS JEFFERSON

Exhibit a work ethic. In college, you're at your best when you demonstrate your work ethic. The same will be true in your career. If you've learned that focused, dedicated work produces your best results in school, carry that lesson over to the world of work. Organizations prefer to hire winners, not slackers. Winners are motivated and reliable. They know how to kick into high gear when necessary. Not only is day-to-day performance important, but so is how you handle yourself at crunch time. Someone once said, "Every job is a self-portrait of the person who did it. Autograph your work with excellence." Your work ethic says a great deal about who you are. And who you are, who you want to be, is the most effective professional you can be. Remember, you're "Going Pro"!

> **It's not so much how busy you are, but why you are busy. The bee is praised; the mosquito is swatted.**
>
> *Marie O'Conner*

walk around, or grab a light snack every half hour during study sessions. Of course, it's important to sit down and get back to work again. Don't let a quick study break to get a snack multiply into several hours of television viewing that wasn't in the plan.

6. **Mix it up.** Put a little variety into your study sessions by switching from one subject to another or from one mode of studying—for example, reading, self-quizzing, writing—to another. Variety helps you fight boredom and stay fresh (unless, of course, you're on the verge of a breakthrough). Even changing locations from time to time, rather than always studying in one place, stimulates your brain to reboot.[24]

7. **Estimate how long it will take.** Before starting an assignment, estimate the amount of time you will need to complete that assignment (just as you do at the start of each chapter of this book), and then compare that estimate with the actual amount of time the assignment took to complete. Getting into this habit helps you develop realistic schedules for future projects.

8. **Vary your study techniques by course content.** Studying productively is more than just learning a few general rules that apply to any type of subject matter. You need to zoom in on whatever subject or discipline it is that you're studying. Look over the pages of your textbook. Does the material synch with your learning style? Is it text-heavy (read/write)? Do graphs or charts explain the text and seem important? Are color-coding or bulleting used to call your attention to particular items (visual)? If the material isn't presented as you'd prefer, what can you do to "translate"? For example, if you're a kinesthetic learner, can you make flash cards? Can you create and complete practice tests? If you learn by listening, can you read the material aloud (aural)? And finally, what kind of exam (multiple-choice, essay, problem sets, etc.) does the material lend itself to? What are you likely to need to know, and what will you be asked to do on an exam? When you study math, it's important to do more than read. Working problem sets helps you actually develop the skills you need. When you study history, you study differently. You might draw a timeline of the events leading up to World War I, for example.[25]

"Disciplined" Studying

Assume you are taking three classes this term: calculus, psychology, and music. For the three textbook pages here, describe how you would go about studying the material, based on what the content in these three subjects requires. Among other things, which particular VARK learning style preferences should be used: V, A, R, and/or K? Fill in specifics about how you would study each subject's textbook page. It's also important to annotate as you read, as shown here. Make notes to yourself in the margins or on sticky notes, reacting, explaining, or summarizing what you've learned or what is still fuzzy. In doing so, you'll be interacting with the material and personalizing it. Make connections; don't just let information float by and hope that something sticks. After you're done, compare notes with your classmates.

---

2   **Chapter P**   Preparation for Calculus

P.1 Graphs and Models

- Sketch the graph of an equation.
- Find the intercepts of a graph.
- Test a graph for symmetry with respect to an axis and the origin.
- Find the points of intersection of two graphs.
- Interpret mathematical models for real-life data.

RENÉ DESCARTES (1596–1650)

Descartes made many contributions to philosophy, science, and mathematics. The idea of representing points in the plane by pairs of real numbers and representing curves in the plane by equations was described by Descartes in his book *La Géométrie*, published in 1637.

Weird looking dude! But SMART!

The Graph of an Equation

In 1637 the French mathematician René Descartes revolutionized the study of mathematics by joining its two major fields—algebra and geometry. With Descartes's coordinate plane, geometric concepts could be formulated analytically and algebraic concepts could be viewed graphically. The power of this approach was such that within a century of its introduction, much of calculus had been developed.

The same approach can be followed in your study of calculus. That is, by viewing calculus from multiple perspectives—*graphically*, *analytically*, and *numerically*—you will increase your understanding of core concepts.

Consider the equation $3x + y = 7$. The point $(2, 1)$ is a **solution point** of the equation because the equation is satisfied (is true) when 2 is substituted for x and 1 is substituted for y. This equation has many other solutions, such as $(1, 4)$ and $(0, 7)$. To find other solutions systematically, solve the original equation for y.

$$y = 7 - 3x \qquad \text{Analytic approach}$$

Then construct a **table of values** by substituting several values of x.

x	0	1	2	3	4
y	7	4	1	−2	−5

Numerical approach

From the table, you can see that $(0, 7)$, $(1, 4)$, $(2, 1)$, $(3, -2)$, and $(4, -5)$ are solutions of the original equation $3x + y = 7$. Like many equations, this equation has an infinite number of solutions. The set of all solution points is the **graph** of the equation, as shown in Figure P.1.

NOTE   Even though we refer to the sketch shown in Figure P.1 as the graph of $3x + y = 7$, it really represents only a *portion* of the graph. The entire graph would extend beyond the page. ■

In this course, you will study many sketching techniques. The simplest is point plotting—that is, you plot points until the basic shape of the graph seems apparent.

EXAMPLE 1   Sketching a Graph by Point Plotting

Sketch the graph of $y = x^2 - 2$.

Solution   First construct a table of values. Then plot the points shown in the table.

x	−2	−1	0	1	2	3
y	2	−1	−2	−1	2	7

Finally, connect the points with a *smooth curve*, as shown in Figure P.2. This graph is a **parabola**. It is one of the conics you will study in Chapter 10. ■

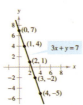

Graphical approach: $3x + y = 7$
Figure P.1

Point plotting— this graph really helps me understand the definition of parabola maybe that's because I'm a visual learner.

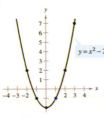

The parabola $y = x^2 - 2$
Figure P.2

How would you study this? *Calculus, 9th Edition, by Ron Larson and Bruce H. Edwards.*

_____

_____

(Continued)

studies of the brain. Case studies lack formal control groups. This, of course, limits the conclusions that can be drawn from clinical observations.

Survey Method

Sometimes psychologists would like to ask everyone in the world a few well-chosen questions: "Do you drink coffee? How often per week?" "What form of discipline did your parents use when you were a child?" "What is the most dishonest thing you've done?" Honest answers to such questions can reveal much about people's behavior. But, because it is impossible to question everyone, doing a survey is often more practical.

In the **survey method,** public polling techniques are used to answer psychological questions (Tourangeau, 2004). Typically, people in a representative sample are asked a series of carefully worded questions. A **representative sample** is a small group that accurately reflects a larger population. A good sample must include the same proportion of men, women, young, old, professionals, blue-collar workers, Republicans, Democrats, whites, African Americans, Native Americans, Latinos, Asians, and so on as found in the population as a whole.

A *population* is an entire group of animals or people belonging to a particular category (for example, all college students or all single women). Ultimately, we are interested in entire populations. But by selecting a smaller sample, we can draw conclusions about the larger group without polling each and every person. Representative samples are often obtained by *randomly* selecting who will be included (▶▶ Figure 1.11). (Notice that this is similar to randomly assigning participants to groups in an experiment.)

How accurate is the survey method? Modern surveys like the Gallup and Harris polls are quite accurate. The Gallup poll has erred in its election predictions by only 1.5 percent since 1954. However, if a survey is based on a biased sample, it may paint a false picture. A *biased sample* does not accurately reflect the population from which it was drawn. Surveys done by magazines, websites, and online information services can be quite biased. Surveys on the use of guns done by *O: The Oprah Magazine* and *Guns and Ammo* magazine would probably produce very different results—neither of which would represent the general population. That's why psychologists using the survey method go to great lengths to ensure that their samples are representative. Fortunately, people can often be polled by telephone, which makes it easier to obtain large samples. ==Even if one person out of three refuses to answer survey questions,== the results are still likely to be valid (Hutchinson, 2004).   *Like me!*

Internet Surveys

Recently, psychologists have started doing surveys and experiments on the Internet. Web-based research can be a cost-effective way to reach very large groups of people. Internet studies have provided interesting information about topics such as anger, decision making,

There's lots of phone polling during a presidential election year to get some idea of who will win. . . . It's important that the sample is representative and nonbiased. I like to learn kinesthetically so maybe I should look up some websites on polling . . .

Survey method The use of public polling techniques to answer psychological questions.

Representative sample A small, randomly selected part of a larger population that accurately reflects characteristics of the whole population.

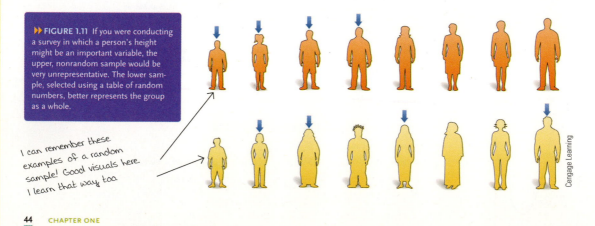

▶▶ **FIGURE 1.11** If you were conducting a survey in which a person's height might be an important variable, the upper, nonrandom sample would be very unrepresentative. The lower sample, selected using a table of random numbers, better represents the group as a whole.

Cengage Learning

I can remember these examples of a random sample! Good visuals here. I learn that way too.

44   CHAPTER ONE

How would you study this? *Psychology: A Journey, 4th Edition by Dennis Coon and John O. Mitterer.*

Measures

As you performed the different meters, you may have lost your place momentarily. Even if you didn't, you can see that it would be difficult to play a long piece of music without losing one's place. For this reason, music is divided into **measures** with vertical lines called **bar lines**.

A bar line occurs immediately before an accented pulse. Thus, duple meter has two pulses per measure, triple meter has three pulses per measure, and quadruple meter has four pulses per measure. The following example shows the common meters again, this time with bar lines included. Notice how much easier it is to read and perform the meter when it is written this way.

Double bar lines have a special meaning: Their two most common uses are to signal the beginning of a new section in a large work and to mark the end of a work. Put double bar lines at the end of any exercises or pieces you write.

MUSIC IN
Action

Hearing Pulse and Meter

As members of the class listen, clap a steady pulse without any noticeable accents. Slowly change the pulse to duple, triple, or quadruple meter. You may want to have a contest to see how quickly members of the class can detect the shift to a measured pulse.

Note Values

Learning to read music involves mastering two different musical subsystems: ==pitch== notation and ==rhythmic== notation. Pitch is indicated by the placement of a note on a five-line staff (the higher the note on the staff, the higher the pitch). You will learn about that later in this chapter. Rhythm, on the other hand, is written with

[handwritten note:] I remember learning about pitch and rhythm as a kid in my piano lessons with Mrs. Sauerbraten—or whatever her name was! Maybe being an aural learner helped me fake my way through all those lessons my parents paid for!

How would you study this? A *Creative Approach to Music Fundamentals, 10th Edition,* by William Duckworth.

Finally, what have you learned about studying and about yourself as a learner by completing this exercise?

© Larry Harwood Photography. Property of Cengage Learning.

9. **Study earlier, rather than later.** Whenever possible, study during the daytime, rather than waiting until evening. Research shows that each hour used for study during the day is equal to one and a half hours at night. Another major study showed that students who study between 6:00 p.m. and midnight are twice as likely to earn A's as students who put off their studying until after midnight.[26] And simply getting enough sleep can help you rachet up your GPA more than you'd expect.

10. **Create artificial deadlines for yourself.** Even though your instructors will have set deadlines for various assignments, create your own deadlines that precede the ones they set. Finish early, and you'll save yourself from any last minute emergencies that may come up, like crashed hard drives or empty printer cartridges.

11. **Treat school as a job.** If you consider the amount of study time you need to budget for each hour of class time, and you're taking twelve to fifteen credits, then essentially you're working a thirty-six to forty-five-hour/week job on campus. Arrive at "work" early and get your tasks done during "business hours" so you have more leisure time in the evenings.

12. **Show up.** Once you've decided to sit down to study, really commit yourself to showing up—being present emotionally and intellectually, not just physically. If you're committed to getting a college education, then give it all you've got! Get help if you need it. If you have a diagnosed learning disability, or believe you might, find out where help is available on your campus. One of the best ways to compensate for a learning disability is by relying on metacognition. In other words, consciously controlling what isn't happening automatically is vital to your success.[27]

These twelve planning strategies are vital to your success in college—and they're crucial as well to your success on the job throughout your professional life.

Sprinting to the Finish Line: How to Study When the Heat Is On

Let's be realistic. Planning is important, but there will be the occasional time when you'll have to find some creative ways to survive the onslaught of all you have to study. You'll need to prioritize your time and make decisions about what to study. When you do need to find a way to accomplish more than is humanly possible, keep these "emergency preparedness" suggestions in mind:

1. **Triage.** With little time to spare, you must be efficient. Consider this analogy: If you're the physician on duty in the ER, and three patients come in at once, who will you take care of first: the fellow with strep throat, the woman with a sprained wrist, or the heart attack victim who needs CPR? Making decisions about priorities is called triage. Of all the material you need to study, ask what is most important, moderately important, and least important. For example, if you are earning an A− in art history, a B+ in geography, and a C− in math, you know which course most needs your attention. Evaluate the material and ask yourself which topics have received the most attention in class and in the textbook. Then focus your study time on those topics, rather than trying to study everything.

2. **Use every spare moment to study.** If flashcards work for you, take your flashcards with you everywhere, like on your daily bus ride or to the laundromat, for example. Organize your essay answer in your head while you're filling up at the pump. It's surprising: Small amounts of focused time do add up.

3. **Give it the old one-two-three-four punch.** Immerse all your senses in the precious little amount of time you have to study: *read, write, listen*, and *speak* the material.

4. **Get a grip on your gaps.** Honesty is the best policy. Rather than glossing over what you don't know, assess your knowledge as accurately as possible, and fill in the gaps.

5. **Cram, but only as the very last resort.** If you're ultrashort on time due to a real emergency, and you have studying to do for several classes, focus on one class at a time. Be aware: If you learn new information that is similar to something you already know, the old information can interfere. So if you're studying for a psychology test that contains some overlap with your sociology test, separate the study sessions by a day. Studies also show that cramming up to one hour before sleeping can help to minimize interference.[28] Nevertheless, continually remind yourself: What's my goal here? Is it to just get through twenty-five pages or is it to truly understand?

A Final Word about Studying and Learning

Albert Einstein said this: "Never regard study as a duty, but as the enviable opportunity to learn . . ." Studying and learning are what college is all about. Take his advice: Consider the opportunities before you to become an educated person, and take advantage of them all.

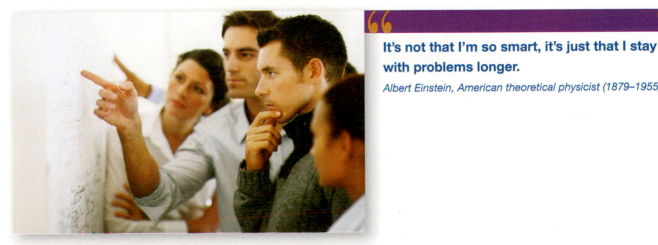

Jacob Wackerhausen/iStockphoto.com

> **It's not that I'm so smart, it's just that I stay with problems longer.**
>
> *Albert Einstein, American theoretical physicist (1879–1955)*

What's In **YOUR** Briefcase?

GET TRULY GRITTY

Besides being the title of a famous novel and award-winning movie, what does "true grit" have to do with you—both in college and on the job? If you look up the word *grit*, you'll find this definition: "firmness of character; indomitable spirit; pluck."[29] People with grit have what it takes to hang in there. They tough things out despite huge obstacles that get thrown in their way. If an instructor in college or a colleague in the workplace says you have true grit, that's a compliment.

"Grit is a willingness to commit to long-term goals and to persist in the face of difficulty. Studies show that gritty people obtain more education in their lifetime and earn higher college GPAs.[30] Think of it this way: In college, grit explains the difference between two students who fail the same calculus test but respond very differently. One throws the exam in the trash can on the way out of the lecture hall and refuses to ever crack open the textbook again. The other vows to study differently and spend more time doing it. "I'm not going to let calculus get the better of me. I'm going to take control of my learning so that it gets the best from me!" See the difference? After college, in the workplace, grit has to do with how you react to being treated unfairly or badly—like being laid off just when you think your job is going particularly well.

The good news is that if you're short on grit, you can get more. Increasing your self-awareness, especially with help from experts, is the way to start. So when unexpected challenges surface—and they surely will—remember the quote earlier in this chapter: "There's a crack in everything. That's how the light gets in." Cracks are just cracks. They don't have to become breaks. And they can shed light on an otherwise dark situation. It's not the challenge itself that counts; it's how you respond to it.

How much grit do you have? Give one piece of evidence from your own experience, either in school or on the job. Identify a time when you showed grit or a time when having more could have helped you.

_____

_____

_____

step 3 INSIGHT *Now* What Do You Think?

At the beginning of this chapter, Tammy Ko faced a series of challenges as a new college student. Now, after learning from this chapter, would you respond differently to any of the questions you answered about the "FOCUS Challenge Case"? Using what you learned in the chapter, write a paragraph ending to Tammy's case study. What are some of the possible outcomes for her?

step 4 ACTION Your Plans for Change

1. How will you put the information from this chapter to good use, not only in this class but in any others you're enrolled in this term?

2. List your learning and personality preferences as you discovered them in this chapter here:

   Multiple Intelligences _____

   VARK _____

   MBTI _____

   What do you think these preferences reveal about you and how you learn?

3. If you apply your learning style to your study style, what will you actually change? Over the course of this term, note whether it helps you become more successful.

chapter 4

Managing Your Time, Energy, and Money

READINESS CHECK

How this chapter relates to **YOU**

1. When your time is limited, and you should be using it to study, what is most likely to derail you, if anything? Please circle one or more responses if any are generally true for you.

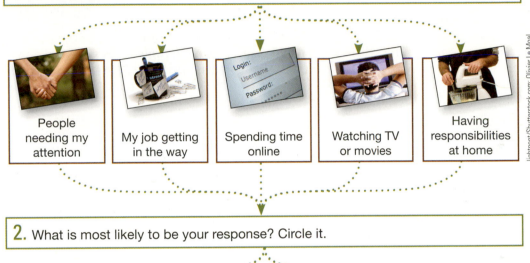

| People needing my attention | My job getting in the way | Spending time online | Watching TV or movies | Having responsibilities at home |

2. What is most likely to be your response? Circle it.

| I have strong will power and focus no matter what. | Even though it's hard, eventually I settle in and focus. | I try to focus, but I can't seem to do it for long. | I give in to the urge to do something else and procrastinate. |

3. What would you have to do to increase your likelihood of success? Will you do it now?

Example: *Actually turn off my phone? Yes!*

_____

_____

How **YOU** will relate to this chapter

What are you most interested in learning about? Put check marks by those topics.

☐ Why time management alone doesn't work

☐ How time management differs from energy management

☐ How to schedule your way to success

☐ How the P word can derail you

☐ How to realistically balance work, school, and your personal life

☐ How to manage your money

● How motivated are you to learn more about getting the right start in college? (5 = high, 1 = low) ___

● How ready are you to read now? ___ (If something is in your way, take care of it if you can, zero in and focus.)

● How long do you think it will take you to complete this chapter? If you start and stop, keep track of your overall time. ___ hour(s) ___ minutes

DEREK JOHNSON

twitter

DerekJ

What are you doing?

Heading to world history class. I have a 12 page paper due in a few weeks! This isn't fair!!

update

Home Profile Find People Settings

As Derek Johnson walked out of his World History class on Wednesday evening, he felt panicked. The instructor had just assigned a twelve-page paper, due one month from today. How could she? Derek thought. *Doesn't she realize how busy most returning students are?* The syllabus had mentioned a paper, but twelve pages seemed downright excessive. He sent a tweet complaining about it from his phone on his way to his next class. Twitter was quickly becoming Derek's favorite way to communicate.

When Derek had decided to go back to college five years after he graduated from high school, he hadn't quite realized what a juggling act it would require. First, there was his family—his wife, Justine, his four-year-old daughter, Taura, and another baby due before winter break. Then there was his job, which was really quite demanding for what he earned. He hoped that an associate's degree in accounting would help him get a job as an accounting assistant and possibly even move into the management ranks, where salaries were higher. Money was tight, and they always seemed to run out before payday. Add to that singing in his church choir, coaching the youth soccer league, competing in cycling races, and working out every morning at the gym. Derek had been a high school athlete, and physical fitness was a priority for him.

His head began to swim as he thought about all his upcoming obligations: his mother's birthday next week, his dog's vet appointment, his brother's visit, the training class he was required to attend

MAKE TO-DO LIST!?

REMEMBER TO BUY MOM A BIRTHDAY GIFT!!!

REMEMBER: COMPUTER TRAINING CLASS FOR WORK ON WEDNESDAY!

Community Center
Gym Schedule

Monday	Tuesday	Wednesday	Thursday	Friday
Open Gym 6:30-8:30	Open Gym 6:30-8:30	Open Gym 6:30-8:30	Open Gym 6:30-8:30	Open Gym 6:30-8:30
Cycling Class 9:00-10:00	Taekwondo Class 9:00-10:00	Taekwondo Class 9:00-10:00	Kick Boxing 9:00-10:00	Cycling Class 9:00-10:00
Taekwondo Class 12:00-1:00	Yoga Class 12:00-1:00	Yoga Class 12:00-1:00	Yoga Class 12:00-1:00	Taekwondo Class 12:00-1:00
Yoga Class 3:00-4:00	Kick Boxing 3:00-4:00	Cycling Class 3:00-4:00	Taekwondo Class 3:00-4:00	Kick Boxing 3:00-4:00

MEMBERSHIP FEES - January 1 - December 31

Children	$10.00
Full-time Student	$30.00
Adult (18 and older)	$50.00
Senior	$40.00

for work. Something had to go, but he couldn't think of anything he was willing to sacrifice to make time for a twelve-page paper. Maybe he'd have to break down and actually do some planning like the *compulsive* students he knew.

Still, the paper was to count as 25 percent of his final grade in the course. He decided he'd try to think of a topic for the paper on his way home. But then he remembered that his wife had asked him to stop at the store to pick up groceries. Somewhere on aisle 12, between the frozen pizza and the frozen yogurt, Derek's thoughts about his research paper vanished.

The following week, the instructor asked the students in the class how their papers were coming along. Some students gave long descriptions of their research progress, the amazing number of sources they'd found, and the detailed outlines they'd put together. Derek didn't raise his hand. Somehow, he never seemed to have enough time to plan—and therefore nothing ever seemed to get done.

A whole week has gone by, Derek thought on his way back to his car after class. *I have to get going!* Writing had never exactly been Derek's strong suit. In fact, it was something he generally disliked doing. Through a great deal of hard work, he had managed to earn a 3.8 GPA in high school—a record he planned to continue. A course in World History—a general education class that was not even a part of his major—was *not* going to ruin things! The week had absolutely flown by, and there were plenty of good reasons why his paper was getting off to such a slow start. Derek didn't waste time, except for occasionally watching his favorite TV shows while he studied and caught up

on e-mail. Regardless, he rarely missed his nightly study time from 11:00 p.m. to 1:00 a.m. Those two hours were reserved for homework, no matter what. The problem, of course, was keeping other things from crowding in.

At the end of class two weeks later, Derek noticed that several students lined up to show the instructor the first drafts of their papers. *That's it!* Derek thought to himself. *The paper is due next Wednesday. I'll spend Monday night, my only free night of the week, in the library. I can get there right after work and stay until 11:00 or so. That'll be five hours of concentrated time. I should be able to write it then.* Despite his good intentions, Derek didn't arrive at the library until nearly 8:00 p.m., and his work session wasn't all that productive. As he sat in his library stall, he found himself obsessing about things that were happening at work. His boss was offering him more hours. Considering that he really did want a degree, should he take on more, even though he didn't really like the job? Finally, when he glanced at his watch, he was shocked to see that it was already midnight! The library was closing, and he'd only written three pages. Where had the time gone?

On his way out to the car, his cell phone rang. It was Justine, wondering where he was. Taura was running a fever, and his boss had called about an emergency meeting at 7:00 a.m. *If one more thing goes wrong . . . ,* Derek thought to himself. His twelve-page paper was due in two days.

HISTORY PAPER OUTLINE

INTRO...

WORLD HISTORY
Fall Semester Syllabus

Instructor: Julia Alexander
Office: Main Hall 320
Email: Julia.Alexander@campusmail.edu
Phone: 555-3424
Office Hours: 12:30-3pm daily

red Textbook:
History, 6th Edition. By William J. Duiker and Jackson J. Spielvogel ISBN: 049556

Exam: 10 @ 10 points each   100pts
nalysis: 100pts
ay: 50pts
                                                        150pts
                                                        100pts

                                                        500pts

vilization and the Fertile Crescent
ne: Agriculture and Mesopotamia
vo: The Nile Valley and the Near East

Civilizations
ee: The World of Homer
: Classical Greece and the Golden Age
Rome: The Rise of the Republic
mperial Rome
Rome: The Fall of the Empire
China and the Far East
The Indian Subcontinent

Expansion

Accounting Associate

Job Description
We are currently looking for a qualified Accounting As educational, and industry experience. This is an entry graduates are encouraged to apply.

Job Responsibilities
- Ensure timely collection of vendor A/R
- Review, correct, and update sub ledger transactions a
- Transaction review
- Vendor follow-up and research
- Vendor disputes
- Inventory audits
- Reconcil

Campus Library

FALL SEMESTER HOURS
Monday – Thursday: 8 am – Midnight
Friday – Saturday: 8 am – 8 pm
Sunday: 10 am – 4 pm

1. What do you have in common with Derek? What time, energy, or money management issues are you experiencing in your life right now?

2. Describe the time-wasters that are a part of Derek's schedule. Do you think procrastination is an issue for

Derek? What's behind his failure to make progress on his paper?

3. Suggest three realistic ways for Derek to balance work, school, and personal life.

Time Management Requires FOCUS

Before diving into the details of time management skills, let's clarify one important point. There's a sense in which the phrase *time management* is misleading. Let's say you decide to spend an hour reading an assigned short story for your literature class. You may sit in the library with your book propped open in front of you from 3:00 to 4:00 p.m. on the dot. But you may not digest a single word you're reading. You may be going through the motions, reading on autopilot. Have you managed your time? Technically, yes. Your planner says, "Library, short story for Lit 101, 3:00–4:00 p.m." But did you get results? Time management expert Jeffrey Mayer asks provocatively in the title of his book: *If You Haven't Got the Time to Do It Right, When Will You Find the Time to Do It Over?*. Now that's a good question!

Time management is not just about managing your time, it's about managing your attention. Attention management is the ability to focus your attention, not just your time, on a designated activity so that you produce a desired result. And that's a big challenge, because research shows that the human mind wanders about half the time[1]. Time management may get you through reading a chapter of your textbook, but attention management will make sure that you understand what you're reading. It's about *focus*. If you manage your attention during that hour, then you've managed your time productively. Without attention management, time management is pointless. And the good thing is that we can train our brains to focus.

Succeeding in school, at work, and in life is not just about what you do. It's about what gets done. You can argue about the effort you put into an academic assignment all you want, but it's doubtful your professor will say, "You know what? You're right. You deserve an A just for staying up late last night working on this paper." Activity and accomplishment aren't the same thing. Neither are quantity and quality. Just because the assignment asked for five pages and you turned in five, doesn't mean that you automatically deserve an A. Results count. So don't confuse being busy with being successful. Staying busy isn't much of a challenge; being successful is.

Here's a list of preliminary academic time-saving tips. However, remember that these suggestions won't give you a surefire recipe for academic success. To manage your time, you must also manage yourself: your energy, your behavior, your attention, your attitudes, *you*. Once you know how to manage all that, managing your time begins to work.

> " *In truth, people can generally make time for what they choose to do; it is not really the time but the will that is lacking.*

> *Sir John Lubbock, British banker, politician, and archaeologist (1834–1913)*

> ➤ Have a plan for your study session; include suggested time limits for each topic or task.

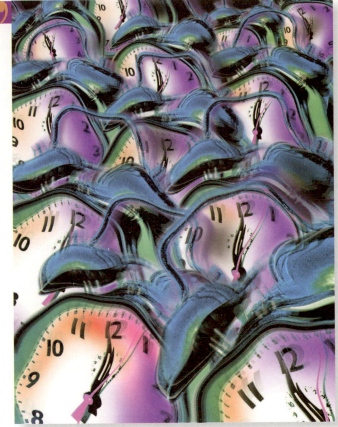

Digital Vision/Getty Images

> Pay attention to what gets you off track. If you come to understand your patterns, you may be better able to control them.

> Turn off your phone or tell other people you live with that you don't want to be disturbed if a call comes in for you. Let them know what time they can tell callers to call you back.

> If you're working on your computer, work offline whenever possible. If you must be online to check sources, don't give in to the temptation to check your social networking account or e-mail every five minutes. According to a recent survey of over one million people, willpower is the one virtue human beings are least likely to recognize in themselves.[2] Whether it's resisting the third cupcake or staying on task to write a paper, willpower is sometimes hard to muster. But it can be cultivated by continually monitoring ourselves so that we're making decisions that are in our own best interest.

> Take two minutes to organize your workspace before beginning. Having the resources you need at your fingertips makes the session go much more smoothly, and you won't waste time searching for things you need.

> Focus. You can't do anything if you try to do everything. **Multitasking** may work for simple matters, such as scheduling a doctor's appointment while heating up a snack in the microwave. But when it comes to tasks that require brainpower, such as studying or writing, you need a single-minded focus. Remember that the more you multitask, the less able you are to focus. Believe it or not, multitasking actually slows you down. It may sound like the solution to time management, but it's not![3]

> Actually use a timer. Forty minutes is thought by some experts to be the optimum amount of time to focus on something before taking a break. It takes thirty minutes to really get in gear, and then you arrive at another ten minutes of optimal productivity. If you aim for more than that, tedium can set in. And use a real, physical countdown timer. When you hear the "ding," you get a real feeling of accomplishment and a bit of relief from stress. Online timing tools can get buried under layers of other software applications. An actual timer can force you to face the challenge.[4]

> Monitor how your life works. There are different ways to manage time, and different ways work best for different people. Think of this analogy: Is time like ice or like water? A hard copy planner is a day-by-day record of solid blocks of time. But in today's world, solid blocks can melt away in seconds as

---

VARK It!

Read/Write: Make a list of all the things that are distracting you the next time you sit down to study. Simply acknowledging them may help you set them aside for a while.

---

multitasking doing two or more tasks at one time

events around us change. Managing time may be less like moving around ice cubes and more like "going with the flow." Many dynamic e-tools are available to help you on a minute-by-minute basis, if you stay on top of how time flows in your life.[5] Whether it's an automatic, audible reminder from something you've entered into your Google calendar or an electronic "personal assistant" like Siri via your iPhone, these reminder systems can help you manage your obligations.[6]

Energy, Our Most Precious Resource

"We live in a digital time. Our rhythms are rushed, rapid-fire and relentless, our days carved up into bits and bytes. . . . We're wired up but we're melting down." So begins the bestselling book *The Power of Full Engagement: Managing Energy, Not Time, Is the Key to High Performance and Personal Renewal*. The authors, Jim Loehr and Tony Schwartz, have replaced the term *time management* with the term *energy management*. Their shift makes sense. Because most of us are running in overdrive most of the time, energy is our most precious resource.

Energy management experts say you can't control time—everyone has a fixed amount—but you can manage your energy. And in fact, it's your responsibility to do so. Once a day is gone, it's gone. But your energy can be renewed.

It's clear that some things are energy *drains:* bad news, illness, interpersonal conflict, time-consuming hassles, a heavy meal, rainy days. Likewise, some things are energy *gains* giving you a surge of freshness: a new job, good friends, music, laughter, fruit, coffee. It's a good idea to recognize your own personal energy drains and gains so that you know how and when to renew your supply.[7] Energy management experts say it's not just about *spending time*, it's about *expending energy:*

> physical energy

> emotional energy

> mental energy

> spiritual energy

Of the four dimensions of energy, let's take a closer look at the first two. To do your very best academically, it helps to be *physically* energized and *emotionally* connected. Physical energy is measured in terms of *quantity*. How much energy do you have—a lot or a little? Emotional energy, on the other hand, is measured by *quality*. What kind of energy do you have—positive or negative? If you put them together into a two-dimensional chart with *quantity* as the vertical axis and *quality* as the horizontal axis, you get something like Figure 4.1.

Thinkstock Images/Photos.com

To do two things at once is to do neither.
Publilius *Syrus*, Maxim 7, *42 B.C.*

FIGURE 4.1

The Dynamics of Energy[8]

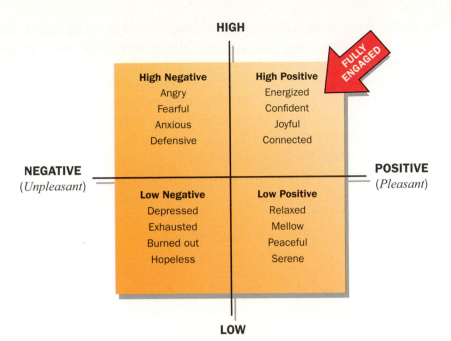

When you're operating in the upper right quarter of the chart, with high, positive energy, you're most productive, which makes sense. The question is, How do you get there? How do you make certain you're physically energized and emotionally connected so that you can do your best academically?

Get Physically Energized

To make sure you're physically energized, try these suggestions.

1. **Snap to your body's rhythm.** Have you noticed times of the day when it's easier to concentrate than others? Perhaps you regularly crash in the middle of the afternoon, for example, so you go for a chocolate fix or a coffee pick-me-up. Everyone has a biological clock. Paying attention to your body's natural rhythms is important. Plan to do activities that require you to be alert during your natural productivity peaks. That's better than plodding through a tough assignment when the energy just isn't there. Use low energy times to take care of mindless chores that require little to no brainpower.[9]

2. **Up and at 'em.** What about 8:00 a.m. classes? Don't use your body's natural rhythms as an excuse to sleep through class! ("I'm just not a morning person. . . .") If you're truly not a morning person, don't sign up for early morning classes. If you are coming off working a night shift, you may need some rest first. Sleeping through your obligations won't do much for your success—and you'll be playing a continual game of catch-up, which takes even more time. Some experts advise that you start your day as early as possible. Marking six items off your to-do list before lunch can give you a real high.[10]

3. **Sleep at night, study during the day.** Burning the midnight oil and pulling all-nighters isn't the best idea either. It only takes one all-nighter to help

VARK It!

Read/Write: Keep a daily journal for a day or two to record your energy levels. Are you groggy all morning? Do you wake up in the evening? Use this journal to figure out your own energy rhythm.

you realize that a lack of sleep translates into a drop in performance. Without proper sleep, your ability to understand and remember course material is impaired. Research shows that the average adult requires seven to eight hours of sleep each night. If you can't get that much for whatever reason, take a short afternoon nap. Did you know that the Three Mile Island nuclear meltdown in Pennsylvania in 1979 and the Chernobyl disaster in the Ukraine in 1986 took place at 4 a.m. and 1:23 a.m., respectively? Experts believe it's no coincidence that both these events took place when workers would normally be sleeping.[11]

4. **"Burn premium fuel."** You've heard it before: Food is the fuel that makes us run. The better the fuel, the smoother we run. It's that simple. A solid diet of carbs—pizza, chips, and cookies—jammed into the fuel tank of your car would certainly gum up the works! When the demands on your energy are high, such as exam week, use premium fuel. If you don't believe this, think about how many people you know who get sick during times of high stress. Watch how many of your classmates are hacking and coughing their way through exams—or in bed, missing them altogether.

Get Emotionally Connected

Physical needs count, to be sure, but emotional connections are part of the picture, too. See whether you agree with these suggestions.

1. **Communicate like it matters.** Sometimes we save our best communicating for people we think we have to impress: teachers, bosses, or clients, for example. But what about the people we care about most in our lives? Sometimes these people get the leftovers after all the "important" communicating has been done for the day. Sometimes we're so comfortable with these people that we think we can let it all hang out, even when doing so is *not* a pretty sight. Communicate as if everything you said would actually come true—"Just drop dead," for instance—and watch the difference! Communicating productively with people we care about is one of the best ways to replenish our energy.

2. **Choose how you renew.** Finish this comparison: Junk food is to physical energy as _____ is to emotional energy. If you answered "TV," you're absolutely right. Most people use television as their primary form of emotional renewal, but, like junk food, it's not that nutritious and it's easy to consume too much. Try more engaging activities that affirm you: singing or reading or playing a sport.[12]

3. **Let others renew you.** Remember that people don't just make demands on your time; they also provide emotional renewal. There's pure joy in a child's laugh, a friend's smile, a father's pat on the back. These small pleasures in life are priceless—prize them!

We've focused on physical and emotional energy here, but remember that all four dimensions of energy—physical, emotional, mental, and spiritual—are interconnected. If you subtract one from the equation, you'll be firing on less than four cylinders. If you are fully engaged and living life to the fullest, all four dimensions of your energy equation will be in balance.

> **There is more to life than increasing its speed.**
>
> —MOHANDAS K. GANDHI,
> INDIAN SPIRITUAL LEADER (1869–1948)

Reason 4: They burn out.

Why do people lose their focus? One reason is because they move so quickly that they never stop to look inside, let alone catch the scenery whizzing by around them. Their goal—whether they know it or not—is to just get through each busy day, cramming in more and more activities and obligations. Eventually, they burn out. Some people think that some form of spirituality can help people rebuild and regain their focus. For you, spirituality may mean a church, a type of organized religion, or simply looking inward to examine your life. According to a national study of 112,232 college students, four out of five first-year students are interested in spirituality, and nearly three-fourths report feeling a sense of connection with a higher power. Nearly half believe that college should help encourage their expression of spirituality.[13] Can college help you examine your values, find inner direction, ponder the meaning of life, and possibly help you slow down long enough to look at the big picture?

TRY It!

Do you think paying attention to your spiritual health has the potential to help you revitalize and sharpen your focus? To help you think about your answer to this question, respond to the items below:

1. It's easy to get caught up in day-to-day details, like kids, jobs, and bills. But many experts believe that you can sharpen your focus by taking time out to consider "life's bigger picture"—through yoga, meditation, prayer, or exercise, for example. Do you practice any of these? Do you think they might help? Why or why not?

2. Think about your college classes. Does "big picture" thinking come up (directly or indirectly) in any of them? If so, which class—and where has your thinking led you?

3. Make a promise to yourself to find time this week to free up your mind and slow down long enough to think more deeply than usual, and then pay attention to the results. What were they? Did your focus improve?

"I'll Study in My Free Time" … and When Is That?

EXERCISE 4.1

Where Did the Time Go?

How do you spend your time? Complete this self-assessment to find out how you spend your time. Fill in the number of hours you spend doing each of the following, then multiply your answer by the number given (7 or 5 to figure weekly amounts) where appropriate.

	Number of hours per day
Sleeping:	_____ × 7 = _____
Personal grooming (for example, showering, shaving, putting on makeup):	_____ × 7 = _____
Eating (meals and snacks; include preparation or driving time):	_____ × 7 = _____
Commuting Monday through Friday (to school and work):	_____ × 5 = _____
Doing errands and chores:	_____ × 7 = _____
Spending time with family (parents, children, or spouse):	_____ × 7 = _____
Spending time with boyfriend or girlfriend:	_____ × 7 = _____

(Continued)

Number of hours per week

At work: _____

In classes: _____

At regularly scheduled functions (church, clubs, etc.): _____

Socializing, hanging out, watching TV, talking on the phone, etc.: _____

Now add up all the numbers in the far right column, and subtract your total from 168, the number of hours in a week.

168 – _____ = _____. *This is the total number of hours you have remaining in your week for that ever-important task of studying. You may wish to revise how much time you spend on other activities of your life, based on whether you're already short on hours without studying factored in.*

Ask ten students when they study, and chances are at least eight will reply, "In my free time." The strange thing about this statement is that if you actually waited until you had free time to study, you probably never would. Truthfully, some students are amazed at how easily a day can race by without their ever thinking about cracking a book. This is why you should actually *schedule* your study time, but to do that, you should first be aware of how you're currently spending those twenty-four hours of each day.

Notice that Exercise 4.1 places studying at the bottom of the list, even though it's vital to your success in college. The exercise reflects a common attitude among college students, namely, that studying is what takes place after everything else gets done. Where does schoolwork rank on *your* list of priorities?

If succeeding in college is a top priority for you, then make sure that you're devoting adequate time to schoolwork outside the classroom. Most instructors expect you to study two to three hours outside of class for every hour spent in class. If it's a particularly challenging class, you may need even more study time. You can use the following chart to calculate the total number of hours you ought to expect to study—effectively—each week:

Credit hours for less demanding classes: _____ × 2 hours = _____ hours

Credit hours for typical/average classes: _____ × 3 hours = _____ hours

Credit hours for more challenging classes: _____ × 4 hours = _____ hours

Expected total study time per week = _____ hours

Remember, just putting in the time won't guarantee that you'll truly *understand* what you're studying. You need to ensure that your study time is productive by focusing your attention and strategically selecting study techniques that work best for you.

VARK It!

Kinesthetic: Try writing each item from your schedule today on sticky notes and arrange them in chronological order. Then try moving the sticky notes around to make the best use of your time and energy.

VARK It!

Visual: Think back over your day yesterday and draw it as a pie chart. If you showed time in class as RED, study time as BLUE, work as GREEN, and free time as WHITE, what would the overall results be? Are you using your time well?

Schedule Your Way to Success

Time Monitor

Can you remember how you spent all your time yesterday? Using the following Time Monitor, fill in as much as you can remember about how you spent your time yesterday, for the complete twenty four-hour period. Be as detailed as possible, right down to thirty-minute segments. If you were multitasking, put down your primary activity, and put an asterisk beside that time block. When you're finished, note how many asterisks are on your chart, and assess your overall productivity.

7:00 a.m. _____	3:00 _____	11:00 _____
7:30 _____	3:30 _____	11:30 _____
8:00 _____	4:00 _____	12:00 a.m. _____
8:30 _____	4:30 _____	12:30 _____
9:00 _____	5:00 _____	1:00 _____
9:30 _____	5:30 _____	1:30 _____
10:00 _____	6:00 _____	2:00 _____
10:30 _____	6:30 _____	2:30 _____
11:00 _____	7:00 _____	3:00 _____
11:30 _____	7:30 _____	3:30 _____
12:00 p.m. _____	8:00 _____	4:00 _____
12:30 _____	8:30 _____	4:30 _____
1:00 _____	9:00 _____	5:00 _____
1:30 _____	9:30 _____	5:30 _____
2:00 _____	10:00 _____	6:00 _____
2:30 _____	10:30 _____	6:30 _____

Now monitor how you use your time today (or tomorrow if you're reading this at night), or your instructor may have you complete this Time Monitor for a several days. Again, be very specific. At the conclusion of your record-keeping for this exercise, go back to Exercise 4.1, and check to see how accurate your estimates were.

There is no one right way to schedule your time, but if you experiment with the system presented in this book, you'll be on the right path. Eventually, you can tweak the system to make it uniquely your own. Try these eight steps to schedule your way to success!

Lame Excuses for Blowing Off Class

Do you find yourself skipping class at times in order to do something else: getting an oil change for your car, soaking up the sun's rays, or socializing with a friend on the phone? If so, ask yourself this: Would you walk into a gas station, put a big bill down on the counter to prepay for a tank of gas, and then put in a dollar's worth and drive off? Absolutely not, you say?

Would you buy a $10 movie ticket and then just toss it in the trash because you decided there was something else you'd rather do on the spur of the moment? No way!

Why, then, would you purchase much more expensive "tickets" to class—the average cost of an hour in class may be as high as $100, $150, or $200 or more—and then toss them in the trash by not attending? Don't you value your money more than that? More importantly, don't you value yourself more than that?

The next time you're tempted to opt out of your scheduled classes, ask yourself whether you really want to throw away money, in addition to the opportunity. Check your priorities, then put one foot in front of the other and walk into that classroom. In the long run, it's the best investment in your own future.

STEP 1: Fill out a "Term on a Page" Calendar. Right up front, create a "Term on a Page" calendar that shows the entire school term on one page. (See Exercise 4.3. This particular activity works best on paper. A month-by-month cell phone calendar won't let you see an entire term at once!) This calendar allows you to see the big picture. You will need to have the syllabus from each of your classes and your school's course schedule to do this step properly. The following items should be transferred onto your "Term on a Page" calendar:

> Holidays when your school is closed

> Exam and quiz dates from your syllabi

> Project or paper deadlines from your syllabi

> Relevant administrative deadlines (e.g., registration for the next term, drop dates)

> Birthdays and anniversaries to remember

> Important out-of-town travel

> Dates that pertain to other family members, such as days that your children's school is closed or that your spouse is out of town for a conference—anything that will impact your ability to attend classes or study

STEP 2: Invest in a Planner. Although it's good to have the big picture, you must also develop an ongoing scheduling system that works for you. Using the "It's all right up here in my head" method is a surefire way to miss an important appointment, fly past the deadline for your term paper without a clue, or lose track of the time you have left to complete multiple projects.

© Larry Harwood Photography. Property of Cengage Learning.

> **Take care of your minutes, and the hours will take care of themselves.**
>
> *Lord Chesterfield, British statesman and diplomat (1694–1773)*

Term on a Page

Take a few minutes right now to create your own Term on a Page, using the charts in Figure 4.2. Go online to download this exercise in Word.

Term _____ Year _____

FIGURE 4.2

Term on a Page

Month:

	Sunday	Monday	Tuesday	Wednesday	Thursday	Friday	Saturday

Month:

	Sunday	Monday	Tuesday	Wednesday	Thursday	Friday	Saturday

Month:

	Sunday	Monday	Tuesday	Wednesday	Thursday	Friday	Saturday

Month:

	Sunday	Monday	Tuesday	Wednesday	Thursday	Friday	Saturday

Month:

	Sunday	Monday	Tuesday	Wednesday	Thursday	Friday	Saturday

Although your instructor will typically provide you with a class syllabus that lists test dates and assignment deadlines, trying to juggle multiple syllabi—not to mention your personal and work commitments—is enough to drive you crazy. You need *one* central place for all of your important deadlines, appointments, and commitments. This central place is a planner—a calendar book with space to write in each day. Most every successful person on the planet uses some kind of planner, whether paper or electronic.

When you go planner shopping, remember that you don't have to break the bank unless you want to. Many new college students find that an ordinary paper-and-pencil daily calendar from an office supply store works best. Having a full page for each day means you can write your daily to-do list right in your planner (more on to-do lists later), and that can be a huge help. Using an online calendar, like Google calendar, can work, too. But remember that unless you have a smart cell phone with Internet access, an online calendar won't be portable, and you'll have to remember to enter events later.

STEP 3: Transfer Important Dates. The next step is to transfer important dates for the whole term from your "Term on a Page" overview to the appropriate days in your planner. It's important to be able to see all of your due dates together to create a big picture, but it's equally important to have these dates recorded in your actual planner because you will use it more regularly—as the final authority on your schedule.

STEP 4: Set Intermediate Deadlines. After recording the important dates for the entire academic term, look at the individual due dates for major projects or papers that are assigned. Then set intermediate stepping-stone goals that will ultimately help you accomplish your final goals. Working backward from the due date, choose and record deadlines for completing certain chunks of the work. For example, if you have a research paper due, you could set an intermediate deadline for completing all of your initial research and other deadlines for the prewriting, writing, and rewriting steps for the paper.

STEP 5: Schedule Fixed Activities for the Entire Term. Next, you'll want to schedule in all fixed activities throughout the entire term: class meeting times and reading assignments, religious services you regularly attend, club meetings, and family activities. It's also a great idea to schedule brief review sessions for your classes. Of course, sometimes you'll be going directly into another class, but ten-minute segments of time before and after each class to review your notes help prepare you for surprise quizzes and improve your comprehension.

STEP 6: Check for Schedule Conflicts. Now, take a final look at your planner. Do you notice any major scheduling conflicts, such as a planned business trip smack dab in the middle of midterm

Janis Christie/Photodisc/Getty Images

> ❝ **Nothing is so fatiguing as the eternal hanging on of an uncompleted task.** ❞
>
> *William James, American psychologist and philosopher (1842–1910)*

exam week? Look for these conflicts now, when there's plenty of time to adjust your plans and talk with your instructor to see what you can work out.

STEP 7: Schedule Flextime. In all the scheduling of important dates, checking and double-checking, don't forget one thing. You do need personal time for eating, sleeping, exercising, and other regular activities that don't have a set time frame. Despite your planner, life will happen. If you get a toothache, you'll need to see a dentist right away. Several times each week, you can count on something coming up that will offer you a chance (or force you) to revise your schedule. The decision of how high the item ranks on your priority list rests with you, but the point is to leave some wiggle room in your schedule. One other good idea is to follow the "two-minute" rule. Do any work items that can be completed in two minutes right then, on the spot. Doing so will free you from nagging details as you plan for bigger items.[14]

STEP 8: Monitor Your Schedule Every Day. At this point, you've developed a working time management system. Now it's important to monitor your use of that system on a daily basis. Each night, take three minutes to review the day's activities. How well did you stick to your schedule? Did you accomplish the tasks you set out to do? Do you need to revise your schedule for the rest of the week based on something that happened—or didn't happen—today? This simple process will help you better schedule your time in the future and give you a sense of accomplishment—or of the need for more discipline—for tasks completed, hours worked, and classes attended.

GOING PRO

BE DISCIPLINED

> **Time is the coin of your life. It is the only coin you have, and only you can determine how it will be spent**
>
> CARL SANDBURG

Manage your time, your money, and yourself. Success in college and in your career is about self-responsibility. You're in charge of your education; you call the shots. If you manage your time and money, you can focus as you should on your courses. If you "spend" unwisely—in either area—you lose your focus and your performance slips. In your career, the same will be true, but the professional aspect of time and money management becomes even more important. For example, you may be required to plan and follow a project schedule and work within a department budget, or you may even be responsible for coming up with next year's budget. Learning to be a budget expert in your personal life may well ensure real success in your professional career. In many ways, your ability to manage time and money will affect your personal and professional future.

To Do or Not to Do? There *Is* No Question

Part of your personal time management system should be keeping an ongoing to-do list. Although the concept of a to-do list sounds relatively simple, here are a few tricks of the trade.

Before the beginning of each school week, brainstorm all the things that you want or need to get done in the upcoming week. Using this random list of to-do

FIGURE 4.3

Time Zones

Important and Urgent: "A" Priorities	Important, but Not Urgent: "B" Priorities
Not Important, but Urgent: "C" Priorities	Not Important and Not Urgent: Scratch these off your list!

items, assign a priority level next to each one. The A-B-C method is simple and easy to use:

A = must get this done; highest priority

B = very important, but not absolutely necessary to get done immediately

C = not terribly important, but should be done right away (time-sensitive)

urgency in need of immediate attention

The two factors to consider when assigning a priority level to a to-do item are *importance* and **urgency**, creating four time zones. Use Figure 4.3 as a guide.[15]

After you've assigned a time zone to each item, review your list of A and B priorities and ask yourself:

1. **Do any of the items fit best with a particular day of the week?** For example, donating blood may be a high priority task for you, yet you don't want to do it on a day when you have a sports event planned. That might leave you with two available days in the upcoming week that you can donate blood.

2. **Can any items be grouped together to make things easier?** For example, you may have three errands to run downtown on your to-do list, so grouping them together will save you from making three separate trips.

3. **Do any A and B priorities qualify as floating tasks that can be completed anytime, anywhere?** For example, perhaps you were assigned an extra-long reading assignment for one of your classes. It's both important and urgent, an A priority item. Bring your book to read while waiting at the dentist's office for your appointment, a B priority. Planning ahead can really help save time.

4. **Do any priorities need to be shifted?** As the days pass, some of your B priorities will become A priorities due to the urgency factor increasing. Or maybe an A priority will become a C priority because something changed about the task. This is normal.

EXERCISE 4.4

So Much to Do—So Little Time

Assume this is your to-do list for today (Monday). Assign each item one of the four time zones described earlier: A, B, and C (and strike through any items that are not urgent and not important). Finally, renumber the items to indicate which you would do first, second, and so forth.

Start time: 9:00 a.m., Monday morning, during the second week of the fall term.

1. _____ Return Professor Jordan's call before class tomorrow. He left a message saying he wants to talk to you about some problems with the assignment you turned in.

2. _____ Pick up your paycheck and get to the bank before it closes at 5:00 p.m. this afternoon.

3. _____ Call your mother to find out how grandma is doing in the hospital.

4. _____ Start figuring out how to go about your new assignment at work. Your boss seems nervous about it.

5. _____ Call your favorite aunt. She lives overseas in a time zone seven hours ahead of yours. Today is a big birthday for her.

6. _____ Stop by the campus celebration with free food today only.

7. _____ Listen to the new music you downloaded yesterday.

8. _____ Leave a note asking your husband or wife/boy- or girlfriend/sibling/child to please stop leaving messes everywhere. It's really aggravating.

9. _____ Read the two chapters in your history textbook for the in-class quiz on Wednesday.

10. _____ Watch the first episode of the new reality TV show you've been waiting for, at 9 p.m. tonight.

11. _____ Write a rough draft of the essay due in your composition class on Thursday.

12. _____ Invite an out-of-town friend to spend the weekend.

13. _____ Return the three library books that are a week overdue.

14. _____ Call your math Teaching Assistant and leave a message asking for an appointment during her office hours to get help with the homework due on Wednesday. Nearly everyone is confused about the assignment.

15. _____ Meet your best friend for dinner for his or her birthday at 6 p.m.

Outline the criteria you used for making your decisions. For example, did you base your answers on personal priorities, locations (combining tasks based on where you need to be to do them), urgency/importance, or some other principle? (Note that this exercise asks you to put these tasks in order, according to whatever principles from this chapter you choose—not to figure out how to multitask and accomplish several at once!) If you choose to call your aunt (5) while writing your essay (11), chances are she'll hear the tapping of the keys and the breaks in the conversation and know exactly what you're doing. It's important to base your choices not only on what's quick or convenient, but also on how much people and priorities mean to you.

Items you've marked with a C must be decided on a case-by-case basis. But don't let their urgency convince you that you should do them before you accomplish items on your A and B lists. As for those not important and not urgent to-do items, scratch them off the list right now. Life is too short to waste time on unimportant tasks. Give yourself permission to focus on what's important. Because time is a limited resource, one of the best ways to guarantee a successful college experience is to use it wisely. If you don't already use these tools on a regular basis, give them a shot. What do you have to lose except time?

How Time Flies!

According to efficiency expert Michael Fortino, in a lifetime, the average American will spend:

> Seven years in the bathroom

> Six years eating

> Five years waiting in line

> Three years in meetings

> Two years playing telephone tag

> Eight months opening junk mail

> And six months waiting at red lights[16]

The bad news is time flies. The good news is you're the pilot.

Michael Altshuler, motivational speaker

What a waste of time! We can't do much about some of these items, but what *can* we do about other time-wasters? Plan—schedule—organize! Think about the issue of control in time management, and write in examples for the following:

1. Things you think you can't control, and you can't: _____
2. Things you think you can't control, but you can: _____
3. Things you think you can control, but you can't: _____
4. Things you think you can control, but you don't: _____
5. Things you think you can control, and you can: _____

Perhaps you wrote in something like *medical emergencies* for (1). You could have written in *family or friends bothering you while you study* for (2). For (4), maybe you could control how much *time you waste online*, but you don't. And for (5), perhaps you wrote in *your attention*. You're absolutely right. But what about (3)? Did anything fit there? Are there things you think you can control, but you can't? Try to think of something that would fit into (3), and then think of creative ways you really could control this situation if you tried.[17] Have you ever thought about how much the issues of control and time management are related?

According to experts, there are four kinds of common problematic time management "P's" in the world. When it comes to time management, control is generally a good thing. You take control and become more productive. But take a look at these four "P's." They exert control in ways that can bring counterproductive results!

> **The Preemptive.** Preemptives believe they are doing their best; in fact, they are continuously ahead of the game. They constantly, compulsively play "beat the clock." They're always way ahead of schedule. So what's wrong with that? Sometimes, nothing. But preemptives can gain a reputation of being non–team players, only out for themselves. They look like they're trying to impress everyone—or someone in particular, like the boss or teacher.

> **The People Pleaser.** People pleasers have the best of intentions, but they take on too much and sabotage their own effectiveness by trying to make others happy. Always saying yes to everyone may mean that there's no time left for their own work. Over time, they can even come to resent the very people they're trying to please and vice versa.

> **The Perfectionist.** Nothing is ever good enough for perfectionists. In effect, what they do is make other people play a waiting game while they continue to tinker with their projects to make them into some ideal they may never reach. They're control freaks, and they lead anxiety-ridden lives.

> **The Procrastinator.** Procrastinators are adrenaline junkies. They put things off until the 11th hour and then make a mad dash for the finish line, trailing a long list of excuses. Often, the root cause of procrastination is fear. Although the perfectionist will only accept an A+, the procrastinator is secretly afraid of not ever being able to achieve an A+. If she doesn't turn in an assignment, she can't find out just how good (or not) she is.[18]

Are you a Preemptive, People-pleasing, Perfectionistic, or Procrastinator?

Do you know people who fit into each of these four problematic time management "P" categories? Do you fit into one of these categories? Work in groups or as a class to brainstorm ways of helping these people improve their time management skills. What advice would you give each type?

Preemptive

Photos.com

People Pleaser

Photos.com

Perfectionist

Photos.com

Procrastinator

Photos.com

_____
_____
_____

_____
_____
_____

The "P" Word. Read This Section Now!… or Maybe Tomorrow…or…

Picture this: You sit down to work on a challenging homework assignment. After a few minutes, you think, *Man, I'm thirsty*, so you get up and get a soda. Then you sit back down to continue your work. A few minutes later, you decide that some chips would go nicely with your soda and you head to the kitchen. Again, you sit down to face the task before you, as you concentrate more on eating than on working. Ten minutes go by and a nagging thought starts taking over: *Must do laundry*. Up you go again to throw a load of clothes in the washer. Before long you're wondering where all the time went. Because you only have an hour left before class, you think, *Why bother getting started now? Doing this project will take much more time than that, so I'll just start it tomorrow*. Despite good intentions at the beginning of your work session, you've just succeeded in accomplishing zip, nada, nothing.

Congratulations! You—like thousands of other college students—have just successfully procrastinated! Researchers define procrastination as "needlessly delaying tasks to the point of experiencing subjective discomfort."[19] And according to researchers, 70 percent of college students admit to procrastinating on their assignments.[20]

You may be in the majority, but alas, in this case, there's no safety in numbers! Academic procrastination is a major threat to your ability to succeed in college. And procrastination in the working world can actually bring your job, and ultimately your career, to a screeching halt. Plenty of people try to rationalize their procrastination by claiming that they work better under pressure. However, the challenge in college is that during some weeks of the term, every class you're taking will have an assignment or test due, all at once, and if you procrastinate, you'll not only generate tremendous anxiety for yourself, but you'll lower your chances of succeeding at any of them.

Who, Me? Procrastinate?

Procrastination is a habit. It may show up as not getting around to doing your homework (if you don't turn it in, you can't get a bad grade on it—which almost guarantees that you'll get a bad grade on it), not vacuuming the carpet because it takes too much energy to lug the machine around, or not getting to work on time because your job is boring. What about you? Think about the following ten situations, and put a check mark next to each one to indicate the degree to which you normally procrastinate:

	Always	Sometimes	Never
1. Doing homework	_____	_____	_____
2. Writing a paper	_____	_____	_____
3. Studying for tests	_____	_____	_____
4. Reading class material	_____	_____	_____
5. Meeting with your academic advisor	_____	_____	_____
6. Texting/e-mailing a friend	_____	_____	_____
7. Playing a game/hanging out	_____	_____	_____
8. Going to see a movie you've heard about	_____	_____	_____
9. Meeting someone for dinner at a restaurant	_____	_____	_____
10. Watching TV	_____	_____	_____

If you are like many students, you checked "always" or "sometimes" more often for the first five items than you did for the last five. But procrastination isn't as simple as not procrastinating when you want to do something and procrastinating when you don't. You may actually hate vacuuming but decide to vacuum the entire house so that you don't have to face studying for a test. There are "layers" of procrastination and many reasons why people procrastinate. Which of these apply to you?

_____ Avoiding something you see as unpleasant   _____ Not realizing how important the task is

_____ Feeling overwhelmed by all you have to do   _____ Reacting to your own internal conflict

_____ Being intimidated by the task itself   _____ Protecting your self-esteem

_____ Fearing failure   _____ Waiting for a last-minute adrenaline rush

_____ Fearing success   _____ Just plain not wanting to

Before you can control the procrastination monster in your life, it's important to understand *why* you procrastinate. Think about all the instances in which you don't procrastinate: meeting your friends for dinner, returning a phone call from a friend, going to the store. Why are those things easy to do, but getting started on an assignment is difficult until you feel the jaws of a deadline closing down on you?[21] The reasons for procrastinating vary from person to person, but once you know your own reasons for putting things off, you'll be in a better position to address the problem from its root cause.

The next time you find yourself procrastinating, ask yourself why. Procrastination hurts your chances for success and gives you ready-made excuses if you don't succeed: "It's like running a full race with a knapsack full of bricks on your back. When you don't win, you can say it's not that you're not a good runner, it's just that you had this sack of bricks on your back."[22] In addition to understanding why you procrastinate, try these ten procrastination busters to help you kick the habit.

1. Keep track (of your excuses). Write them down consistently, and soon you'll be able to recognize them for what they are. Own your responsibilities—in school and in the rest of your life.

2. **Break down.** Break your project into its smaller components. A term paper, for example, can be broken down into the following smaller parts: prospectus, thesis, research, outline, small chunks of writing, and bibliography. Completing smaller tasks along the way is much easier than facing a threatening monster of a project.

3. **Trick yourself.** When you feel like procrastinating, pick some aspect of the project that's easy and that you would have to do anyway. If the thought of an entire paper is overwhelming you, for example, work on the bibliography to start. Starting with something—*anything*—that will get you into the rhythm of the work.

4. **Resolve issues.** If something's eating away at you, making it difficult to concentrate, take care of it. Sometimes you must deal with a bossy friend, your kids vying for your attention, or something equally intrusive. Then get down to work.

5. **Get real.** Set realistic goals for yourself. If you declare that you're going to finish a twelve-page paper in five hours, you're already doomed. Procrastinators are sometimes overly optimistic. They underestimate how much time something will take. Make it a habit to keep track of how long assignments take you in all your courses so that you can be increasingly realistic over time. And be specific. Instead of writing, "Finish Chapter 10" in your planner, write exactly what you need to do: "Finish reading Chapter 10, answer the discussion questions at the end, and e-mail my responses to my instructor."

6. **Capture killer B's.** You're working on Task A when Task B presents itself—perhaps it's a text or an e-mail, something that seems important at the time. Immediately capture the threatening "Killer B" by writing it in a paper notebook that's always by your side. Why paper? If you use an online journal, you'll be tempted to wander further online. You may end up in Timbuktu. com and make countless stops along the way.[23]

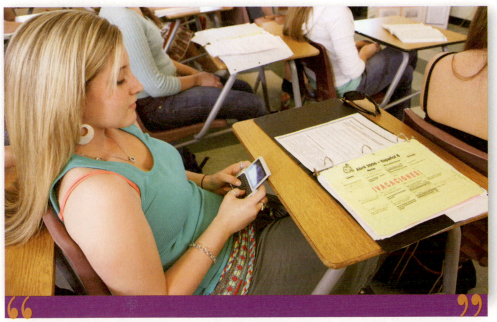

Things which matter most should never be at the mercy of things which matter least.

Johann Wolfgang von Goethe, German writer and scholar (1749–1832)

7. **Make a deal with yourself.** Even if it's only spending fifteen minutes on a task that day, do it so that you can see progress.

8. **Overcome fear.** Many of the reasons for procrastinating have to do with our personal fears. We may fear not doing something perfectly, or failing completely—or even the responsibility that comes with success to keep succeeding. But as Susan Jeffers, author and lecturer, states, "Feel the fear, and do it anyway!"

9. **Get tough.** Sometimes projects simply require discipline. The best way to complete a tough task is to simply dig in. Become your own taskmaster; "crack the whip" and force yourself to focus on those things that are high priorities, but perhaps not your idea of fun.

10. **Acknowledge accomplishment.** We're not talking major shopping sprees at Neiman Marcus here. We're talking reasonable, meaningful rewards that match up with how much effort you invested. Go buy yourself a small treat, call your best friend in another state, take a relaxing soak in the bathtub, or do something to celebrate your accomplishments—big and small—along the way. Acknowledgment, from yourself or others, is a great motivator for tackling future projects.

Beyond Juggling: *Realistically* Manage Work, School, and Personal Life*

Your personal time management needs depend on who you are and how many obligations you have. Today's college students are more diverse than ever. Increasing numbers of college students are also parents, part-time employees or full-time professionals, husbands or wives, community volunteers, soccer coaches, or Sunday school teachers. How on earth can you possibly juggle it all?

The answer? You can't. According to work-life balance expert Dawn Carlson, juggling is a knee-jerk coping mechanism—the default setting when time gets tight and it seems that nothing can be put on the back burner. If you, like millions of others, feel overworked, overcommitted, and exhausted at every turn, you may have already learned that you can't juggle your way to a balanced life. It's impossible.[24]

Now for the good news. Balance among work, school, and personal life is possible. All of us have three primary areas of our lives that should be in balance, ideally—meaningful work (including school), satisfying relationships, and a healthy lifestyle. In addition to work and relationships, we all need to take care of ourselves. See what you think of these five rebalancing strategies. The idea is you can't have it all, but you can have it better than you do now.

Alternating

If you use this strategy, your work-life balance comes in separate, concentrated doses. You may throw yourself into your career with abandon, and then cut back or quit work altogether and focus intensely on your family. You may give your job 110 percent during the week but devote Saturdays to physical fitness or to your kids or to running all the errands you've saved up during the week. Or you save Tuesdays and Thursdays for homework and go to classes Mondays,

*Adapted from Sandholtz, K., Derr, B., Buckner, K., & Carlson, D. (2002). *Beyond juggling: Rebalancing your busy life.* San Francisco: Berrett-Koehler Publishing.

Wednesdays, and Fridays. People who use this strategy alternate between important things, and it works for them. An alternator's motto is "I want to have it all, but just not all at once."

Outsourcing

Outsourcing, or paying someone else to do something for you, is another solution. An outsourcer's motto might be "I want to have it all, not do it all." This strategy helps you achieve work–life balance by giving someone else some of your responsibilities—usually in your personal life—to free up time for the tasks you care about most. If you have enough money, hire someone to clean the house or mow the lawn. If you don't, trade these jobs among family, friends, or neighbors who band together to help each other. Of course, there are ways this strategy could be misused by college students. Don't even think about outsourcing your research papers by having someone else write them or downloading them from the Internet with a charge card! Warning: This practice will definitely be hazardous to your academic health! In fact, your college career may be over!

Bundling

Bundling is efficient because it allows you to "kill two birds with one stone." Examine your busy life and look for areas in which you can double dip, such as combining exercising with socializing. If your social life is suffering because you have too much to do, take walks with a friend so that you can talk along the way. A bundler's motto is "I want to get more mileage out of the things I do by combining activities."

Techflexing

Technology allows us to work from almost anywhere, anytime, using technology. If you telecommute from home several days a week for your job, you might get up early, spend some time on e-mail, go out for a run, have breakfast with your family, and then get back on your computer. In the office, you use instant messaging to stay connected to family members or a cell phone to call home while commuting to a business meeting. Chances are you can telecommute to your campus library and do research online, register for classes online, and pay all your bills online, including tuition. Use technology, and the flexibility it gives you, to your advantage to merge important aspects of your life.

Simplifying

People who use this strategy have decided they don't want it all. They've reached a point where they make a permanent commitment to stop the craziness in their lives. The benefit of simplifying is greater freedom from details, stress, and the rat race. But there are trade-offs, of course. People may have to take a significant cut in pay in order to work fewer hours or at a less demanding job. But for them, it's worth it.[25]

These five strategies, used separately or in combination, have helped many people who are dealing with work, school, and family commitments at the same time. They all require certain trade-offs. None of these strategies is a magic solution.

But the alternative to rebalancing is more stress, more physical and emotional exhaustion, more frustration, and much less personal satisfaction. If you focus on rebalancing your life—making conscious choices and course corrections as you go—small changes can have a big impact. Work–life balance isn't an all-or-nothing proposition. It's an ever-changing journey. So take it one step at a time.

> Our attraction to a world of infinite possibility, information and complexity is here to stay. The challenge is how to participate productively in this new and turbulent world, and not be paralyzed by it.
>
> *David Allen, time management expert*

ONLINE TechKnow

Where did all the time go? Scheduling yourself productively is important in any college or career work, but it's especially crucial when you're working online:

- **Note your potential for peak performance.** Ever had a friend who was a "morning person" or a "night-owl"? Each of us has high energy times, and times during the day when we're zoned out on "auto-pilot." Learn to recognize when you're at your best, and find ways to schedule your online working sessions during those peak periods.

- **Read the "fine print."** You wouldn't buy a car without knowing the details of the contract, would you? When you sign up for an online course, your syllabus is your contract. It'll pay to read it carefully and note how much time this course will require, including reading, research, projects, tests, chats, and forums.

- **Make a calendar for yourself.** Write down exactly when online assignments must be done. Then mark on your calendar when you'll need to start each project ahead of time, and how long you estimate it will take you to get it done. Refer to this calendar every day—develop a partnership between yourself and your calendar as your main ally.

- **Work ahead.** What about cramming for tests? What about writing up assignments mere minutes before a deadline? In both cases, you'll do your best online work if you work ahead and submit assignments early. Use your contract (your syllabus) and your calendar wisely here—mark these tests and tasks at the beginning of the course and get them done ahead of time.

Improve Your Grade
Online Flashcards
Glossary

Time Is Money!

EXERCISE 4.7

How Fiscally Fit Are You?

Have you ever heard the phrase "Time is money"? Before leaving the subject of time and energy management, let's look at how you manage your money as well. How good are you at managing your finances? Check one of the three boxes for each statement, to get a sense of how financially savvy you are.

	Always true of me	Sometimes true of me	Never true of me
1. At any given moment in time, I know the balance of my checking account.			
2. I use my credit card for particular types of purchases only, such as gas or food.			
3. I pay off my bills in full every month.			
4. I know the interest rate on my credit cards.			
5. I resist impulse buying and only spend when I need things.			
6. I have a budget and I follow it.			
7. I put money aside to save each month.			
8. When I get a pay raise, I increase the proportion of money I save.			
9. I keep track of my spending on a daily or weekly basis.			
10. I don't allow myself to get pressured by others into buying things I don't really need.			

Look over your responses. If you have more checks in the "Never true of me" column than you do in either of the two others, you may be able to put the information you're about to read to good use!

© Larry Harwood Photography. Property of Cengage Learning.

> **Don't tell me where your priorities are. Show me where you spend your money and I'll tell you what they are.**
>
> *James W. Frick (1924–), Former Vice President, University of Notre Dame*

People say that "time is money." It's true. If you're so efficient with your time that you can call more customers or sell more products, then time does equal money. If your company is the first to introduce a hot new kind of cell phone or a zippy fuel-efficient car, you win. Even if better models come out next year, they may fall flat because people have already invested.

Both time management and money management are key to your college success.

Studies show that working too many hours at a paid job increases your chances of dropping out of college.[26] Many students find themselves working more so that they can spend more, which in turn takes time away from their studies. They may take a semester off from college to make a pile of money and then never come back. Although there's evidence that working a moderate amount can help you polish your time and energy management skills, the real secret to financial responsibility in college is to track your habits and gain the knowledge you need to make sound financial decisions.

VARK It!

Kinesthetic: Use a free online budget tool such as Mint.com, or create an Excel spreadsheet to track your monthly budget. Look for opportunities to cut your spending.

Create a Spending Log

Take a look at this student's spending log, then complete one for yourself. Money has a way of slipping through our fingers. Choose one entire day that is representative of your spending, and use the chart on the next page to keep track of how you spend money. Write down everything from seemingly small, insignificant items to major purchases, and explain why you made each purchase. Your log may look something like this student's:

TIME	ITEM	LOCATION	AMOUNT	REASON
8–9 A.M.	coffee and bagel	convenience store	$3.50	overslept!
9–10 A.M.	computer paper	office supply store	$2.50	English paper due
10–11 A.M.	gas fill-up	gas station	$65.00	running on fumes!
11 A.M.– 12 P.M.	burger and fries	fast-food restaurant	$6.00	lunch on the run
12–1 P.M.	toiletries, etc.	drugstore	$18.00	out of stock
1–2 P.M.	bottled water	convenience store	$2.50	forgot to bring
2–3 P.M.	supplies	bookstore	$12.00	forgot to get earlier

(Continued)

TIME	ITEM	LOCATION	AMOUNT	REASON
3–7 p.m.	WORK			
7–8 p.m.	pizza	pizza place	$12.00	meet friends
8–9 p.m.	week's groceries	grocery store	$61.50	cupboard is bare!
9–10 p.m.	laundry	laundromat	$5.00	washer broken
10–11 p.m.	STUDY TIME			
11 p.m.– 12 a.m.	weekend movie, online tickets, DVDs, cell phone upgrade	Internet retail websites, phone service	$129.00 $20.00	friend's recommendations, need more minutes

This student has spent $337 today without doing anything special! When you analyze his expenditures, you can find patterns. He seems to (1) forget to plan, so he spends money continuously throughout the day, (2) spend relatively large amounts of money online, (3) be particularly vulnerable late at night, and (4) spend money grabbing food on the run. These are patterns he should be aware of if he wants to control his spending. He could pack food from home to save a significant amount of money, for example. Now create your own chart.

TIME	ITEM	LOCATION	AMOUNT	REASON
8–9 a.m.				
9–10 a.m.				
10–11 a.m.				
11 a.m. – 12 p.m.				
12–1 p.m.				
1–2 p.m.				
2–3 p.m.				
3–4 p.m.				
4–5 p.m.				
5–6 p.m.				
6–7 p.m.				
7–8 p.m.				
8–9 p.m.				
9–10 p.m.				
10–11 p.m.				
11 p.m.–12 a.m.				

What patterns do you notice about your spending? What kinds of changes will you try to make to curb any unnecessary spending?

The Perils of Plastic

The "newly minted" Credit Card Act of 2009 has changed some things about how credit cards work. In 2008, before the law went into effect, college students carried a balance of $3,173 (a ten-year high), and a full 82 percent kept paying on a balance every month.[27] Under the new law, credit cards cannot be issued to people under the age of 21 unless they have an adult co-signer or can show proof that they have enough income. So younger college students will need permission from parents or guardians to increase their credit limits. And those under 21 will be protected from "sneaky" credit card offers unless they opt to get them. If you're in this younger category, read up on credible Internet sites about the new law and the protections and restrictions it provides. If you already have a credit card or plan to get one, however, keep this general advice in mind.

1. **Think about the difference between needs and wants.** You may think you need particular things so that your friends will like you ("Hey, let's stop for a burger"), so that you have a new item (like a new car you can't afford), or so that you look fabulous (like pricey manicures). Here's a rule of thumb: If buying something simply helps you move from acceptable to amazing, it's not an emergency. Do you really need a mocha latté every day? A regular old cup of coffee a day sets you back $500 per year!

2. **Leave home without it.** Don't routinely take your credit card with you. Use cash and save your credit card for true emergencies or essentials, like gas and groceries. Do you really want to risk paying interest on today's ice cream cone years from now?

3. **Don't spend money you don't have.** Only charge what you can pay for each month. Just because your credit card limit is $2,000 doesn't mean you need to spend that much each month. A vacation that costs $1,000 will take 12 years of minimal payments to pay off at an 18 percent interest rate. And that $1,000 trip will eventually cost you $2,115! One piece of good advice is to "live like a student while you are in school so you don't have to live like a student after you graduate."[28]

4. **Understand how credit works.** It's important to know the basics. According to one source, "Only 15% [of college students] have any idea how much their interest rate is, and fewer than one in 10 students know their interest rate, late fee and over-limit fee amounts."[29]

   Here are some terms you need to know:

   > **Credit reports.** Your credit history is based on (1) how many credit cards you owe money on, (2) how much money you owe, and (3) how many late payments you make. Bad grades on your credit report can make your life difficult later.

   > **Fees.** Credit card companies charge you in three ways: (1) annual fees (a fee you must pay every year to use the card); (2) finance charges (a charge for loaning you the money you can't pay back when your bill is due); and (3) late fees (for missing a monthly payment deadline). Think about what's most important to you—no annual fee, frequent flyer miles, or a lower interest rate—and shop around!

   > **The fine print.** How can you learn more? Read your credit card contract carefully. Credit card companies must give you certain important information, which is often on their website. Go to the Federal Reserve website

for vital, bottom-line information, and search online to find out more about ways the new law could affect you.[30]

5. Track your expenses. All kinds of tools—technology-based and otherwise—can help you discover where your money actually goes. To control your spending, use a credit card with caution or use a debit card.

6. If you're already in financial trouble, ask for help. Talk to an expert who can help you figure out what to do.[31]

BOX 4.2

Top Ten Financial Aid FAQs

Financial aid. Like all good things, you have to know how it works. You can think of financial aid as complicated and time-consuming, or it can be the one thing that keeps you in school. Take a look at these questions students often ask about the mysteries of financial aid. Most students need financial help of some kind to earn a college degree. Here is some information to help you navigate your way financially.[32]

1. **Who qualifies for financial aid? Almost everyone!** You may not think you qualify for financial aid, but it's a good idea to apply anyway. You won't know until you apply, and some types of aid are based on criteria other than your income and assets.

2. **What does FAFSA stand for?** FAFSA stands for Free Application for Federal Student Aid. You apply online at fafsa.gov, or you can get a copy of the application by calling 1-800-4-FED-AID.

3. **What types of financial aid exist?** You can receive financial aid in the form of scholarships, fellowships, loans, grants, or work-study awards. Generally, scholarships and fellowships are for students with special academic, artistic, or athletic abilities; students with interests in specialized fields; students from particular parts of the country; or students from minority groups. Typically, you don't repay them. Loans and grants come in a variety of forms and from several possible sources, either federal or state government or private organizations. Loans must be repaid, but there are many loan programs to pay down your student loans if you pursue fields such as teaching, nursing, or public service. In addition, if you qualify for a need-based work-study job on or off campus, you can earn an hourly wage to assist in your educational expenses.

4. **When should I apply?** You can apply for financial aid any time after January 1 of the year you intend to go to college, but be mindful of your school's priority filing date to ensure you meet that deadline, as grant funds are limited. The FAFSA will require tax information from the previous year. Remember, you must be enrolled by the start of classes to receive funds.

5. **Do I have to reapply every year?** Yes. Your financial situation can change over time. Your brothers or sisters may start college while you're in school, for example, which can change your family's status.

6. **How can I keep my financial aid over my college years?** Assuming your financial situation remains fairly similar from year to year, you must demonstrate that you're making progress toward a degree in terms of credits and a minimum GPA. Remember that if you drop courses, your financial aid may be affected based on whether you're considered to be a full-time or part-time student.

7. **Who's responsible for paying back my loans?** You are. Others can help you, but ultimately the responsibility is yours and yours alone. If your parents forget to make a payment or don't pay a bill on time, you will be held responsible.

8. **If I leave school for a time, do I have to start repaying my loans right away?** Most loans have a grace period of six or nine months before you must begin repayment. You can request a forbearance or deferment if you need to postpone payments beyond your grace period.

9. **If I get an outside scholarship, should I report it to the Financial Aid office on campus?** Yes. They'll adjust your financial aid package if necessary, but the rules require that scholarships must be processed through the financial aid office.

10. **Where can I find out more?** Your best source of information is in the Office of Financial Aid right on your own campus. Or you can get information online at studentaid.ed.gov. Or call the Federal Student Aid Information Center at 1–800–433–3243, and ask for a free copy of *The Student Guide: Financial Aid* from the U.S. Department of Education.

What's In **YOUR** Briefcase?

WORK EFFICIENTLY

Imagine yourself off to a great start, impressing everyone, especially your boss, in your long-awaited career after college. But something is gnawing at you. You can't help but notice your stress level inching up. One day, when you power up your office computer, you immediately see 250 new e-mails that weren't there yesterday. Aaaak!!! When you have multiple projects with deadlines, the bottom line question becomes "Which task do you do first when you're totally overwhelmed?"

Some people choose to become "workaholics". They come in early, leave late, and take work home with them. However, working more doesn't mean you care more or get more done. It just means you work more.[33] Instead of working harder, how about working smarter?

Try putting a whiteboard on your wall and spending the first hour prioritizing your day. Shut the door, turn everything off, and list your goals for the day by creating small boxes to represent your three main projects. Then explore how they can be chunked into smaller subprojects, and look for relationships among them and patterns across them. You'll be able to save yourself time and accomplish much more. Your whiteboard will help you prioritize prioritizing (and no, that's not a typo). You're moving the process of prioritizing right up to the top of your to-do list.

By prioritizing first, you're guaranteeing that you'll make greater headway than you would otherwise. You're working smarter, not harder. At the end of the day, you can look back at your "wake" in the imaginary river of your work life, satisfied with how far you've come from the shoreline. As someone once said, "Efficiency is intelligent laziness." Figure it out now. It's all about working smarter and getting things done.[34]

How can you practice prioritizing now to develop the skills you'll need in your eventual career?

_____

_____

step 3 INSIGHT *Now* What Do You Think?

At the beginning of this chapter, Derek Johnson, a frustrated and disgruntled student, faced a challenge. Now after reading this chapter, would you respond differently to any of the questions you answered about the "FOCUS Challenge Case"? Using what you learned in the chapter, write a paragraph ending to Derek's case study. What are some of the possible outcomes for Derek?

step 4 ACTION Your Plans for Change

1. What's the most important thing you learned in reading this chapter?
2. How will you apply the information you've learned to yourself to improve your time, energy, and money management?

chapter 5

Thinking Critically and Creatively

How this chapter relates to YOU

1. When it comes to thinking critically and creatively in your college classes, what do you find the most challenging, if anything?

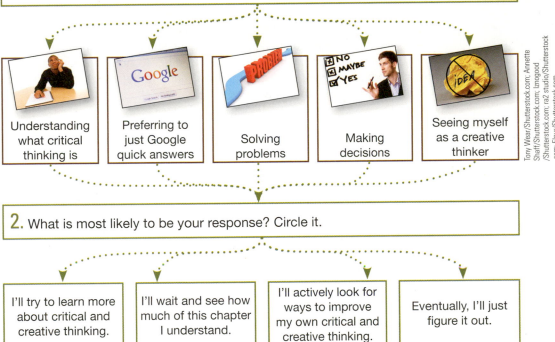

Understanding what critical thinking is

Preferring to just Google quick answers

Solving problems

Making decisions

Seeing myself as a creative thinker

2. What is most likely to be your response? Circle it.

I'll try to learn more about critical and creative thinking.

I'll wait and see how much of this chapter I understand.

I'll actively look for ways to improve my own critical and creative thinking.

Eventually, I'll just figure it out.

3. What would you have to do to increase your likelihood of success? Will you do it this term?

Example: *Really focus on this topic as the foundation for success in college. Yes!*

How YOU will relate to this chapter

What are you most interested in learning about? Put check marks by those topics.

☐ How critical thinking and creative thinking are defined

☐ How a four-part model of critical thinking works

☐ How to analyze arguments, assess assumptions, and consider claims

☐ How to avoid mistakes in reasoning

☐ What metacognition is and why it's important

☐ How to become a more creative thinker

● How motivated are you to learn more about getting the right start in college? (5 = high, 1 = low) ___

● How ready are you to read now? ___ (If something is in your way, take care of it if you can; zero in and focus.)

● How long do you think it will take you to complete this chapter? If you start and stop, keep track of your overall time. ___ hour(s) ___ minutes

Desiree Moore

Anke van Wyk/Shutterstock.com

Simply put: Desiree Moore was a perfectionist. Her friends said she was "detail oriented." Her family said she was compulsive. Truthfully, though, she hadn't been all that successful in high school; her assignments were always turned in late, if at all, because they were never "finished." She'd always ask her teachers how long a paper should be and what topic she should write about. She wanted to get things right. Her teachers always advised her to stop "tweaking": "You spend so much time revising your assignments that nothing ever gets done." But she found it hard to take their advice.

High school had been so stressful that when she graduated, she took the first job that came along, as a receptionist for a small law firm. When the two lawyers announced they were going to retire, she started to job hunt immediately. She found another job as a telemarketer. But being hung up on all day wasn't all that much fun, so eventually she quit. She tried waiting tables and cleaning houses, but those jobs didn't hold much appeal either. Before she knew it, more than a few years had gone by, and Desiree realized she didn't have much to show for it. She needed more specialized skills in order to get a better job. When she thought back over all the jobs she'd had since high school, she realized that working with the two lawyers had been her favorite. So, Desiree decided to become a paralegal by earning a two-year degree at the big career college in town. She would be the first person in her family to go to college! It was a good career field, and she could investigate legal cases, draft documents, and do research working alongside an attorney.

Her first semester consisted of two night classes: "Introduction to Paralegal Careers" and "Paralegal Ethics." But "Paralegal Ethics" was a very challenging course. The instructor, Mr. Courtney, a retired lawyer himself, had announced on the first day of class that he believed in the Socratic method of teaching, by asking questions of students instead of lecturing. "Socrates, perhaps the greatest philosopher of all time," he announced the first day, "is the 'father' of critical thinking. In this class, you'll learn to think critically. *Learning to think* is what college is all about." Mr. Courtney began every class session with a hypothetical story, and he always randomly chose a student to respond. His openings went something like this:

An attorney has just finished law school and opens a law office. He hires a legal

© Larry Harwood Photography. Property of Cengage Learning.

© Cengage Learning

© Cengage Learning

Paralegal Associate's Degree Program

Courses offered:

- Introduction to the Law
- Torts & Personal Injury
- Contracts
- Legal Research, Writing & Civil Litigation
- Paralegal Ethics
- Criminal Law
- Business Law & Bankruptcy
- Constitutional Law and Criminal Procedure
- Employment Law
- Environmental Law

Paralegal Ethics Syllabus

Instructor: Samuel Courtney
Email Address: S.Courtney@campusmail.edu
Office Hours: MWF 8am–10am
Office Location: Main Hall 1020
Text: *Legal Ethics for Paralegals and the Law Office* (1st Edition) by Laura Morrison

Class Content:
- Understand ethical issues that paralegals may face
- Review the universal concepts of professional responsibility and ethical practices
- Define the roles of paralegals versus attorneys
- Recognize what activities constitute the
- Discuss possible solutions to ethical dilemmas

Class Method: Since philosophy is an important part of law, for our class method we will turn to one of the founding fathers of critical and philosophical thinking: Socrates. Consequently, we will be using the "Socratic method" when approaching course material. This means that instead of giving a lecture, I will ask you, the students, questions in order to create a lively discussion.

Grading: This course will include 3 exams, each worth 20% of your overall grade. There will also be 5 quizzes during the semester, all of which contribute to another 20% of your grade.

What's In **YOUR** Briefcase?

EXAMINE YOUR THINKING

Consider a job that you've held in the past. If someone asked you to come up with five adjectives that describe the most memorable boss you've ever had, what words would come to you? Words like *encouraging, smart, visionary, responsive,* or *supportive*—or words like *hasty, unfair, mean, hypocritical,* or *irrational*? What do all the words you think of have in common? Were they mainly *positive* or *negative*?

When asked this question, most people go in one direction: either entirely positive or negative. No one ever says, "What I really love about my boss is his critical nature. He doesn't miss a single mistake I make."[22] It's natural to lean one way or the other; that's one reason why critical thinking skills are a useful tool in the workplace. They can help you adjust your thinking appropriately and keep you from getting locked into particular patterns, especially negative ones.

In the workplace, the most desirable kind of thinking is "realistic optimism." It's not blind faith or false hope; it's looking for the best in things and then working to make them happen. It's accepting what's going on around you, but at the same time admitting what needs to be changed. It's about resilience, "getting back on the horse," and trotting on. It's a productive pattern of thinking.[23]

If "realistic optimism" sounds like an oxymoron to you, have faith! Remember the words of the environmentalist and founder of Patagonia, the well-known outdoor gear company: "There's no difference between a pessimist who says, 'Oh, it's hopeless, so don't bother doing anything,' and an optimist who says, 'Don't bother doing anything, it's going to turn out fine anyway.' Either way, nothing happens." It's your thinking and your career, and you're in the driver's seat. You want to do things, go places, and make things happen. That's what it's all about.

How does this section apply to your current or a recent job? Can you think of an example of how "realistic optimism" could help you in a real-life scenario from your work experience?

_____

_____

_____

At the beginning of this chapter, Desiree Moore, a frustrated student, faced a challenge. Now, after reading this chapter, would you respond differently to any of the questions you answered about the "FOCUS Challenge Case"? Using what you learned in the chapter, write a paragraph ending to Desiree's case study. What are some of the possible outcomes for Desiree?

step
4 ACTION Your Plans for Change

1. What's the most important thing you learned in reading this chapter? Why did it have an impact on you?

2. What will you change about the way you try to learn in your classes or perform on the job as a result of reading it?

chapter 6 Learning Online

READINESS CHECK

How this chapter relates to YOU

1. When it comes to online learning, using technology, and doing research for your college classes, what are you most concerned about, if anything?

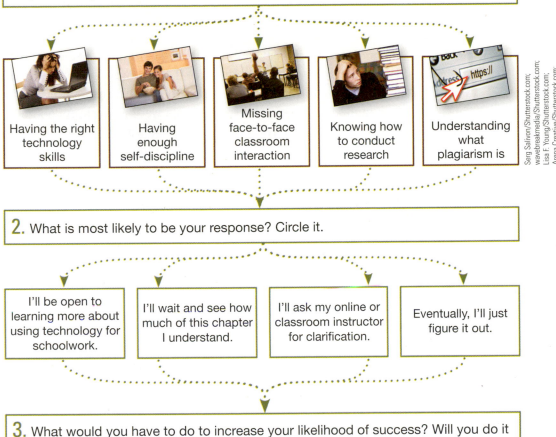

Having the right technology skills

Having enough self-discipline

Missing face-to-face classroom interaction

Knowing how to conduct research

Understanding what plagiarism is

2. What is most likely to be your response? Circle it.

I'll be open to learning more about using technology for schoolwork.

I'll wait and see how much of this chapter I understand.

I'll ask my online or classroom instructor for clarification.

Eventually, I'll just figure it out.

3. What would you have to do to increase your likelihood of success? Will you do it this term?

Example: *Increase my self-discipline to be successful at online tasks. Yes!*

How YOU will relate to this chapter

What are you most interested in learning about? Put check marks by those topics.

☐ How to develop useful strategies for online classes

☐ How to use technology to become more academically successful

☐ How to cultivate your research skills

☐ What information literacy skills are and why they're important

☐ What plagiarism is and how to avoid it

● How motivated are you to learn more about getting the right start in college? (5 = high, 1 = low) _____

● How ready are you to read now? _____ (If something is in your way, take care of it if you can, zero in and focus.)

● How long do you think it will take you to complete this chapter? If you start and stop, keep track of your overall time. _____ hour(s) _____ minutes

DARIO JONES

CLM/Shutterstock.com

Ever since grade school, Dario Jones had been called a geek. It was a label he hated, but, honestly, most people probably thought of him that way. As a kid, Dario lived for computer games. He played them nearly every waking hour. In high school, he'd shower in record time, throw on whatever clean clothes he could find, and use any spare minutes for computer games. When he got home, he'd log right back on again. His Dad tried threatening him: "You'll lose your eyesight and flunk out of school." Once when he was younger, he faked a sore throat and played World of Warcraft at home for a week while his parents were at work. As he got older, his Dad warned: "You'll never get a date." But Dario wasn't worried. Online relationships were enough. Real-life relationships were too much trouble. After high school, he joined the Army, and now that he was finally back from 18 months in Afghanistan, his cyber life was much more exciting than ever. Dario spent more time—even sacrificing precious hours of sleep—surfing the Internet, envisioning how he could improve websites, and grooming his Facebook page than he spent talking to any living being.

Then one day the obvious truth dawned on him. Now that he was a civilian, he was going to have to get a job—plain and simple. He had joined the Army because he really didn't know what he wanted to do next, and he figured he'd gain some skills there. But now that he was home, he wondered how those skills would translate into a different career—and whether he had the right skills.

Eventually, Dario made a decision. He would use his G.I. benefits and go to college. Because he was such a technology fan, maybe being a web designer would be a good field for him. And as he Googled opportunities, he found that he could get an entire degree online! What could be more perfect than that? Sitting in real classrooms with all those college kids didn't appeal to him at all. Besides, now that he was back from some pretty intense experiences while deployed, fighting for parking spots and being in crowded classrooms would just add to his stress, and that was something he didn't need. The images of the past 18 months were still very much alive in his memory. Besides, online courses had to be easier than real classes, and that one thing sealed the deal.

CLIPAREA/Custom media
Shutterstock.com

Robert Kyllo/Shutterstock.com

Ben Mitchell/Shutterstock.com

Jack Haefner/Shutterstock.com

© Larry Harwood Photography. Property of Cengage Learning.

Mike Margol/PhotoE

136

But Dario quickly discovered that his considerable tech skills might not be enough. Besides that, all three classes had major assignments that would require a serious time commitment. The first week, he stayed up late, listening to online lectures, downloading handouts, and posting responses on the discussion board. Then before he knew it, he got an e-mail from the instructor in his toughest class, "Fundamentals of Internet Business," reminding him that he needed to post two of his own responses to her questions and respond to two classmates' comments each week. "Your comments need to be substantive, Dario, not just quick entries like, 'I really liked the online lecture for Chapter 6' or 'Good point, Keisha.' And you need to keep up," she wrote. "I didn't hear from you for two weeks." *That kind of criticism is a definite turn-off*, Dario thought to himself. If he hadn't already paid tuition, he would have been tempted to drop out of the course entirely.

The worst part was that his toughest class required a research paper. The assigned topic was Globalization and Internet Commerce. Even though he had always considered himself to be a technology expert, frankly, he didn't know where to start. *Step one*, Dario thought to himself, *is to Google*. He always Googled everything: the directions to a new Mexican restaurant—his favorite food—or some little-known fact that he wondered about, like how many Chihuahuas were sold in the United States last year. (He had just bought one.) But when he Googled "Internet Commerce," he got 22 million hits. *Better regroup*, he advised himself.

But how? Should he go to a real library or try to do his research online in the comfort of his own apartment? Physically going to a library seemed unnecessary when so much information was available online. Then he had a flash of inspiration: Wikipedia. He found a page on "Electronic Commerce." At least that was a start—that is, until he looked at his instructor's handout on the assignment. Students were discouraged from using Wikipedia as a primary research source. The handout said, "Information literacy is required." He got another idea: He'd close Wikipedia and go back to Googling. This time he'd try "Electronic Commerce." *Ah, only 7 million hits this time*. He was on a roll. He plugged in "E-Commerce," "E-Business," and "Globalization." He tried "Global Issues," but before he knew it, he found himself knee-deep in articles about "Global Warming." He was so far afield now that he couldn't find his way back to his topic. Should he shut everything down and start over or just give up?

At the last minute, Dario panicked. He found a few useful things online, and cut and pasted from the Internet until he'd filled five pages. At least he had something to turn in. He wondered if this was the way to do research and whether he'd broken any rules. *Well, I can always go back into the military*, he thought to himself. But to be honest, he really wanted to make an entirely new life for himself as a civilian.

Yuri Samsonov/Shutterstock.com

Luciana Bueno/Shutterstock.com

Christopher John Coudriet/Shutterstock.com

© Cengage Learning

Fundamentals of Internet Business
CS 112

Research Paper Guidelines

TOPIC: Globalization and Internet Commerce

For this assignment you will write a 10 page research paper investigating relationship between globalization and Internet commerce. You should focus on how globalization has affected Internet commerce, but how th relationship may be a two-way street. In other words, look at how Int commerce has changed the pace of globalization in the 21st century.

POTENTIAL AREAS OF RESEARCH FOCUS:

- What is Globalization?
- Free Trade
- ational Corporations

© Cengage Learning

Fundamentals of Internet Business
CS 112

Instructor: Dr. Greg Otis
Office: Hansford Hall 230
Office Hours: T, W 2:00–4:00 PM

Description:
The Internet has fundamentally changed the landscape of the business world. Today, commerce conducted on the Internet plays a major role in the

1. In your view, is Dario addicted to technology? Can being too dependent on technology be a problem? Why?

2. Do you have anything in common with Dario? For example, do you think (or have you found) that online classes are easier or harder than face-to-face courses? Why?

3. The instructor's assignment required "information literacy." What is information literacy? Dario was tech-savvy, but did he have the right skills? Why or why not?

4. Did Dario plagiarize his paper—or did he simply find the sources he needed and use them? Give the reasons behind your answer.

Taking Online Classes: E-Learning versus C-Learning

What do an American soldier just back from Afghanistan, a single mother of twin toddlers in California, and a victim of cerebral palsy in New York have in common? All three are taking the same online course in psychology. Instead of c-learning (traditionally, in the classroom), they're engaging in **distance education** or e-learning (electronically, online). E-learning is one kind of technology you may well run into during your time in college.

Of course, most of your college courses are hybrids, or blended, courses: they each have an online component and a classroom component. You e-mail your professor, use software to track your progress, upload assignments, and download handouts, but you still go to a physical classroom with classmates once or twice a term, or perhaps even every week. That's why they're called hybrid (like cars: part electricity and part gasoline) or blended (when mediated and face-to-face learning are meshed) classes. If you haven't already, chances are you'll be engaged in distance learning in a totally online environment for at least one of your college classes. In fact, 65 percent of college students whose institutions offer online courses have already taken at least one.[1] Distance education, as totally online classes are sometimes called, is gaining momentum fast at many colleges, and the demand for these courses hasn't peaked yet.[2]

What are the differences between e-learning and c-learning? E-learning is sometimes defined as structured learning that takes place without a teacher at the front of the room. If you're an independent, self-motivated learner, e-learning can be a great way to learn, because *you* are in control.

> **You control when you learn.** Instead of that dreaded 8:00 a.m. class—the only section that's open when you register—you can schedule your

Hybrid, or **blended,** courses are part online and part on-ground in varying proportions.

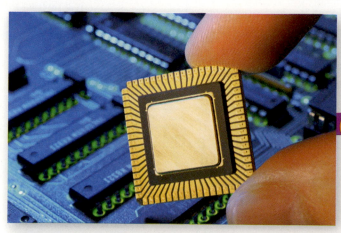
Stockbyte/Getty Images

> " It was not so very long ago that people thought that semiconductors were part-time orchestra leaders and microchips were very small snack foods.
>
> *Geraldine Ferraro, Democratic politician, 1935–2011*

e-learning when it's convenient for you. If you want to do your coursework at midnight in your pajamas, who's to know?

> **You control how you learn.** If you are an introvert, e-learning may work well for you. You can work thoughtfully online and take all the time you need to reflect. If you are an extravert, however, you may become frustrated by the lack of warm bodies around. Jumping into threaded discussions and chatting online may satisfy some of those needs, but you may miss real people sitting next to you. If you're a kinesthetic learner, the keyboard action may suit you well. Because you're working independently, you can do whatever you need to do to accommodate your own learning style.

> **You control how fast you learn.** You know for a fact that students learn at different rates. With e-learning, you don't have to feel you're slowing down the class if you continue a line of questioning or worry about getting left in the dust if everyone else is way ahead of you.

E-learning can be a very effective way to learn, but it does require some adjustments. Here are some suggestions for making the best of your online learning opportunities:

1. **Work hard.** Many students think that fully online courses will be easier than going to class. After all, you won't have to shower, get dressed, drive through traffic, and cruise the campus for fifteen minutes to find a parking spot. These factors, in and of themselves, should be big time savers. Unless your class requires a webcam (to record yourself for an online public speaking class, for example), you're virtually invisible. But think about it this way: in an online course, you will have to do many of the things that your instructor normally does for you. In a classroom, she may simply walk around and pass out handouts. Online, you'll have to locate them on the course website, download them, and print them out yourself. You'll need to read everything carefully, both the items posted on the course management shell itself (like the course calendar, syllabus, reminder messages, instructions for each assignment) and every document you download. Instead of taking a seat in the classroom to listen to your professor lecture at the front of the room, you will have to get the information yourself by downloading lecture notes, PowerPoint slides, or videos of your instructors' lectures. Some studies show that students work harder and longer online. The belief that online courses are easier is a myth.

2. **Keep up.** Even though you may be "invisible" in online courses, you can't "hide." You'll likely have to keep up by posting regularly to the class blog or online discussion board and comment on your classmates' posts every week. Dario from this chapter's Challenge case received an e-mail from his instructor, asking where he was. If you decide to "take a vacation" in the middle of your online course, your instructor may inquire about your whereabouts, too. Just as you'd do for a face-to-face class, consider setting aside a specific time each week for your online course, like Tuesday and Thursday afternoons, and commit to reserving that time for online coursework.

3. **Get advice from other online students.** The first time you take an online course, ask a friend or classmate who has experience with this type of course for advice. That person may save your hours of online wandering with a few

simple tips. Besides finding out how to navigate the course online, ask what student services are available online, like advising, tutoring, financial aid, enrollment, and tuition payments.

4. Communicate your needs to your instructor. If this is your first online course, ask your instructor for a general assessment of how much time he expects you to set aside each week. Think about the three hours or so you usually spend per week in a face-to-face class or lab, and use that as a rule of thumb. (Of course, specifics depend on what else you have going on and your individual learning style preferences. And when you begin to see the grades you earn on the assignments you turn in, you may decide to invest more time on your own.) Remember, too, that your instructor won't be able to see your "huh?" looks when you don't understand something. Take direct action by e-mailing her, for example, instead of hiding behind your computer screen and hoping for the best. "The best" usually doesn't come to you; you'll have to work for it. On the other hand, before you fire off a quick question, reread the assignment. It may be that you just missed something simple, and your question is actually unnecessary.

5. Stay in touch with other students in the course. Rather than isolating yourself, which is a mistake, use e-mail to communicate with your cyber classmates to build an online **learning community**. They may be able to clarify an assignment or coach you through a tough spot.

learning community group of students who help one another learn.

> "Any occurrence requiring undivided attention will be accompanied by a compelling distraction.
>
> *Robert Bloch, American fiction writer, (1917–1994)*

6. Take notes. When you're sitting through an in-class lecture, you handwrite notes to review later. Likewise, if you're reading lecture notes online, open a Word document and switch back and forth for your own note-taking purposes. Or open an e-tool, like evernote.com, which can work well for note taking.

7. Keep your antivirus program up to date. When you upload assignment files, you run the risk of infecting your instructor's computer with whatever viruses your computer may have. Make sure your antivirus software is up to date!

8. Create a productive learning environment. Because you'll most likely do your e-learning at home, make sure the environment is right for learning. If your computer is next to the TV or your kids are acting up to get attention, move to another location that's calm, properly lit, and quiet.

9. Use each login session as an opportunity to review. Begin each online session by reviewing what you did or how much progress you made last time. Physically logging on can become a signal to take stock before moving forward with new course material.

10. Organize, organize, organize! In your face-to-face classes, you can keep courses separate in your mind by remembering where the different classrooms are located, for example, and who your classmates and teachers are. By contrast, in online courses you usually sit down in front of your same computer, and you might never even meet your classmates or teacher. You'll have to find ways to separate and organize materials for each class either physically by using hard copy files or electronically by using folders on your computer or thumb drive.

11. **Call on your time management skills.** Create a "Term-on-a-Page" master calendar, mark the due dates for each class, and review it at the beginning of every week. If your e-course is self-paced, you'll need to plan ahead, schedule due dates, and above all discipline yourself to make continual progress. For many students, this very thing is the biggest challenge of online courses. The instructor isn't there with you, insisting that you turn in assignments. If you're sharing a computer with other family members, you'll need to create a master schedule of who can use the computer when. Remember that you may need to be online at particular times to engage in class chats or discussions.

12. **Have a back-up plan.** Technology crashes from time to time, and system **platforms** go down, sometimes just when you need them. Get to know your campus tech support staff, and don't hesitate to contact them in an emergency. Work ahead, so that you don't fall behind if the dreaded "blue screen" suddenly appears, signaling a tech failure. Watch for campus e-mails about system down time for scheduled upgrades, and work around it. In other words, take responsibility. If your paper is late because you left your thumb drive in the car, and your car is at your sister's house, expect to have points deducted. Most online instructors abide by syllabus rules, and they expect you to do the same.[3]

platform the course management system (CMS) your campus uses, like Blackboard or Moodle, sometimes with a title for your school, like "GBTConline".

EXERCISE 6.1

A Day in the Life of an Online Student

You wake up and look out the window. It's a beautiful day, and—lucky you—it's your day off from work! While having your morning coffee, you log on to Facebook. You see a few new posts on your wall and some new pictures from last weekend. You check your e-mail and find a tempting new Groupon, a few e-mails from friends, and an e-mail from the instructor of your online class. Oh no, you think. I haven't done anything for my online class in a while, and there's a big assignment due tomorrow! With a sigh you glance out the window one more time. It looks like you won't be able to spend the day relaxing outside like you thought.

Assume this is what your day looks like. For each entry in your hypothetical "day timer," look at the obstacles that may get in your way, and describe how you'll address them.

8:00 a.m.

You pour yourself another cup of coffee and sit down to work on your online course, but you start to wander, electronically. Maybe you should see how many of your friends "like" the new photos you uploaded to your Facebook page. Before you know it, an hour and a half has gone by and you get up to get a snack.

SOLUTION:

_____

_____

10:00 a.m.

You successfully get yourself back on task, but you've hit another snag. You have the syllabus somewhere, and you have lots of questions about the assignment. Your instructor gave you her contact info, but you can't afford to wait very long for a response.

SOLUTION:

_____

_____

(Continued)

10:30 a.m.

Now that you have clarification on the assignment, you dig into your work. You need to find four different sources for your research, but you're not having much luck. You try one Google search after another, but the websites don't seem to have what you're looking for.

SOLUTION:

_____

_____

11:00 a.m.

You've finally located some reliable and useful resources for your assignment. As you continue to work, you find yourself copying and pasting a useful word here and there into your paper. Pretty soon, you're clicking and dragging phrases, then sentences into your assignment. *Am I plagiarizing?* you wonder.

SOLUTION:

_____

_____

12:00 a.m.

You're working hard, finding good resources, and using them ethically. Your phone rings. It's one of your friends, inviting you to lunch and a movie this afternoon. You glance at your watch. You've been working on this project for a couple of hours now; haven't you earned a little break?

SOLUTION:

_____

_____

7:00 p.m.

Looking back on the day, you've accomplished a lot. You've coped with understanding the assignment clearly, finding good resources and using them well, and managing your time. You're pretty happy with your work, but you wish there was a way to get some feedback on the assignment before you e-mail it to your instructor.

SOLUTION:

_____

_____

11:00 p.m.

Turn in for the night. Tomorrow is a new "Day in the Life of an Online Student."

Technology Skills: Wireless, Windowed, Webbed, and Wikied

Ah, technology . . . Does it make our lives simpler or more complicated? Like Dario, are you pulled into games like World of Warcraft? Do you live to text? Do you run, not walk, to any nearby computer to check your Facebook account? Or, on the other hand, do you hate the thought of facing your e-mail after you haven't had access for awhile? Did you find yourself answering "yes" to any of these questions—or maybe answering "yes" to all of them?

Many of us have a love–hate relationship with technology: We love the convenience but hate the dependence. But in college, your techno-skills will be another key to your success. You'll need to know things like how to produce an essay in Microsoft Word, how to give a PowerPoint presentation, and how to use course management systems like Blackboard. "Whoa! Wait a minute," you say. "I'm no expert at all of that!" You don't have to be an expert, but you do need to know the basics and be willing to learn more. Dario considered himself to be a technology expert, but his expertise was more about *entertainment* than *education*. In college, you'll be using technology to enhance your education.

Your college may have invited you to enroll with a Twitter or Facebook invitation. Your school will provide you with an e-mail account and send you official college documents, like your tuition bill and weather alerts, over e-mail. You will take entire courses or parts of courses online so that you can learn on your own time at your own pace. Many of your instructors will use course management systems, YouTube clips, streaming video, and websites in the classroom to increase your learning. (And the good news is that many college students say it helps.[4]) So the time to start building your skills is now! Just how useful is the Internet to college students? The answer is that just like anything else, the Internet has pros and cons.

The Internet: The Good, the Bad, and the Ugly

The Good Students who enter college right after high school are the leading consumers of digital technology in the United States.[5] In one study, 79 percent of college students reported that the Internet has had a positive impact on their college academic experience.[6] For many of us, the Internet is how we get our news, our research, our entertainment, and our communication. When it comes to all the potential benefits of the Internet, think about advantages like these:

> **Currency.** While some of the information posted on the Internet isn't up to date, much of it is current. This is especially important during a crisis or a national emergency, for example, when it's important to get news fast. Reports, articles, and studies that might take months to publish in books or articles are available on the web as soon as they're written.

currency timely

> **Availability.** The Internet never sleeps. If you can't sleep at 2:00 a.m., the Internet can keep you company. It can be a good friend to have. Unlike your real instructor, who teaches other classes besides yours and attends marathon

> **Technology is nothing. What's important is that you have a faith in people, that they're basically good and smart, and if you give them tools, they'll do wonderful things with them.**
>
> *Steve Jobs, founder of Apple Computer*
> *(1955–2011)*

arek_malang/Shutterstock.com

meetings, Professor Google is always in. For the most part, you can check your e-mail or log onto the Internet from anywhere, any time.

scope range, capacity

> **Scope.** You can find out virtually anything you want to know on the Internet, from the recipe for the world's best chocolate chip cookie to medical advice on everything from **A**thlete's Foot to **Z**its. (Of course, real human beings are usually a better option for serious questions.)

> **Interactivity.** Unlike other media, the Internet lets you talk back. You can write a letter to the editor of a newspaper and wait for a reply, or you can push buttons on your phone in response to an endless list of menu questions ("If you want directions in English, press 1 . . .") and finally get to a real-live human being. But the Internet lets you communicate instantly and constantly. You can instant message to your heart's content, if you want to; add to your Facebook page daily; or edit a Wikipedia entry whenever you like.

> **Affordability.** The number of Internet users worldwide now tops 2 billion; 273 million Americans are on the Net today.[7] For most of us, when it comes to the Internet, the price is right. After you buy a computer and pay a monthly access fee, you get a great deal for your money.

The Bad Too much of a good thing—anything—can be bad. When something becomes that central to our lives, it carries risks. Here are some Internet dangers worth thinking about:

> **Inaccuracy.** Often we take information presented to us at face value, without questioning it. But on many Internet sites, the responsibility for checking the accuracy of the information presented there is yours. Bob's Statistics Home Page and the U.S. Census Bureau's website are not equally valid. Not everything published online is true or right.

> **Laziness.** It's easy to allow the convenience of the Internet to make us lazy. Why go through the hassle of cooking dinner when you can just stop for a burger on the way home? The same thing applies to the Internet. Why not just do what Dario did and find information somebody else has already posted on the Internet, and use it? What's wrong with that? For one thing, if you don't give the rightful author credit, that's plagiarism, which can give you a zero on an assignment or even cause you to fail a course. But another thing worth considering is that the *how* of learning is as important as the *what*. If all you ever did was cut, paste, and download, you wouldn't learn how to do research yourself. College helps you learn skills you will need later—critical thinking, research, and writing skills, for example—in your career. You may never have to give your boss a five-page paper on the humor of Mark Twain—as you might your literature instructor—but you may need to write a five-page report on your customers' buying trends over the last six months.

> **Overdependence.** A related problem with anything that's easy and convenient is that we can start depending on it too much. National studies report that many of us lack basic knowledge. We can't name the Chief Justice of the Supreme Court or the President of Pakistan. Without even realizing it, we may think: Why bother learning a bunch of facts when you can just check quickly online? Are we so dependent on the Internet that we're relying on it for information we should learn or know?[8]

VARK It!

Visual: Monitor the time you spend online for one day. Draw a pie chart showing the time you spent online and doing other things (school, work, TV, etc). Do the results surprise you?

VARK It!

Kinesthetic: Find the browsing history on your web browser. How many of the websites are time-wasters and how many were used for work or school?

Teo Lannie/PhotoAlto Agency RF Collections/Getty Images

The Ugly The Internet can be used in foul ways. Spam, viruses, spyware, and phishing cost American consumers billions of dollars in damage last year, affecting 40 percent of U.S. households.[9] Take a look at one student's social networking page in Figure 6.1 to see whether you can guess where things are headed.

Like the hypothetical Victoria Tymmyns (or her online name, VicTym) featured in Figure 6.1, some students publish inappropriate, confidential, and potentially dangerous information on their social media pages. Victoria has posted her address, phone numbers, and moment-by-moment location. Look at the final entries on her page to find out what potential threat she may be facing. Aside from the risk of serious harm, other types of "danger" can result from bad judgment, too. What some students post just for fun can later cost them a job opportunity. If your webpage has provocative photos of you or descriptions of rowdy weekend activities that you wouldn't want your grandmother to see, remove them! (Employers regularly check these sources for insider information on applicants.) "Living out loud," as social networking is sometimes called, requires constant vigilance so that the details of your life aren't on display. Some recent research indicates that younger users are more sensitive to keeping things offline than older users.[10] To avoid "social insecurity," keep these five useful suggestions in mind:

1. Use a password with at least eight letters and numbers, like FO34$&CuS.

2. Don't include your full birth date. Identity thieves can use this information.

3. Take advantage of privacy controls. Use the options provided to you, like choosing the "Friends Only" option. Be sure not to check the box for "Public Search Results." Search engines can find your Facebook profile on and off Facebook if you do.

4. You wouldn't put a "No One's Home" sign on your door, so don't post it as your status.

5. Don't post your child's name in a caption. If someone else does, remove it.[11]

What does all of this have to do with you? Everything! It's important to remember that the Internet itself is neutral. It can be used constructively or destructively, based on the choices you make. It can be an exciting, invigorating, essential part of your college experience. Use it wisely!

ISpy.com

RMSU

[View More Photos of Me](#)

Status   edit

Doin' shots at Annie Oakley's!

RMSU Friends

425   friends at RMSU   See All

Seymore Bonz   N.O. Body

Friends in Other Networks

Cal (12)
UF (40)
CMU (6)
KSU (7)
RMSU (425)

Basic Info

Name: **Victoria Tymmyns**
Looking For: **A Good Time**
Residence: **Pine Valley 456**
Birthday: **June 12, 1995**

Contact Info

Email: **VicTym@rmsu.edu**
AIM Screenname   **VicTym**
Mobile: **719.111.1112**
Current Address: **123 Fake St.**
    Great Bluffs, CO 80900

Personal Info

Activities: **Drinkin' at "Annie Oakley's" every Fri. night**
    Karaoke at "All That Jazz" every Sat. night.

Favorite Artists: **Adele, Mariah Carey, Bruno Mars**
Favorite Shows: **Walking Dead, Big Bang Theory, New Girl**

Work Info

Company: **Common Grounds on Corner Mountview**
Schedule: **Work M – F 7AM – 2PM**

The Wall

 N.O. Body wrote: at 11:00am August 1, 2014
Saw u dancing at Annie Oakley's!! Whatta hottie! We should meet.

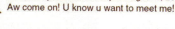

N.O. Body wrote: at 1:00pm August 1, 2014
Aw come on! U know u want to meet me!

 N.O. Body wrote: at 3:02pm August 1, 2014
Still no response? What's up? Do u wanna play or not?

 Seymore Bonz wrote: at 4:27pm August 1, 2014
R we still hookin up w/the gang at Annie Oakley's tonight?
Meet you guys at the front door at 10.

N.O. Body wrote: at 5:20pm August 1, 2014
Sounds fun. Maybe I'll see u there.

 Bay-Bee Face wrote: at 10:17pm August 2, 2014
Can you believe how we much we rocked last night? What was the deal with that guy
who kept staring at us? He gave me the creeps!! You switched shifts w/Mary right?
Working at 4?

 N.O. Body wrote: at 12:39pm August 2, 2014
Gee, BTW u were dressed, I just assumed u liked being stared at… U looked really
amazing at work.

 N.O. Body wrote: at 2:21pm August 3, 2014
What's the matter sweetheart? U looked unhappy to see me at work today. Why
didn't u talk to me? BTW, nice house u got. Who knew you lived in such a nice neighborhood.

 N.O. Body wrote: at 12:57pm August 5, 2014
Nice dog u have. Ur parents must be outta town—no one's been home all night.

 N.O. Body wrote: at 7:26pm August 5, 2014
U never showed up for ur shift today. I waited all day for u. Saw your friends.
They said somebody poisoned your dog. That's a shame—such a yappy
little thing. I hate stuck-up women. Guess I'll just have to find u in person…

FIGURE 6.1

Fictional Ispy.com page

Companion, M. (2006). Victoria Tymmyns Ispy.com. Used with permission.

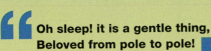

> **Oh sleep! it is a gentle thing,**
> **Beloved from pole to pole!**
>
> —SAMUEL TAYLOR COLERIDGE,
> ENGLISH CRITIC AND POET (1772–1834)

Reason 6: They're exhausted.

Let's face it: It's hard to focus when you're dead tired. You're so weary that you can't get your eyes to focus, much less your brain. What's keeping you up at night? Worry? Financial stress? Internet games? According to sleep experts, you should be getting seven or more hours per night, or a minimum of forty-nine hours per week. Some students, like Dario from the FOCUS Challenge Case, choose to stay up until the wee, small hours of the morning. Or perhaps you have a baby at home who keeps you up at night or a job working the night shift. Life happens. But the choices you make—whatever the situation—will determine the degree to which you can focus when you need to.

TRY It!

Keep a sleep log for a week. When you wake up, write down the number of hours of sleep you've gotten.

Sun.	Mon.	Tues.	Wed.	Thur.	Fri.	Sat.

Are you surprised to see the actual numbers? Is there much variation from night to night? From weekdays to weekends? Formulate a new strategy to become better rested. Scientists now know that the amount of sleep you get can affect your ability to focus, your health, your weight, and your grades![12]

Use Technology to Your Academic Advantage

Despite the pros and cons, technology plays a big role in all of our lives, especially the lives of college students and career professionals. The truth of the matter is that technology skills are increasingly important in all academic disciplines—as well as any profession.[13] A recent study of 3,000 students at 1,179 two-year colleges and universities reports that technology use is widespread in higher education. See how many of these items apply to you. For example:

Technology Ownership

87% of students own a laptop
70% of students own a USB thumb drive
67% own a Wi-Fi device or have access to Wi-Fi
66% own a stationary gaming device
62% own an iPod
55% own a smartphone

Technology Use

99% of students use e-mail
93% of students use text messaging
90% use Facebook
85% download videos
85% read Wikis
73% use a course management system like Blackboard
72% read blogs
70% use the Internet
70% engage in online forums or bulletin boards
55% use e-books or e-textbooks[14]

What academic benefits does technology provide? In one major study, students noted that it helps them:

> Access resources and information.
> Simplify administrative tasks (enrolling for classes, paying tuition bills, etc.).
> Track progress in classes.
> Communicate with instructors and classmates.
> Make learning more engaging and relevant.[15]

How Tech-Savvy Are You?

Let's look at some specific technology applications you'll need to know in college, including types of software, search engines, course management systems, and other class-related possibilities. Match the examples on the right to the descriptions on the left.

a.

b.

c.

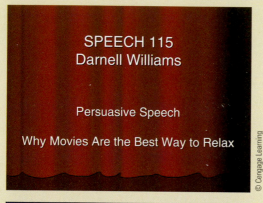

d.

e.

f.

g.

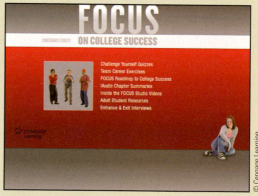

h.

1. _____ Internet Domain Extensions

Internet hostnames after the period in the URL (Uniform Resource Locator) describe where websites come from:

.gov = U.S. government (such as www.irs.gov, the Internal Revenue Service [or IRS])

.edu = education (such as www.gbtc.edu, Great Bluffs Technical College)

.org = organizations or businesses (such as www.democratic.org, the Democratic Party, or nonprofit organizations, like www.americanheart.org, American Heart Association)

.mil = military (such as www.defenselink.mil, U.S. Department of Defense)

.com = commercial, buying and selling (such as www.realtor.com, National Association of Realtors)

.net = network or Internet provider (such as www.earthlink.net)

.int = international organizations (such as Interpol, Council of Europe, or NATO)[16]

2. _____ Software

College will require you to use several standard software applications to do your academic work:

Microsoft Word allows you to type, edit, alphabetize, index, footnote, and do many other things to prepare papers for your classes.

Microsoft PowerPoint, used as an electronic visual aid for oral presentations, allows you to create an on-screen guide for your listeners (and you, if you glance at it periodically and subtly for clues).

Microsoft Excel spreadsheets are good for tabulating, record keeping, and organizing. The industry standard for these applications is generally the Microsoft products listed here, although other possibilities exist. If you need help learning any of these applications, your campus techies, your instructors, or online tutorials (which can easily be found by Googling) can help. If you're a techie yourself, you can venture into other software applications like Flash, Camtasia, or iMovie to make your academic work look even more professional.

3. _____ Search Engines

Different search engines work best for different purposes, but these three are the most popular recommendations:[17]

Google (www.google.com) has a well-deserved reputation as the best search engine you can use. Its size is not disclosed anywhere, but it's generally thought to have the largest assets to search and 900,000,000 unique visitors per month.

Bing (www.bing.com) a Microsoft alternative to Google, organizes your responses to help you make better informed decisions. It is used by 165,000,000 unique visitors a month.

Yahoo (www.yahoo.com) can also help you get excellent search results, or allow you to use any of the other specialized search features.

4. _____ Wikis

Wikis are today's online, editable encyclopedias. (The word wiki means "fast" in the Hawaiian language.) Wikipedia is the largest of these sites, and anyone can add information or change content (currently at 21 million articles in more than 280 languages on the Wikipedia site). On the other hand, be aware that inaccurate information can be added just as easily as accurate information. Never consider Wikipedia to be the final word on anything.

5. _____ Course Management Systems

Many of your college classes will be conducted partially or wholly online, using a course management system, like Blackboard, eCollege, or Moodle. These shells help organize the online component of classes, and most students report having positive experiences with them. How do students use course management systems?

- To track grades, assignments, and tests
- To take sample tests and quizzes (or real ones)
- To get the course syllabus
- To turn in assignments online
- To access readings and other course materials
- To post to an online discussion[18]

6. _____ Blogs

Web logs, or blogs, can be thought of as online journals that are typically one person's reactions to current events or cultural issues, for example. Or you can think of them as websites that someone changes every day.[19] Your instructors may post a question or comment and ask you to blog your responses online and to respond to your classmates' blogs. Everyone can get to know you by your online personality, and some students say they become better writers by reading other students' responses to their writing. And professional blogs can be a great way to stay current on the career you go into.

7. _____ YouTube

YouTube is a video-sharing website where you can upload and watch video clips. You may want to insert one into a presentation you create as a class assignment or post one yourself related to your life as a student.

8. _____ Textbook Websites

Textbook websites, like the one you're using for *FOCUS on College and Career Success,* can contain information and activities to enrich your learning experience, like videos, quizzes, and iAudio chapter summaries. Use these resources to help you master course material.

Other Need-to-Know Technology Definitions

VPN (Virtual Private Network): You may need to go through particular steps to connect to your campus databases from home. Tech experts on your campus can show you how to do this, or there may be an online tutorial on your campus's website.

Podcasts: Many professors now record their lectures for you to review later. Or you can listen to *FOCUS on College and Career Success* and other textbooks' iAudio summaries for each chapter online.

PDF files: Using Adobe technology, you can create and edit documents that are formatted on your computer screen just as they would appear if they were published. PDFs look very professional, and there may be a time when you are asked to create one for a particular class.

Web 2.0: Web 2.0 is not a new version of the Internet. It refers to creative uses of it, like Facebook, Wikis, and blogs, where instead of just reading passively, users help create the content.

Viruses, Worms, and Trojan Horses: Pranksters (or vicious cyber attackers, for that matter) can infiltrate campus technology systems and infect individual computers or shut down a campus system entirely. The solution? Don't open attachments with suspicious names or ones from people you don't know. And keep your antivirus software up to date!

Mobile Apps: Apps, short for "applications," are Internet-based programs that allow you to work, read, or communicate online from your smartphone or other portable electronic device. In today's world, people are busy and don't stay in one spot. They want to work, learn, and study from anywhere at anytime.

QR Codes: QR (short for "quick response") codes are two-dimensional bar codes that you can scan, for example, from your cell phone (if you download an app). The code will take you to a website immediately for more information.

Tablet Computing: Mobile devices such as the iPad are seen as having rich potential for use as learning tools. There's no cell phone ringing or text message binging, and the image is larger, so you can do more with it. Both Mobile Apps and Tablet Computing are seen as the hottest trends in educational technology.[20]

Dropbox: Dropbox is a free (or paid) service that lets you store your files on the Internet, access them from anywhere, and share them with anyone.

Writing Effective Online Messages

Being a professional student doesn't just apply to how you act in class, like asking questions if you're unclear or turning in your assignments on time. Online communication has particular rules you must follow. For example, when you're writing discussion board posts in a hybrid or online course, it's important to be civil. "How could anyone ever possibly think that?" as a post to a classmate's entry may be honest, but it's hardly collegial. Instead, why not say, "That's something I hadn't thought of. Can you explain more about it?"? Think about the Golden Rule of online posts: How would you feel if a classmate shot down a good idea of yours? Be respectful. When classmates post an idea, they're putting their egos on the line—or so it feels. Remember that you can disagree with a classmate online, but never disrespect him or her personally. "I thought we were always supposed to use good grammar on this discussion board. Jerome's posts are full of mistakes." There's no need to put Jerome on the spot. On the other hand, using good grammar and correct spelling will be important to your instructor, so be conscientious in that regard.

Another thing your instructor will insist on is that your posts are sufficiently informative. When you are in a hurry, it's tempting to write as little as possible, like "Alicia is right on target!" as your entire entry. Tell why. Mention parts of her argument you agree with, and explain your endorsement. A discussion board is a place for online, back-and-forth dialogue, not Tweet-like comments for other people to decipher.

Of course IMs and text messages are used more often in social contexts than academic ones, but some of the same rules apply. "Breaking up" with your romantic partner by sending a text message would probably be perceived as a cowardly "low blow." Simply put: Certain situations call for certain types of messages.

E-mail that you send your instructor has netiquette (online etiquette) standards you should follow, too. Take a look at these widely accepted rules for academic settings:

1. **Don't send a message you don't want to risk being forwarded to someone else.** Doing so has caused many a fretful night. ("Aaaaakkk! What have I done?")

2. **Don't hit the "send" key until you've given yourself time to cool off, if you're upset.** You may want to edit what you've written.

3. **Don't forward chain e-mails.** At the very least, they're a nuisance, and sometimes they're illegal.

4. **Don't do business over your school e-mail account.** Sending all 500 new students an invitation to your family's restaurant grand opening is off-limits. Besides, sending messages to lots of people at once is called "spam," and it can really gum up the works.

5. **Don't spread hoaxes about viruses or false threats.** You can get into big trouble for that.

6. **Don't type in all CAPS.** That's called SHOUTING, and it makes you look angry.

7. **Don't be too casual.** Use good grammar and correct spelling. Your instructors consider e-mails to be academic writing, and they'll expect professionalism from you. "Hey Prof, this is a heckuva of a cool class!" may sound enthusiastic, but it's not professional. Language that you use for texts and IMs is not appropriate for academic correspondence.

8. **Don't forget important details.** Include everything the reader needs to know. For example, if you're writing to an instructor, give your full name and the name of the course you're writing about. Professors teach more than one class and have many students.

9. **Don't hit the "Reply to All" key, when you mean to hit the "Reply" key.** Many e-mail message writers have been horrified upon learning that hundreds or thousands of people have read something personal or cranky that was meant for just one reader.

10. **Don't forget to fill in the subject line.** That gives readers a chance to preview your message and decide how soon they need to get to it.

VARK It!

Read/Write: Read through some of your last texts, IMs, posts, or tweets. Have you made any of the mistakes listed on this page?

How *Not* to Win Friends and Influence People Online

All four of these e-mail messages from students violate the rules of netiquette. See whether you can identify the rule number above that's been violated in each case.

From Matt

Professor X,

I just looked at the online syllabus for Academic Success 101. Why didn't you tell us that our first paper is due on Monday? I will be very busy moving into a new apartment this weekend. Writing an essay for your class is the last thing I want to have to think about.

Rule:_____

From Tiffany

Prof X,

i didn't know u were makin us write a paper over the weekend. i won't be able to do it. i hop you don't mind.

Rule:_____

From Xavier

PROFESSOR X,

I CAN'T GET MY PAPER DONE BY MONDAY. LET ME KNOW WHAT I SHOULD DO.

Rule:_____

From Dameon

Hey, Section 3

Can you believe our instructor? She assigns a big writing assignment after only one day of class! Who in their right mind would be remotely interested in sitting in their crummy little room writing a bunch of meaningless junk, when we haven't even learned anything yet? What kind of teacher are we stuck with here? Somebody out there respond to me, OK? I'm totally hacked off!

Rule:_____

As a class, discuss your responses. Do you all agree on which rules were broken in the four examples provided? See whether you can create some new ones that violate other rules.

Research Skills and Your College Success

VARK It!

Visual: Download or ask for a map of your library. Identify the locations of various resources, such as computers, reference books, librarian's area, study rooms, and so on.

Many of your class assignments in college will require you to conduct research. Why? Aren't you in college to learn from your instructors? Why do they ask *you* to do research on your own?

There are unanswered questions all around us in everyday life. Some questions are simple; others are complex. How much time will it take to get across town to a doctor's appointment during rush hour? What can you expect college tuition to cost by the time your kids are old enough to go? What are the chances that someone you know who has cancer will survive for five years? Research isn't necessarily a mysterious thing that scientists in white coats do in laboratories. Research is simply finding answers to questions, either real questions you encounter every day or questions that are assigned to you in your classes. Doing research on your own can be a powerful way to learn, sometimes even more so than hearing answers from someone else, even if those people are your instructors. Going off to a research expedition in the library may sound like exhausting busywork, but the skills you stand to gain are well worth the effort.

Conducting research teaches you some important things about how to formulate a question and then find answers. And it's not just finding answers so that you can scratch a particular assignment off your to-do list. It's about learning an important process. When you get into the world of work, your instructors won't be there to supply answers, so knowing how to figure things out on your own will be key to your success. So, exactly what is college-level research?

What Research Is *Not*	What Research Is
Research isn't just going on a "search and employ" mission. It's not just seeing what all you can find and then using it to check off an assignment on your to-do list.	**Research starts with a question.** If an assignment is broad, as Dario's was, you must come up with a specific question to research yourself. (More about that later.)
Research isn't just moving things from Point A (the library) to Point B (your paper).	**Research is a process with a plan.** A plan was something Dario lacked. He jumped in without a question—or a plan.
Research isn't random rummaging through real or virtual files to find out something.	**Research is goal-oriented.** You've formulated a question, developed a plan, and now you begin to find answers by using both online sources and ones that sit on your library's shelves.
Research isn't doing a quick Internet search. The cutting and pasting Dario did to fill up his five pages is actually plagiarism!	**Research often involves breaking a big question into several smaller ones.**[21]

ONLINE TechKnow

"It's on the Web, so it must be true!" Part of information literacy skills is evaluating the accuracy and usefulness of information you come across. As you read materials you find during online research for college or on the job, be careful to check the accuracy and authority of your sources.

- **Examine each article and each claim carefully to see where it comes from originally.** What original research came up with that finding? How reputable is the original source—can you find information about that source from other places?

- **Effective news editors follow this rule:** before a claim can be believed, it must be verified by two independent sources. Sometimes what looks like two sources is really only one source repeated. You may need to search for au-

thenticity online before you use information that's readily available.

- **What about Wikipedia?** Many professors consider it a useful starting point in your research, but won't accept it as a critical reference. Best not to cite it in backing up your research. The best way to use Wikipedia is to use the bibliography and links at the bottom of the page, and do further research from there.

- **When you've been at your online research for a long time**—say over a half-hour—then it pays to take a break and think about what you've been finding. You'll find that short breaks strengthen your ability to critically assess what you've found.

- **Rule of thumb?** Don't use anything as a reference unless it has an author listed.

Improve Your Grade
Online Flashcards
Glossary

© Larry Harwood Photography. Property of Cengage Learning.

Navigating the Library

You've probably heard this since you were a child: "The library is your friend." As a young child, it was exciting to go to the library, choose a book, check it out with your own library card, and bring it home to read. Now, being "exiled" to the library to do research for a paper may seem like torture that can ruin a perfectly good weekend. But if you look at things differently, it can be a mind-expanding trip into places unknown. The truth is that in college the library should be more than just a friend. It should become your best friend! Beyond navigating the web to find research for your assignments, as many students do, it's important to learn your way around the actual, physical space of the library on your campus. The library has many useful resources, including real, very knowledgeable librarians who are there to help you. Asking a reference librarian for help can save you hours of unproductive digging on your own. Here are some of the resources your library offers and how you should use these resources when you're assigned a research project:

> **Card Catalog.** Explore your library's catalog that lists all of the books available to you. Card catalogs used to be actual cards in file cabinet drawers, but now most libraries put all the information about their holdings online. Go to your college's website, and from there you can find your way to your college library's home page. Click the library's catalog button. Let's say Dario follows these instructions and finds this book in his campus library's catalog: *The Global Internet Economy*, edited by Bruce Kogut. Cambridge, MA: MIT Press, 2003. The call number for the book is HC79.I55 G579, based on the Library of Congress classification system, which most college libraries use. (Some libraries, like your community's public library, may use the Dewey Decimal system. One advantage of the Library of Congress system is that books usually have the same number, no matter which library you find them in. That's not always true for the Dewey Decimal system.) The Library of Congress number identifies this item as a book about economics and information technology. Now, after identifying other possible useful books, Dario needs to make his way to campus and find the actual book on the shelf.

> **Databases.** If you go to your library's home page, you can link to the list of online databases it subscribes to. Databases identify articles from academic journals and sometimes contain entire articles online. Generally, different databases exist for different disciplines, for example:

Education	**ERIC** (Educational Resources Information Center)
Psychology	**PsycINFO™**
Business	**Business Source Premier**

But more general databases also exist. Dario might want to search through these:

Academic Search Premier

WilsonWeb OmniFile Full Text Mega

The key to making the most of databases is to find the right search words to plug into the database's search engine. That's where a short coaching session with a real reference librarian can be enormously helpful. You can have productive results or no results at all, just by slightly altering the search words you enter. Also, check Google Scholar online. It will search academic literature, including journal abstracts and articles, dissertations and theses, and books, across many different disciplines.

> **Stacks.** Physically walk through the stacks or collections of books and periodicals (journals, magazines, newspapers, and audiovisual resources, for example). Get to know the stacks in your library, and figure out how to find what you need. Look for the Library of Congress numbers posted on signs at the end of each row of books. When Dario finds the book he's looking for, he's likely to find other books in the library's "HC" section that would also be useful to him. That's why even though doing online research is convenient, there's no substitute for "being there."

VARK It!

Kinesthetic: Go to your library and explore a section you've never seen before. What did you find? Could it be useful in the future?

GOING PRO

BE RESOURCEFUL

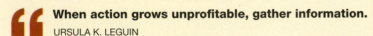

When action grows unprofitable, gather information.
URSULA K. LEGUIN

Know how to gather information and use it. In college, you're asked to develop your research skills. It's easy to think that each paper for a class is just another assignment to check off the list, when you're actually developing skills that will be critical to your success later. Whether in college or on the job, you don't just string together pieces of information when you do research for a paper or project. You analyze research through the "eyes" of the problem you're trying to address and your perspective on it. Then you weave ideas together to make an effective argument or proposal, and you anticipate counter-arguments and competing ideas as you develop yours. When the boss wants your thoughts on a new day-care program for your fellow employees, of course you'll want to research what works in similar organizations. What are the most common options out there? But you'll also want to consider the special needs of your colleagues, anticipate possible problems, and develop a proposal that takes both your research and your analysis into account.

Information Literacy and Your College Success

Much of the research you do for your college assignments will take place online. Information literacy is defined as knowing *when* you need information, *where* to find it, *what* it means, *whether* it's accurate, and *how* to use it. Simply put, it's "the ability to use technology to solve information problems." Information literacy includes five components, as seen in Figure 6.2. Think about them as a step-by-step process as we work through Dario's assignment.[22]

The Top Five Research Mistakes First-Year Students Make: Advice from a Reference Librarian

Are you guilty of any of these common mistakes first-year students make?

1. **Selecting a topic that is too broad.** Students often start out with a very general topic, and sometimes have a hard time narrowing the focus. Trying to write a paper on "recycling" sets you up for an impossible task. Entire books have been written on that subject. Figuring out which words to use can be tricky, too. If you search Google or databases by entering the word "green," you'll get everything from "lime, mint, olive, and avocado" (meaning shades of green, not foods) to "Kermit, the frog." Brainstorming different search words and noting the usable results is half the battle.

2. **Taking short cuts.** Major search engines are a great place to start, but don't stop there. Just using Google or Foxfire is the equivalent of academic "wimping out," like just grabbing something quick from a vending machine when there's so much more nutritious and satisfying food out there. Libraries buy many different electronic databases that have a wealth of information: articles, books, and book chapters, for example. Learn how to use these library databases and really mine them for information. Finding useful information takes time and patience!

3. **Devoting too little time.** Students frequently underestimate how long the research process will take. There are multiple steps required to doing thorough research. It's not a last-minute process, and procrastination isn't the answer. Even if you write like a pro, you can't complete a research paper in an hour or two. Just getting in materials you've ordered from another library can take several weeks.

4. **Not evaluating sources.** Many students don't look closely enough at the sources they find, and then they end up making poor choices or using the first items that come up in search results. Instead, as you scan your results, look for hints about authenticity and accuracy. Compare your findings with other authoritative sites. Note the domain extension (like .gov, for example). One hit may lead you to another, which leads you to yet another. Evaluate your search results and be selective about what you use. Not all sources are created equal; make sure yours are credible ones that support your argument.

5. **Copying and pasting.** Students sometimes use someone else's work without correct and thorough documentation of the source, especially when time is running out. You can end up plagiarizing unintentionally just because you don't understand how to cite your sources. Or you may intentionally cut and paste to save yourself time and effort. But either way, you're putting your academic success at high risk.

The biggest mistake students make is not asking the reference librarian for help at the beginning of the research process! That's why librarians are there—to provide guidance and help with all of the above. Continue reading this chapter for more strategies on making the most of your research time.[23]

Step 1. Define

Define what the assignment requires of you. Dario was assigned a *research* paper. He wasn't being asked to **summarize** or *evaluate* a topic. He was asked to *find out about it.* But "Globalization and Internet Commerce" is a huge topic. He must narrow it down and decide which specific research question (or questions) he wants to focus on.

If you were assigned the paper Dario was assigned, and you knew very little about "Globalization and Internet Commerce," you might start as he did, by Googling your topic to help you define it. But the Internet is huge and unstructured. There's really no way to organize that much information into simple, neat categories.[24] And how do you whittle down 22 million hits? According to a recent study, less than 1 percent of Google users look further than the first page of their Google results, regardless of how many hits they get![25]

summarize condense a longer work into a few essential statements

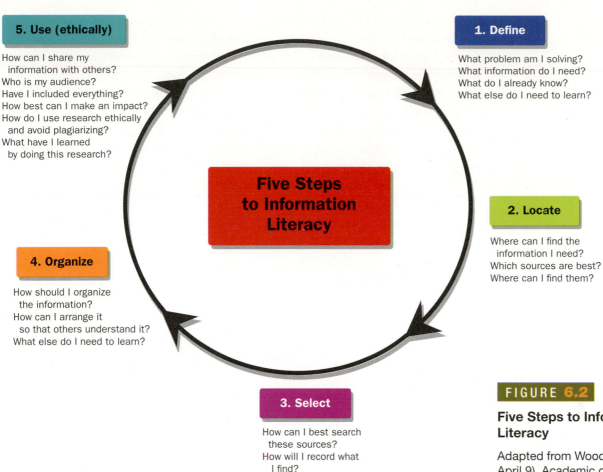

5. Use (ethically)

How can I share my
  information with others?
Who is my audience?
Have I included everything?
How best can I make an impact?
How do I use research ethically
  and avoid plagiarizing?
What have I learned
  by doing this research?

1. Define

What problem am I solving?
What information do I need?
What do I already know?
What else do I need to learn?

**Five Steps
to Information
Literacy**

2. Locate

Where can I find the
  information I need?
Which sources are best?
Where can I find them?

4. Organize

How should I organize
  the information?
How can I arrange it
  so that others understand it?
What else do I need to learn?

3. Select

How can I best search
  these sources?
How will I record what
  I find?
How will I give credit to
  the sources?

FIGURE 6.2

**Five Steps to Information
Literacy**

Adapted from Wood, G. (2004,
April 9). Academic original
sin: Plagiarism, the Internet,
and librarians. *The Journal of
Academic Librarianship,* 30(3),
237–242. Reprinted by permission of Elsevier; Samson, S.
(2010, May). Information literacy
learning outcomes and student
success. *Journal of Academic
Librarianship, 36*(3), 202–10.

VARK It!

Multimodal (Visual/Aural):
Think about a current assignment
for a class, and use this figure
to talk through the questions for
each step. Picture how you will
actually move from one step to
the other.

If you don't know anything about the topic you need to research—absolutely nothing at all—the Internet is a great place to start. You can type in "globalization" and "Internet commerce," and within the blink of an eye, information appears. The problem is that you now have too much information, and the challenge is knowing what to do next. Your college instructors will insist you go beyond the Internet and avoid relying too much on encyclopedias and Wikipedia. College requires you to do more research than you've probably done before, and to do it differently.

Dario could have used the websites that Google brought up to help him *define* a specific research focus, instead of being overwhelmed by the number of hits. Consider these more focused research topics or questions, which Google or Wikipedia could have led him to:

1. **Five Reasons to Go Global with Your Website** (Why is it a good idea?)

2. **Online Retail Businesses Will Explode over the Next Ten Years** (Where will it go in the future?)

3. **Three Problems with Doing E-Business Internationally: Language, Shipping, and Money** (What are the challenges of trying to make it happen?)

Let's take that last focused topic and run with it. Suppose you have an online business and you want to attract customers from around the world to expand it. That's a good idea, but how will you deal with translating what's on your website to other languages? How will you ship your product overseas for a reasonable cost? How will you deal with the exchange rate between the U.S. dollar and the currency used in other countries? Now we've taken a big, broad topic ("Globalization and Internet Commerce") and broken it down into three specific questions or subtopics to research. Your preliminary Google and Wikipedia searches can help you identify what the smaller chunks of your topic could be.

But they can't do *all* the work for you, and you can't stop there, as Dario did. You have to know what to do next. (If you think this process is challenging, you're not alone. In one study, only 35 percent of college students knew how to narrow a Google search![26])

Step 2. Locate

If you've identified electronic sources, **bookmark** them in a file labeled with the name of your project. If they're print resources, physically find them in the library. If they're not available in your own campus library, see whether it participates in an interlibrary loan agreement among libraries. Your own library may be able to borrow the resource from another library. (But be aware that this process may take up to two weeks or so. That's why it's important to start your research projects early!)

Step 3. Select

The Information Age surrounds us with huge amounts of data of all kinds. With so much information available, how do we know what to believe? Whether or not it's true, we tend to think that if something is on television or in a book or online, it must be important. But in any of these cases, we need to exercise our critical thinking skills and turn them into critical searching skills. Just because information is published doesn't automatically make it right or true. In particular, some of the so-called research you encounter online may be bogus, containing inaccuracies or bias. You must read, interpret, and evaluate research to decide whether to use it. Use these five criteria to evaluate any website you come across:

1. **Currency.** How up to date is the information? Some websites don't list a date at the bottom of the screen (where copyright information is often found). If you don't see one, try using other hints on the site to get at how old the information is ("According to a study published in 1995 . . ."). You may find that you need to search for something more up to date.

2. **Accuracy.** How accurate is the information presented? If a website makes an unbelievable claim ("Grow a new head of hair in just six weeks!") or presents shaky statistics to make a case, it's important to be skeptical. Take responsibility to validate the information elsewhere.

3. **Authority.** Does the sponsor of the website have the credentials to post the information you see? Chances are "Steve's Picks" or "myfavoritemovies .com" is a collection of one person's opinions. Compare that to a film reviewer's site with information compiled by a professional film critic for a major newspaper. Which one would you trust more? You may not agree with Steve or the professional film critic, but one has credentials, and the other doesn't.

Plans are only good intentions unless they immediately degenerate into hard work.

Peter Drucker, management expert (1909–2005)

4. **Objectivity.** Does the website sponsor have a reason to convince you of something, or is it presenting unbiased information? If the site wants you to order something online because it claims to have better products than those you can buy at a store, for example, you should be suspicious.

objectivity ability to not take sides, being neutral

5. **Coverage.** If a website just presents one side of an issue or a very small piece of a larger picture, check to make sure you're getting all the information you need. If you're left wondering, *But what about . . . ?* you're probably having the right reaction.

EXERCISE 6.4

Critical Searching on the Internet

With these five criteria in mind, choose one of the following two assignments to complete. Each one will ask you to use your critical searching skills.

Assignment 1: Create a list of three websites that pertain to your intended major. (If you're not sure of your major right now, choose one to explore anyway.) Evaluate the websites, using the five criteria, to see which ones seem most useful to you as a student.

Assignment 2: Compare websites with contradictory information. Choose a controversial subject such as abortion, the death penalty, religion, politics, or some other subject of interest. Find three websites on your topic and compare them on the five criteria. Which of the three websites gets the highest marks? Why?

Step 4. Organize

Now that you have located the information you need, using a variety of sources, and selected those that will be most useful to you in your research project, it's time to organize. Dario's paper will be easier to write now that he has created three subtopics: language, shipping, and money. He should begin taking notes on index cards or highlighting pieces of information he wants to quote word-for-word (giving credit to the author) or paraphrase (putting information into his own words). He can literally put the index cards, printed articles, and photocopied pages from books he found while doing his research into three piles and work from those. Organization is the key to an excellent research paper.

To help you keep track of the sources you find, you should follow these suggestions.

Make sure you pay attention to details. Write the name of the book or article, author, place of publication, publisher, date, or URL at the top of an index card with your notes or on a photocopied page of information you plan to use. Here's an example of what two index cards (of the same paragraph) would look like:

Don't agonize. Organize.

Florynce Kennedy, American lawyer and African American activist

Hans Neleman/Comet/Corbis

Direct Quote

"The Internet has caused drastic shifts in business practice. Customer service calls are outsourced to India today not just because labor costs are low there. Labor costs have always been low in India, but international telephone calls used to be expensive. Calls about airline reservations and lingerie returns are answered in India today because it now takes almost no time and costs almost no money to send to India the bits representing your voice." Blown to Bits, p. 12.

Paraphrase

The Internet has changed the way we do business. Now people in places like India handle things like our airline reservations and lingerie returns, because the technology of cell phones has made long distance cheap.

If you have ideas of your own that don't come from any book, write them on cards or pages, too, and label them, "My Own Ideas."

> **Learn how to use Google Docs,** if you don't know how. Google Docs can serve as an alternative to index cards in some ways. For example, if you're called away on a trip and you plan to work on a paper for a class while you're away but forget to bring the stack of cards, you're out of luck. Google Docs, on the other hand, can be accessed via the Internet from anywhere. Simply create a gmail account for yourself, if you don't already have one, and choose the "Documents" tab. There you'll find all the documents you saved while doing research using your school library's online databases. You can open the articles, categorize them by subtopics, open them, or print them out. It's a great organizational tool for busy students.

> ❝ ❞
>
> **Work is either fun or drudgery. It depends on your attitude. I like fun.**
>
> *Colleen C. Barrett, President Emeritus and Corporate Secretary, Southwest Airlines*

EXERCISE 6.5

Technology Project: Group Ad

Working with two or three classmates and using PowerPoint, Flash, or iMovie, create a television ad (as professional-looking as possible) for the course for which you're using this book. Use text, images, and music. The advertisement shouldn't be long—two or three minutes, or the length of the song you use—but it should describe what the course is about and why other students should take it. Be as creative as you like! Once you've created your presentation, play your ad for the class.

Step 5. Use (ethically)

You've done your research, and now it's time to share it with the world (or at least your instructor) either through the written word, the spoken word, or both. One of the most important things you can learn as a new student is not only how to *use* your research, but how to use *your* research. Some students think that because the Internet is out there, why not just use it? Other people have already made volumes upon volumes of prior research available. They've "been there; done that." Why reinvent the wheel? The reason is because the Internet is simply a tool, just like your library's online databases are tools. You must learn how to use the tool—the Internet—ethically. If your boss asks you for a report on the job, cutting and pasting from the Internet is unlikely to be an option. You must conduct your own research, analyze it, and compile it for a written report or oral presentation. We'll focus on developing speaking and writing skills elsewhere, but learning how to use the Internet ethically is a good place to start now.

Downloading Your Workload: The Easy Way Out?

EXERCISE 6.6

Plagiarism Survey[27]

When you're doing research for a class assignment, have you ever asked yourself questions like these? Jot down your own responses, and then see whether you can find the answers as you continue reading this section. Then discuss them as a class.

1. How do I put things into my own words?
2. How do I give credit to sources I use?
3. How do I do research methodically in steps so that I don't run out of time, leaving plagiarism as an attractive alternative?
4. If an assignment feels as though it's busy work that has nothing to do with my life, is plagiarism really such a bad thing?
5. Isn't anything published on the Internet free, valid, and available to use?

Source: Wood, G. (2004, April 9). Academic original sin: Plagiarism, the Internet and Librarians. *The Journal of Academic Librarianship, 30*(3), 237-242. Reprinted by permission of Elsevier.

One of the trickiest aspects of writing papers for your college courses can be expressed in these three words: *What is plagiarism?* First, you should understand the difference between *intentional* and *unintentional* plagiarism. Intentional plagiarism is deliberately downloading a paper from an online source or cutting and pasting text from a website or book, as Dario did, for example. However, you run the risk of committing unintentional plagiarism if you don't understand what plagiarism is or you forget which book you used, so you don't cite the words you've borrowed from someone else. Intentional plagiarism is cheating, pure and simple. Technology today makes plagiarism all too convenient and easy, but by the same token, finding plagiarism in students' papers has become easy for instructors, too. The bottom line? Follow the guidelines you get from your instructors. And if you don't understand them or your instructor assumes you already know them,

> **The first principle is that you must not fool yourself, but you are the easiest person to fool.**
>
> *Richard P. Feynman (1918–1988), Nobel Prize Winner, Physics, 1965*

VARK It!

Read/Write: Reread a recent paper or assignment you've completed. Did you use your resources ethically, or might you have intentionally or unintentionally plagiarized?

ask questions. Both intentional and unintentional plagiarism can hurt you academically. These FAQs will help.

Q1: If I just list all the sources I used in writing a paper in the bibliography, won't that cover everything? List all your sources in the bibliography at the end of your paper, but also mention that they are others' ideas as you present them. Generally, it's a good idea to cite the original author soon after you present that idea in your paper. In a research paper, it's also useful to name the authors ("According to Staley, college success skills are critical in the first year of college.") Each discipline uses a particular format to cite references. These are called *style sheets*, such as:

> *MLA* (Modern Language Association) is often used in the humanities (English, art, and philosophy, for example).

> *APA* (American Psychological Association) is often used in the social sciences (psychology, communication, and sociology).

> *Chicago Manual of Style* is used in history.

Check with your instructor if you're not certain which one to use, and Google these terms to find the specifics of formatting.

Q2: Must I cite all my sources if I just put ideas into my own words? Yes, you must cite all your sources, even though you may think that your paper looks cluttered. In academic writing, you must cite all the information you use, whether you paraphrase it, quote it, or summarize it. Some students are even taught bad habits in high school, for example, "It's not plagiarism if you change every fifth word," so they write papers with a thesaurus close by. Unfortunately, that's not the way it works. Try reading what you'd like to paraphrase, and then cover the text with your hand and write what you remember. In this case, you'd still need to cite the reference, but because you're paraphrasing, you wouldn't use quotation marks.

VARK It!

Aural: With another aural learner, discuss the perils of plagiarism, and how you can work to avoid plagiarizing.

Q3: But I didn't know anything at all about this subject before I started this assignment. Does that mean I should cite everything? Some ideas are common knowledge that need not be cited. For example, it's a well-known fact that the Civil War lasted from 1861 to 1865. If you cited this piece of common knowledge, who would you cite? Generally, however, your motto should be, "Better safe than sorry." As a rule, you must cite quotations, paraphrases, or summaries. If you use the exact words of someone else, put quotation marks around them, or if they're longer than four lines, indent them in a block. (And generally, only use long quotes if something has been said in a remarkable way.) Also cite specific facts you're using as support and distinctive ideas belonging to others, even if you don't agree with them.

© Torsten Silz/AFP/Getty Images

> **Borrowed thoughts, like borrowed money, only show the poverty of the borrower.**
>
> *Lady Marguerite Blessington, English socialite and writer (1789–1849)*

Q4: I've been doing a lot of reading for this paper. Now I'm not really sure which ideas came from others and which are my own. How do I avoid plagiarism? The best solution here is to take careful notes as you do your research and document where you found each piece of information. Avoid cutting and pasting text. That practice can backfire later when you can't remember what you've extracted and what represents your own thoughts and wording.

What's In **YOUR** Briefcase?

"WRITE" YOUR REPUTATION

You've just graduated from college and landed a great job. All that hard work paid off. But now what? How will people in—for example—a large company begin to form an impression of you? The simple answer is that they will *listen* to you—in meetings, during presentations, and while hanging around the proverbial water cooler. But how else will they judge you and your work? One way you may not have thought about yet provides great opportunity, but also significant risk. It can do you in quickly. At times it's ever so subtle; at other times it's totally in your face.

Imagine this example. Your new boss asks, "Can you get an e-mail out about that new policy?" As the eager company newbie, you reply, "Sure." You quickly compose an e-mail message to send out to everyone in the organization: **The new company policy will go into effect soon**. *Short and sweet*, you think and hit the "send" key. But immediately, you get back a barrage of e-mails from other employees, "What company policy?" "There's a new company policy?" "What new shenanigans is the corporate office up to now?" The request from your boss sounded simple enough. But in your short, sweet message, you've just communicated something relatively meaningless: some new policy from somewhere is about to start sometime. Will your new colleagues assume you're uninformed, unthinking, or unconscious? Think about how composing that one message could start to shape your company reputation right out of the gate.

Instead, you could have sent out an e-mail message like this: **The new software system to report travel expenditures, which has been mandated by the corporate office in response to violations of company travel policy, will go into effect on November 1, 2013, upon the recommendation of the general manager's task force appointed to examine ways to streamline operations and cut company waste**. This message certainly isn't guilty of leaving out all the good stuff like the first one. In fact, you've overloaded your sentence with "TMI"—so much extraneous verbiage that most people will have to read it twice, if they read it at all. Your colleagues may assume you're as boring and stuffy as your message. Even people who haven't met you yet are forming an impression of you through your writing.[28] To make sure that people form the right impression of you, your writing must be clear, powerful, and bold. And actually, if you put some thought into it, the texting and tweeting you do now can help you develop the clear and concise business writing skills you'll need later.[29] (Our second bolded example above wouldn't fly as a tweet, would it? Too many characters.) Writing short, eye-catching, lively messages that people actually *will* read speaks volumes about your potential on the job. If you rock, make sure your writing rocks, too. That kind of writing tells people how effective you will be and "writes" your reputation for ongoing career success.

Looking at the two unsatisfactory messages above, rewrite the e-mail message one more time. Try to create a clear, concise, and effective message.

_____

_____

_____

Now look back at your answers to the Plagiarism Survey in Exercise 6.6 at the beginning of this section and see whether you would change any of them.

EXERCISE 6.7

Plagiarism or Not?

In your opinion, is the following passage plagiarized? Compare these two examples:

Original passage: A new Northwestern University study provides the first biological evidence that bilinguals' rich experience with language "fine-tunes" their auditory nervous system and helps them juggle linguistic input in ways that enhance attention and working memory.

Source: Leopold, W. (2012, April 30). Bilingualism fine-tunes hearing, enhances attention. *Science Daily.* Available at http://www.sciencedaily.com/releases/2012/04/120430152033.htm.

Student paper: Bilinguals' use of more than one language fine-tunes their auditory nervous system and helps their attention and working memory.

Has this student committed plagiarism? Why or why not?

step 3 INSIGHT *Now* What Do You Think?

At the beginning of this chapter, Dario Jones faced a series of challenges as a new college student taking three online classes. Now after learning from this chapter, would you respond differently to any of the questions you answered about the FOCUS Challenge Case? Using what you learned in the chapter, write a paragraph ending to Dario's case study. What are some of the possible outcomes for Dario?

step 4 ACTION Your Plans for Change

1. Identify one new thing you learned in reading this chapter. Why did you select the one you've selected? How will it affect what you do in your college classes?

2. How much experience have you had conducting research? What sounds most challenging about the process?

3. How would you describe your technology skills? If you haven't had much experience with technology, how do you plan to increase your skills? If you have technology experience, how will you use your knowledge to your advantage in your college classes?

chapter 7

Engaging, Listening, and Note-Taking in Class

© Larry Harwood Photography. Property of Cengage Learning.

How this chapter relates to **YOU**

1. When it comes to engaging, listening, and note-taking in your college classes, what do you find most challenging, if anything?

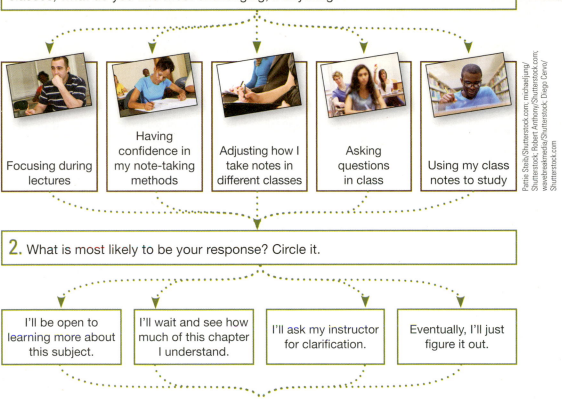

Focusing during lectures

Having confidence in my note-taking methods

Adjusting how I take notes in different classes

Asking questions in class

Using my class notes to study

Pattie Steib/Shutterstock.com; michaeljung/ Shutterstock; Robert Anthony/Shutterstock.com; wavebreakmedia/Shutterstock; Diego Cervo/ Shutterstock.com

2. What is most likely to be your response? Circle it.

I'll be open to learning more about this subject.

I'll wait and see how much of this chapter I understand.

I'll ask my instructor for clarification.

Eventually, I'll just figure it out.

3. What would you have to do to increase your likelihood of success? Will you do it this term?

Example: *Discipline myself to focus in class. Yes!*

_____

_____

How **YOU** will relate to this chapter

What are you most interested in learning about? Put check marks by those topics.

☐ How to get engaged in class

☐ How to listen with focus to different kinds of lecture styles

☐ How to take good notes

☐ How to adjust your note-taking system and why

☐ How to ask questions in class

☐ How to use your notes to achieve the best results

● How motivated are you to learn more about getting the right start in college? (5 = high, 1 = low) ____

● How ready are you to read now? ____ (If something is in your way, take care of it if you can, so you can zero in and focus.)

● How long do you think it will take you to complete this chapter? If you start and stop, keep track of your overall time. ____ hour(s) ____ minutes

Rachel White

© Cengage Learning

Every child goes through "child development" and this process includes: walking, talking... children go through milestones at predictable time periods.

2 month old babies explore environment, this is cognative development, and emotional development is smiling and taking turns.

Language development is when a baby learns first words, or learning parts of the body knowing when.

fine and gross motor skills: fine skills are when a child uses small muscles like drawing.

fine

gross

Understanding **CHILD** Development **8th** Edition

© Cengage Learning

Rachel White's Caring Hands Childcare

State Certified In-Home Childcare Service Open 7:30am–5:30pm Nutritious Meals, Preschool Curriculum

Call Rachel White 719-555-5103 for an appointment

TAKE ONE!!!

Caring Hands Childcare 719-555-5103
Caring Hands Childcare 719-555-5103
Caring Hands Childcare 719-555-5103
Caring Hands Childcare 719-555-5103
Caring Hands Childcare 719-555-5103
Caring Hands Childcare 719-555-5103
Caring Hands Child...
Caring Hands 719-555-...
Ca...
7...
Car...
7...

© Borodaev/ShutterStock.com

Bondarenko/Shutterstock.com

All she ever wanted to be was a Mom. Rachel White loved kids. When she was one herself, she helped raise her six younger brothers and sisters. Her parents worked hard to support the family, so Rachel took over her mom's duties. With each new baby, Rachel got better at distinguishing between whiney cries, hurt cries, and hungry cries. It was Rachel who cooked their dinner most nights and took them to the park on Saturdays. It was almost as if they were Rachel's children. In fact, sometimes she pretended they were.

So as a senior, Rachel dropped out of high school and married her boyfriend, Mike. He loved kids, too, and when they found out they were expecting, he was as happy as she was that the "baby" was actually "babies." Twins ran in Mike's family, and it wasn't long until they had a real family with a little boy and a girl. But now with another baby on the way, Rachel realized that Mike's income wouldn't be enough. She

wanted a big family like the one she'd grown up in, and she knew that getting an education was the best answer. The ideal career for a stay-at-home mom, she thought, would be to open a day care center in her own home. An associate's degree in Early Childhood Development would provide credentials. So she studied at night, earned her GED, and enrolled in two evening classes at her local career college. Mike would be so proud of her.

Despite a 40-minute commute in heavy traffic, Rachel was excited about her first class, Child Development I, as a new college student. But right away, several things caught her off guard. The young instructor was new to teaching, spoke with a foreign accent, and raced through the lecture. Because she'd been out of school for a while, Rachel felt as though she had forgotten

© Larry Harwood Photography. Property of Cengage Learning.

how to be a student. As the instructor talked, she tried to take notes as quickly as she could, but how was she supposed to know what was important enough to write down? She looked around: What were other students writing? Was she the only one who couldn't keep up? The lecture began:

Child development is a process every child goes through. This process involves learning and mastering skills like sitting, walking, talking, skipping, and tying shoes. Children learn these skills, called developmental milestones, during predictable time periods. Children develop skills in five main areas of development: First, let's look at cognitive development. This is the child's ability to learn and solve problems. For example, this includes a two-month-old baby learning to explore the environment with hands or eyes or a five-year-old learning how to do simple math problems. Second, social/emotional development is the child's ability to interact with others, including helping themselves and self-control. Examples of this type of development would include a six-week-old baby smiling, a ten-month-old baby waving bye-bye, or a five-year-old boy knowing how to take turns in games at school. Third, speech and language development is the child's ability to both understand and use language. For example, this includes a 12-month-old baby saying his first words, a two-year-old naming parts of her body, or a five-year-old learning to say "feet" instead of "foots." Children also learn both fine and gross motor skills. Fine motor skills are the child's ability to use small muscles, specifically their hands and fingers, to pick up small objects, hold a spoon, turn pages in a book, or use a crayon to draw. Gross motor skills, on the other hand, are the child's ability to use large muscles. For example, a six-month-old baby learns how to sit up with some support, a 12-month-old baby learns to pull up to a stand holding onto furniture, and a five-year-old learns to skip.*

Rachel tried to pay attention to the instructor's words and copy down the

writing scribbled all over the board, but her mind seemed to drift to the flyers she'd create for her new day-care business, or whether she should call Mike at the break to tell him the twins seemed to be coming down with a cold. Why was it so hard to focus? Rachel wondered whether she should bring her laptop to take notes that way, but somehow she knew she wouldn't be able to resist the temptation to check her Facebook page every 15 minutes or so. Information seemed to fly out of her instructor's mouth at mach speed, and frankly, she used the foreign accent as an excuse for her troubles. Taking notes that quickly was just plain impossible. She tried giving her instructor quizzical looks to communicate "Slow down, please," but the instructor probably couldn't see Rachel's face in the back of the room.

Because she didn't catch all of what the instructor was talking about, asking questions in class would only prove that she wasn't paying attention. Trying to read and take notes from the textbook chapters *before* class was hard with her active and noisy kids. Instead, she tried to look like she was paying attention in class so that no one knew that her brain wasn't really there.

Rachel had thought about trying to stop in during her instructor's office hours sometime, but she hated the thought of rush-hour traffic. She could try making an appointment at another time, but did she really want to discuss how hard it was to concentrate in the class? It was too late in the term to drop the class, and she needed the credits for her degree. Still, she had to figure something out or this course was going to spoil her dream.

1. Do you have anything in common with Rachel? If so, how are you managing the situation so that you can be successful?

2. In terms of the title of this chapter—Engaging, Listening, and Note-Taking in Class—how is Rachel doing? In your view, is she likely to pass the course? Why or why not?

3. List five mistakes Rachel is making.

4. Now list five things that Rachel should do immediately to improve her childhood development classroom experience.

Get Engaged in Class

engagement emotional and psychological commitment to a task

No, this chapter isn't about buying a ring and getting down on one knee. It's about your willingness to focus, listen, discuss, ask questions, take notes, and generally dive into your classes. It's about being a full participant in your learning, not just a spectator sitting on the sidelines. It's about not just memorizing information for exams and then forgetting it. You see, the secret to college success hinges on this one word: **engagement**.

Think about this analogy. How did you learn to swim? Did you watch swimming on TV? Did you get advice from your friends about swimming? Did you just Google it? No, you probably jumped in and got wet, right? The same thing is true with your college classes. The more willing you are to jump in and get wet, the more engaged you'll be in the learning process.

Follow the Rules of Engagement

Just as is the case with most places you can think of, college classrooms have rules about how to behave. You don't find people yelling in church or staring at other people in elevators or telling jokes at funerals. There are rules about how to behave in a variety of contexts, and college classrooms are no exception. In fact, the rules of engagement described here are a part of what this book calls academic professionalism, and preparing for class beforehand is at the top of the list. Despite their best intentions, some college students "shoot themselves in the foot" without meaning to. They believe they're ready for college and motivated to achieve, but within the first few weeks of the term, they miss class (25%), turn in an assignment late (33%), or don't turn in an assignment at all (24%).[1] Although not all students see the value of academic professionalism and preparation, do more than your classmates—dare to prepare! If you follow these rules of engagement, your classes will be much more enjoyable, enriching learning experiences.

1. **Look ahead.** By checking your course syllabus before class, you'll be prepared for the upcoming topic. You'll also avoid the "oops" factor of sitting down, looking around, and noticing that everyone else knows something you don't about what's supposed to happen today.

2. **Do the assigned reading.** If you have a reading assignment due for class, do it, and take notes as you read. Write in the margins of your textbook or on sticky notes. Or take notes using one of many convenient online note-taking tools while you read. Question what you're reading, and enter into a mental conversation with the author. Having some background on the topic will allow you to listen more actively and participate more

When you can do the common things of life in an uncommon way, you will command the attention of the world.

—*George Washington Carver, 1864–1943, horticulturist, chemist, and educator*

© Larry Harwood Photography. Property of Cengage Learning.

You cannot truly listen to anyone and do anything else at the same time.

M. Scott Peck, American author, (1936–2005)

intelligently during any discussion: *Yes, I remember the chapter covering that topic,* you'll think when the instructor begins talking about something you recognize. Instead of hearing it for the first time, you'll *strengthen* what you've already read. According to one study, as few as one-third of your classmates will have done the assigned reading prior to class.[2] That little-known fact isn't a reason to excuse yourself from reading; instead it gives you insider information on how you can shine in class by comparison.

3. **Show up physically.** Not only is attending class important for your overall understanding of the material, but it may move your grade up a few notches. Even if attendance isn't required by your instructor, require it of yourself. Research says that missing classes is definitely related to your academic performance. And once you give yourself permission to skip one single class, it becomes easier to do it the next time, and the time after that. Studies indicate that on any given day, approximately one-third of your classmates will miss class, and that most students think that several absences during a term is "the standard."[3] Exercise good judgment, even if your classmates don't! Besides the importance of being there, it's essential to be on time and stay for the full class session. Students who arrive late and leave early are annoying not only to the instructor but also to their classmates. To everyone else, it looks like they don't value the other students or the class content. How would you like dinner guests to arrive an hour late, after you'd slaved over a hot stove all day? Your instructors have prepared for class, and they feel the same way. Build in time to find a parking place, hike to the building where class is held, or stop for a coffee. Do everything you can to avoid coming late and leaving early.

4. **Show up mentally.** Showing up means more than just occupying a seat in the classroom. It means thinking about what you bring to the class as a learner on any particular day. Do a mental readiness check when you arrive in class. If you're not ready, what can you do to rally for the cause?

5. **Choose your seat strategically.** Imagine paying $150 for a concert ticket, just like everyone else, and then electing to sit in the nosebleed section as high up and far away from the action as you could get. Sitting in the back means you're more likely to let your mind wander and less likely to hear clearly. Sitting in the front means you'll keep yourself accountable by being in full view of the instructor and the rest of the class. What's the best spot for great concentration? Front and center, literally—the "T zone"! In one study, students who sat at the back of a large auditorium were six times more likely to fail the course, even though the instructor had assigned seats randomly![4]

6. **Bring your tools.** Bring a writing utensil and notebook with you to every class. Your instructor may also ask you to bring your textbook, calculator, a blue book or scantron form for an exam, or other necessary items. If so, do it. Question: How seriously would you take a carpenter who showed up to work without a hammer, nails, and screwdriver? Get the point?

7. **Be aware that gab is not a gift.** In class, talking while others are speaking is inappropriate. And it's certainly not a gift—especially to your instructor. In fact, side conversations while your instructor is lecturing or your classmates are contributing to the discussion are downright rude. If you're seated next to a gabber, don't get sucked in. Use body language to communicate that you're there to learn, not to gab. If that's not enough, politely say something like "I really need to pay attention right now. Let's talk more later, okay?" Don't let other students cheat you out of learning.

8. **Choose to engage.** Engagement isn't something that just happens to you while you're not looking. It's a choice you make, and sometimes it's a difficult choice because the material isn't naturally appealing to you, or the course is a required one you didn't choose, or you're just in a bad mood. Choose to engage anyway. Instead of actively choosing to disengage in class by sleeping through lectures, surfing the Internet, or texting friends, choose to engage by leaning forward, listening, finding your own ways to connect to the material, and thinking of questions to ask. For many students, texting on their cell phones during class is particularly tempting. There's a reason why people are asked to turn off their cell phones before concerts, athletic events, or movies. Imagine being in a jam-packed theater trying to follow the film's plot, with cell phones going off every few seconds. You've paid good money to see a film. The same thing goes for your college classes.

9. **Focus.** After sitting down in class each day, take a moment to clear your head of all daydreams, to-do's, and worries. Take a deep breath and remind yourself of the opportunity to learn that lies ahead. Think of yourself as a reporter at a press conference, listening carefully because you'll be writing a story about what's going on. You *will* be writing a "story"—often in response to an essay question on an exam!

10. **Maintain your health.** Being sick can take its toll on your ability to concentrate, listen well, and participate. Prevent that from happening by getting enough sleep, eating well, and exercising. Remember, *energy management* is key to your ability to focus.

Listening with Focus

Listening with focus is more than just physically hearing words as they stream by. It's actually a complicated process that's hard work. You can't listen well when your energy is zapped, when you've stayed up all night, or when your stomach is growling fiercely. Focused listening means that you are concentrating fully on what's going on in class.

"Easy Listening" Is for Elevators— Focused Listening Is for Classrooms

Stores, restaurants, and elevators are known for their programmed, background easy listening music. Chances are you hardly notice it's there. Listening in class, however, requires actual skill, and you'll be doing a great deal of it as a college student. Experts estimate that the average student spends 80 percent of class time listening to lectures.[5]

Many of us think that listening is easy. If you happen to be around when there's something to listen to, you can't help but listen. Not so! Did you know that when you're listening at your best, your breathing rate, heartbeat, and body temperature all increase? Just as with physical exercise, your body works harder when you're engaged in focused listening. When all is said and done, listening is really about energy management.

Here are some techniques for improving your listening skills in the classroom. Read through the list, then go back and check off the ones you're willing to try harder to do in class this week.

> **Calm yourself.** Take a few deep breaths with your eyes closed to help you put all those nagging distractions out of your mind during class time.

> **Be open.** Keep an open mind and view your class as yet another opportunity to strengthen your intellect and learn something new. Wisdom comes from a broad understanding of many things, rather than from a consistently limited focus what's going on in your own world.

> **Don't make snap judgments.** Remember, you don't have to like your instructor's wardrobe to respect his knowledge. Focus on the content he's offering you, even if you don't agree with it. You may change your mind later when you learn more. Don't jump to conclusions about content *or* style.

> **Assume responsibility.** Speak up! Ask questions! Even if you have an instructor with an accent who's difficult to understand, the burden of understanding course content rests with you. You will interact with people with all sorts of accents, voices, and speech patterns throughout your life. It's up to you to improve the situation.

> **Watch for gestures that communicate "Here comes something important!"** Some typical examples include raising an index finger, turning to face the class, leaning forward from behind the lectern, walking up the aisle, or using specific facial expressions or gestures.

> **Listen for speech patterns that subtly communicate "Make sure you include this in your notes!"** For example, listen for changes in the rate, volume, or tone of speech, longer than usual pauses, or repeated information.

> **Uncover general themes or roadmaps for each lecture.** See whether you can figure out where your instructor is taking you *while* he's taking you

© Larry Harwood Photography. Property of Cengage Learning.

VARK It!

Read/Write: Read this list of suggestions for improving your listening skills aloud. Choose one item to focus on, and coach yourself about how you'll do it.

there. Always ask yourself, "Where's he going with this? What's he getting at? How does this relate to what was already said?"

> **Appreciate your instructor's prep time.** For every hour of lecture time, your teacher has worked for hours to prepare. Although she may make it look easy, her lecture has involved researching, organizing, creating a PowerPoint presentation, overheads, or a podcast, and preparing notes and handouts.

Listen Hard!

It's estimated that college students spend ten hours per week listening to lectures.[6] Instructors can speak 2,500–5,000 words during a fifty-minute lecture. That's a lot of words flying by at breakneck speed, so it's important to listen correctly. But what does *that* mean?

Think about the various situations in which you find yourself listening. You often listen to empty chit-chat on your way to class. "Hey, how's it going?" when you spot your best friend in the hallway is an example, right? Listening in this type of situation doesn't require a lot of brainpower. Although you wouldn't want to spend too much time on chit-chat, if you refused to engage in any at all, you'd probably be seen by others as odd, withdrawn, shy, or stuck up.

You also listen in challenging situations, some that are emotionally charged; for example, a friend needs to vent, relieve stress, or verbalize her anxieties. Most people who are blowing off steam aren't looking for you to fix their problems. They just want to be heard and hear you say something like "I understand" or "That's too bad."

Listening to chit-chat and listening in emotionally charged situations require what are called **soft listening skills**. You must be accepting, sensitive, and nonjudgmental. You don't have to assess, analyze, or conclude. You just have to be there for someone else.

But these two types of listening situations don't describe all the kinds of listening you do. When you're listening to new information, as you do in your college classes, or when you're listening to someone trying to persuade you of something, you have to pay close attention, think critically, and ultimately make decisions about what you're hearing. Is something true or false? Right or wrong? How do you know? When you're listening to a person trying to inform you or to persuade you, you need **hard listening skills**. In situations like these, you must evaluate, analyze, and decide.[7]

One mistake many students make in class is listening the wrong way. They should be using their hard listening skills, rather than sitting back and letting information float over them. Soft listening skills don't help you in class. You must listen intently, think critically, and analyze carefully what you're hearing. It's important to note that neither listening mode is better than the other. They are each simply better suited to different situations. But soft listening won't get you the results you want in your classes. You don't need to be there for your instructor; you need to be there for yourself.

You may find many of your classes to be naturally fascinating learning experiences. But for others, you will need to be convinced. Even if you don't find Intro to Whatever to be the most engaging subject in the world, you may find yourself fascinated by your instructor. Most people are interested in other people. What makes him tick? Why was she drawn to this field? If you find it hard to get interested in the material, trick yourself by paying attention to the person delivering the message. Sometimes focusing on something about the speaker can help you

Sharpen *Your* FOCUS

> **Speed is the blessing (and the curse) of the modern age. It is our drug of choice.**
>
> —EDWARD M. HALLOWELL, M.D., *CRAZY BUSY*

Reason 7: They are always rushing.

Are you hooked on speed? Do your days whiz by as you rush from thing to thing? Time management expert Edward Hallowell writes, "We go fast not just because we're busy, but because speed is fun. Speed grips attention. Speed excites. Speed speeds you out of boredom. Nothing is boring if it's fast enough." But what do we sacrifice when we choose to speed through life? The ability to focus! Focus is what is required when we need to zero in on important things. Ask yourself whether slowing down occasionally could help you truly sharpen your focus.

TRY It!

As you go through this week, make a point of slowing down—and accomplishing more. Keep a record of something you do each day—slower, longer, and better—by consciously remembering that "slow and steady wins the race."

Sunday _____

Monday _____

Tuesday _____

Wednesday _____

Thursday _____

Friday _____

Saturday _____

---

focus on the subject matter, too. And you may just find out that you actually do find this class to be valuable. Although tricking yourself isn't always a good idea, it *can* work if you know what you're doing and why.

Get Wired for Sound

Increasingly instructors are providing podcasts and videocasts of their lectures so that you can *preview* the lecture in advance or *review* it after class. Some textbooks (like this one) offer chapter summaries you can listen to on the subway, in the gym, at home during a blizzard, or in bed while recovering from the flu, via your computer or digital-audio player.

Regardless of your learning style, recorded lectures allow you to re-listen to difficult concepts as many times as needed. You can take part in the live action in class and take notes later while re-listening to the podcast. In one study, students who re-listened to a lecture one, two, or three times increased their lecture notes substantially each time.[8] Of course, recorded lectures aren't meant to excuse you from attending class, and in order to take advantage of them, you actually have to find time to listen to them. They're supplemental tools to *reinforce* learning for busy students on the go, which is virtually *everyone* these days.[9]

> **The most basic and powerful way to connect to another person is to listen. Just listen. Perhaps the most important thing we ever give each other is our attention.**
>
> *Rachel Naomi Remen, physician and author*

© Larry Harwood Photography. Property of Cengage Learning.

Identify Lecture Styles So You Can Modify Listening Styles

Regardless of how challenging it is to listen with focus, being successful in college will require you to do just that—focus—no matter what class or which instructor. Sometimes your instructors are **facilitators**, who help you discover information on your own in new ways. Other times they are **orators**, who lecture as their primary means of delivering information. If you're not an aural learner, listening with focus to lectures will be a challenge for you.

Chances are you won't be able to change your instructors' lecturing styles. And even if you could, different students react differently to different lecture styles. But what you can do is expand your own skills as a listener—no matter what class or which instructor. Take a look at the lecture styles coming up and see whether you recognize them.

> **The Rapid-Fire Lecturer:** You may have found yourself in a situation like Rachel's with an instructor who lectures so fast it makes your head spin. Listening and taking notes in a class like this are not easy. By the end of class, your hand aches from gripping your pen and writing furiously. Because there'll be no time to relax, you'll need to make certain you're ready for this class by taking all the suggestions in this chapter to heart. Read ahead so that you recognize points the instructor makes. Also take advantage of whatever **supplementary** materials this teacher provides in the way of audio support, online lecture notes, or PowerPoint handouts.

> **The All-Over-the-Map Lecturer:** Organization is not this lecturer's strong suit. Although the lecture may be organized in the lecturer's mind, what comes out is difficult to follow. In this case, it will be up to you to organize the lecture content yourself.

> **The Content-Intensive Lecturer:** This lecturer, determined to cover a certain amount of material in a particular amount of time, is hardly aware that anyone else is in the room. This teacher may use specific language related to the subject, which you will need to learn rapidly to keep up. Prepare yourself for a potentially rich learning environment, but be sure to ask questions right away if you find yourself confused.

> **The Review-the-Text Lecturer:** This lecturer will follow the textbook closely, summarizing and highlighting important points. You may assume it's not important to attend class, but watch out for this trap! Receiving the same information in more than one format (reading *and* listening) can be a great way to learn.

> **The Active-Learning Lecturer:** This lecturer may choose not to lecture at all or to alternate between short lectures and activities, exercises, and role plays. Although you may find it easier to get engaged in this type of class, and you'll most likely appreciate the teacher's creativity, remember that you are still responsible for connecting what happens in class to the course material itself. You will need to read, digest, and process the information on your own outside of class.

facilitators guides

orators public speakers

supplementary extra

Sophie Louise Davis/
Shutterstock.com

iStockphoto.com/narvikk

VARK It!

Aural: With a partner, discuss the pros and cons of each lecture style. Do either of you have instructors that use any of these styles?

Kuzma/Shutterstock.com

Mladen Mitrinovic/
Shutterstock.com

arkadymar/Shutterstock.com

BOX 7.1

Listening Tips If English Is Your Second Language

It's normal to feel overwhelmed in the classroom as a new student, but especially if your first language isn't English. The academic environment in higher education can be stressful and competitive. It's even more stressful if you're also dealing with a new and different culture. You will need to give yourself time to adapt to all of these changes. In the meantime, here are some suggestions for improving your ability to listen well in class:

- Talk to your instructor before the course begins. Let her know that English is not your native language, but that you're very interested in learning. Ask for any suggestions on how you can increase your chances of success in the class. Your instructor will most likely be willing to provide you with extra help, knowing you're willing to do your part to overcome the language barrier.

- Try to get the main points of your instructor's lecture. You don't have to understand every word.

- Write down words to look up in the dictionary later. Keep a running list and check them all after class. Missing out on one important term can hurt your chances of understanding something else down the line.

- Don't be afraid to ask questions. If you're too uncomfortable to ask during class, make use of your instructor's office hours or e-mail address to get your questions answered. Also, teaching assistants and peer tutors may be available to help you.

- Use all support materials available for the class. Find out whether your instructor posts his notes on the course website or if they are available as handouts. Some instructors offer guided notes or skeleton outlines for students to fill in throughout the lecture. Some large lectures are videotaped for viewing by students at a later time. Make full use of podcasts of lectures, if they're available, so that you can listen more than once to portions you found confusing in class. Use any tools available to help reinforce lecture content.

- Team up with a classmate whose native language is English. Clarify your notes and fill in gaps.

- Form a study group with other classmates. Meet on a regular basis so that you can help one another. Remember: just because your native language isn't English doesn't mean you don't have something to offer the other members of your study group.

- Be patient. It will take some time to adjust to the accents of your various instructors. After a few weeks of class, you'll find it easier to understand what is being said.

- Practice your English comprehension by listening to talk radio or watching television or movies. You'll hear a variety of regional accents, for example, and broaden your understanding of American culture.

- Take an English as a Second Language course if you think it would help. It's important to keep up with the academic demands of college, and further development of your English skills may improve your comprehension and boost your confidence.

- If you continue to feel overwhelmed and unable to cope after several weeks in school, find out whether your campus has an International Students Office, and enlist support from people who are trained to help.[10]

Turn Listening Skills into Note-Taking Skills

How Well Do You Listen?

Now that you've read about focused listening, see how the following statements apply to you. Check the box that most applies to what you usually do in the classroom. Use this self-assessment to develop a plan for improvement, particularly so that you're listening at your best to take careful, useful notes.

Listening Statements:	Always True of Me	Sometimes True of Me	Never True of Me
I stay awake during class so that I can take good notes to use later while studying.	☐	☐	☐
I maintain eye contact with the speaker.	☐	☐	☐
I don't pretend to be interested in the subject.	☐	☐	☐
I understand my instructor's questions.	☐	☐	☐
I try to summarize the information in my notes.	☐	☐	☐
I look for organizational patterns in the lecture and identify them in my notes (e.g., causes and effects, lists of items).	☐	☐	☐
I set a purpose for listening, like trying to capture all the key ideas and examples that explain them.	☐	☐	☐
I don't daydream during class, leaving gaps in my notes.	☐	☐	☐
I try to predict the lecturer's next main point.	☐	☐	☐
I take notes regularly.	☐	☐	☐
I don't let external distractions such as loud noises, late-arriving students, and so on, interfere with my note-taking.	☐	☐	☐
I try to determine the speaker's purpose.	☐	☐	☐
I recognize that the speaker may be biased about the subject, but I don't let that affect my note-taking.	☐	☐	☐
I write down questions the instructor poses during class.	☐	☐	☐
I copy down main points and examples from the board or screen.	☐	☐	☐
Total check marks for each column:	☐	☐	☐

Add up the check marks in each column to learn the results of your analysis. Pay particular attention to the total in the "Always True of Me" column.

13–15 "Always True of Me": You're probably an excellent listener, both in the classroom and in other situations. Keep up the good work.

10–12 "Always True of Me": You are a good listener, but you need to fine-tune a few of your listening skills.

7–9 "Always True of Me": You need to change some behaviors so that you get more out of your classes.

6 or less "Always True of Me" or 7 or more "Never True of Me": You need to learn better listening skills if you want to achieve academic success in college.[11]

Listening in class is one thing. Taking notes is quite another. You must be a good listener to take good notes, but being a good listener alone doesn't automatically make you a good note-taker. Note-taking is a crucial and complex skill, and doing well on tests isn't based on luck. It's based on combining preparation and opportunity—in other words, knowing how to take useful notes in class that work for you.

Actually, one reason that note-taking is so important in the learning process is that it uses all four VARK categories: *visual* (you see your instructor and the screen, if overheads or PowerPoint slides are being used), *aural* (you listen to the lecture), *read/write* (you write what you see and hear so that you can read it later to review), and *kinesthetic* (the physical act of writing opens up a pathway to the brain). Have you ever thought about it that way before?

According to one study, 99 percent of college students take notes during lectures, and 94 percent of students believe that note-taking is important.[12] These are good signs, but are these students taking notes correctly, as a result of focused listening? If 99 percent of college students are taking notes, why isn't nearly everyone getting straight A's? Here are some reasons:

> Students typically only record less than 40 percent of the lecture's main content ideas in their notes.[13]

> Only 47 percent of students actually review their notes later to see what they've written.

> Only 29 percent edit their notes later by adding, deleting, or reorganizing material.

> A full 12 percent do nothing other than recopy them verbatim.

> Some students never do anything with their notes once they leave class![14]

 ## GOING PRO

BE CLEAR

> **A mighty thing is eloquence . . . nothing so much rules the world.**
> ~POPE PIUS II

Speak and write well. Both college and career success may require more emphasis on these skills than any others. In today's world of abbreviated text messages (ays = Are you serious?; lol = laugh out loud; u = you; brb = be right back) and empty conversation ("And she's going. . . and I'm like . . . you know . . . whatever . . ."), you can become a super star on the job by just speaking and writing well. For example, if the boss wants someone to brief the staff on a new procedure, who will she choose? Someone who speaks like a high school student, or the person who sounds like an experienced professional? The ability to use both spoken and written language well—the language of educated and successful professionals—communicates to your colleagues and your supervisors that you think clearly and work effectively. And when the boss wants someone to deal with customers, partners, and suppliers, who will the boss choose? Those who are hard to understand and sound inexperienced, or those who have a solid command of the language and use it to clearly get their points across?

And in addition to speaking and writing well, learn to listen to what's really being said and why. With practice, you can listen past the bravado or baloney and get to the real message. We learn in the competitive world of business that poor speaking, writing, and listening skills will lead people to take their business elsewhere. When you communicate effectively and professionally, you help your organization succeed—and that helps you succeed!

Does note-taking make a difference? Absolutely. During lectures, it serves two fundamental purposes: It helps you understand what you're learning at the time and it helps you preserve information to study later. In other words, both the *process* of note-taking (as you record information) and the *product* (your notes themselves) are important to learning. There is strong evidence that taking notes during a lecture leads to higher achievement than not taking notes, and working with your notes later increases your chances for academic achievement even more. Studies show that if you take notes, you have a 50 percent chance of recalling that information at test time versus a 15 percent chance of remembering the same information if you didn't take notes.[15]

Different Strokes for Different Folks: Note-Taking by the System and Subject

Now that we know just how important listening and note-taking are, let's ask a crucial question. Exactly how do you take *good* notes? Interestingly, when it comes to note-taking, "Different strokes for different folks" is literally true. Different note-taking systems work best for different lecture styles, different learning styles, and different subjects—math versus history, for example. If your instructor uses a "Rapid-Fire" lecture style, you'll need to write quickly, perhaps using abbreviations, no matter which note-taking system you use. If your instructor is an "All-Over-the-Map" lecturer, you may have to create the connections on paper as she talks about all kinds of ideas.

No matter which note-taking strategy you choose to use in a particular situation, an important question to ask is: What constitutes good notes? The answer is: writing an accurate, complete, organized account of what you hear in class (or read in your textbook, which is discussed later in this chapter). How do you know if your notes are good? Show them to your instructor and get input, or assess your strategy after you see your results on the first exam. Your note-taking skills should steadily improve as you evolve as a student.[16]

However you decide to take notes in a particular class, it's good to have some general goals:

1. **Capture main ideas.** Listen for an organizing pattern. Has the instructor been covering the subject by major time periods? Has she been listing contributors to the field by specific discoveries? What's her system? Listen for verbal clues your instructor emphasizes or repeats several times, notice what he writes on the board, or watch for major bullets or itemized steps on the screen. In the lecture Rachel was trying to focus on in class, her instructor made it easy to recognize main points by numbering them, "first," "second," and so forth. If portions of the lecture are highlighted verbally, these portions are probably important. Listen for signal words and phrases such as "There are three reasons . . . ," "On the other hand . . . ," "For example . . . ," and "In summary . . . ."

2. **Note whether a handout accompanies lecture materials.** If so, chances are that the information is considered to be important. If the instructor interrupts the lecture to give more detailed examples from a handout, he must consider doing so important enough to take up class time. Keep all handouts, and assume they'll be worth reviewing at exam time.

3. **Write down examples or key words from stories that will help anchor the main points.** If you were a classmate of Rachel's, you might not remember exactly when the social/emotional milestone begins to develop in children, but writing down the instructor's story about something funny her own little girl did may help trigger your memory.

4. **When in doubt, write it down.** If you're not sure whether to write something down, use the motto "Better safe than sorry." If you don't know a word the instructor uses, leave a blank to show you omitted something, or sound it out as you're writing and come back to it later. Put the lecture in your own words for the most part, but write down formulas, definitions, charts, diagrams, and specific facts verbatim. Also, write down good points made by classmates. Not all the words of wisdom in class will come from your instructor. If you've prepared for class by reading the assignment and listened to the lecture, and a classmate makes a point during a discussion that adds new information, write it down!

5. **Consider your learning style preferences.** If you're a visual learner, a note-taking system that works well for you may not work particularly well for a classmate who has a different learning style. Drawing all over your paper may help you see connections, whereas a classmate next to you is writing the same information down in a structured outline format. If a note-taking system seems awkward to you even after you've tried it for awhile, you may be better off trying a different one.

6. **Create a shorthand system that works.** When you're taking notes quickly, as you often do in class, you won't have time to write out every word your instructor utters. Use abbreviations or a shorthand system that you create for yourself. The last thing you want is to look at your notes as you begin to study for an exam and wonder what you meant by a string of letters that makes no sense now. So make an abbreviation "dictionary" for yourself that you use regularly, like this:

Symbol	Meaning	Example
→	leads to, produces, causes, makes	Practice → perfect.
←	comes from, is the result of	Tsunamis ← earthquakes
↑	increased, increasing, goes up, rises	Taxes ↑ 100% last year.
↓	decreased, decreasing, lowering	Salaries ↓ 10% this year.
#	number	Retry problem #3.
@	at	Due @ 4:00 p.m.
/	per	25 miles/gallon
p	page	Read p. 99.
pp	pages	Study pp 99–105.
¶	paragraph	Revise ¶ #4.
w/o	without	They revised w/o reading carefully.
?	question	Answer ? 1.
w/i	within	There are problems w/i the tax laws.

(*Continued*)

VARK It!

Read/Write: Add to this list by creating a few more abbreviations for one of your toughest classes, for example, hypothesis = hyp.

Symbol	Meaning	Example
i.e.	that is	The SAT, i.e., a college entrance exam, is challenging.
e.g.	for example	Professionals, e.g., doctors and lawyers, have advanced degrees.
etc.	et cetera, so forth	Clinton, Reagan, etc., were popular presidents.
b/c	because	We pay taxes b/c it's the law.
b/4	before	Incidents b/4 the attack.
esp.	especially	Tobacco, esp. cigarettes, causes cancer.
min.	minimum	The min. wage may go up.
max.	maximum	The max. number of people in an elevator is 8.
gov't.	government	The gov't. helped the people.
ASAP	as soon as possible	Complete your certificate program ASAP.
wrt	write	wrt #3 (write number 3)
yr/yrs	year, years	She's 18 yrs old.

Based on http://www.essayzone.co.uk/blog/how-to-take-lecture-notes-quickly-common-abbreviations-and-symbols-for-students/

When you write down your ideas you automatically focus your full attention on them. Few if any of us can write one thought and think another at the same time. Thus a pencil and paper make excellent concentration tools.

—*Michael Leboeuf, American business author*

So what are the various note-taking methods? What are the steps involved in using each one? Knowing your options, developing your skills, and learning flexibility as a note-taker are keys to your success.

Outlining

Outlining is probably the oldest, and perhaps the most trusted form of taking notes. The problem, of course, is that not all instructors speak from an outline. Rachel's instructor probably did, and if Rachel had been able to focus, outlining may have worked well. Here's what Rachel's notes would have looked like. She'd listen for key points, like the five developmental milestones, and list examples beneath each one, like this:

Child Development 1, Week 4

1. *Child development involves learning and mastering skills like sitting, walking, talking, skipping, and tying shoes.*
   A. *Developmental milestones are learned during predictable time periods.*
   B. *Children develop skills in five main areas of development:*
      1. *Cognitive development: ability to learn and solve problems.*
         a. *two-month-old baby learning to explore the environment with hands or eyes*
         b. *five-year-old learning how to do simple math problems*

(Continued)

---

2. Social/emotional development: ability to interact with others, including helping themselves and self-control.
   a. six-week-old baby smiling
   b. ten-month-old baby waving bye-bye
   c. five-year-old boy knowing how to take turns in games at school
3. Speech/language development: ability to both understand and use language.
   a. 12-month-old baby saying his first words
   b. a two-year-old naming parts of her body
   c. a five-year-old learning to say "feet" instead of "foots"

She's listed the instructor's main points and several examples below each point to help her remember what it's about. At the end of the lecture, she could have included a **summary** of her notes. Summarizing is an excellent way to make sure you've understood the gist of all the information you've written down.

summary a condensed version of the main points

Summary:

Children reach developmental milestones in five areas at fairly predictable ages. These five areas are cognitive, social/emotional, speech/language, fine motor skills, and gross motor skills.

Of course, if your instructor's lecture is less organized, you can elect to use an informal variation of outlining, like listing bullets, and perhaps even color-coding them so they're easier to remember, as shown here:

Child Development 1, Week 4

Child development = learning & mastering skills
- sitting
- walking
- talking
- skipping
- tying shoes

Children develop skills in five main areas of development:
1. Cognitive development: ability to learn and solve problems.
2. Social/emotional development: ability to interact with others, including helping themselves and self-control.
3. Speech/language development: ability to both understand and use language.

VARK It!

Visual: Color-code a set of class notes to mark important themes (blue highlighter for main points, yellow highlighter for examples, etc.).

Even if your instructor is flashing PowerPoint slides on the screen, don't count on your memory to do all the work. You have to take notes yourself to help the information stick.

The Cornell System

The Cornell system of note-taking, devised by educator Walter Pauk, suggests this. On each page of your notebook, draw a line from top to bottom about one and a half inches from the left edge of your paper. (Some notebook paper already has a red line there.) Take notes on the right side of the line. Your notes should include main ideas, examples, short phrases, and definitions, for example—almost like an outline.

Leave the left side blank to fill in later with key words or questions you'd like answered, as Rachel has done in Figure 7.1. After class, as you review your notes, put your hand or a sheet of paper over the right side and use the words or questions you've written on the left side as prompts to see whether you can remember what's on the right side.[17] By doing this to recall the lecture, you can get a good idea of how much of the information you've really understood.

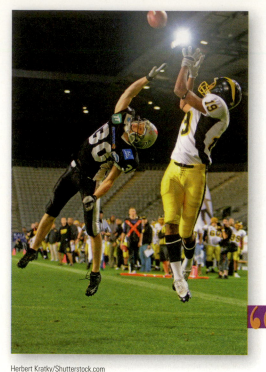

Herbert Kratky/Shutterstock.com

> **Luck is what happens when preparation meets opportunity.**
>
> *Darrell Royal, football coach*

FIGURE 7.1

Child Development Milestones: Cornell System Example

KEY WORDS AND QUESTIONS	SHORT PHRASES, EXAMPLES, DEFINITIONS
Child development	—Every child goes through.
	—learning and mastering skills (sitting, walking, talking, skipping, tying shoes, etc.)
Developmental milestones	— predictable time periods
Five main areas of development	1. Cognitive development
	Ability to learn and solve problems
	—two-month-old baby learning to explore the environment with hands or eyes
	—five-year-old learning to do simple math
Was it five main areas or six?	2. Social/emotional development
	Ability to interact with others, including helping themselves and self-control
	—six-week-old baby smiling
	—ten-month-old baby waving goodbye
	—five-year-old knowing how to take turns in games at school

© Cengage Learning

Mind Maps

An alternative to the Cornell system, or a way to expand on it, is to create mind maps. Mind maps use both sides of your brain: the logical, orderly left side and the visual, creative right side. What they're particularly good for is showing the relationships among ideas. Mind maps are also generally a good note-taking method for visual learners, and even the physical act of drawing one may help you remember the information, particularly if you're a kinesthetic learner. To give mind mapping a try, here are some useful suggestions:

1. **Use extra-wide paper (11 × 17 inches or legal size).** You won't want to write vertically (which is hard to read) if you can help it.

2. **Write the main concept of the lecture in the center of the page.** Draw related concepts coming from the center.

3. **Limit your labels to key words so that your mind map is visually clear.**

4. **Use colors, symbols, and images to make your mind map livelier and more memorable.**

5. **Consider using software such as MindManager, MindManuals, Mind-Plugs, MindMapper, or MindGenius, which are all powerful brainstorming and organizing tools.** As you type, these programs will anticipate relationships and help you draw a mind map on screen.

FIGURE 7.2

Child Development Milestones: Mind Map Example

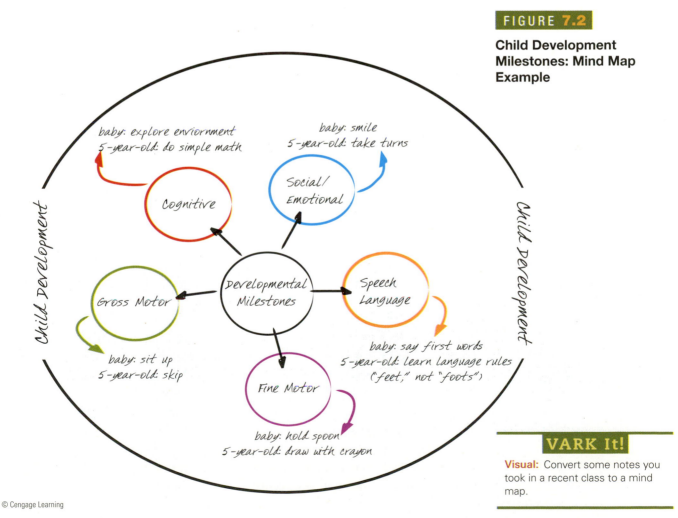

VARK It!

Visual: Convert some notes you took in a recent class to a mind map.

© Cengage Learning

Jupiterimages/Photos.com

© 2014 Cengage Learning

Note-Taking on Instructor-Provided Handouts

PowerPoint Miniatures Some instructors provide full-text lecture notes online or copies of their PowerPoint slides (three or six miniatures on a page). Instructors may hand out PowerPoint miniatures in class before the lecture, so you can follow along; hand them out after the lecture so that you still have to take your own notes but have the print outs of the miniatures as back-up; or e-mail them as attachments (see Figure 7.3). If you have copies of the PowerPoint slides to use during class, write in specifics on the lines provided next to each slide miniature, more or less as you would if you were using the Cornell System. Put down examples that are discussed in class but don't appear on the slide, or a story that will help you remember a main point on a slide. If they're handed out after class, transfer your own notes to the PowerPoint fill-in lines. If they're e-mailed to you before or after class, make sure you use them. They're "insurance" that you have access to what appeared in class on the screen. Tools such as these can be a valuable resource if you remember to use them. Don't rely on PowerPoints your instructors provide to the extent that you skip taking notes yourself in class altogether. Although it's helpful to have them available as a tool, you still need to take notes on your own to help you process the information you're listening to in class.

Guided Notes Your instructor may actually help you to pay attention in class by providing what are called "Guided Notes," or copies of lecture outlines or PowerPoint miniatures with key words missing, so that you must listen closely to "fill in the blanks." In one study, students in a college algebra class who used guided notes with problem sets they worked out together in groups liked their math class and did much better than comparable students who weren't using guided notes.[18]

Parallel Note-Taking Because many instructors today provide e-support for lectures, either through web notes, hard copies of onscreen slides, lecture outlines, or a full transcript, parallel note-taking may be particularly useful, if you go about it in the right way.[19] Here's how it works, ideally.

If they're available, print out lecture notes before class and bring them with you, preferably in a ring binder. As your instructor lectures, use the back (blank) side of each page to record your own notes as the notes from the ongoing, real-time lecture face you. You can parallel what you're hearing from your instructor with your own on-the-spot, self-recorded notes, using a Cornell format on each blank page. It's the best of both worlds! You're reading, writing, and listening at

[Fill in the blank page during actual lecture.]	[Print out instructor's notes and place in binder.]
My In-Class Lecture Notes	**Instructor's Lecture Notes**

Every child develops skills like learning to sit up, walk, talk, skip, and tie shoes.

These are called developmental milestones, and they happen to most children around the same age.

Children learn skills in five main areas of development: cognitive, social/emotional, speech/language, fine, and gross motor skills:

Child development is a process every child goes through. This process involves learning and mastering skills like sitting, walking, talking, skipping, and tying shoes. Children learn these skills, called developmental milestones, during predictable time periods. Children develop skills in five main areas of development: First, let's look at cognitive development. This is the child's ability to learn and solve problems. For example, this includes a two-month-old baby learning to explore the environment with hands or eyes, or a five-year-old learning how to do simple math problems. Second, social/emotional development is the child's ability to interact with others, including helping him or herself and self-control. Examples of this type of development would include a six-week-old baby smiling, a ten-month-old baby waving bye-bye, or a five-year-old boy knowing how to take turns in games at school.

FIGURE 7.4

Child Development Milestones: Parallel Note-Taking Example

VARK It!

Read/Write: What is your system for taking notes? E-mail your notes to another R/W learner from class—and compare your notes and your methods.

the same time, fully immersing yourself in immediate and longer-lasting learning. Figure 7.4 illustrates how parallel note-taking might look for Rachel in her childhood development class.

Note-Taking by the Book

So far this chapter has discussed taking notes in class. What about taking notes as you read from a textbook? Is that important, too? The answer: absolutely! It's easy to go on auto-pilot as you read and have no idea what you read afterward! Instead, take notes in the margins, on sticky notes, or better yet, keep a spiral-bound notebook next to you, and fill it with your own words as you read. Jot down questions, summarize main points, or use the Cornell System. Actually, the best thing to do is to read a section, close the book, and write down what you remember. You'll prove to yourself what you absorbed and what you didn't. Then you can dive back into the textbook again and clarify concepts that are still fuzzy.[20]

Note-Taking by the Subject

Beyond figuring out which note-taking style seems to "fit" you best, think about times when the subject dictates that you vary your note-taking style. In your American History class, it may make sense to take your notes along a timeline of the beginning of World War II, for example (see Figure 7.5). Because your instructor and your textbook report key events that took place during World War II chronologically, along a time line, you might want your notes to reflect that.

However, in your college algebra class, you may want to take notes very differently. Let's say, for example, that your instructor lectures by working problems on a white board or by projecting them on the screen. Then you are asked to work a problem and then talk it over with a classmate next to you. You may want to divide up your notes into columns by proposing a solution and then showing how you arrived at your answer. Having a record of how you worked a problem can be a valuable aid

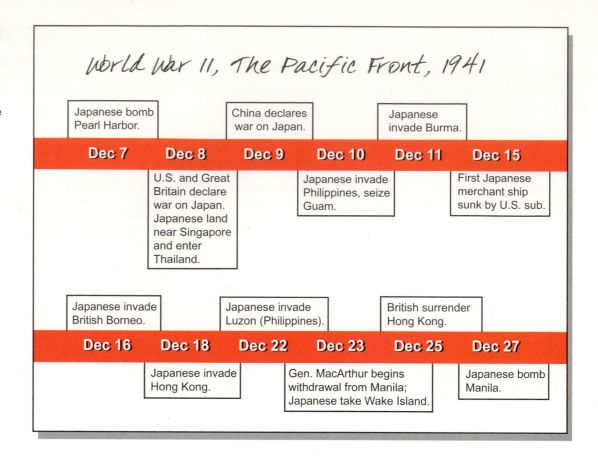

later when you're studying for a test that will probably contain algebra problems very much like the ones you solve regularly in class. Write everything down, and skip a few lines if there's something you want to fill in later (see Figure 7.6).

Mind mapping, on the other hand, is particularly useful in geology, physiology, biology, psychology, and education courses, where relationships among concepts are important.[21] Some students may make the mistake of thinking that mind maps are "scribbling," but the process of making connections on paper helps you make those same connections in your brain. Successful note-taking does mean "different strokes for different folks"—and different subjects. Be sure to make the right choices about which note-taking system makes the most sense for the course material being presented.

VARK It!

Kinesthetic: Would Exercise 7.2, which combines all four VARK preferences, help you remember course material? Why?

EXERCISE 7.2

"Focused" Multitasking

One reason it's hard to focus in class is because of distractions. Like Rachel, you may be tempted to check your Facebook account or text someone about something that pops into your mind. Being pulled in different directions at once is what happens when you multitask. It breaks your concentration and disrupts your learning. Try this experiment instead. Let's call it "Focused Multitasking," meaning that all your attention is directed at one thing. Before you listen to an in-class lecture, divide into groups, with each group trying out a different note-taking strategy presented in this chapter. For example, Group 1 members should use outlines. Group 2 should use the Cornell System, Group 3 should create mind maps, and so on. Then begin the lecture. The lecture could be your instructor lecturing about this chapter of FOCUS. Or it could be something different, like listening to an NPR podcast that the instructor or the whole class chooses. You are intentionally using all of your VARK preferences at once to focus on a single topic. After the lecture, take a quiz provided by your instructor and see which note-taking group's method earns the highest score!

Determine which of the x values are solutions to the equation

$$x^4 + x^3 - 5x^2 + x - 6 = 0$$

a) $x = -3$,   b) $x = -2$,   c) $x = 1$,   d) $x = 2$

STEPS TO SOLUTION	CALCULATIONS	RESULTS
1) Try answer a Substitute –3 into the equation for x and see if the equation is satisfied.	$(-3)^4 + (-3)^3 - 5(-3)^2 + (-3) - 6 \overset{?}{=} 0$ $81 \quad -27 \quad -45 \quad -3 -6 = 0$ $0 = 0$	YES, because both sides are 0.
2) Try answer b Substitute –2 into the equation for x and see if the equation is satisfied.	$(-2)^4 + (-2)^3 - 5(-2)^2 + (-2) - 6 \overset{?}{=} 0$ $16 \quad -8 \quad -20 \quad -2 -6 = 0$ $-20 \neq 0$	NO, because the two sides are unequal.
3) Try answer c Substitute 1 into the equation for x and see if the equation is satisfied.	$(1)^4 + (1)^3 - 5(1)^2 + 1 - 6 \overset{?}{=} 0$ $1 \quad +1 \quad -5 \quad +1 -6 = 0$ $-8 \neq 0$	NO, because the two sides are unequal.
4) Try answer d Substitute 2 into the equation for x and see if the equation is satisfied.	$(2)^4 + (2)^3 - 5(2)^2 + 2 - 6 \overset{?}{=} 0$ $16 \quad +8 \quad -20 \quad +2 -6 = 0$ $0 = 0$	YES, because both sides are 0.

FIGURE 7.6

Math Note-Taking Example

From http://www.math .armstrong.edu/MathTutorial /exerciseSoln/ LinearEqSoln /LinearEq1Soln/13LinearEq1.html

Ask and You Shall Receive

Even if you listen carefully to every word your instructor utters, it's likely you won't understand them all. After all, your instructor is an expert in the subject you're studying, and you're new to it. At some point or other, you'll need to ask questions. Even though that makes sense, not all students feel comfortable asking questions in class. Why? See whether you've excused yourself from asking questions for any of these reasons:

> I don't want to look stupid.

> I must be slow. Everyone else seems to be understanding.

> I'm too shy.

> I'll get the answer later from the textbook.

> I don't think my question is important enough.

> I don't want to interrupt the lecture. The instructor's on a roll.

> I'm sure the instructor knows what he's talking about. He must be right.

Tomas Rodriguez/Solus/Corbis

If any of these reasons for not asking questions in class applies to you, the good news is . . . you're in good company. Many students think this way. The bad news, of course, is that your question remains unasked, and therefore unanswered.

The next time you find yourself in a situation where you don't understand something, consider these points.

1. **Remember that you're not in this alone.** Chances are you're probably not the only person in class who doesn't understand. Not only will you be doing yourself a favor by asking, but you'll also be helping someone else who's too shy to speak up.

2. **Ask academically relevant questions when the time is right.** As opposed to "Why do we need to know this?" or "Why did you make the test so

EXERCISE 7.3

How Much Does Asking Questions Help?

To demonstrate the value of asking questions, try this in-class exercise. A student volunteer, or class "lecturer," will briefly replace the instructor to describe to the rest of the class two different, simple figures she draws herself. Each figure should take up a full piece of paper. The rest of the class must then reproduce the drawings as accurately as possible on their own paper as the class "lecturer" describes each figure during two rounds. The point of the exercise is to replicate the two figures the class "lecturer" has drawn as accurately as possible from her description alone. The lecturer can't show the class her drawings; she must simply describe them.

Round 1: The volunteer should turn her back to the group (so she can't see them and they can't see her), hiding her paper from view, and give the class instructions for drawing Figure 1. No questions from the group are allowed. Keep track of the exact amount of time it takes for the rest of the class to listen to the instructions and complete the drawing. If this were an exam, the class would have to redraw the figure as closely as possible to the original to get an "A."

Round 2: Next, the volunteer should now turn around and face the class, giving instructions for drawing Figure 2. Students may ask questions of the "lecturer" to make sure they're getting the drawing right. Again, note the exact amount of time taken.

After both rounds of the exercise are done, the "lecturer" should ask class members whether they think their drawings look like the two originals, and count the number of students who think they drew Figure 1 correctly and the number of students who think they drew Figure 2 correctly. Then the "lecturer" should show the two original figures as drawn, and count the number of students who actually drew Figure 1 and Figure 2 correctly. Finally, as a group discuss the two rounds and the value of asking questions in lecture classes. Even though questions take more time, the results are usually much better.

Elapsed Time	# Think Correct	# Actually Correct
Round 1		
Round 2		

hard?" ask questions to clarify information. Don't ask questions designed to take your instructor off on a **tangent** (to delay the **impending** quiz, for example). If you're really interested in something that's not directly related to the material being covered, the best time to raise the question would be during your instructor's office hours.

tangent a sudden change of subject

impending upcoming

3. **Save _personally_ relevant questions for later.** If your questions relate only to you (for example, you were ill and missed the last two classes), then don't ask in class. Set up an appointment with your instructor. You can also get answers by researching on your own, visiting or e-mailing your instructor, seeking out a teaching assistant or tutor, or working with a study group.

4. **Build on others' questions.** Your instructor isn't the only person who speaks in class. You must apply what you're reading in this chapter to listening to your classmates, too. Listen to the questions other students ask. Use their questions to spark your own. Perhaps another student has a unique way of looking at the issue being discussed that will spark an idea for a follow-up question from you. To your instructor good questions indicate _interest_, not _ignorance_.

Remember, your college education is an investment in your own future. You're here to learn, and asking questions is a natural part of that learning experience. Don't be shy—put that hand in the air!

VARK It!

Visual: As a visual learner, was this exercise easy for you because you could "picture" the images?

ONLINE **TechKnow**

When you're lost, you ask for directions, right? When you're not sure what to do or how to do it in your online coursework, or on the job, ask for help.

- If you're not sure how to access information or use an online tool, ask your instructor. Remember, in an onground class, you can often benefit from the questions of others in the class. In an online environment, you don't have the benefit of other warm bodies around, so ask your instructor directly.

- If something isn't working the way you're told it should, ask your instructor or your IT help desk.

- If you're not sure what's required to fully complete an assignment, read your syllabus carefully. Usually, instructors are very helpful in describing exactly what they want—and don't want—in an assignment. But if reading the syllabus still leaves you with questions, go online to ask your instructor.

Taking notes for online courses can benefit from online technology. Such note-taking software as Evernote, Google

Notebook, and Knowledge Notebook allow tremendous flexibility in taking, organizing, linking, and accessing notes, Web pages, images, sounds, and other data on your computer and phone. While working an online assignment in one window, you can take notes in another. Or if you prefer, you can toggle back and forth from readings to notes.

- You can import items from Webpages, add notes, images, to-do lists, PDFs, and more.

- You can search for printed or even handwritten text in images.

- You also have the ability to share these notes with classmates.

In an online environment, such note-taking software is a natural strength that you should take advantage of.[22]

Improve Your Grade
Online Flashcards
Glossary

Using Lecture Notes

Taking good notes is only part of the equation. To get the most value from your notes, you must actually *use* them. As soon as possible after class, take a few minutes to review your notes. If you find sections that are unclear, take time to fill in the gaps while things are still fresh in your mind. One instructor found that students who filled in any missing points right after class were able to increase the amount of lecture points they recorded by as much as 50 percent. And students who worked with another student to reconstruct the lecture immediately after class were able to increase their number of noted lecture points even more![23]

This part of the note-taking process is often overlooked, yet it is one of the most helpful steps for learning and recall. If you don't review your notes within twenty-four hours, there's good evidence that you'll end up *relearning* rather than *reviewing*. Reviewing helps you go beyond just writing to actually making sure you understand what you wrote. These three techniques help you get the best use of your notes: manipulating, paraphrasing, and summarizing.

> **Manipulating** involves working with your notes by typing them out later, for example. Some research indicates that it's not writing down information that's most important. Manipulating information is what counts. Work with your notes. Fill in charts, draw diagrams, create a mind map, underline, highlight, organize. Cut a copy of the instructor's lecture notes up into paragraphs, mix them up, and then put the lecture back together. Copy your notes onto flash cards. Manipulating information helps develop your reasoning skills, reduces your stress level, and can produce a more complete set of notes to study later.[24]

> **Paraphrasing** is the process of putting your notes into your own words. Re-copy your notes or your instructor's prepared lecture notes, translating them into words you understand and examples that are meaningful to you. Paraphrasing is also a good way to self-test or to study with a classmate. If you can't find words of your own, perhaps you don't really understand the original notes. Sometimes students think they understand course material until the test proves otherwise, and then it's too late! Practice paraphrasing key concepts with a friend to see how well you both understand the material. Or ask yourself, *If I had to explain this to someone who missed class, what words would I use?*

VARK It!

Multimodal: As a multimodal learner, you have an advantage because you are flexible. But you may have to use your two or three preferred modalities in order to be confident that you have learned something. Is this true for you?

EXERCISE 7.4

Note-Taking 4-M

Practice your note-taking skills by doing this. Immediately after class, or during the lecture if your instructor allows, compare notes with a classmate by following these four steps:[25]

1. **Matching**—Look for content areas where your notes match those of your classmates.

2. **Missing**—Look for content areas where one of you has missed something important, and fill in the gaps.

3. **Meaning**—Talk about what this lecture means. Why was it included in the course? Do you both understand the lecture's main points?

4. **Measuring**—Quiz each other. Measure how much you learned from the lecture. Give each other some sample test questions to see whether you understand important concepts.

> **Summarizing** is a process of writing a brief overview of all of your notes from one lecture. Imagine trying to take all your lecture notes from one class session and putting them on an index card. If you can do that, you've just written a summary. Research shows that students who use the summarizing technique have far greater recall of the material than those who don't.

Some students think that simply going over their notes is the best way to practice. Research shows that simply reading over your notes is a weak form of practice that does not transfer information into long-term memory.[26] You must actually *work with* the material, rearrange or reword it, or condense it to get the most academic bang for your buck. Active strategies always work better than more passive ones.

What's In **YOUR** Briefcase?

INCREASE YOUR SPQ

Do you know people like this? When you start a story, they one-up you: "Oh, you think that's something? You should hear what I did. . . ." They spend their time (and yours) bragging about what they've done and how good they are at things. They "dot" every sentence with an "I." Let's face it: They're just plain annoying. Everything is about them.

Other people are humble. When it comes up in conversation that they won a full scholarship to your school, and you say, "Wow! That's incredible!" they say, "Oh, it was just good luck." When they get the top grade on the economics test that everyone else failed, they say, "I don't know. I just remembered stuff and wrote it down." You stand amazed.

But once you're settled into that new job after college, you have to show your stuff. No one will know exactly what you're capable of, nor can they read your mind (or your growing résumé) on a day-to-day basis. In order for your career to survive—and to thrive—you need high SPQ. What is SPQ? It's a fairly new fun, pop concept: Self-Promotion (Intelligence) Quotient. It's vital to your career, and getting good at it can be a challenge.[27] It's not bragging; it's realizing what you have to offer and letting others know about it without turning them off. SPQ requires not only communication skills, but finesse. And it's not necessarily about being a superstar at one particular thing. It's recognizing your own particular blend of abilities—the combination of characteristics that makes you unique.

Start noticing exactly what makes you unique, and be prepared to talk about it, as if you were creating your own personal "brand." If you have a particular skill, become known as the go-to person for it. ("Ask Maria; she's great with PowerPoint!") Like an athlete, "play back" incidents in your head and remember what you did well (or not). Don't be afraid to speak up, even if you're an introvert. On the other hand, don't forget to ask questions of others and listen carefully to what they have to say about themselves. Volunteer for visibility by offering to write, speak, or run a meeting. Connect other people so that you become known as a networker. Use the pronoun "we" more than you use its complement, "I." (Rarely is anything accomplished by a single individual in isolation.) And finally, be generous in your praise of others; it will come back to you.[28]

What makes you unique? What makes up your personal "brand," and how you can let others know about it?

_____

_____

_____

At the beginning of this chapter, Rachel White, a frustrated student, faced a challenge. Now after reading this chapter, would you respond differently to any of the questions you answered about the "FOCUS Challenge Case"? Using what you learned in the chapter, write a paragraph ending to Rachel's case study. What are some of the possible outcomes for Rachel?

1. What is the single most important point you will take from this chapter?
2. Do you have a class like Rachel's? What are you doing to cope?

Reading, Writing, and Presenting

READINESS CHECK

How this chapter relates to **YOU**

1. When it comes to reading, writing, and presenting in college, what do you find most challenging, if anything?

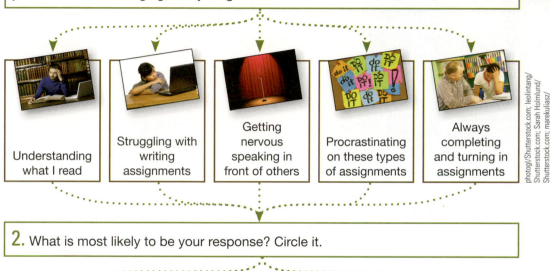

Understanding what I read	Struggling with writing assignments	Getting nervous speaking in front of others	Procrastinating on these types of assignments	Always completing and turning in assignments

2. What is most likely to be your response? Circle it.

I'll be open to learning how to improve my skills.	I'll wait and see how much of this chapter I understand.	I'll get help from a support center on campus.	Eventually, I'll just figure it out on my own.

3. What would you have to do to increase your likelihood of success? Will you do it this term?

Example: Get help from an on-campus coach or tutor. Yes!

_____

_____

How **YOU** will relate to this chapter

What are you most interested in learning about? Put check marks by those topics.

☐ Why reading is important

☐ How to build reading skills

☐ How to read right

☐ How the writing process works

☐ What the seven C's (writing) and seven P's (presenting) are

☐ How to make your PowerPoint pop

● How motivated are you to learn more about getting the right start in college? (5 = high, 1 = low) ____

● How ready are you to read now? ____ (If something is in your way, take care of it if you can, zero in and focus.)

● How long do you think it will take you to complete this chapter? If you start and stop, keep track of your overall time. ____ hour(s) ____ minutes

Katie Alexander

College would be a lot more fun if it weren't for all the reading and writing required. That was Katie Alexander's take on things. She wasn't much of a student, actually. She much preferred playing softball or volleyball with her friends to sitting in one spot with a book propped open in front of her. Reading for fun wasn't something she'd ever even consider doing—at least not reading books. To Katie, reading seventy five text messages a day was necessary; reading books was boring. *Anyway, why read the book when you can just watch the movie?* she always asked. Katie was an energetic, active, outgoing person, and "doing" and "socializing" were her things. Academic pursuits, like reading textbooks, writing papers, and giving presentations, definitely weren't.

Actually, this was Katie's second attempt at college. She'd gone to a small liberal arts school right after high school, but the self-discipline required just wasn't there. A specialist at the college officially diagnosed dyslexia, a learning disability that affects reading skills, and Katie became discouraged and dropped out. Working as a server for two years at a restaurant in her neighborhood helped her earn enough money to go back to school. She loved the people part of her waitressing job, and thought a hospitality degree from the college close to home would be the right choice for her. Besides, how much reading would she possibly have to do for a career like that?

Because of her dyslexia, reading and writing papers were hard work for Katie. She was smart enough to make it in college—she was sure of that—and this time

around, she was more motivated. But reading a long assignment, page by page, made her fidgety, and after she read something, she found it hard to summarize what it had been about. Reading took her a long time, so long that her mind wandered wherever it seemed to want to go. She found it hard to focus, and things just didn't seem to stick. Before she knew it, she was off in some other world, thinking about her friends, or her schedule at work, or everything else she had to do. Writing papers was just as hard, if not harder.

Back in grade school, Katie had been labeled as a slow reader. She was never in the top reading group, and although she resented the label, she didn't quite know what do to about it. The last time reading had actually been a subject in school was sixth grade. Now, eight years later, she was enrolled in a developmental reading class. Would it really help her?

© Larry Harwood Photography. Property of Cengage Learning.

Text Message:

Katie, want to catch a baseball game this weekend? I've got 2 free tickets!! ~B

Sept 6th, 8:10 pm

MalibuBooks/Shutterstock.com

Photos.com

Katie

Waxen/Shutterstock.com

1027

PAY TO THE ORDER OF Great Bluffs Technical College $ 2159 00

9-13-13 DATE

Two thousand one hundred and fifty nine + 00/00 DOLLARS

FOR

Katie Alexander

:222222222: 000 111 555 1027

Katie's sister, Amanda, had always been an excellent student who loved to read, especially now that she'd gotten an e-reader for her birthday. Katie always wondered if Amanda's love of reading was due to the fact that she had been in a wheelchair since a car accident in the third grade. She couldn't be active or play sports. Katie's best friend, Brittney, however, had a different strategy. "There's so much required reading in all my classes that I don't even know where to start," Brittney admitted, "so I just don't do it. I go to class, listen to the lectures, and write down what the instructor has said on the essay tests. Katie, just learn to 'play the game'!"

Besides her developmental reading class, Katie was enrolled in two other classes: history and introduction to psychology. She knew she'd have plenty of reading to do there, and her friend Brittney's strategy definitely wasn't going to work. Professor Harris-Black had assigned a shocking number of chapters to read in their thick psychology textbook for the first exam. She didn't even go over the reading in class, and her lectures were about all sorts of things, much of which wasn't even related to the reading. Whenever Katie sat down to read a chapter, she found what to her were unfamiliar words and long, complicated phrases. The instructor had suggested that students read with a dictionary at their sides, but who'd ever want to keep stopping to look up words? You'd never finish!

With a midterm exam coming up in her psychology class next week, not to mention a paper and presentation due in her history class, Katie was beginning to panic. She'd only read one of the nine chapters assigned. In fact, she hadn't made it through the first chapter when she got discouraged and gave up. She knew the essay questions would be challenging. Winging it wouldn't work, and choosing to "watch the movie" instead of reading the book wasn't an option. Exactly what did psychology have to do with hospitality, she puzzled, and why did she have to take this course in the first place?

The night before the test, Katie decided to get serious. She sat down at her desk, armed with her yellow highlighter. As she began reading, however, she realized she didn't know exactly what to highlight because she didn't really understand what she was reading. Looking back at the page she had just finished, she saw that she had basically highlighted everything.

Exasperated, Katie told herself that she couldn't go to bed until she'd finished reading everything, no matter when that was. She started with the second chapter, because she'd read the first one, and by morning she'd be as ready as possible. Anyway, whether or not she did well wasn't up to her—it was up to Professor Harris-Black. She was the one making up the test.

Getting a good grade on her Introduction to Psychology midterm exam was probably out of the question, but if she could just manage to pass, Katie knew she would have to settle for that. On the other hand, she secretly hoped that maybe she'd just luck out.

Charles Brutlag/Shutterstock.com

Psychology
Recommended Reading List

Treating the Troubled Family
Ackerman, N.W.
The Care and Feeding of Ideas
Adams, J. L.
Kinds of Minds
Dennett, D.C.
The Dreaming Brain
Clifford, James
Guilty by Reason of Insanity
Lewis, D.O.
The Evolution of Consciousness
Ornstein, R.
Beginner's Guide to Jungian Psychology
Robertson, R.
Anger: The Misunderstood Emotion
Tavris, C.

Lars Lindblad/Shutterstock.com

© Cengage Learning

Study Strategies for Students with Dyslexia

- **Take advantage of multi-sensory learning methods**
  - Study diagrams, look at charts
  - Listen to the instructor's words
  - Combine sensory input to create a more complete picture of the info...

- **Read through superficially first**
  - Look at the title page and intro
  - Note the major headings and bullets
  - Skim through the text to get the main ideas

- **Read out loud**
  - Read out loud while highlighting, then read what you've highligh...
  - Listen to your voice as you emphasize important points

- **Organize your workspace**
  - Categorize papers and books for each subject
  - Color-code assignments and papers to make organization ea...

- **Improve your work methods**
  - Brainstorm at the beginning of a project
  - Set priorities and outline your work strategy

- **Prepare for tests**
  - Be sure to attend all classes leading up to the test
  - Listen for clues and try to determine the format of the t...
  - Get a good night's sleep
  - Take your time

```
ST# 34   OP#        TE#        TR#
          005749801035         3.38
          007065200750         2.97
          007065200750         2.97
          006025835503        14.96
          068113176369         4.97
          002340035457         0.93
          005963148202         3.87
          002340035458         0.93
          005920000731         0.93
                  SUBTOTAL     35.91
               HST 15%          4.88
                     TOTAL     40.79
           DEBIT  TEND         40.79
             CHANGE DUE         0.00
                 RT
GST/HST
Metro Sports Equipment
PURCHASE TRANSACTION RECORD
       40.79
CHEQUING    ************
RRN #:
AUTH #:
00 APPROVED-THANK YOU
TERMINAL ID:
```

Adisa/Shutterstock.com

1. Do you have anything in common with Katie? If so, in what ways, specifically?

2. Katie is probably an intelligent student, but she has decided that she dislikes reading, so she avoids it. How important will reading be as she continues to pursue a college degree? Is she likely to succeed her second time around?

3. How would you characterize Katie as a student? Identify five specific problems described in this case study that could interfere with her college success.

4. Identify three specific things Katie should do to get her college career on track.

Who Needs to Read?

What's so important about reading? Teachers seem to think it's important, but times have changed, haven't they? Now you can just skim predigested information on websites, get a summary of the day's news from television, and watch movies for entertainment. Who needs to read? Look around the next time you're in a doctor or dentist's waiting room. You'll see some people staring at the TV screen mounted on the wall, others plugged into iPods, and still others working with their smart phones. A few may be skimming through magazines, but does anyone ever pick up a book to actually read it cover to cover anymore? Does it matter?

> **No matter how busy you may think you are, you must find time for reading, or surrender yourself to self-chosen ignorance.**
>
> *Confucius, Chinese philospher, 551–479 B.C.E.*

Tomasz Trojanowski/Photos.com

> **Make use of time, let not advantage slip.**
>
> —WILLIAM SHAKESPEARE

Reason 8: They miss opportunities.

When it comes to succeeding in college, you may feel like you're in the middle of a whirlwind, with obligations swirling around you. Everything's a blur, and you begin to lose your focus. You try hard: You buy a planner, fill in due dates, color code the level of priority of various items, and devote a good amount of time to getting yourself organized. Then you lose the planner or leave it in your car. You can't find the time to actually use the planner you've planned to use. Follow through and remember Shakespeare's wisdom: "let not advantage slip"! Turn opportunities into advantages, and keep your focus sharp.

TRY It!

Of course you're busy, but if you took five minutes—or even three—to review your planner before going to bed each night, time management might actually become a habit, rather than something you just can't find the time to do. Try reviewing your planner at the end of each day for one week, note your success by checking off each day you do it, and report your results in class.

Sunday	☐	Thursday	☐
Monday	☐	Friday	☐
Tuesday	☐	Saturday	☐
Wednesday	☐		

The answer, according to many experts, is a definite yes, it does matter![1] Reading helped create civilization as we know it and taught us particular ways of thinking.

One fairly predictable result of doing anything less often is that eventually you may not do it as well. Practice helps you improve. Even an Olympic athlete who doesn't stick with training gets rusty after a while. As students read less, their reading skills deteriorate, and they don't enjoy doing it. On the other hand, the better you get at reading, the more you may enjoy it. Falling down every ten minutes the first time you get on skis isn't all that much fun, but once you can zip down the mountain like a pro, you begin to appreciate the sport.

Like Katie from the "FOCUS Challenge Case," reading may not be your favorite pastime. You may feel about reading like many people do about eating cauliflower. You know it's good for you, but you'd prefer to avoid it. However, this chapter wouldn't be worth its weight in trees if it didn't try to convince you otherwise. One aspect of reading Katie particularly dislikes is that reading is not a social or physical activity. You can read with someone else in the room, of course, or talk about what you read afterward with other people, but basically, reading is something you do alone. It's a solitary activity that involves you, words on a page, an invisible author, and your brain. You need to do it with a minimum of physical movement. Reading while playing a game of volleyball would be tough to pull off.

If you enjoy reading, congratulations! When you settle in with an exciting novel, you can travel to the far corners of the Earth, turn back the clock to previous centuries, or fast-forward to a future that extends beyond your lifetime. Whether or not you enjoy reading, it will be one of the primary skills you need to cultivate in college. According to one study, 85 percent of the learning you'll do in college requires careful reading.[2] First-year students often need to read and comprehend 150–200 pages per week in order to complete their academic assignments.[3]

VARK It!

Aural: Why do (or don't) you enjoy reading? Talk through three reasons aloud with a classmate. Does listening to his or her arguments change your thinking at all?

BE KNOWLEDGEABLE

> **Learn everything you can, anytime you can, from anyone you can—there will always come a time when you will be grateful you did.**
> ~SARAH CALDWELL

Study up. In college, you are encouraged to learn deeply, not just memorize facts. Transfer this principle to the workplace. On the job, learn the ins and outs of your industry. If, for example, you are a healthcare or law enforcement professional, strive to know more than just the details of your day-to-day work. Learn about your department's history, what your employing agency stands for, its vision and values, and the reputation it has earned from customers, clients, and citizens. It's easy to get tunnel vision and lose sight of the bigger picture. But when you keep up on your profession, and even on new events—the "news"—of what's happening in your industry, you show your colleagues and supervisors that you care about your job and your organization's future. All other things being equal, when there's a promotion coming up, the person who has shown a pattern of "studying up" on the organization will be the person most often promoted.

primary sources works written by authors themselves, like the autobiography of Benjamin Franklin (that he wrote himself)

scholarly research articles in academic journals, like the studies about reading and college students, footnoted at the end of the last paragraph

What's more, reading skills go hand in hand with writing and presenting skills, which makes them even more important. The better you get at reading, the more likely you are to achieve academic success. Many of your classes will require intensive reading of complex material, including **primary sources** by original authors and **scholarly research**. If you complete reading assignments, and your classmates don't, think about how much ahead of the nonreaders *you* will be! But how do you learn to become a better, college-ready reader?

Build Your Reading Skills

Some people think reading should be second nature since we've all been doing it for many years now. Someone may understand an article they've just read immediately, whereas others ask, "How did you know that?" about something in the same passage. Learning to understand the process helps. In this chapter, we will look at some clues to help you become a better reader. It's not always as easy as it looks, especially in college. Books and articles you need to read for your classes are often challenging, and they can require a lot of self-discipline to read. Sometimes you may need to read a section or an entire chapter more than once! Perhaps you're in a developmental reading class to boost your skills. Or perhaps a language other than English is your native tongue. If so, this chapter can be especially useful to you.

Recognize the Building Blocks of English

One way to become a better reader is by gaining a deeper understanding of how English works. If you've been speaking it all your life, it seems natural. You open your mouth and speak, without pausing to think over every word choice. But even for many people who learned to speak English as children, *reading* English is a bigger challenge. Just what are some of the specific challenges?

Zedcor Wholly Owned/
PhotoObjects.net/Jupiter Images

Sounds English is spoken as a first or second language by 1.8 billion people. It's the designated "official" language in fifty four countries.[4] English varies somewhat from one region of the country to another. If you live in the South, "pa" (as in "I'll have a slice of apple 'pa'") may be something you eat for dessert; in another part of the country, it's what you call your dad. The sound "tsk" you make when you mean "What a shame . . . " (tsk, tsk . . .) is an actual sound that might be the first sound in a word in other languages. In fact, when you were a six-month-old baby, you could pronounce most any sound that exists in any language. But as you learn to speak as a young child, you discard sounds that aren't a part of your native language.

You already know a good deal about English that you're not even aware you know. If you entered a contest to name a new laundry detergent, you'd automatically use the "rules" for how English operates. For example, you know that you can't clump too many consonants together at the beginning of an English word, and you know that some sounds just don't go together, like "f" and "z." You'd never come up with "Buy new Fzuthoox!" People in the supermarket couldn't even pronounce it to ask a stocker, let alone find it on Aisle 9. If you're a new speaker of English, go to a website on English sounds and play the MP3 files. You can hear "pure" English online.[5]

Syllables Things get more complicated when sounds combine into syllables, like prefixes or suffixes. Some syllables are easy to understand, like the difference between the prefixes *pre-* and *post-* in preseason game versus postseason game. Or you know when you see the word *co-presenters*, that more than one person will be speaking. Other times, syllables are just plain puzzling. For example, typically, the prefix "in-" means "not." But why do *flammable* and *inflammable* mean exactly the same thing? Or when someone says your help is *valuable* or *invaluable*, why are both remarks equally complimentary? Go figure. Learning basic prefixes, suffixes, and word roots can help you decipher unfamiliar words you encounter in your reading.

Zedcor Wholly Owned/
PhotoObjects.net/Jupiter Images

Spelling Here's where many of us get tripped up—and spellcheck isn't always the solution. (Did you notice the missing letter in the word spelled by the blocks?) To make things especially messy, English has many exceptions to its rules.

Zedcor Wholly Owned/PhotoObjects.net/Jupiter Images

Vocabulary Reading is about words. That's why it's important to put some muscle into your vocabulary. When you study a foreign language, your first task is to learn new vocabulary words so that you have something to say: "What time is it?" or "Where is the train station?" or "How much does this cost?" It's just as important, especially in college, to fill your mind with new words, too.

PhotostoGO.com

One of the best things you can do to become a better reader is to make friends with your dictionary. Even though it's annoying to stop every few minutes to look up a word, it's absolutely necessary. Sometimes it's important to break your stride, stop, and look up a word or

> **Force yourself to reflect on what you read, paragraph by paragraph.**
> *Samuel Taylor Coleridge, British poet (1772–1834)*

phrase because what follows in the reading is based on that particular definition. Other times, these strategies might be appropriate:

> Keep a stack of blank index cards next to you, and write down the unknown word or phrase, the sentence it appears in, and the page number. Then when you have a sizable stack, or when you've scheduled a chunk of time, look up the whole stack.

> Try to guess the word's meaning from its **context** that helps to reveal its meaning. Remember Lewis Carroll's "Jabberwocky" poem from *Through the Looking-Glass?* Even though the poem contains fabricated words, when you read it, you infer that something was moving around sometime, somewhere, right?

context words, sentences, and/or paragraphs around an unknown word that help you unlock its meaning

> **'Twas brillig** ['*twas* usually indicates a time, as in 'twas daybreak],
>
> **and the slithy toves** [we don't know what *toves* are, but *slithy* sounds like a combination of slimy and slithering]

Often you can infer a word's meaning from how it's used or from other words around it, but not always. Many of your courses will require you to learn precise meanings for new terms. If you can't detect the meaning from the context, use your dictionary—and see it as a friend rather than an enemy.

EXERCISE 8.1

Word Hunt

You'll notice that this book defines some words that relate to your college education in the margins. That's not only a convenience; they're included to help remind you to stop and look up words as you read assignments for your other courses. Which other words are you looking up on your own as you read FOCUS? Highlight all the additional words you needed to look up in this chapter, and bring your list to class to compare with your classmates' lists.

Learn to "Read between the Lines"

We can move beyond the realm of sounds and words into the realm of sentences, inferences, and main ideas. Being a good reader is like being a good detective. You have to watch for subtle clues and draw conclusions.

Inferences Combining words into "complete thoughts" gives us sentences, and they can be complicated, too. The mere arrangement of words in a sentence can make a difference. From sentences and paragraphs, we create meaning and make **inferences**. For example, language experts talk about the difference between active and passive voice, often detectable by how words are arranged. For example:

inference a conclusion reached from hints or clues about something

Mom (noticing the dent in the front fender): "Did you drive the car?"
You: "Yes, I drove the car." (Active voice, as in "I admit it.")

Compare that answer with "Um, the car was driven [by me]." (Passive voice, as in "the car was practically driving itself . . . ")

There's an inference (or conclusion) behind Mom's question, right? The dent is most likely your fault. Even a slight change in intonation or emphasis can make a difference in what two nearly identical sentences mean. Take this sign, for example, hanging in the men's room of a restaurant: "We aim to please. You aim, too, please."

Two-Way Inferences

Part I. *Find a photo for this quote and bring it to class with you.*

> *"The secret of joy in work is contained in one word— excellence. To know how to do something well is to enjoy it."*
>
> —Pearl Buck, Pulitzer Prize-winning American author, 1892–1973

Part II. *Find a quote for the photo on the right and write it in the caption box below.*

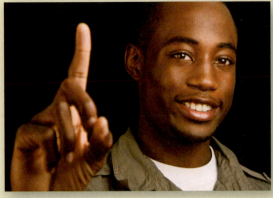

drbimages/iStockphoto.com

Main Ideas Reading longer sections of text requires that we look beyond sentences, down into the "guts" of a passage. This is where reading becomes interesting. How do you move beyond sounds, syllables, and words—the building blocks of language—toward understanding? The place to start is by finding the **main idea**. How do you do that?

> Look for hints that identify the topic or subject being discussed.
> Look for words and phrases that are repeated.
> Look for a thesis statement or topic sentence that summarizes the passage.
> Look for evidence of the author's opinion on what's being written about.

How do you know whether the main idea is worth buying into? Where can you find the evidence that supports the idea and makes it believable?

> Look for statistics, testimony from an expert, or examples.

And how do you detect inferences?

> See whether you can uncover a generalization that could be made after reading the passage.
> Ask how the passage overall relates to you.

main idea central message a writer is trying to get across

VARK It!

Read/Write: After you read these four bullet points to the right, cover them with your hand and list them elsewhere. How many did you remember? How did you do it? Was it by looking for the main idea in each one?

Outside of a dog, a book is man's best friend.
Inside of a dog, it's too dark to read.

Groucho Marx, American comedian, actor, and singer (1890–1977)

Andersen Ross/Brand X Pictures/Jupiter Images

Read Right!

What do we know about reading? How *should* you tackle your many reading assignments in college? Consider these twelve essential points:[6] As you read, put check marks next to items you see as potential areas of improvement for yourself as a reader.

1. _____ **Understand what being a good reader is all about.** Reading isn't a race. Remember the old children's story about the tortoise and the hare? The turtle actually won the race because he plodded along, slowly and steadily, while the rabbit zipped all over the place and lost focus. The moral of that story applies to reading, too. Reading is a process; understanding is the goal. The point isn't simply to make it through the reading assignment by turning pages every few minutes so that you can finish the chapter in a certain amount of time. Reading requires you to back up occasionally, just like when you back up a DVD to catch something you missed: "What did he say to her? I didn't get that."

   Students sometimes mistakenly think that good readers are speed-readers, when it's really about focus.[7] Science fiction writer Isaac Asimov once wrote, "I am not a speed reader. I am a speed understander." On the other hand, reading too slowly can be a problem, too. If you chew (with your eyes) on every word and huff and puff along as you go, your mind can wander. Before you know it, you've let a thousand other thoughts intervene, as Katie Alexander did, and you have no idea where you are. The average reader reads at a rate of approximately 250 words per minute, with a 70 percent comprehension rate. Time yourself on an upcoming paragraph in this chapter, and then see whether you can talk through what you've just read and convince yourself that you understand it.[8] The point is to be efficient so that you can actually get all your reading done for all your classes.

VARK It!

Read/Write: Make a list of which of the twleve items in this section you agree to work on. When you get to class, read a classmate's list and see what reading challenges you have in common.

EXERCISE 8.3

Keeping a Reading Log

Is there a book you'd really like to read? Perhaps it's a book about which people say, "Oh, the book is much better than the movie!" Perhaps it's an author you've heard about: a famous politician, actor, or singer. Select a book to read for pleasure this month, and keep a reading log of how many pages you read each day and how long you stick with it. After you finish the book, write a letter about the book and the process of reading it to your instructor and classmates. There's evidence that reading something you choose yourself can be an important force in becoming a better reader![9]

2. _____ **Take stock of your own reading challenges.** Which of the following are reading issues for you? Rank order your top five, with 1 as your most difficult challenge.[10]

___ boredom	___ surroundings	___ vision	___ fear	___ speed
___ fluency	___ comprehension	___ fatigue	___ time	___ level
___ amount	___ retention	___ interest	___ laziness	___ motivation
___ vocabulary	___ attitude toward reading	___ finding the main point	___ estimating reading time	___ reading everything the same way

© Larry Harwood Photography. Property of Cengage Learning.

Many people find reading challenging. You may have worked with an impatient teacher as a youngster, or you may have been taught using a method that didn't work well for you—factors that still cause you problems today. Reading involves visually recognizing symbols, transferring those visual cues to your brain, translating them into meaningful signals—recording, retaining, and retrieving information (here's where your memory kicks in)—and finally using these meanings to think, write, or speak. Reading challenges can be caused by *physical factors* (your vision, for example) and *psychological factors* (your attitude). If you want to become a better reader in the future, it's a good idea to assess honestly what's most challenging about the process for you right now.[11]

3. _____ **Adjust your reading style.** You shouldn't read a magazine (flip through and find something interesting) the same way you scan a quick text message or devour a novel that you just can't put down. Reading requires flexibility. Contrast these two situations: reading the menu on the wall at your local fast-food joint and poring over the menu at a fancy, high-end restaurant. You'd just scan the fast-food menu in a few seconds, wouldn't you? You wouldn't read word by word and ask: "Is the beef in that burger from grass-fed cattle?" "What, exactly, is in the 'special sauce'?" If you did, the counter clerk would probably blurt out, "Look, are you going to order something or not?" That kind of situation requires quick skimming. But you'd take some time to study the menu at a pricy restaurant you might go to with friends and family to celebrate a special occasion. It's an entirely different situation, and the information is more complicated. And if it's a fancy French restaurant, you might even need to ask the definitions of some terms like *canard* (duck) or *cassoulet* (a rich, hearty stew). That kind of situation requires slow, considered study, word by word. You're going to pay for what you choose, and you want the best results on your investment. That's true about college, too. You're investing in your college classes, so reading right is important!

You'll face an enormous amount of reading in your combined college classes. The question is, what's fast food (to carry through with the example) and what's fine dining? According to research on reading, good readers know the difference and adjust their reading styles.[12]

Reading a popular new detective novel is something you could whip through, but reading the first chapter of your philosophy textbook would require more concentration. Likewise, some of the reading you'll do in college is fast food. You just need to skim to get the main points and then move on to the next homework item on your agenda. However, much of the reading you'll do in college is fine dining. That's why it's important to devote more time to reading and studying than you think you'll actually need. You'll be able to "digest" what you're reading much better.

4. _____ **Have a "conversation" with the author.** In every book you read, the author is trying to convince you of something. Take this book, for example. We have been engaged in a conversation all the way through. What do you know about me? What am I trying to persuade you to think about or do? Even though I'm not right in front of you in person on every page, you are forming impressions of me as you read, and I'm either convincing you to try the suggestions in this book or I'm not. As you read any book, argue with the author ("That's not how I see it!"), question her ("What makes you say that?"), agree with her ("Yes, right on!"), relate something she said earlier to something she's saying now ("But what about …?"). Instead of just coloring with your yellow highlighter, scribble comments in the margins, or keep a running **commentary** in a notebook. Reading is an active process, not a passive one in which the words just float by you. In fact, mark up this page right now! How do you decide what's really important? One thing you can do is ask your instructor in this course to show you his or her mark-ups in this book, and see whether the two of you agree on what's important.

5. _____ **Dissect the text.** Whether you did it virtually online or physically in a real lab, dissecting or cutting up those little critters in your biology class helped you figure out what was what. The ability to dissect text is important in reading. As you read and make notes in the margins, write "what" and "why" statements. Try it: beside each paragraph on this page, write a one-sentence summary statement, a "what" statement. Put the author's words into your own words. Then write another sentence that focuses on why the paragraph is included. Does the paragraph contain *evidence* to make a point? Is it an *example* of something? If you can tackle this recommendation, you'll do wonders for yourself when exam time rolls around.

commentary a record of your opinion

> " It matters, if individuals are to retain any capacity to form their own judgments and opinions, that they continue to read for themselves. "
>
> *Harold Bloom, literary critic*

EXERCISE 8.4

Marginal Notes

Go back through the section of this chapter on reading that you've just finished. Make notes to yourself in the margins (or on another sheet of paper) about why you underlined a word, phrase, or section. Why did you consider that part to be important? Knowing the answers to these questions is more important than the act of "coloring."[13]

6. _____ **Make detailed notes.** You'll be much more likely to actually master a challenging reading assignment if you keep a notebook beside you and take full-blown notes as you read. Go back and forth, detailing main points and supporting evidence. Or go online and use a note-taking tool like evernote.com. The old rule of thumb still applies: read, close the book, and write down what you remember. Then go back into the book and check.[14] The physical act of writing or typing can help you remember it later.

7. _____ **Put things into context.** Reading requires a certain level of what's called **cultural literacy**. Authors assume their readers have a common background. They refer to other books or current events, or historical milestones, and unless you know what they're referring to, what you're reading may not make sense to you. An example you might be familiar with is how the television show *Seinfeld* made real words that everyone now knows and uses, out of fake ones: *yada yada yada*, for example. Those words are now part of our cultural literacy that have meaning for you and everyone you know, probably, but may not for people from another culture. They know the literacy of their own culture instead.

cultural literacy core knowledge—things that everyone knows—that helps put things into context and give them meaning

8. _____ **Don't avoid the tough stuff.** Much of the reading you'll do in college includes complicated sentences that are difficult to work your way through. When you read complex passages aloud, you may stumble because you don't immediately recognize how the words are linked into phrases. But practicing reading aloud is one way you can become more conversant with difficult language. Many instructors teach their students a common approach to reading and studying called SQ3R:

Survey—Skim to get the lay of the land quickly.

Question—Ask yourself "what," "why," and "how" questions. What is this article or chapter about? Why is it included? How might I use this information?

Read (1)—Go ahead now and read the entire assignment. Make notes in the margins or even create a study guide for yourself.

Recite (2)—Stop every now and then and talk to yourself. See whether you can put what you're reading into your own words.

Review (3)—When you've finished, go back and summarize what you've learned.

Try it right now with this section of the chapter, "Read Right."

Survey—What is this section of the chapter about, generally? When you preview a chapter or section of a textbook, look for color, highlighting, italics, layout, bullets—anything that communicates, "This is important!"

Question—What's the point of including it? Why is it here? How can it help you?

Read (1)—Now read the bullets in this section carefully, making "what" and "why" comments in the margins.

Recite (2)—At the conclusion of each bullet, summarize the point out loud, and decide whether this is an item you should put a check mark next to, indicating that it's something you should work on.

Review (3)—When you're finished with the whole section, see whether you can summarize what you've learned from reading it.

Parents should play an inestimable role in children's learning to read and learning to love to read.

—*Barbara Swaby, Literacy expert*

© Larry Harwood Photography. Property of Cengage Learning.

9. _____ **Learn the language.** Every discipline has its own perspective and its own vocabulary. In many of the introductory classes you take, you'll spend a good deal of time and effort learning terms to be used in classes you'll take later. In order to study *advanced* biology, everyone has to learn the same language in *introductory* biology. You can't be calling things whatever you want to call them. You call it a respiratory system, but your classmate calls it a reproductive system. In college you will be introduced to various subjects or disciplines as you take what are often called general education or core courses. It's important to get to know a discipline.

10. _____ **Bring your reading to class.** Some of your instructors will infuse the outside course readings into their lectures. They may preview the readings in class, talk about their importance, or create reading worksheets for use in small groups. If they don't, however, it's up to you to integrate them. Bring up the reading in class, ask questions about it, and find out how it relates to particular points in the lecture. Doing so is an important part of being responsible for your own learning.

11. _____ **Ask for a demonstration.** If a textbook reading assignment for a course baffles you, ask your instructor for a mini-lesson in how to proceed. Sometimes all it takes is for the teacher to give the entire class (or just you) some pointers. For example, the instructor may help you come up with "what" and "why" statements or tell you where she would stop to write something in the notebook she keeps beside her.

12. _____ **Be inventive!** Students who are the best readers invent strategies that work for them. Perhaps you're an auditory learner. Reading assignments aloud might drive people you live with crazy (so find a place where you can be alone), but it might be the perfect way for you to learn. If you're a kinesthetic learner, you might make copies of particular passages from your textbook and lecture notes, and build your own scrapbook for a course. Or cut up the instructor's lecture notes into small puzzle pieces and reassemble them. Using what you know about yourself as a learner is a big part of college success, so don't just do what everyone else does or even follow your instructor's advice word for word, if it doesn't work for you. Figure out what does, and then do it!

> **Reading is to the mind what exercise is to the body.**
>
> *Joseph Addison, British politician and writer (1672–1719)*

Channel Chooser

Today's wide array of technology options requires that we choose how to communicate on a minute-by-minute basis. Your grandparents used to make long-distance calls (which were expensive) or write snail-mail letters. Besides talking face-to-face, those were the primary options. Today, you can call someone, fire off a text, send an e-mail or Tweet, or post on his Facebook wall, for example. The particular choices you make send a message about you and whether you are a competent communicator. The bottom-line question is this: Is one channel more appropriate than another for a specific message? Look at the following scenarios, decide which particular communication channel you'd choose for each situation, and then explain why. Here's an example:

A student employee who has worked with you for two years wins a prestigious college award. You want to congratulate her. Which channel would you choose, and why?

- a. Phone call
- b. Text message
- c. E-mail
- d. Facebook post
- e. Written note
- f. Face-to-face conversation
- g. Tweet
- h. Other

E. I'd send her a handwritten note because that's more personal and special.

Now try some on your own. Be prepared to defend your choices during a class discussion.

1. You need your instructor's approval on the thesis statement you've written for your first essay in English class. You're having trouble coming up with something. _____

2. You want to break up with your romantic partner of six months. You just found out something disappointing that makes you feel hurt and angry. _____

3. You want to let other students know about an exciting campus event this weekend. It is free and open to everyone. _____

4. Your last college tuition bill contained a major error. It's a big mess. _____

5. The low grade you earned on your history paper counted for a large portion of your overall grade and may put you on academic probation. You need to ask your instructor to reconsider.

   _____

6. You want to tell your boss you're not coming in to work today because something came up.

   _____

7. You want to thank your favorite professor for a great learning experience this term.

   _____

Write Right!

Although your reading skills will be critical, they are only one of the several types of communication skills you will need in college. Good writing skills will be essential, too. The question we'll explore next is how to build the writing skills you'll need. If you can do that, you're well on your way to successful outcomes.

An old Doonesbury cartoon may very well hang on the wall in the Writing Center on your campus. It shows two college students. One is tapping away at a typewriter and mutters, "Man, have I got a lot of papers due!" as he types the paper's opening: "Most problems, like answers, have finite resolutions. The basis for these resolutions contain many of the ambiguities which conditional man daily struggles with. Accordingly, most problematic solutions are fallible. Mercifully, all else fails; conversely hope lies in a myriad of polemics. . . ." The other student is looking over his shoulder and asks, "Which paper is this?" to which the writer replies, "Dunno, I haven't decided yet." Obviously, cranking out college papers just for the sake of getting them done isn't the best idea. But, unfortunately, it happens.

Why do some students put off writing assignments? Is it because they worked with a cranky writing teacher in the past? Are they afraid of producing something less than perfect? Have they been unsuccessful at previous writing projects? Or, like Katie, do they simply dislike writing? As shown in the cartoon dialogue above, it's tempting to start with something so general that it could work for literally any paper. Or you may fall into a boring habit, like starting every paper with the dictionary definition for whatever you're writing about. Or perhaps you don't even get that far. You may simply stare at the blank screen until it's time to do something else and move on.

When you have an important writing assignment to do, how do you get started? Many students just sit down at their computers and start typing at midnight the night before the paper is due—hoping for a flash of inspiration—and thereby end up sabotaging themselves. They avoid the upfront work and rationalize that they work better under pressure or they enjoy the adrenaline rush of a tight deadline. But ask yourself this: Would you invite your girlfriend out for dinner before

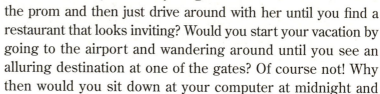

> **I do not like to write—I like to have written.**
>
> *Gloria Steinem, journalist and political activist (1934–)*

the prom and then just drive around with her until you find a restaurant that looks inviting? Would you start your vacation by going to the airport and wandering around until you see an alluring destination at one of the gates? Of course not! Why then would you sit down at your computer at midnight and just start typing? Sure, eventually you will have filled enough pages to reach the assignment's required length, but it's not just about quantity; it's about quality. Quality writing takes patience, focus, and attention to detail. Writing and critical thinking are linked. When you write, you're thinking on paper. Doing it well will help you become a better critical thinker and learner in all your courses.[15]

Writing as a Process

How should the writing process work, ideally? It should involve three basic stages: prewriting, writing, and rewriting.

Prewriting

Think of this analogy: When you speak, you may not know exactly which words will come out, but you have some idea of what you want to say before you open your mouth, right? Just as you prethink what you're going to say, you must prewrite what you're going to put down on paper. In order to do that, you must ask yourself questions like these:

1. **What is the assignment asking me to do?** Let's say one assignment asks you to summarize interviews with three English instructors on campus, to find out what makes them effective teachers. And another assignment asks you to compare and contrast teaching English with teaching math. You'd

> **Finis origine pendet (The end depends on the beginning.)**
>
> *Manlius, first century Roman poet*

go about these two writing papers differently. Zero in on the verbs in the assignment—*summarize* versus *compare* and *contrast,* in this case. The specifics of the assignment must be crystal clear to you, and if you're given a choice of topic, pick something that really interests you.

2. **Who is my audience, and what do I want them to know or do?** You write differently for different audiences—for your composition class or for your blog on being a college student, for example. If you're writing for your blog readers, you may aim for catchy phrasing, short sentences, and an intriguing title. Once you know who you're writing to or for, then you can ask: *What do I want them to know? Am I trying to inform, persuade, or entertain them?* You'll write differently, depending on your specific purpose.

3. **Can I compose a strong thesis statement?** Your paper's **thesis** statement should be the specific argument you're making, summarized into one sentence, ideally. For example, in your paper about good teaching, you might begin with a thesis statement like, "Being a good English teacher requires knowledge, patience, and enthusiasm." Formulating a strong thesis is half the battle.

thesis your main points, summed up in a sentence (or two); what you intend to "prove" in your paper

---

EXERCISE 8.6

Getting Started

The mystery writer Agatha Christie once said, "The secret of getting ahead is getting started." Look at the topics below, and choose one of them. Write the first paragraph for an essay on the topic. If you do this exercise in class, your instructor may only give you one minute, for example, to get something down on paper. When it comes to getting started, one of the biggest challenges is commitment. You have an idea that could go in a dozen different directions, but in order to get started, you have to settle on one direction and run with it. If you do this exercise on your own, set a timer so that you're forced to commit to something. Give it your best effort, and use correct grammar and spelling. The point of the exercise is to practice getting started, which is sometimes the most difficult part of a writing assignment.

   A. *Why I will (won't) be quitting Facebook*

   B. *Why I love to read (or don't)*

   C. *Why writing is good therapy (or why writing stresses me out)*

   D. *Why public speaking is (or isn't) my strong suit*

Now look back at what you have written. Give your paragraph a grade (based on your own standards), or trade with a classmate who chose the same option (A, B, C, or D), and explain the grade you've assigned to him or her. What is the grade based on? Does the writing have a topic sentence that can be identified? Is there a clear thesis statement? If your instructor thinks there is time, try another option. Practicing the art of getting started (when the threat is low because no real grade will be assigned) can be a helpful exercise.

4. Have I done enough research? If you've followed the guidelines provided in your instructor's handout about the assignment, ask: Do I have enough support for my thesis? Have I gathered enough statistics, expert testimony, and examples to persuade my reader?

5. Set in-between target dates for the three stages of writing, even if your instructor doesn't. Some instructors will ask to see your work at each stage of the writing project. If you try to print your paper at 9:50 a.m. for your 10 a.m. class, you can count on something going wrong, like your printer cartridge shriveling up or your hard drive plummeting to an untimely death. To beat the odds, schedule in-between deadlines for yourself for prewriting, writing, and rewriting to keep the project moving along.

Writing

Have you ever experienced writer's block, or nowadays, the "tyranny of the blank screen"? You sit down to write and suddenly go blank? Whatever you call it, you'll be relieved to know there are ways around it.

Some professional writers resort to downright weird strategies to get themselves going. Victor Hugo supposedly wrote in his study at the same time every day—naked! His servant was ordered to lock away all Hugo's clothes until he had finished each day's writing.[16] Apparently, the method worked—look at *Les Misérables.* The paperback version has 1,488 pages! But this technique may not be well received by the people you live with. Just write freely about whatever comes into your head, whether it's on target or not. But how do you start doing that? Take a look at these techniques for starting the writing process.

1. Begin by writing what's on your mind.

> *I'm having trouble starting this paper because there's so much to talk about in terms of good teaching. When I think back over all the English teachers I've ever had, a few really stand out. Mrs. Hampton, in seventh grade, was definitely the worst teacher ever, but Mr. Evans, in eighth grade, was the complete opposite. Just what was it that made him so good? I think it was his knowledge, patience, and enthusiasm. Maybe identifying these three characteristics will help me decide what makes a good English instructor in college.*

Now stop and look at what you've written. Based on your "stream of consciousness," you now have the beginnings of a paper about how being a teacher requires knowledge, patience, and enthusiasm. You're on your way.

2. Begin with the words, "The purpose of this paper is . . ." and finish the sentence. You may be surprised by what comes out of your fingertips.

3. Work with a tutor in your campus Writing Center. Sometimes talking through the assignment with someone else can help, particularly if that person is a writing expert. Or talk it through with a family member.

4. Change the audience. If it helps, assume you're writing your paper to someone who sharply disagrees with you or to a middle school student who just asked you a question. Sometimes thinking about your audience—instead of the topic in the abstract—helps you zero in on the writing task.

ONLINE TechKnow

In "Lazy eyes: How we read online," Michael Agger has come up with a clever list of suggestions for successful online writing:

- Bulleted lists
- Occasional use of **bold** to prevent skimming
- Short sentence fragments
- Explanatory subheads
- No puns
- Did I mention lists?

While amusing, these suggestions are also useful. Writing that will be read online should be easy to read from a small screen—and these suggestions can help busy readers better manage online reading. For reading online coursework or professional sources more effectively, try these suggestions:

- **Choose a default font** designed for screen reading, e.g., Verdana, Trebuchet, Georgia.
- **Minimize reflections.**
- **Use a good monitor.** Don't make it too bright or have it too close to your eyes.

- **Read when you can focus best.** Choose those times of the day when you know you're sharpest for reading, retaining, and learning.
- **Rest your eyes** for 10 minutes every 30 minutes.
- **Take action.** When you've read something you know will be useful, use it right away. Experience strengthens understanding and retention.
- **Be aware of visual cues. Bold text,** *italics*, lists, charts, and graphs can be especially helpful when scanning or reviewing online material.
- **Print out or bookmark pages of special interest.** And be sure to develop a well-organized filing system.
- **Take notes.** Find a useful online note-taking tool (such as Evernote™) or physically write down in your own words what you've found important.
- **Avoid Internet distractions.**[17]

Improve Your Grade
Online Flashcards
Glossary

---

5. Play a role. Imagine yourself as a nationally-known education guru or a network newscaster deciding what to include on the evening news. Separate yourself from the task, and see it from another perspective.

Rewriting

Rewriting is often called "revision," and that's a powerful term. It means not merely changing, but literally re-seeing, re-en*vision*ing your work. Sometimes students think they're revising when they're actually just editing: tinkering with words and phrases, checking spelling, changing punctuation. But the word revision actually means more than that. It means making major organizational overhauls, if necessary. According to many writing experts, that's what you must be willing to

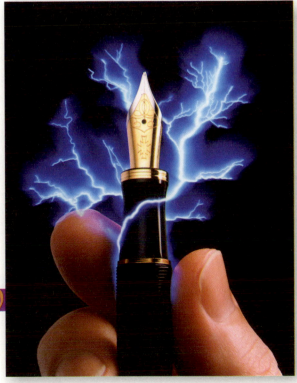

Myron Jay Dorf/Cusp/CORBIS

> ❝ I must write it all out, at any cost. Writing is thinking. It is more than living, for it is being conscious of living. ❞
>
> *Anne Morrow Lindbergh, American writer and aviation pioneer (1906–2001)*

do. You're on a search and destroy mission, if that's what it takes.[18] Try these suggestions for rewriting to see whether they work for you:

1. **Leave it alone.** To help you see your paper as others will see it, set it aside for a while. If you can wait an hour, a day, or a weekend before revising, you'll have distanced yourself long enough to see your writing for what it is, and then improve it. Of course, this suggestion isn't meant to serve as an excuse for a late paper ("I couldn't turn my paper in today because I need to wait before I rewrite."). That won't fly. But coming back later can provide "Aha!" moments. (*What? I wrote that? What was I thinking?*)

2. **Ask for feedback.** One way of discovering how your writing will affect others is simply to ask them. Share your writing before it becomes final.

3. **Edit ruthlessly!** Cutting a favorite phrase or section may feel like lopping off an arm or a leg. But sometimes it must be done. The goal here is to produce the best paper possible, even if it's painful!

4. **Decide on an organizational format.** If you were writing about the three qualities of good English instructors, you'd want to use a *topical* format. Your paper would be organized into three major chunks. If you were writing about the differences between good English instructors and good math instructors, you'd use a *compare and contrast* format. If you were going to present solutions to other instructors about the problems in making English and math classes more exciting, you'd use a *problem-solution* format. Decide how best to present your information, and then follow the format you choose.

5. **Proofread, proofread, proofread!** You may think you have just written an unbelievable essay, but if it's full of mistakes, your instructor may pay more attention to those than to your paper's brilliant ideas. Sometimes it also helps to proofread out loud. Somehow, hearing the words, especially if you're an aural learner, makes errors more obvious. Be proud of the document's final appearance—paper clean, type dark and crisp, margins consistent, headings useful, names and references correct, no spelling errors. And remember that spellcheck, for all its convenience, can let you down. If the word you use is an actual one, but not the right on, it will give its approval, regardless. (Did you catch the spelling error in that last sentence? Spellcheck didn't.)

One more tip. Throughout these three stages, be prepared to move fluidly from one to the other at the slightest provocation. If you're rewriting and you come across some <u>prewriting</u> information (as in *new research*) copy it down and fit it in. If in the <u>prewriting</u> stage you think of <u>writing</u> that strikes you as powerful—a good argument or a well-constructed phrase—write it down.[19]

Build a Better Paper: The Seven C's

In many ways, writing is like building. But instead of using nails, planks, and sheetrock to construct our communication, we use words, sentences, and paragraphs. Here are seven suggestions—all of which begin with C to help you remember them.[20]

1. **Be <u>C</u>lear.** Unfortunately, the English language gives you endless opportunities to write something quite different from what you mean. You can flip

---

VARK It!

Visual: Think about all the organizational formats you know about. Can you develop symbols that help you understand them, like these?

■■■ or ⟷ or ?/☺

VARK It!

Aural: Read the essay in Exercise 8.7 aloud. Before reading the explanation that follows it, can you identify its major problem?

What's in an A?

Take a look at this first-year student's essay and offer the writer advice.

Assignment: Describe a problem you have faced as a first-year student and identify a possible solution.

Last summer, I worked for a bank in my hometown to earn money for college. I was told to show up for the interview at 8:30 a.m. I usually don't get up that early, so on Thursday night, I set my alarm clock, my cell phone alarm, and my clock radio to make sure I didn't miss it. Afterward, I thought that I had really hit it off with the interviewer. When I first got the job on a Friday, I was thrilled. Imagine me working for a bank! I thought that sounded like a prestigious job. When I told my Dad about getting the job, he said that he thought banks really shouldn't hire young people because they don't know the value of money. I decided he was probably kidding around.

But after my first week at Citizen's National Bank, I found myself bored stiff. Counting bills and tallying numbers really aren't that interesting. I did meet this girl named Nicole, and she was kind of cool, but everyone else at the bank was a little standoffish, including my supervisor, Ned. I didn't want to have a strained relationship with my supervisor, so I was friendly with him and serious about getting my work done. But by the following Wednesday, I was ready to quit. I heard about an opening at the coffee shop close to my house that included free food. So that's where I ended up. The moral of this story is to only take a job if you are really interested in the work. And I've definitely decided not to major in accounting.

What's the main problem with this essay? The writer has written about a problem she faced as a first-year student. The essay contains no grammatical errors. But is it likely to earn an A? Actually, the assignment calls for a problem-solution organizational pattern. Instead, it follows a chronological pattern (and then this happened, and then this . . .). What is the writer's thesis statement? Is it the next-to-the last sentence? *Only take a job if you are really interested in the work.* Instead of telling a story from start to finish, how would the essay change if the writer had asked a question like this: What mistakes do students make when looking for a job to help them pay for college? Then the writer could have organized the essay around the thesis statement (only take a job if you are really interested in the work) and found evidence, including her own experience, to back up the claim. Paying attention to the specific requirements of an assignment is the first step in earning a good grade.

through your thesaurus and use a word that sounds good, but isn't recognizable (as in *profundity*, below), or you can write a convoluted sentence that can't be understood. Compare the problems in these two sentences, both of which are unclear:

> *The profundity of the quotation overtook its author's intended meaning.*

> *The writing was profound, but on closer examination, not only was it devoid of content but it was also characterized by a preponderance of flatulent words.*

Yes, many of us will be able to figure out what these sentences mean, though perhaps we'll need to check the dictionary. Sometimes beginning college students decide they must write to *impress* rather than to *express*. They assume instructors like this kind of complicated writing. They think it sounds more academic. Instructors see through that trick. Mean what you say, and say what you mean.

2. Be Complete. Ask yourself what your reader needs to know. Sometimes we're so close to what we're writing that we leave out important information,

What's another word for Thesaurus?

—*Steven Wright, American comedian*

or we fail to provide the background the reader needs to get our meaning. Put yourself in your reader's shoes (or in this case, eyes).

3. Be Correct. If your writing has many grammatical, spelling, and punctuation errors, readers may get the sense that you don't know what you're writing about either. If grammar and punctuation aren't your strong points, ask someone you know who's a crackerjack writer to look over your first draft.

4. Be Concise. In the past, you may have used tricks like enlarging the font or increasing the margins to fill an assigned number of pages. But college students sometimes face the opposite problem: they find that writing less is more challenging than writing more. Think of this formula: A given idea expressed in many words has relatively little impact. But that same idea expressed in few well-chosen and well-combined words can stick in your memory. You could say:

> *"Whether or not a penny, or any amount of money, is earned or saved, it has the same or at least a similar value, fiscally speaking, in the long run."*

Compare that writer's tendency to "run off at the mouth" with Ben Franklin's concise expression:

> *"A penny saved is a penny earned."*

5. Be Compelling. Your writing should be interesting, active, and vivid, so that people want to read what you have to say. Compare these two headlines. Which article would you want to read?

> ❯ *Protests against tuition increases have been led by college student leaders.*
> ❯ *Student leaders urge campus-wide protests over tuition hikes.*

The sentences create different images, don't they? The first sentence makes the situation sound like something that happens every day. The second sentence uses the active voice *(leaders urge campus-wide protests)* instead of the passive voice *(protests have been led),* and the second sentence uses a more descriptive verb *(urge* versus *lead)* and noun *(hikes* versus *increases).* Of course, you can go too far *(Campus leaders spearhead fiery student fury over radical tuition upsurge).* But this principle is a good one to remember.

6. Be Courteous. Courtesy is important in any kind of writing. E-mail and texts are often places where people are discourteous to one another in writing—perhaps because distance gives them courage or they're just plain cranky. Having a meltdown on paper or your computer screen is rarely the right choice.

Steve Cole/Photodisc/Getty Images

> ❝ ❞
>
> **A C essay is an A essay turned in too soon.**
>
> *John C. Bean, Professor of English, Seattle University*

7. Be Convincing. You'll be a more successful writer if you support your views with solid evidence and credible testimonials. Give specific examples to illustrate your point—anecdotes, testimonials from experts, experiences, analogies, facts, statistics—and your writing will be more persuasive.

Keep these seven C's in mind. The secret to learning to think in college is to become a better writer. As you're learning critical thinking skills, you'll also become a more clear, complete, correct, concise, compelling, courteous, and convincing writer.

EXERCISE 8.8

Paper Submission Checklist

Before you turn in a written assignment, make sure you go through this checklist. Consider it to be "insurance" that your paper is fully ready. If you checked the "No" box for any item, explain why in the margin. For example, if you checked "no" for item 3 under "Structure," you might write that the assignment required your opinion, rather than research.

Structure

	Yes	No
1. Did you use a normal-sized font (12-point) and one-inch margins?	☐	☐
2. Did you follow APA or MLA stylesheet rules if doing so was a part of your assignment?	☐	☐
3. Did you include a list of references (bibliography)?	☐	☐
4. Did you number the pages, as instructed, format the title page correctly, and so on?	☐	☐

Content:

	Yes	No
1. Reread the assignment. Did you do what the assignment asked you to do?	☐	☐
2. Did you write for the appropriate audience? (Are you writing for your instructor or for another student or group of students, for example?)	☐	☐
3. Does your paper have a clear thesis statement?	☐	☐
4. Did you do enough research?	☐	☐

5. Circle the organizational pattern you used:

problem–solution, chronological, topical, cause and effect, other (please explain).

_____

	Yes	No
6. Is your writing clear, complete, correct, concise, compelling, courteous, and convincing? Circle the "C's" that are particularly strong.	☐	☐

Process

	Yes	No
1. Have you received feedback on your paper, either formally from a campus Writing Center tutor or informally from someone you know who is a good writer?	☐	☐
2. Have you edited your paper after reading and rereading it (after allowing some time to pass), or after reading it aloud?	☐	☐

3. Other (as indicated by your instructor): _____

4. Based on the grading criteria your instructor has discussed for this paper, what grade would you assign it? Why?   Ⓐ Ⓑ Ⓒ Ⓓ Ⓕ

_____

_____

BOX 8.1

Ten Ways to Oust Speaking Anxiety

High anxiety. It's the curse of many a speaker. Although doing your best on a writing assignment can certainly generate stress, giving a presentation is an even more personal, more immediate look at you and your work. There you are, up front, doing your thing. If you can harness your anxiety and actually look forward to opportunities to speak, you'll build more confidence and get better at doing it. See whether you think the items on this checklist of fear-suppressing suggestions might work for you.

1. **Ready, set, go.** Being unprepared will cause your anxiety to skyrocket, and winging it won't help your presentation fly! The best antidote to anxiety is to prepare, prepare, prepare!

2. **Dress for success.** Confidence in your physical appearance can increase your confidence overall. Wearing a tee shirt that makes a questionable statement or displays a swear word to get attention won't help your grade. Dress up a little; show the audience they're worth the extra effort!

3. **Lighten up.** Humor can ease tensions, both for your audience and for you. But say something funny that occurs to you at the moment, rather than repeating a joke you read on the Internet.

4. **Don't be a mannequin.** Move around. Use gestures. Look at your audience. Talk as if you were having a conversation with each individual in the room alone. Be real, be yourself, and you'll feel more confident. Let your personality shine through.

5. **Practice in your presentation room.** Doing so can help put you at ease during your actual speech.

6. **Find some guinea pigs.** When you practice your presentation, do it in front of a live audience to prepare yourself for natural distractions, like people coughing or sneezing. Practice in front of your best friend or your family. Research indicates your grade is likely to go up.[21]

7. **Channel your energy.** Harness your fear, and turn it into positive energy that makes you more dynamic.

8. **Visualize success.** When you see yourself giving your presentation in your mind's eye, visualize success, not failure.

9. **Remember that mistakes are made to be corrected.** If disaster strikes, remember that how you handle it is what's important. Perhaps you fear making a "tip of the slung." Don't worry; instead, make the most of a few moments of lightheartedness!

10. **If you can't shake it, fake it.** If your nerves get the better of you, fake it. Pretend you're confident. Before you know it, your confidence may actually begin to rise.

In a Manner of Speaking . . .

When your assignment involves a presentation, instead of or in addition to, a paper, your public speaking skills will be on the line. You may be thinking something like this: *I'm not going to be a public speaker. I'm going to be a surgeon. I'll spend all my time hunched over an unconscious person lying on an operating table. All I'll need to know how to do is hold a scalpel with a steady hand.* But is that really true? What about the communicating you'll need to do with totally conscious hospital administrators, other doctors, and patients before and after surgery?

Most people think of public speaking as an episode, a one-time event. You stand up to give a speech, and when you're finished, you sit down. But actually, there's a sense in which all the speaking we do is public. By contrast, what would *private* speaking be? Thinking? On the job, you'll communicate with others every day. Unless you join a profession that requires you to take a vow of silence, you'll be speaking publicly all the time!

When you prepare for a presentation in one of your classes, what is your primary goal? To impress your instructor? To amaze your classmates? To get your presentation over with? How about to give the very best presentation you can give?

Many of the suggestions in this chapter apply to both writing and speaking. As both a writer and a speaker, you should be clear, complete, correct, concise, compelling, courteous, and convincing. You should choose an organizational pattern and use it to help your audience understand what you're saying. (Unlike reading a written paper, they only have one chance to hear your words go by.) You must have a strong thesis in a speech, just as you must in a paper. But let's examine some other advice that relates primarily to speaking. Use these suggestions to create winning presentations that set you apart in all your courses.[22]

1. **Purpose.** What is the purpose of your presentation? Often the purpose is given to you directly by your instructor: Prepare a five-minute speech *to inform*. . . . But other assignments will allow you to select your own purpose: "The Trials and Tribulations of a Student Mom" (to inform), "Sustainability in an Age of Materialism" (to persuade), "Five Sure-Fire Ways to Flunk Out of College . . . Not!" (to entertain), "How Being Class President Can Change Your Life" (to inspire). Knowing exactly what you're trying to accomplish helps!

2. **People.** Who will be your listeners? Generally, you'll be speaking to an audience of students in your classes, right? But what are their specific characteristics as they relate to your purpose? For example, if you're addressing parents and friends at graduation, you might create a different speech than the one you'd present to your co-members of a student club.

> **The trouble with talking too fast is you may say something you haven't thought of yet.**
>
> *Ann Landers, syndicated advice columnist (1918–2002)*

3. **Place.** Where will you deliver your presentation? The location of your presentation may affect its tone and style. A presentation you might give to a group of tourists at a national park would allow you to be informal, and your visual aid would be the scenery around you. But if you gave the same presentation as a geography major to high school seniors, you'd be more formal and scholarly, using a PowerPoint presentation or maps in the classroom.

4. **Preparation.** How should you prepare your speech? Developing the content of a speech is often similar to writing a paper. You'll need to develop a thesis statement and find support for each point by researching examples, statistics, and expert testimonies. Depending on the assignment, you might write out your speech or create a set of PowerPoint slides with talking points. Or you may find it helpful to create a storyboard, a map, or a flowchart of your slides on paper before moving to the screen (see Figure 8.1). Then, after you know your basic format, you'll need to come up with an attention-grabbing introduction and a memorable conclusion. Or think about it this way: One of the best ways to prepare is to make sure your presentation is SHARP. SHARP stands for stories, humor, analogies ("this" is like "that"), references (or quotes), and pictures/visuals.[23] SHARP is a good formula for a successful presentation, one that your audience will remember. Imagine that you decided to give a presentation about "exiting from college and finding a job."

FIGURE 8.1

Storyboarding a PowerPoint

You might start with a horrendous story (S) about a plane trip you just took, where you ran through three airports but missed all three connections (H); compare a plane trip to the journey in college toward a "career destination" (A); include the quote "Map out your future, but do it in pencil. The road ahead is as long as you make it. Make it worth the trip" (Jon Bon Jovi); and include this photo you took with your cell phone camera on the plane.[24] You'd have the makings of a very SHARP presentation.

iStockphoto.com/Baran Özdemir

5. **Planning.** What planning should you do? For example, are visual aids available, or do you need to bring your own? Is there a plug in the room, if you need one? Should you bring a backup of your presentation on a flash drive? Should you test the LCD projector to make any necessary adjustments? Many a speaker has been unnerved at the last minute by some overlooked detail.

6. **Personality.** How can you connect with the audience? How can you demonstrate your competence, charisma, and character to your listeners? Eye contact is important. Look at each person individually, if possible. Inspire trust by telling a story or relating your topic to some aspect of your own experience. Rather than playing a role, act natural and be yourself.

7. **Performance.** This last P relates to delivering your presentation. Rehearsal is important (although too much rehearsal can make your presentation sound sing-songy and memorized). Beware of bringing a full written draft to the podium. If you do, you may be tempted to read it, which is the last thing you want to do. Aim for a dynamic delivery, both verbally and nonverbally, that helps keep your listeners listening.

One final thing: After you've finished a paper or presentation, you're not really done. It's time to sit back and think about what you've accomplished. Are you pleased with your work? What have you learned? What will you do differently next time? If you do this every time you finish a project, you'll build your skills over time and take them with you to your other college classes, a university, or the world of work.

BOX 8.2

PowerPoint or PowerPointless? Five Ways to Make Your PowerPoint Pop

College presentations usually involve visual aids, often electronic ones. These e-tools can serve as helpful cues for you during your presentation. Although you'd never want to simply read your slides to an audience, glancing quickly at a slide can serve as a cue card and remind you of what you want to say. But how professionally your visual aids are created and used can make or break your presentation—and your grade. Your instructor may allow you to use Keynote (for Macs), Prezi (an online tool that moves and shows the relationships between concepts), or PowerPoint, the industry standard. Each of these tools has pros and cons, but the one we'll concentrate on here is PowerPoint. PowerPoint is an excellent and neutral tool. How you use it makes all the difference. Bulleted words or phrases with the same PowerPoint background, one after the other, aren't nearly as engaging as SHARP ones, Prezi's (prezi.com), or Keynote presentations delivered from your iPad, using an iPhone app as a slide advancer. Start to perfect your skills now by considering these five ways to make your PowerPoint "pop."

1. **DO use your whole brain.** When it comes to designing PowerPoint presentations, the challenge is to combine useful information with attractive design. Think of it as using both sides of your brain—your logical left hemisphere and your creative right hemisphere. For example, if you're giving a presentation on teaching young children, you might want to use a font that looks *like this* (children's writing) on your title slide. (Just make sure it's legible from a distance. A good rule of thumb is to use 24-point font size or larger and keep your fonts simple unless you have a particular reason to change them.) You also might want to include a high-quality graphic like this one here.

2. **DO use color to your advantage.** Choose an attractive color scheme and stick to it. That doesn't mean that every background on every slide must be the same. In fact, if you do that, your listeners may die of boredom. But if your title slide is blue, orange, and white, then use one, two, or all three of these colors in some hue or shade on every slide. Some speakers create PowerPoint presentations that seem fragmented and messy because the individual slides aren't connected visually.

3. **DON'T crowd your slides with text.** Your listeners won't pay attention to you if they're spending all of their time reading. Be kind, and spare them the trouble by limiting the text on your slides. Some of the most deadly PowerPoint presentations are those in which the speaker turns around, faces the screen, and flies through slide after slide. The only way your listeners can live through that is if oxygen masks drop from the overhead compartments!

4. **DON'T let your slides steal the show.** Always remember that YOU are the speaker. Your slides shouldn't be so fascinating that your audience ignores you. Gunshots and screaming sirens shouldn't be used as sound effects unless, of course, you're speaking on gun control or ambulance response times. Any special effects should be used sparingly to make a point, rather than to shock your listeners.

5. **DO include a bibliography slide, both for words and images.** Some students assume that plagiarism only pertains to writing papers. Not so! Always give credit where credit is due. List your references, either on individual slides (if you use a direct quote, cite it) or on one slide at the end.

ardni/Shutterstock.com

What's In **YOUR** Briefcase?

COMMAND CRUCIAL CONVERSATIONS

Imagine this: You're appealing to your professor to change an exam grade: "Why did you give me a D? Now I'm going to lose my scholarship." "Open mouth, insert foot." Often during challenging conversations, you know intuitively that your communication choices are crucial. You also know intuitively (by that sinking feeling in the pit of your stomach) when you've said the wrong thing. Unfortunately, by implying that your poor grade is your professor's fault, you've probably "failed the test." You're unlikely to get the results you were seeking. There are ways in which crucial conversations are tests of our communication skills, and it's clear that most of us don't always know how to get the "grade" we want.

When is a conversation crucial instead of just plain important? Crucial conversations are said to be those with results that could potentially change the quality of your life. According to experts, crucial conversations have three components: high stakes, strong emotions, and differing opinions—a potentially toxic triangle.[25]

At times like these, results are on the line, and sometimes our communication skills don't rise to the occasion. We underreact with silence; overreact with a meltdown; or choose a safe, but inappropriate, medium (like sending a text message that says, "The wedding is off," for example). Other times, we somehow get it right. The question is this: How do we develop the communication skills we need for these inevitable crucial conversations? When we're at our best, we demonstrate a willingness to speak up when we disagree, deal with issues head-on rather than resorting to the "silent treatment," and dive into dreaded conversations with bravery and resolve rather than fear. Underneath it all is this advice: "Engage brain before opening mouth." Intentionality and planning make a crucial conversation work.[26]

In your coming career, crucial conversations will be nothing short of crucial. When you're seeking an opportunity, responding to criticism, giving your boss feedback, asking a difficult teammate to cooperate, or requesting help, your career may be on the line. How well you communicate will make all the difference.

Can the lesson you just identified be applied to your future career in the workplace? If so, how?

_____

_____

_____

3 INSIGHT *Now* What Do You Think?

At the beginning of this chapter, Katie Alexander, a frustrated and disgruntled student, faced a challenge. Now after reading this chapter, would you respond differently to any of the questions you answered about the "FOCUS Challenge Case"? Using what you learned in the chapter, write a paragraph ending to Katie's case study. What are some of the possible outcomes for Katie?

4 ACTION Your Plans for Change

1. What, in particular, from this chapter will you put to the test immediately in some other class?

2. In what ways might the information in this chapter help you become more successful in this class? What results are you expecting and how will you achieve them?

Developing Memory, Taking Tests

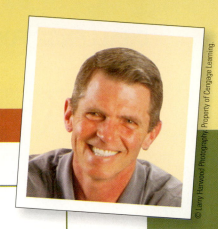

READINESS CHECK

How this chapter relates to **YOU**

1. When it comes to memorizing material for tests and taking exams in college, what do you find most challenging, if anything?

Focusing on test material

Developing good memorization strategies

Going completely blank when I see the test

Not showing what I really know on tests

Getting nervous about exams

2. What is most likely to be your response? Circle it.

I'll be open to learning how to improve my skills.

I'll wait and see if this chapter helps me.

I'll get help from a support center on campus.

Eventually, I'll just figure it out on my own.

3. Talk to a specialist about possible test anxiety to increase your likelihood of success? Will you do it this term?

Example: Talk to a specialist about possible test anxiety. Yes!

How **YOU** will relate to this chapter

What are you most interested in learning about? Put check marks by those topics.

☐ How your memory works like a digital camera

☐ How to improve your memory, using twenty different techniques

☐ Why you should change your thinking about tests

☐ What to do before, during, and after a test

☐ What text anxiety is and what to do about it

☐ How to take different kinds of tests differently

☐ How cheating can hurt your chances for success

• How motivated are you to learn more about getting the right start in college? (5 = high, 1 = low) ____

• How ready are you to read now? ____ (If something is in your way, take care of it if you can; zero in and focus.)

• How long do you think it will take you to complete this chapter? If you start and stop, keep track of your overall time. ____ hour(s) ____ minutes

KEVIN BAXTER

Darko Kovacevic/
Shutterstock.com

©Larry Harwood Photography. Property of Cengage Learning.

As he got ready for work one morning, it finally hit him. He took a long, close look at himself in the mirror, and frankly, he didn't like what he saw. Kevin Baxter was a forty-year-old father of three who was dissatisfied with his life. Yes, he earned a decent income as a construction foreman, and yes, his job allowed him to work outdoors. To Kevin, being cooped up in an office from eight to five every day was something he'd always wanted to avoid. Being outdoors, where you could see the sky, feel the sunshine, and breathe fresh air, was what made him feel alive. The world outside was where he wanted to be, yet at the same time, he knew the world inside his head was withering away. Kevin realized he hadn't really learned much since high school. *I feel brain-dead; that's the best way to describe it,* he frequently thought. *I've run out of options, and I'm stuck.*

Clearly, dropping out of college his first semester twenty-two years ago had been the wrong decision for him. But at the time, he'd convinced himself that he wasn't college material. Besides, college had seemed so expensive, and he desperately wanted to be on his own and begin a life with Carol, his high school sweetheart. Unfortunately, that hadn't worked out well, either. Now he was a single dad whose children lived out of state. He very rarely saw them. Nothing had quite turned out as he had planned.

But in a way, his divorce had jolted him into a midlife crisis. He needed to change things, and going back to college to earn a degree in architecture was the right decision for him now. He was sure of it. Working in construction, he frequently saw flaws in the architects' plans, and he'd often come up with better ideas. *This is a chance to start over again,* he thought to himself, *and I'm going to do it right this time.* So at forty, he quit his construction job and enrolled in the local college. His first-term courses consisted of Introduction

Nadezda/Shutterstock.com

Buturlimov Paul/Shutterstock.com

Image copyright Ingvar Bjork, 2010. Used under copyright from Shutterstock.com.

Image copyright Dmitriy Shironosov, 2010. Used under copyright from Shutterstock.com.

chapter 10
Building Relationships, Valuing Diversity

READINESS CHECK

How this chapter relates to YOU

1. When it comes to building relationships and valuing diversity in college, what do you find most challenging, if anything?

Developing emotional intelligence

Communicating in important relationships

Appreciating the varied aspects of diversity

Developing cultural intelligence

Understanding the impact of globalization

2. What is most likely to be your response? Circle it.

I'll be open to learning how to improve my skills.

I'll see whether this chapter helps me.

I'll pay particular attention to these issues in my classes.

Eventually, I'll just figure it out on my own.

3. What would you have to do to increase your likelihood of success? Will you do it this term?

Example: Find a mentor, counselor, or instructor to talk about these issues. Yes!

How YOU will relate to this chapter

What are you most interested in learning about? Put check marks by those topics.

- ☐ Whether your emotional intelligence can be improved
- ☐ How to improve communication with people you care about
- ☐ Why diversity enriches our lives
- ☐ What cultural intelligence is and why it's important
- ☐ How globalization changes our world

- How motivated are you to learn more about getting the right start in college? (5 = high, 1 = low) ____
- How ready are you to read now? ____ (If something is in your way, take care of it if you can, zero in, and focus).
- How long do you think it will take you to complete this chapter? If you start and stop, keep track of your overall time. ____ hour(s) ____ minutes

Serena Jackson

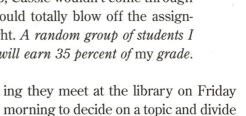

As Professor Arnold read the group members' names aloud for the assigned presentations in Introduction to Mass Media on Monday, it was all Serena could do to keep her cool. She listened intently: "Group 1: Jessica Andrews, Jordan Nelson, Cassie Phillips, and Serena Jackson." Even as the names were coming out of Professor Arnold's mouth, Serena could see how it would all play out. Jessica would want to run the group, Cassie wouldn't come through on her part, and Jordan would totally blow off the assignment. *Great*, Serena thought. *A random group of students I don't even know very well will earn 35 percent of my grade.* It just didn't seem fair.

They had the last fifteen minutes of class to exchange cell phone numbers and e-mail addresses, which everyone did. There was even some excitement in the room. At least the group presentations would break the repetitive cycle of weekly lectures. But the very thought of speaking in front of the class made Serena's heart race, and now with questionable teammates, things were looking grim. She'd only earned a B on the first exam, and she desperately needed an A in this class to balance out the C she knew she'd get in calculus.

Serena sent off an e-mail to the group on Wednesday, suggesting they meet at the library on Friday morning to decide on a topic and divide up the work. Jessica wrote back immediately, "I work off campus on Friday mornings." Cassie took her time, but she finally replied on Sunday, "I'm out of town this weekend. Let's wait until next week." Jordan didn't write back at all. "You e-mailed me?" he said with a puzzled look on his face in class on Monday. "Oh, I never check my e-mail. I only respond to texts." Serena planned to catch everyone's attention to set a new meeting time as class let out, but Cassie wasn't there, and the other two had bolted by the time she zipped up her backpack.

On Tuesday morning, it was Jessica who texted everyone: "Meeting in UC 213 tomorrow at 2. I know that works for three of us." *Three of us?* Serena asked herself. No one had even checked with

Dmitry Rukhlenko/Photos.com

© Larry Harwood Photography. Property of Cengage Learning

Source: YouTube, LLC

her. Were they working around her? Her calc class met from 1:15 to 3:30, and she couldn't afford to skip it. She texted back, "I have class then." "No worries," Jessica replied. "We three will get started. Then we can just circulate a PowerPoint, and talk through it for the actual presentation." Serena replied, "I could meet at 4. Can you?" "No, Cassie has a doctor's appointment, and I have a student government meeting." What was the group's topic? Who was doing what? Were they trying to exclude her, or did it just seem that way? Sometimes Serena felt slightly uncomfortable being the only minority student in this class, and at her school, that happened fairly often.

Although she didn't want to bother Professor Arnold, Serena finally decided to alert her to the group's issues. But when she dropped by during office hours, Professor Arnold defended the assignment. "I know group projects can be challenging," she said. "But you'll be working through team issues like these in the workplace in a few years—and you'll be 'graded' on the team's results. I could step in and try to fix things, but you four should work through it yourselves. It's good practice for '*the real world.*'" Although Serena knew Professor Arnold was right in the long run, her wisdom didn't help right now.

At least the group had updated her after they met. Jessica's e-mail read, "We only had time for a half-hour meeting, but we decided our presentation would be about the best Super Bowl commercials of all time. Cassie and I will research the communication and marketing databases, Jordan will find examples of commercials on the Internet, and your job will be doing the PowerPoint slides."

A week before their presentation was due, the group finally managed to agree on a time that everyone could meet—a waste of time, as it turned out. No one was prepared. Jessica spent the meeting time texting her boyfriend. Jordan was on his phone with somebody, and Cassie sat there scarfing down a huge burrito. Somehow they managed to get nothing done in an hour and twenty minutes. The presentation was next Monday, and no one else seemed to be the least bit interested in doing a good job. "Group projects are a pain," Jessica tweeted after class. "Let's just get through it." What Serena's mother had always told her appeared to be true: "If you want to get something done *right*, do it yourself." But "doing it herself" wasn't an option for Serena's group project, and, most likely, neither was getting an "A."

Intro to Mass Communication

Professor Karen Arnold

Oleksiy Mark/Photos.com

Vjom/Shutterstock.com, Source: Twitter, Inc.

9:15 AM

Home Tweet

Jessica
@twitter

Group projects are a pain. Let's just get through it.

27 seconds ago

Home   Connect   Discover   Me

© Cengage Learning

Name: Serena Jackson C

MAT 181
CALCULUS 1
Test One

1. $\frac{d}{dx}(x^n) = nx^{n-1}$ ✓

2. $\frac{d}{dx}(\sin^{-1} u) = \tan x$ ✗

3. $\frac{d}{dx}(\sin x) = \cos x$ ✓

4. $\frac{d}{dx}(\ln u) = \frac{1}{u}\frac{du}{dx}$ ✓

5. $\frac{d}{dx}(\sec x) = \sec x + \cos x$ ✗

6. $\frac{d}{dx}(\cot^{-1} x) = \neq x$ ✗

Intro to Mass Communication
Syllabus

Class: COMM 1015
Instructor: Arnold, Jennifer   **Office:** N507 **Ph:** 867-5309
Bldg: Centennial Hall **Room:** 324 **Days:** MT **Time:** 01:40PM-04:20PM

Textbook: Straubhaar, Joseph; LaRose, Robert; Davenport, Lucinda. *Media Now: Understanding Media, Culture, and Technology,* 8th Ed. Boston: Cengage Learning.
ISBN: 1133311369

Overview: This survey course will explore mass communication media, its structures, theories, and functions, and how media interacts with modern life. COMM 1015 will also delve into the history of mass media and the future of mass media in the face of new technologies.

Grading:

Assignment:	Points Possible:
Reaction Papers - 10 total	
Class Participation	50
Exam 1	50
Exam 2	100
Group Project	100
TOTAL:	300
	600

Course Schedule:

Week 1

1. Do you have anything in common with Serena? As you read her story, do you identify with portions of it—or do you know anyone else in college who would?

2. Serena's life is complicated, just like the lives of many college students. Identify five specific problems described in this case study that could interfere with her college success.

3. To have done so well in school, Serena must be an intelligent person. But is her emotional quotient (EQ) different from her intelligence quotient (IQ)? Why or why not?

4. Identify three things Serena should do to get her college success and her life on track.

The Heart of College Success

EXERCISE 10.1

How Would You Respond?

Read these five scenarios and identify your most likely reactions.[1]

1. You peer over a classmate's shoulder and notice she has copied your online response from a class chat and submitted it as her paper in the course, hoping the instructor won't notice. What do you do?
   a. Tell the student off to set the record straight, right then and there.
   b. Tell the instructor that someone has cheated.
   c. Ask the student where the research for the paper came from.
   d. Forget it. It's not worth the trouble. Cheaters lose in the end.

2. You're riding on a plane that hits a patch of extreme turbulence. What do you do?
   a. Grab hold of the person in the next seat and hold on for dear life.
   b. Close your eyes and wait it out.
   c. Read something or watch the movie to calm yourself until things improve.
   d. Panic and lose your composure.

3. You receive a paper back in your toughest course and decide that your grade is unacceptable. What do you do?
   a. Challenge the instructor immediately after class to argue for a better grade.
   b. Question whether you're really college material.
   c. Reread the paper to honestly assess its quality and make a plan for improvement.
   d. Deemphasize this course and focus on others in which you are more successful.

4. While kidding around with your friends, you hear one of them tell an offensive, racial joke. What do you do?
   a. Decide to ignore the problem and thereby avoid being perceived as overly touchy.
   b. Report the behavior to your advisor or an instructor.
   c. Stop the group's conversation. Make the point that racial jokes can hurt and that it's important to be sensitive to others' reactions.
   d. Tell your joke-telling friend later that racial jokes offend you.

5. You and your romantic partner are in the middle of a heated argument, and you're losing your temper. What do you do?
   a. Stop, think about what you're trying to communicate, and say it as clearly and neutrally as possible.
   b. Keep at it because if the issue generated that much emotion, it must be important to get to the bottom of it.
   c. Take a twenty-minute time out and then continue your discussion.
   d. Suggest that both of you apologize immediately and move on.

College is a time of transition; it can be an emotionally challenging time. Even if you're a returning student who's been on your own for years, college will require you to make some major adjustments in your life. Trying to do so without the internal resources you need may be overwhelming, as it was for Serena Jackson in the "FOCUS Challenge Case." When it looked as if the relationship that was most important to her was falling apart, so did she.

> ## Our emotions are the driving powers of our lives.
>
> *Earl Riney, American clergyman (1885–1955)*

Here's a fundamental truth: College isn't just about your head. Yes, academics are the reason you're in college, but your heart plays a critical role in your success, too. From friends to family members, to professors, to romantic partners, how you handle relationships can make or break you academically. Emotional reactions to troubling circumstances have the raw potential to stop you dead in your tracks. As may be the case for Serena Jackson, who most likely has the *academic* skills required for success, *nonacademic* issues can interfere.

In college and in life, your EQ (emotional quotient), or *emotional intelligence*, can be just as important as your IQ (intelligence quotient). Studies show that first-year students often feel overwhelmed and lonely. Begin now to refine the emotional skills you'll need to face whatever challenges come your way.

Perhaps you've found yourself in settings such as those described in Exercise 10.1. You might need more actual details to make the best choice in these five scenarios, but according to some experts, choice (c) is the most emotionally intelligent one in each case. Do you agree? How do *you* make decisions such as these? What constitutes an emotionally intelligent response?

© Larry Harwood Photography. Property of Cengage Learning

What Is Emotional Intelligence?

Many experts believe that intelligence takes many forms. Rather than a narrow definition of intelligence, they believe in Multiple Intelligences: Linguistic, Logical-Mathematical, Spatial, Kinesthetic, Musical, Interpersonal, Intrapersonal, and Naturalistic.[2] Emotional intelligence may well be a combination, at least in part, of *intrapersonal* and *interpersonal* intelligences.

Emotional intelligence is a set of skills that determines how well you cope with the demands and pressures you face every day. How well do you understand yourself, empathize with others, draw on your inner resources, and encourage the same qualities in people you care about? Emotional intelligence involves having people skills, a positive outlook, and the capacity to adapt to change. Emotional intelligence can propel you through difficult situations.

The bottom line? New research links emotional intelligence to college success, and learning about the impact of EI in the first year of college helps students stay in school.[3] Or consider this research finding: strong emotional intelligence helps you achieve a higher GPA when you take online courses.[4] That makes sense because the self-discipline required is related to the very definition of EI.

As you read about the five scales of emotional intelligence, begin thinking about yourself in these areas. As each scale is introduced, ask yourself whether you agree or disagree with the sample statement from a well-known emotional intelligence instrument as it pertains to you.[5]

VARK It!

Read/Write: Summarize the definition of emotional intelligence in a 140-character tweet. Some people think using Twitter can potentially help you condense your thoughts and make you a better writer.

Intrapersonal Skills (Self-Awareness)

"It's hard for me to understand the way I feel." Agree or disagree?

Are you in tune with your emotions? Do you fully realize when you're anxious, depressed, or thrilled? Or do you just generally feel up or down? Are you aware of layers of emotions? Sometimes we show *anger,* for instance, when what we really feel is *fear.* Are you emotionally strong on your own, rather than depending on others for your happiness? Do you realize that no one else can truly make you happy, that you are responsible for creating your own emotions? How well do you understand yourself and what makes you tick?

Interpersonal Skills (Relating to Others)

"I'm sensitive to the feelings of others." Agree or disagree?

Are you aware of others' emotions and needs? Do you communicate with sensitivity and work to build positive relationships? Are you a good listener? Are you comfortable with others, and do you have confidence in your relationships with them?

Stress Management Skills

"I feel that it's hard for me to control my anxiety." Agree or disagree?

Can you productively manage your emotions so that they work *for* you and not *against* you? Can you control destructive emotions? Can you work well under pressure? Are you in control, even when things get tense and difficult?

Adaptability Skills

"When trying to solve a problem, I look at each possibility and then decide on the best way." Agree or disagree?

Are you flexible? Do you cope well when things *don't* go according to plan? Can you switch to a new plan when you need to? Do you manage change effectively? Can you anticipate problems and solve them as they come up? Do you rely on yourself and adapt well?

General Mood

"I generally expect things will turn out all right, despite setbacks from time to time." Agree or disagree?

Are you optimistic and positive most of the time? Do you feel happy and content with yourself, others, and your life in general? Are you energetic and self-motivated? Do people tell you you're pleasant to be around?

Source: From EQ-i:HEd. Used by permission of Multi-Health Systems Inc.

Emotional intelligence affects every part of our lives. For example, researchers study related concepts: "hardiness," "**resilience**," and "**learned optimism**."[6] Some people are more resistant to stress and illness. Hardy, resilient, optimistic people are confident, committed to what they're doing, feel greater control over their lives, and see hurdles as challenges. Emotional intelligence is part of the reason why.

resilience the ability to bounce back from difficulties

learned optimism a way of thinking that helps you stay optimistic and potentially improves your mental and physical health

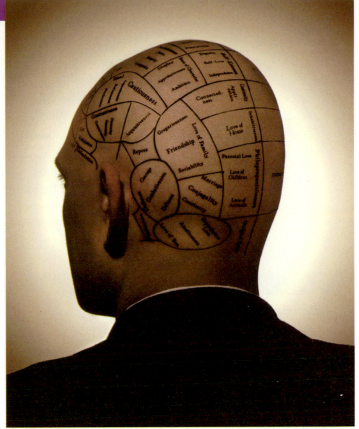

William Whitehurst/Corbis Edge/Corbis

Looking back at the "FOCUS Challenge Case," we can see that Serena Jackson probably lacks strong emotional intelligence. Her level of skill in these five areas may help explain her difficulty controlling her moods, managing stress, adjusting to college, and being positive and optimistic about working through her problems. Will she be academically successful? What do you think?

Emotional intelligence and its five scales are important in all aspects of life, including your future career.[7] When *Harvard Business Review* first published an article on the topic in 1998, it attracted more readers than any article in the journal's previous forty years. When the CEO of Johnson & Johnson read it, he ordered copies for the company's 400 top executives worldwide.[8]

Why? Emotional intelligence is a characteristic of true leaders. Immediately after the first shock of the September 11, 2001, tragedy, the world tuned in to a press conference with New York's Mayor Rudy Giuliani. He was asked to estimate the number of people who had lost their lives in the World Trade Center collapse that day, and his reply was this: "We don't know the exact number yet, but whatever the number, it will be more than we can bear." In that one sentence, Giuliani demonstrated one of the most important principles of true leadership. Leaders inspire by touching the feelings of others.[9]

Can Emotional Intelligence Be Improved?

Everyone wants well-developed emotional intelligence, but how do you get it? Can EI be learned? Although researchers admit that genes definitely play a role, most experts believe that emotional intelligence can be increased. One of the most convincing pieces of evidence is from a study that followed a group of students over seven years. Students assessed their emotional intelligence, selected particular areas to strengthen, and then each created an individual plan to develop them. Seven years later, their competencies remained high.[10]

If you believe what this chapter says about the importance of emotional intelligence and college success, you're probably asking yourself what you can do

VARK It!

Visual: To help you remember the five EI scales, select a photo or image of your own to represent each one.

about it. Are the skills related to emotional intelligence something *you* can work to improve?[11] And if so, how?

Seek honest input from others. It's hard to be objective about yourself. But it is possible to ask for the opinions of others who interact with you regularly. How do they see you? Use other people as coaches to help you see which aspects of your emotional intelligence need strengthening.

Find an EI mentor. A mentor on the job is someone who's older and more experienced than you are and can help you navigate your way through tough problems and manage your college or professional career. Mentors help, and an EI mentor—someone with EI skills you admire—can provide you with important advice about handling challenging emotional situations. Develop a personal relationship with someone whose wisdom you admire, be honest about your problems, and follow the guidance you get.

> **What's going on in the inside shows on the outside.**

Earl Nightingale, success consultant

Robert Recker/zefa/Corbis

Complete an assessment tool. Other than just feeling up or down, or thinking back on on how you handled problems when they came up, is there a way to know more about your own emotional intelligence? The oldest and most widely used instrument to measure emotional intelligence is the Emotional Quotient Inventory, the EQ-i, from which the sample statements for the five scales we have been discussing come. The instrument asks you to respond to various statements by indicating that they are "very seldom true of me" to "very often true of me," and the results provide you with a self-assessment of your emotional intelligence on each of the five major scales and subscales within them.

As a part of the course for which you're using this textbook, you may have an opportunity to complete the EQ-i or a similar instrument. Check your college's Counseling Center, too, to see if it offers EI assessment tools for students. You can also locate plenty of informal instruments online. They may not be valid, however, so be cautious about fully trusting their results.

Work with a counselor to learn more. Some areas of emotional intelligence may be too challenging to develop on your own. You may need some in-depth, one-on-one counseling to work on areas that need enrichment. Recognize that doing so isn't a bad thing. Instead, you are taking advantage

> **People are lonely because they build walls instead of bridges.**
>
> —JOSEPH F. NEWTON, WELL-KNOWN CROSS COUNTRY COACH AND AUTHOR

Reason 10: They don't have enough support.

A famous Barbara Streisand song starts like this, "People, people who need people . . . are the luckiest people in the world." Don't we *all* need people? Building relationships is a critical part of our lives because many of our most basic needs can only be met by other people. It takes people to fulfill our need to belong, for example, and people to meet our need to be held in high esteem by others.

With that in mind, take a look at this formula: relationships ↓ = ability to focus ↓. Do you agree? We need healthy, productive relationships in our lives, and when a major problem or conflict erupts, it's easy to get derailed. We may stress out, lose sleep, overindulge, obsess, and temporarily lose our ability to focus. *"Should I have said that?" "Did he take that the wrong way?" "Why can't I stop thinking about the stupid fight we had last night?"* In one study of college students' sleeping habits, worrying about relationships was the reason most often cited for not getting enough sleep.[12] Remember this advice: To keep your focus sharp, keep your relationships strong. It's hard to focus when a problem relationship pushes to the forefront of your mind.

TRY It!

Think about the three most important relationships in your life—your romantic partner, your mom, your best friend, or your kid brother, for example. Fill in their names on the lines below. Put a + (things are great!), ✓ (things are okay), or – (this relationship needs work!) beside each entry. If any of the three relationships earned a minus sign, list three ways in which you may be contributing to the problems in the relationship—and what you can do to improve the relationship and thereby improve your ability to focus.

1) _____ 2) _____ 3) _____

a.　　　　　　　a.　　　　　　　a.

b.　　　　　　　b.　　　　　　　b.

c.　　　　　　　c.　　　　　　　c.

of the resources available on your campus and working toward the growth that can come during your college years.

Be patient with yourself. Learning to become more sensitive to someone else's emotions in a close relationship isn't something you can get better at overnight, using cookbook techniques. Building emotional skills is a gradual process that involves becoming aware, acting on your new awareness, and noting the results over time.

Keep at it: Developing your emotional intelligence should be a long-term goal. It's safe to say that EI is something all of us can strengthen, if we're willing to work at it. Relationships that are important to us require the best of our emotional intelligence skills. In fact, studies show that the way in which we provide emotional support is strongly related to how satisfied we are with our relationships.[13]

BOX 10.1 Soft Skills Are Hard!

Emotional intelligence isn't just important for individuals; it plays a role in teamwork. "It unlocks productivity and creativity in a way that nothing else does. Specifically, an effective team must know how to play the EI equivalent of three dimensional chess. It must be mindful of the emotions of its members, its own group emotions or moods, and the emotions of other groups and individuals outside its boundaries."[14] That's a challenge, and in all truthfulness, not all groups reach that level of self- and other-awareness.

Think of it this way: a group's IQ isn't the sum total of the IQ of each of its members (Tom = 110 + Katie = 125 + Jillian = 115 + Brent = 130 for a grand total of 480). High group intelligence—or "collaborative intelligence"—brings an entirely new level of rational thinking and creative ideas. In the same way, a group's emotional intelligence is more than just the sum total of the EI of all its members. It's a new level of productivity that results from uniting sensitive, tactful people who trust one another, believe in their task, capitalize on their strengths, and realize that they need one another to do their best.[15]

Sometimes emotional intelligence is referred to as "soft skills." These skills aren't based in hard science, facts, or numbers. Instead, they involve values, judgment, and sensitivity. As a matter of fact, however, soft skills are hard! It's hard to work with a "difficult" teammate and get good results. It's hard to work under a tyrant of a boss and perform at your best, or rebuild a working relationship after a colleague has "backstabbed" you during a meeting. Anyone can learn new "hard skills," but those who rise to the top of their careers are those with the best soft skills. Interestingly, a survey of Microsoft business leaders rated soft skills as more valuable than academic qualifications![16] Ask anyone who has had a long career: "What are the most difficult issues you have faced over your years on the job?" It's unlikely the answer will have anything to do with the actual job itself ("I just couldn't seem to learn Excel. It totally stumped me!" or "I'll tell you, those cavities in the back molars are really hard to reach!") Instead, you're likely to hear a story about a co-worker who made life difficult until one or the other of you eventually moved on. Soft skills are tested day in and day out, so learning more about them now, while you're in college, is excellent preparation for upcoming challenges.

Catherine Yeulet/Photos.com

> 66 **By gaining and mastering communication and other soft skills and developing your own emotional intelligence, you'll become the person everyone wants to work with.** 99
>
> *Dan Schwabel,* Promote Yourself: The New Rules for Career Success

Communicating in Important Relationships

Friends

Think of all the kinds of communicating you do—and with whom. For example, you have friends you care about. You may think the primary thing friends help you do is fill up your spare time. But new research shows that friends can actually help you fight illness and depression, boost your brain power, and even prolong your life. In one study, students were taken to the bottom of a steep hill while wearing a heavy backpack. They were asked to guess how steep the hill was. Students standing next to friends, rather than by themselves, thought the hill looked much less

> 66 **I'm very loyal in relationships. Even when I go out with my mom I don't look at other moms.** 99
>
> *Garry Shandling, comedian*

steep, and friends who had known each other longer guessed it was even less steep. Researchers wrote that "People with stronger friendship networks feel like there is someone they can turn to. Friendship is an undervalued resource. The consistent message of these studies is that friends make your life better." If that's true, then how you communicate with them is more important than you may even realize.[17]

Family

Or consider family members. These people make up the core of who you really are. Your kid brother may drive you crazy at times, and a parent may seem to smother you, but generally, these people care about you most. Often we "let it all hang out" with family members, perhaps because we know they'll overlook our flaws. When we're tired or stressed, this is often where we "veg" or vent. But because of the central, lasting role they play in our lives, they deserve more quality communication than we sometimes give them.

Classmates/Instructors

Classmates and instructors, too, deserve your best communication, even when you disagree with what they're saying in class. You may see your instructors as either friendly or unfriendly, but you'll need to make the first move to get to know them, rather than the other way around. Take the initiative to meet them during their office hours, and bring up points from class that you'd like to know more about. You'll want to get to know your classmates, too, to make your classes more engaging. You're likely to work with them on class projects. Do some of your best communicating here. Chances are your group-mates—and the group's grade—will depend on it. Participate, do your part, and keep your word. No one will appreciate it if you promise to come to every planning meeting outside of class and turn out to be a no-show every week. Group work in your college classes is a great place to practice the exact skills that are required of you in the workplace. Whatever the type of important relationship—friends, family, classmates, or instructors—how you communicate is vital. Some would go so far as to state this broad opinion: the quality of your communication directly affects the quality of your life. Do you agree?

> **Piglet sidled up to Pooh from behind. "Pooh!" he whispered." "Yes, Piglet?" "Nothing," said Piglet, taking Pooh's paw. "I just wanted to be sure of you."**
>
> A. A. Milne, British author (1882–1956)

Romantic Partners

Beyond friends, family, classmates, and instructors, think about how very important communication is in romantic relationships. If you're in a romantic relationship right now, you may have wondered from time to time whether it's truly a good one. In one study, 94 percent of college students reported having been in love, and over one-third reported three or more past love relationships.[18] Perhaps it was love at first sight, and you immediately announced to your friends or family that this was the one for you. Instead, perhaps right now you're with

Walt Disney/Courtesy Everett Collection

someone you've never really gotten to know very well; you're going through the motions. The relationship is convenient, fun for the time being, but you're just filling up time with someone you're not really interested in, long term. If you're not in a romantic relationship at all right now, perhaps you're on the lookout for someone with potential. If you look around at others' relationships, you only see what those two people choose to display. It's not easy to know exactly what characterizes a healthy relationship. What does it take? A study of 21,501 couples across the country compared the answers of the happiest couples to those of the unhappiest.[19] The areas of maximum difference between the two groups were found on responses like the following.

	Happy Couples	Unhappy Couples
1. My partner is a very good listener.	83%	18%
2. My partner does not understand how I feel.	13%	79%
3. We have a good balance of leisure time spent together and separately.	71%	17%
4. We find it easy to think of things to do together.	86%	28%
5. I am very satisfied with how we talk to each other.	90%	15%
6. We are creative in how we handle our differences.	78%	15%
7. Making financial decisions is not difficult.	80%	32%
8. Our sexual relationship is satisfying and fulfilling.	85%	29%
9. We are both equally willing to make adjustments in the relationship.	87%	46%
10. I can share feelings and ideas with my partner during disagreements.	85%	22%

[Note: numbers do not total 100 percent because of the study's design.]

Look at the highest percentages in the "Happy Couples" column. These results point to an all-important truth: Communication is at the heart of every quality relationship.

In relationships we sometimes communicate in ways that aren't productive. The work of communication specialist Deborah Tannen focuses on miscommunication between men and women. Remember the *Seinfeld* episode in which George's date asks him whether he'd like to come up to her apartment for coffee when he takes her home? George completely misses the point and replies that he never drinks coffee late at night. She meant, "Would you like to continue our date?" but he took the question at face value. Later he kicked himself for being so slow witted. Trying to "listen between the lines" in romantic relationships is a challenge. We say one thing and mean another, or we hope romantic partners can read our minds and then resent it when they do.

Productive Communication

The classic work of psychiatrist Dr. George Bach and others can help relational partners communicate more openly and honestly and meet conflict head on. He described types of **"crazymaking"** that cause communication breakdowns and, at their worst, relationship failures. See whether you recognize people you know—romantic partners or even friends—in these six types of crazymakers.[20]

> The TRAPPER: *Trappers* play an especially dirty trick by requesting a desired behavior from the other person and then attacking when the request is met.

"crazymaking" communicating in dishonest, underhanded, and, in the long term, damaging ways

GOING PRO

BE PERSONABLE

 There are two types of people – those who come into a room and say, 'Well, here I am!' and those who come in and say, 'Ah, there you are.'
~FREDERICK COLLINS

Polish your people skills. Your college instructors may assign group projects in your classes to help you learn teamwork skills. Good teamwork skills are key to a successful career in any area! People can be difficult to work with, yet people are the way work gets done. So treating your colleagues with respect, with civility, and with openness is one of the cornerstones to professional success. Beyond these fundamentals, however, consider the value of forming friendships and of building your personal and professional network. Keep in touch with those you've gone to school with and worked on the job with. Help your colleagues when you can—and rely on them for help when you need to.

> The BLAMER: *Blamers* are more interested in whose fault the problem is than they are in solving it.

> The MINDREADER: *Mindreaders* try to solve the problem by telling their partners what they're *really* thinking.

> The GUNNYSACKER: *Gunnysackers* save grudges. They fill up proverbial gunnysacks and then dump all the contents on their partners at some "opportune" moment.

> The HIT-AND-RUN FIGHTER: *Hit-and-run fighters* attack and then leave the scene quickly, without giving their partners a chance to explain or defend themselves.

> The "BENEDICT ARNOLD": *Benedict Arnolds* like to stir up trouble behind the scenes by playing "let's you and someone else fight."

If you think you're a victim of crazymaking communication, what should you do about it? Try these five suggestions:

1. **Step back and try to figure out the situation.** Is the crazymaker making a request of you (to be more open, reliable, or responsible, for example)? If so, is the request reasonable, and are you willing?

2. **Become aware of the feelings behind the crazymaking.** Is your partner feeling powerless or afraid, for example?

3. **Try not to respond with anger, even though it's difficult.** Piling more wood on the fire certainly won't help to put it out.

4. **Check out your assumptions with the other person.** Ask, "Are you feeling frustrated? Is that what this is about? What would you like me to do?"

5. **Try and reach a mutually agreeable solution by changing communication patterns that aren't productive.** Once you've identified any unproductive communication habits, you can work on improving your skills as well as your relationships. The following five suggestions are a place to start. These recommendations work for any type of close relationship—friends or romantic partners.

Choose wisely. When it comes to selecting someone you may want to build a future with, as a friend or romantic partner, don't settle. Seek someone who shares your values, whose background is compatible, but who is different enough to make life interesting. Choose someone who values productive communication as much as you do.

Let go of unrealistic expectations. Remember that although people live happily ever after in movies, what's really true is that all relationships have ups and downs. We're human; we make mistakes as communicators. One blip on the screen, as they say, doesn't necessarily indicate that the whole program should be scrapped. Instead, working on problems together strengthens your relationship.

Don't ignore small problems. You take your car in for a checkup every so many thousand miles to prevent major breakdowns. It's a good idea to do the same with relationships you care about. Keep the channels of communication open, and talk about small issues before they turn into giant ones. Experts say that doing interesting new things together—going on a vacation, for example—can trigger renewed romantic love.[21] In the same way, going through an intense experience with a friend may strengthen your relationship.

Pay attention to your own communication. You can't change someone else, but you can change your own communication: "Although it takes two to have a relationship, it takes only one to change its quality."[22] Get rid of an annoying behavior or change your conflict style. Be more tolerant of someone else's communication faults, too. Communicate your needs; relationships aren't guessing games. Check, don't assume. Remember that listening is one of the highest compliments you can pay someone. (You're important to me!) Instead of attacking, own your emotions by using the X-Y-Z formula: When you do X in situation Y, I feel Z. ("When you tease me [X] in front of other people [Y], I feel embarrassed and never know how to react [Z]" as opposed to "You always embarrass me! Stop it, will you?")[23] Working to increase your emotional intelligence doesn't mean denying all negative feelings; that would mean cutting off part of your psyche! How you choose to communicate those negative feelings is where the "paying attention" comes in. It's also often best to work through difficult problems in face-to-face settings when you can. Texts, e-mails, and Facebook posts aren't always the most productive way to communicate when a message is really sensitve and important.

Take the high road. Don't give in to momentary temptations that may lead to regret and possibly the end of a relationship with great potential. Without trust as the foundation of your communication, little else matters. If your friend is truly your friend, don't join in when someone else is badmouthing her. And if you've promised yourself to someone, keep your promise.[24]

> **At the extreme, we are so enmeshed in our connections that we neglect each other.**
>
> *Sherry Turkle, from* Alone Together: Why We Expect More from Technology and Less from Each Other

Managing Conflict: Life Is Not a Sitcom

Bad relationships can hurt your job performance, your finances, your physical and mental health—even your life span.[25] Conflict with romantic partners, or with anyone you're close to—family or friends, for example—can bring on major stress that affects your academic performance, not to mention your overall happiness.[26]

Unfortunately, movies and television often communicate—subtly or not so subtly—that conflict can be resolved by the end of the show. Just lighten up or settle down and you can resolve almost any problem. And if you can't, just swallow, take a deep breath, and move on. But life isn't like that, nor should it be. Managing the conflict in your life takes time, energy, and persistence. It requires understanding your natural tendencies, considering why you communicate as you do, and making good choices as a communicator.

If you've ever monitored yourself during a particularly heated conflict, you may remember doing something like this: yelling in anger at someone at the top of your lungs, being interrupted by a phone call and suddenly communicating calmly and quietly to the caller, and then returning to the original shouting match after you hang up.

Why? We make *choices* as communicators. Sometimes our choices are productive ones, and sometimes they aren't. It's important to remember that we *do* choose what we say and how we behave. Our choices affect both the *process*—how things go during the conflict—and the *product*—how it turns out in the end. Negative choices produce destructive conflict that includes personal attacks, name calling, an unwillingness to listen, or the crazymaking strategies described earlier in this chapter. Positive choices are much more likely to bring productive conflict that helps us learn more about ourselves, our partners, and our relationships.

Just like healthy relationships, unhealthy ones have identifying characteristics, too. Although every relationship can teach us something important about future ones, some red flags are worth our attention. Here are three to think about.[28] If you see these danger signals, it may be time to end the relationship or to devote more time and energy toward improving it.

Danger signal 1: "All we ever do is fight!" This point seems obvious, but sometimes it's so obvious that it's overlooked. All some couples talk about is how much they disagree or how wrong things are between them. As a general rule, if 50 percent or more of what you talk about is devoted to managing conflict, sit up and take notice. When so much of your time is spent walking on eggshells to avoid conflict, getting things out on the table during conflict, or smoothing things over afterward, there's little time or energy left to talk about anything else.

Danger signal 2: "Let's dig in deeper!" Can you imagine anyone saying something like this: "We've been going out for two years now, but we're just not getting along. I think if we got engaged, we'd both be more committed." Or consider a couple who is unhappily married, who say, "Maybe we should have a baby. That would bring us closer together." Whoa! Statements such as these are danger signals. Relationships should escalate (or reach the next level of commitment) when we're satisfied with them, when we find them fulfilling, and when we are ready to take the next step together. Trying to force intimacy

VARK It!

Read/Write: The next time you're involved in an important conflict, try writing down your thoughts on paper before discussing them out loud.

VARK It!

Kinesthetic: Think about a favorite TV show in which two people are often in conflict. Can you determine each person's conflict style?

VARK It!

Multimodal (Aural/Kinesthetic): Listen carefully to friends talking or look at their Facebook pages this week to see signs of these danger signals.

What's Your Conflict Style?

For each of the following statements, please rate your response on a scale of 1 to 5, with 1 representing "strongly agree" and 5 representing "strongly disagree."

Strongly Agree	Agree	Not Sure	Disagree	Strongly Disagree
1	2	3	4	5

1. _____ I usually end up compromising in conflict situations. (CO)

2. _____ Someone always loses in a conflict. (CP)

3. _____ I usually let other people "win" in conflicts because I often feel less strongly about the outcome than they do. (AC)

4. _____ When I really care about a relationship, I devote unusual amounts of time and energy into coming up with creative solutions so that each of us can get what we want. (CL)

5. _____ "Don't rock the boat" is a good philosophy. (AV)

6. _____ "Winning" in conflict situations gives me a real "high." (CP)

7. _____ Sacrificing what I want so that someone else can achieve a goal is often worth it. (AC)

8. _____ It's possible for both parties to "win" in conflict situations. (CL)

9. _____ Sometimes you have to settle for "part of the pie." (CO)

10. _____ I try to avoid conflict at all costs. It's not worth it. (AV)

Now find a partner in class and compare your responses. Circle the items on which the two of you differed most, for example, where one of you marked a "1" and the other a "5." See whether you can explain your own choice and also come to understand your partner's thinking. On how many items did you differ? If the answer is "several" or "many," you might experience substantial conflict as coworkers or romantic partners.

People often come at conflicts using differing styles. Not only do you disagree on the topic at hand—whatever it is—but you approach conflict itself differently. This quick quiz is based on a well-known, five-part model of conflict styles (see Figure 10.1). In our version of the model, the horizontal axis is labeled "Concern for Other" (or cooperativeness) and the vertical axis is labeled "Concern for Self" (or assertiveness).[27]

Where are your highest scores? Notice the letters at the end of the ten statements.

If you like to win and care most about your own goals, you **compete (CP)**.

If you care more about the other person's goals, and give in, you **accommodate (AC)**.

If you don't care about your goals or your partner's, you **avoid (AV)**.

If you care somewhat about both and are willing to settle for "part of the pie," you **compromise (CO)**. *Strictly speaking, when you compromise, neither of you gets exactly what you want.*

If you care about your own goals and your partner's, and you're willing to devote the time and energy required to reach a win–win solution, you **collaborate (CL)**.

What's your style? Do you have a conflict style you're most comfortable with? Do you fall into the habit of using one style, even if it's not productive in particular situations? Flexibility is the key to managing conflicts productively, and if the relationship really counts, collaboration is the ideal.

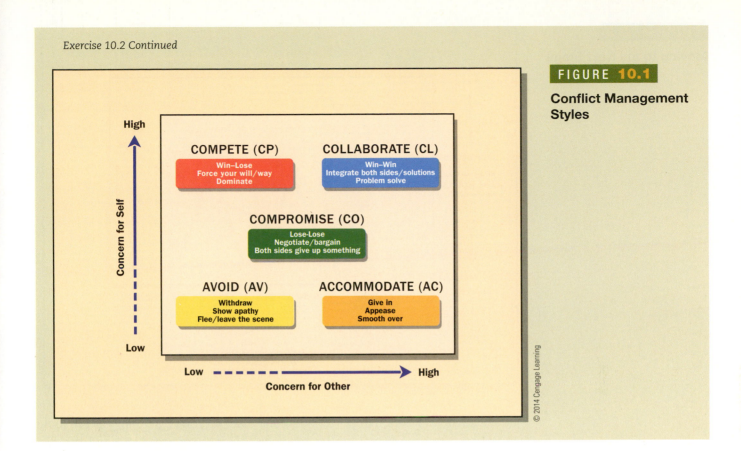

FIGURE **10.1**

Conflict Management Styles

© 2014 Cengage Learning

doesn't work. Although this point makes sense, it's surprising how many couples fall into this trap.

Figure 10.2 provides a visual example of a traditional pattern of relationship stages in our society. (Of course, the steps don't always occur in this order, nor are they even these particular steps.) At each step, the couple is making a decision about staying together. Ideally, relationships should escalate naturally along Line A; however, sometimes people mistakenly force themselves to escalate unnaturally along Line B.

Danger signal 3: "This relationship just isn't worth it!" From two unique individuals, a third thing—a unique relationship—is born. The relationship you create with one person is different from the one you'll create with anyone else. Not only are *you* different in many ways, but *your relationship* with each of these individuals is unique, too. Relationships, like individuals, have their own attitudes, values, and sensitivities.

At some point, you may decide that a relationship just isn't worth it anymore. The costs outweigh the rewards. The relationship is suffocating or lifeless. You find yourself thinking

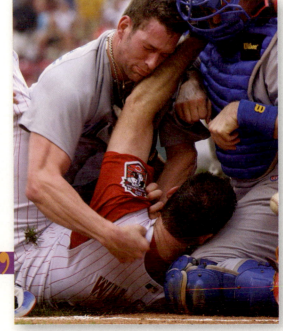

AP Photo/Al Behrman

> **Gettin' good players is easy. Gettin' 'em to play together is the hard part.**
>
> *Casey Stengel, major league baseball player and manager (1890-1975)*

Managing Conflict: Life Is Not a Sitcom **273**

FIGURE **10.2**

Moving to the Next Stage

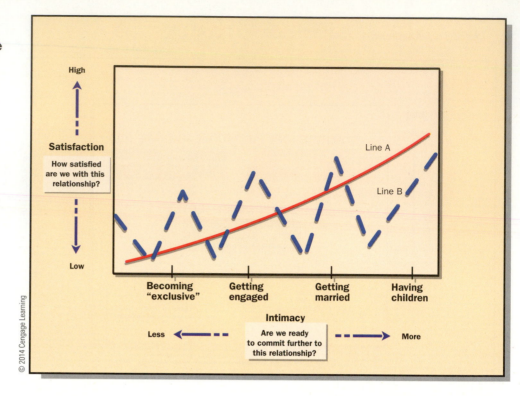

© 2014 Cengage Learning

about having a relationship with someone else, or you're actually on the lookout for a new one. It may be best to face this fact squarely and end the dissatisfying relationship honestly, rather than allowing another one to develop in secret. When relationships end, the quality and quantity of communication between the two people change. But as the golden oldie goes, "Breaking Up Is Hard to Do," and applying all the emotional intelligence you can muster will help you through it.

EXERCISE 10.3

Part I: Twenty Five Things We Have in Common

Conflict is based on differences. Two people each want different things—or two people want the same thing, but only one can have it. But when you think about it, we have many things in common as human beings. Try this experiment: work with three classmates (in a group of four), and when your instructor announces, "Go," begin listing things that all four of you have in common. The first group to reach twenty five items wins! After the exercise, discuss the kinds of things you listed and how easy or hard it was to create a list of twenty five different items.[29]

Part II: What's the Difference?

Now find a single partner to work with on this part of the exercise. Individually, list all the various ways in which you differ: age, height, gender, eye color, birth place, and so on. When your instructor calls "time," read your lists aloud. The point of the exercise is to begin a discussion on the meaning of diversity, to explore its many different facets—beyond just external appearance—and to appreciate the fact that each individual is unique.[30] Now look back at Part I of this exercise, "Twenty Five Things We Have in Common." Was it easier to find commonalities or differences? Why?

Diversity Makes a Difference

Your Views on Diversity

What are your views on diversity? Look at the following ten statements, and indicate the extent to which you agree or disagree.

Strongly Agree	Agree	Not Sure	Disagree	Strongly Disagree
1	2	3	4	5

1. Race is still a factor in hiring decisions today. _____
2. Multiculturalism implies that all cultures have equally valid viewpoints. _____
3. Workforce diversity improves the quality of work. _____
4. The number of male versus female corporate CEOs is nearing the halfway mark in the United States. _____
5. In some situations, sexual orientation is a justifiable basis for discrimination. _____
6. All cultures tend to see the rest of the world through their own cultural lens. _____
7. Feminism is a set of beliefs held by females. _____
8. A global perspective ensures objectivity. _____
9. Religious persecution is a thing of the past. _____
10. There is less racism in the United States today than there was ten years ago. _____

As you continue reading this section of the chapter, search for points relating to these topics. Also, your instructor may wish to use these ten items to begin a discussion in class.

You see a sticker on a passing car's bumper: "Celebrate Diversity." Diversity is a word that's used often these days. But what does it mean? **Diversity** is a term that relates to differences between human beings based on race, ethnicity, age, culture, physical features and abilities, mental capability, socio-economic status, religion, politics, sexual orientation, geographic region, gender identity, and points of view.

diversity the ways in which people differ from one another

You may be American, male, white, 21, heterosexual, tall, athletic, smart, good-looking, and from a well-to-do family—and inadvertently, without ever realizing it, think anyone who isn't like you is somehow "less" than you are. It's not that you intend to look down on others. In fact, some of these traits identified above aren't chosen ones; they're qualities a person is born with or grew up with. But others unlike you may see you very differently. You see yourself as "fortunate"; they may see you as "privileged." **Perceptions** are important in discussions about diversity. Perceptions influence our interactions with others, and sometimes perceptions can lead to bias. Let's take a closer look:

perceptions an awareness of people, things, and qualities around you

Type of Diversity	Possible Perceptions	Things to Consider
Age Diversity	"Those youngsters with all the tattoos and piercings! What do they know?"	Trends change, and outward expressions vary from one generation to the next.
	"Older drivers! They're so slow!"	Reaction times slow down, and vision can worsen.
Gender Diversity	"I'm all for women's rights, but a female president? I'm not sure we're ready for that!"	Actually, in recent presidential races several women rose to prominent roles at the top of their parties.
	"Why would a guy want to be a nurse? That's a woman's job."	Nursing is a top career field for men or women, now and in the future.
Geographic Diversity	"The South is so backwards."	Southerners are proud of their traditions.
	"Northerners are such snobs."	Regional accents can carry particular stereotypes.
Physical Diversity	"Boy, if I only had a handicapped sticker, I could park anywhere on campus."	Physical challenges warrant access capability.
	"That professional signer in class is really distracting!"	In-class signers help deaf students follow lectures and discussions—like a language translator.
Sexual Orientation Diversity	"Call me homophobic, but all *my* friends are straight."	Homophobia can be a highly negative hidden bias.
	"Bisexual? How can somebody be attracted to both sexes? That's just not normal!"	College is a time to become aware of differences, including things you may never have been exposed to.
Religious Diversity	"Religious people are unthinking."	Religious beliefs are highly personal, and spirituality in some form can bring balance and meaning.
	"I'm glad I was raised believing in the right religion."	Although it can be natural to see your family traditions as "right," realize that others may feel equally strong about theirs.

You must look into people, as well as at them.

Lord Chesterfield,
British statesman (1694–1773)

Each of us is a unique human being. Some of us are taller, some are shorter, some are older, some are younger. Some aspects of our uniqueness are visible. It's not hard to tell the difference between someone who's five feet tall and someone who's seven feet tall or someone who's twenty years old versus someone who's eighty. But other aspects of our uniqueness aren't as obvious. Would people necessarily know your religion, your sexual orientation, or even your race just by looking at you? If you had a stack of photos—a headshot of every student who attends your school—could you sort them by race into the same stacks they'd sort themselves into? Anyone can tell an Asian American from an African American just by looking. Or so they may think.

Race is often the first thing people think of when they hear the word *diversity*. But some experts say race is a relatively modern idea. Centuries ago, people tended to classify other people by status, religion, or language, for example, not by race. Actually, most of us are a blend of ethnicities, and how we perceive

Facing the Race Issue

Take a look at the faces below. Can you categorize them into common racial types: White, Black, Hispanic/Latino, Native American, or Asian? After you've identified each one, check the answers below. How accurate were you? Does this activity confirm the point above that although race is used as a common identifier, it isn't an easy or accurate way to classify people?[33]

Answers: (top row): B, H, NA, A, H and (bottom row): B, H, H, W, W.

From top left: iStockphoto.com/Jacom Stephens; iStockphoto.com/billnoll; iStockphoto.com/Thomas Gordon; iStockphoto.com/Goldmund; iStockphoto.com/Jacom Stephens; iStockphoto.com/Lisa Marzano; iStockphoto.com/Jason Lugo; iStockphoto.com/Roberto A Sanchez; iStockphoto.com/TriggerPhoto, iStockphoto.com/LajosRepasi

ourselves may be different from the way others see us. People may assume that a Pacific Islander with light brown skin, dark hair, and dark eyes, for example, is Hispanic. And a classmate you may assume is white may think of himself as black. Or consider this: If you have a Chinese mother and a white father, you may not know which "race box" to check on standard forms. Should you choose Mom or Dad?[31] Biologists tell us that there's more variation within a race than there is between races. Race isn't biological, they say, but *racism* is real.[32]

Although you or some of your classmates may have grown up in communities with less racial, ethnic, or cultural diversity than others, you have probably experienced the multicultural nature of our society in many different ways, even in terms of food, music, and clothing, for example. The media have introduced you to aspects of diversity, and perhaps you've even traveled to other parts of the United States or the world yourself.

> **I take as my guide the hope of a saint: In crucial things, unity; in important things, diversity; in all things, generosity.**
>
> *George H. W. Bush, forty-first president of the United States*

© Larry Harwood Photography. Property of Cengage Learning.

tolerance a fair, objective attitude toward differences

ethnicities groups of people who share a culture, language, and possibly a religion

discrimination bias that results in unfair treatment

stereotypes commonly held unfavorable beliefs about people

proactive planning ahead, rather than simply reacting

prejudice a general, unfavorable opinion held without specific evidence

But here's the challenge: Have experiencing diversity and learning about it in school truly made a difference in the way you think and act? Do you choose to diversify your awareness, your relationships, and yourself as a person? Do you think that discrimination no longer exists in our multicultural society?

Many college students today do believe that racial discrimination is no longer a problem. *Been there; done that*, they've concluded. We may think of ourselves as more "highly evolved" than Americans of past decades, but are we? If you see an interracial couple, do you take a second look without even thinking about it? Are we truly bias-free in this day and age?

According to a recent survey, "helping to promote racial understanding" was considered "essential" or "very important" by only slightly more than one-third of incoming first-year students.[34] In another study, students were asked to identify the five most critical and two least critical outcomes of a college education from a list of sixteen possibilities. Tolerance and respect for people of other races, ethnicities, and lifestyles were identified as among the least important goals for college learning.[35] Why do you think they responded that way? Do they think they've already achieved these goals, or do they think they're less important for other reasons?

If you conducted a survey on your campus to find out whether discrimination exists, you might be surprised at the results. Research continues to show that minority students report experiencing discrimination at higher rates than majority students. Many of us downplay the prejudice all human beings harbor to one extent or another. Our brains are "programmed" to group people that are alike and standardize our views about these groups, resulting in stereotypes. Sometimes, we feel safe around others like us and fear those unlike us. Appreciating individuals for what they are, instead of stereotyping, could drastically change the way we think and act. If you open up your thinking to new possibilities, all kinds of new options present themselves. Imagine a band made up of only trombones, a meal with nothing but string beans, a song played on one note, or a world where everyone looks exactly like you. Diversity enriches our lives. Prejudice stunts our thinking.

A University of Michigan study demonstrated that students who had more positive interactions with diverse peers, and in particular took a college course on diversity, were more likely to be academically self-confident, more personally proactive, and more likely to develop better critical thinking skills.[36] Learning to deal effectively with diversity can actually change you as a college student! Prejudice, or looking down on people just because they are different, isn't a good vantage point. If a classmate who's unlike you were the son or daughter of a famous actor, would that change your view? Prejudice sneaks up on us and limits our ability to grow as human beings.

Appreciate the American Mosaic

It's becoming more and more impossible to draw clear lines between what separates us physically. Actress Jessica Alba has a mother with French and Danish roots and a Mexican-American father; Keanu Reeves is Hawaiian, Chinese, and Caucasian; Mariah Carey is Black, Venezuelan, and Caucasian; and Johnny Depp is Cherokee and Caucasian.[37] The woman in the photo below is Noemie Lenoir, who is of African and European descent and one of the world's highest paid mixed-race models. Most of us are a blend, but diversity is about more than physical appearance. Each of us is a unique human being.

Actually, college is a perfect time to learn more about diversity—in the classroom and beyond it. Classrooms are becoming more diversely populated; it's true. Diversity in higher education gives you an opportunity to expand your world view and develop empathy for others who have vastly different experiences.

Aside from meeting students who are different from you in college, taking advantage of diversity can help you become a more sophisticated thinker, one who can see problems from multiple perspectives, and a better prepared employee, ready to hit the ground running in today's highly diverse workplace. Appreciating diversity also helps us become better citizens. Diversity is what our society is based on. In a democratic society such as ours, citizens must be able to recognize and endorse creative solutions to complex problems. A former chief justice of the U.S. Supreme Court, Charles Evans Hughes, once said, "When we lose the right to be different, we lose the privilege to be free."

One mistake many college students make is not taking advantage of what diversity offers them. Because people often tend to feel comfortable with others like them they join groups of people just like themselves, based on religion,

We have become not a melting pot, but a beautiful mosaic. Different people, different beliefs, different yearnings, different hopes, different dreams.

Jimmy Carter, thirty-ninth president of the United States

Venture/Wireimage/Getty Images

EXERCISE 10.6

Circles of Awareness

Each of us has a cultural identity. How do we see ourselves, and how do others see us? Write your name in the center of the drawing, and then label each of the surrounding circles with a word that represents a group you identify with. You may use categories like age, gender, ethnicity, social, political, and so forth. After your drawing is labeled, your instructor will ask you to circulate around the room and find three classmates who have listed at least three of the same subgroups. After that, you will be asked to find three students who listed at least three categories that you did not. In the second group you formed, based on differences, use the activity to discuss diversity, differences among individuals and groups, and how awareness can change behavior. Look over everyone's list, and to diversify your thinking, select one group on someone else's list, but not on yours. Find out more about that group or decide to attend a group meeting to raise your awareness of what you think the group is like, and what it's actually like.[38]

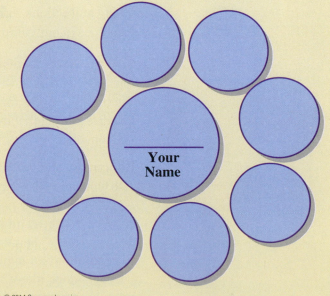

© 2014 Cengage Learning

Appreciate the American Mosaic   279

sexual orientation, or majors, for example. You can choose to belong to the Young Republicans; the Gay, Lesbian, Bisexual, Transgender (GLBT) student group; or the Chemistry Honor Society. Joining a group of like students assures you a place where people accept you for who you are, and you feel comfortable. Think about the groups you belong to and what they say about you.

Of course, being comfortable and feeling accepted are important. But instead, imagine choosing to join groups composed of very different types of people. Consider what philosopher and educator John Dewey once said, "Conflict . . . shocks us out of sheep-like passivity," or the words of a famous American lawyer, Louis Nizer, who once put it like this: "Where there is no difference, there is only indifference." Valuing diversity relates directly to your empathy skills and your emotional intelligence. What about stretching ourselves to learn fully what diversity has the potential to teach us?[39]

Imagine you were engaged in a service-learning project for a class, working in your local soup kitchen. It's easy to criticize a homeless person and think, "Why doesn't he just get a job?" But when you actually sit down and share a bowl of soup across the table, you might see things differently. You might hear stories of personal illness, family tragedy, unbelievable trauma—a list of bad luck coincidences you'd never even think of. Rather than assigning all homeless people to a group with a negative label, learn more about the individuals that make up that group. You might change your views.

One professor says this: "I tell my students to keep in mind that everything they see is a snapshot. That guy drinking from a bottle in a paper bag, he's a photograph. How did he get to where he is? From there, we can share some of the rage at the inherent **injustice** that awaits so many of our poor children as they grow up. As we examine people, the snapshots become a motion picture that links the past, present, and future—what was, what is, what can be."[40]

Choose a stereotype you recognize, one you suspect you believe if you're honest, and decide what you can do to test it. Ask yourself whether it affects your thinking and actions. For example, are you aware of these facts about continuing stereotypes in our culture?

> **Sexism is still an issue in corporate America.** In 2012, twenty of America's top 500 companies were run by a woman, up from one out of forty in 1995. Then, only one of those companies had a female CEO; by 2003, seven did. Experts predict that by 2020, it could be one in five; however, the numbers are still lopsided.[41]

> **Racism is still an issue in hiring decisions.** A recent Gallup poll asked: "Do you feel that racial minorities in this country have job opportunities equal to whites, or not?" Among whites, the answer was 55 percent yes and 43 percent no. (The rest were undecided.) Among African Americans, the answer was 17 percent yes and 81 percent no. You might also be shocked to read about an experiment in which fake applicants of one race were 50 percent more likely to be called for interviews than applicants of another race, based solely on whether their names sounded like they belonged to a particular racial group! As one *Wall Street Journal* reporter noted, "Someday Americans will be able to speak of racial discrimination in hiring in the past tense. Not yet."[42]

VARK It!

Visual: Go back through this chapter, and note the images tied to particular quotes that you are most likely to remember.

injustice unfair action or treatment

> **Discrimination and stereotypes persist.** Students with disabilities report a "chilly classroom climate" for students with disabilities in higher education.[43] According to one college president, "With all [the change in racial demographics], diversity has become the largest issue behind unrest on campus, accounting for 39 percent of student protests."[44] A recent study of closeted and out gay and lesbian college students reported that these students perceived unfair treatment and a need to hide their identity from most other students. Both groups reported experiencing a similar amount of antigay attacks.[45] In 2010, 6628 total hate crime incidents were reported in the United States, according to the U.S. Department of Justice. Racially motivated crimes accounted for approximately 47 percent; religious bias accounted for 20 percent; bias against sexual orientation for 19 percent; bias against disabilities for .6 percent; and bias against ethnicity or national origin accounted for 13 percent.[46] People still harm one another out of hatred for differences they may not understand.

Diversity makes a difference, and as educator Adela A. Allen once wrote, "We should acknowledge differences, we should greet differences, until difference makes no difference anymore." What can we do about it? Raising awareness is a first step on the road to recognizing the reality and the richness of diversity.

What's Your CQ?

EXERCISE 10.7

Diagnosing Your Cultural Intelligence[47]

These statements reflect different aspects of cultural intelligence. For each set, add up your scores and divide by four to arrive at an average. As you answer, think about your answers in each category as they compare to the other two categories.

Rate how much you agree with each statement, using this scale:

1 = strongly disagree   **2 = disagree**   **3 = neutral**   **4 = agree**   **5 = strongly agree**

____ Before I interact with people from a new culture, I think about what I'm going to communicate.

____ If I come up against something unexpected in a new culture, I use the experience to think about how I should respond in other cultures in the future.

____ I plan how I'm going to relate to people from a different culture before I even meet them.

____ When I'm communicating in a new culture, I have a clear sense of whether things are going well or not.

____ **Total divided by 4 = ____ COGNITIVE CQ**

____ It's easy for me to change my body language (eye contact or posture, for example) to match that used by people from a different culture.

____ I can change my expression when I need to interact with people from another culture.

(Continued)

____ I can modify my speech (for example, accent or tone) when interacting with people from another culture.

____ I can easily change the way I act when a cross-cultural situation seems to require it.

____ **Total divided by 4 = ____ PHYSICAL CQ**

____ I have confidence that I can deal well with people from another culture.

____ I am certain that I can make friends with people from a culture that's different from mine.

____ I can adapt to the lifestyle of another culture when I need to fairly easily.

____ I am confident that I can deal with a cultural situation, even if it's unfamiliar.

____ **Total divided by 4 = ____ EMOTIONAL/MOTIVATIONAL CQ**

Generally, an average lower than three identifies an opportunity for improvement, and an average greater than 4.5 identifies a true CQ strength.

An advertisement for an international bank gets the point across well. It shows a picture of a grasshopper. Below the grasshopper are these three sentences that describe three different cultural views of grasshoppers: USA—Pest, China—Pet, Northern Thailand—Appetizer.[48] One insect, three cultural perspectives. Americans tend to shoo away pesky grasshoppers. But if you travel to China, be careful of stepping on one that may be someone else's beloved pet. And if you travel to Northern Thailand, try not to look disgusted when you see fried grasshoppers on the appetizer plate.

America   **China**   **Northern Thailand**

iStockphoto.com/Antagain; iStockphoto.com/Diane Diederich   iStockphoto.com/Antagain; iStockphoto.com/jclegg   iStockphoto.com/Antagain; iStockphoto.com/frytka

---

VARK It!

Kinesthetic: Tour your campus to find examples of art, music, or literature from other cultures.

Just as individuals have emotional intelligence, they also have cultural intelligence. Some of us are more naturally sensitive to cultural differences, and we know how to handle ourselves. But all of us can grow our cultural intelligence with training and preparation. EQ relates to self-awareness and relationship skills; CQ relates to awareness and responses to other cultures (and subcultures of our own culture). EQ and CQ are linked.

Here's a definition: cultural intelligence is an outsider's seemingly natural ability to interpret someone's unfamiliar and ambiguous gestures the way other people of that culture would.[49] CQ has three components that involve your head, your body, and your heart. All three work together to help you interact in a foreign culture—or a subculture that's new to you within your own larger culture. Think, for example, about taking a job in a new culture, either by transferring overseas or by entering an organization with different rules: "Casual Fridays," "Bring Your Dog to Work Day," "Follow Strict Communication Rules and Always Go Through Your Boss," or "Choose Your Own Project to Work on One Day a Week" (if you work for Google). These rules might be different for you, and you'd need good CQ skills to adapt. Or think about entering a subculture you're unfamiliar with: like being "straight" and having a gay best friend, or marrying someone of another ethnicity. CQ can be broken down into three parts, all of which work together:

1. **Cognitive quotient (head):** Do you understand the differences between another culture and your own? Before entering a new culture, do you think before you act? Do you learn about the culture in advance of interacting with its members so that you don't make embarrassing mistakes?

2. **Physical quotient (body):** Do you watch for behaviors that are different in other cultures? Do you mimic the gestures and customs of the people? Do you shake hands correctly? Do you notice whether the culture is "high touch" or "low touch"? Do you adopt their habits so that you earn their trust?

3. **Emotional/motivational quotient (heart):** Do you empathize with people from this culture? Can you imagine what it's like to be a member of this culture? Do you want to connect despite your differences? This aspect of CQ is thought to be most like EQ.

To have good CQ skills, you must be more than a "mimic," simply repeating what you see and hear in another culture. You must be a "chameleon," taking on what it's like to be a member of that culture. You must—through your head, your body, and your heart—prove to others that you have entered their world. Not only are CQ skills important within the American culture, they're also important in today's global society. How culturally intelligent are you? CQ is a natural extension of EQ, and the suggestions for how to improve your EQ apply to strengthening your CQ. If your cognitive quotient is low, read up about other cultures.

VARK It!

Aural: Talk with an international student on your campus about how college life in the United States differs from what a student would experience in his or her home country.

VARK It!

Kinesthetic: If you have a Facebook account, look at the pages of three people you know who have traveled to another country. Can you find examples of cultural differences they describe?

ONLINE TechKnow

A virtual group project—torture or opportunity? When you're assigned to an online project team, here are a few steps you should take to make sure you and your teammates have the best possible chance to produce a good product:

- Get contact information from each of your team members as soon as they are identified and get in touch right away. It's important to have more than one possibility. If an e-mail doesn't get answered, try a text.

- Make sure you all understand what is required of the team and of each individual. If you're unsure of something, or suspect your teammates don't know, work with them right away to clarify that point.

- Identify individual roles and responsibilities immediately.

- Set up a time line for accomplishing tasks or milestones as the team moves toward the final project completion date.

It's important to make sure everyone on the team understands what's coming, so consistent communication is a must! If you're not hearing from one or more of your teammates, get in touch right away. In your team work and in more general online class interaction, reliability and clarity are very important. Don't leave your teammates holding the bag! Decide to jump in and work together to create something that earns all of you the grade you'd like.[50]

Improve Your Grade
Online Flashcards
Glossary

If your physical quotient is low, watch for differences in gestures or movements and find out what they mean. If your emotional/motivational quotient is low, ask others for input, for example, or find a CQ mentor.

Think Globally; Act Locally

The 1972 United Nations international conference on the human environment in Stockholm was the origin of the phrase "Think Globally, Act Locally." Perhaps you've heard it. Simply put, it originally meant "Do what you can to 'save the environment.'"

Today the phrase takes on added meaning. True, recycling is becoming the norm, and **sustainability** is the goal of modern corporations. But beyond environmental concerns, the world is characterized by networks of connections across continents and distances. As citizens of the world, we are all connected, if not geographically, then economically, militarily, socially, financially, and technologically. The General Electric website allows users to select from forty different

sustainability the practice of meeting our needs now without compromising the ability of future generations to meet theirs (Brundtland Commission of the United Nations, March 20, 1987)

Cut and Deal Ltd/Index Open/PhotoLibrary

languages. Google offers an interface in over 130 languages.[51] By 2003, 66 percent of all e-commerce spending originated outside of the United States, and now nearly two-thirds of all Internet users live in Asia and Europe.[52] A famous song title once made the claim: "We Are the World."

What's In **YOUR** Briefcase?

MAKE IT PERSONAL

Have you ever been accused of taking things personally? Your spouse looks askance at your new, multitone hair color or your ever-so-stylish "runway" outfit, or your best friend makes a confusing, offhand comment about something that's dear to your heart. "How dare she?" you think to yourself! When you tell the story to your best friend, she provides a reality check, "Oh, lighten up. You don't have to take it personally."

People count. We care about what they think of us. But what about the often overlooked reverse point of view? They care, too. People prop us up, validate us (or not), and meet our personal needs—and we do the same for them. Even though we know it, we don't always show it. It explains why some very intelligent, highly capable people fail and why misunderstandings are common. It's not so much that people always take things personally; it's that they sometimes forget to make things personal.

Consider this scenario: You're on a team with a colleague who's a bear to work with. She may be the hardest worker in the company, have the best ideas, and sport a sales record that no one can touch. But ultimately, she fails miserably in your organization and moves to another one . . . again. She moves from job to job, and she just can't figure out why she's not seen as successful. But to her, the job is all about the work. The people she works with are invisible to her. She doesn't realize that the people are how the work gets done. According to one career expert, "There's a simple reason for it: we rarely take the time to pause, breathe, and think about what's working and what's not. There's just too much to do and no time to reflect." Making things personal is about listening carefully to the layers of communication and remembering that people count. Actually, it's less about time and more about mindset. Appreciate your differences, explore your commonalities, and above all, remember that work, like the rest of life, is about building productive relationships.[57]

Here's a recommendation: At the end of every workday, take five minutes to reflect not only about the work but also about your coworkers. Ask yourself these three questions:

1. What went well today and what didn't?

2. What lessons from today will help me do a better job tomorrow?

3. Who contributed to my success? Is there someone I should update or thank? If so, do it.[58]

Doing so will not only help you do your best, but it will do the same for others. Remembering to "make it personal" will affect your career more positively than you can possibly imagine now.

Think about a time that you were involved in a college project (a group presentation, for example) when things either did or didn't work well. Which principles you've just read about were (or would have been) important?

_____

_____

_____

The education you get now must prepare you to solve the problems of the future. It will require you to look beyond the walls of your classrooms and refine your skills in terms of how relationships work, how diversity impacts our lives, and how to be culturally intelligent. It will require you to think and act both globally *and* locally. The course for which you're using this textbook is a good place to start.

step 3 INSIGHT *Now* What Do You Think?

At the beginning of this chapter, Serena Jackson faced a series of challenges as a new college student. Now after reading this chapter, would you respond differently to any of the questions you answered about the "FOCUS Challenge Case"? Using what you learned in the chapter, write a paragraph ending to Serena's case study. What are some of the possible outcomes for Serena?

step 4 ACTION Your Plans for Change

1. Do you fall into any of the communication traps you read about in this chapter? If so, which ones? What will you do to change the way you communicate in important relationships?

2. This chapter asserts that diversity makes a difference. Do you believe that statement? In what ways can learning to appreciate diversity change how you interact with others? How can these communication skills pay off in the future? What will you do to refine them further?

3. Is cultural intelligence something you've ever thought about before? What role might it play in your future personal or professional life?

Choosing a College Major and Career

READINESS CHECK

How this chapter relates to **YOU**

1. When it comes to choosing a college major and career, what do you find most challenging, if anything?

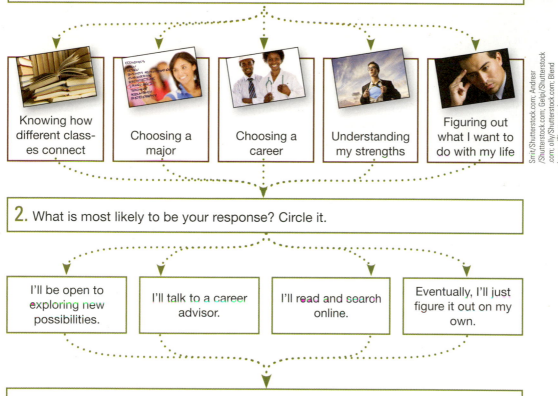

Knowing how different class-es connect

Choosing a major

Choosing a career

Understanding my strengths

Figuring out what I want to do with my life

2. What is most likely to be your response? Circle it.

I'll be open to exploring new possibilities.

I'll talk to a career advisor.

I'll read and search online.

Eventually, I'll just figure it out on my own.

3. What would you do to increase your likelihood of success? Will you do it this term?

Example: Talk to a career advisor on campus. Yes!

How **YOU** will relate to this chapter

What are you most interested in learning about? Put check marks by those topics.

☐ Why "college in a box" isn't an accurate view of coursework

☐ How the disciplines connect in the Circle of Learning

☐ How to choose a major and career

☐ How to follow your bliss, conduct research, and take a good look at yourself

☐ What a SWOT analysis is

☐ How to analyze your "Academic Anatomy"

● How motivated are you to learn more about getting the right start in college? (5 = high, 1 = low) ___

● How ready are you to read now? ___ (If something is in your way, take care of it if you can, zero in and focus.)

● How long do you think it will take you to complete this chapter? If you start and stop, keep track of your overall time. ____ hour(s) ____ minutes

Ethan Cole

Jorge Folha/Shutterstock.com

One thing was certain: Ethan Cole was unsure. Unsure of his abilities, unsure of which major to choose, unsure of what he wanted to do with his life, unsure of himself. Unsure of almost everything.

Ethan came from a good family, and he actually got along pretty well with his parents. They both had decent jobs, worked long hours, and overall they had been good to him. Compared with many of his friends, he came from a "happy home." But frankly, his parents weren't all that interested in the details of his life. When he announced one day as a high school senior that he wanted to attend the college in town, they said, "What for?" When he said he didn't know, they replied, "Well, you'll figure it out." And that was that. He enrolled the next day.

The only thing Ethan was sure of was that skateboarding was his life right now. It's all he wanted to do and all he ever thought about. He'd look at a curve on a window frame or an arc in a picture and imagine what skating on it would feel like. All his friends were skateboarders, too, and he read skateboarder magazines and dreamed of the day he might even go pro. He

© Larry Harwood Photography. Property of Cengage Learning.

TheSupe87/Shutterstock.com

realized not many people make a living at it, but a few really talented athletes did, and maybe—just maybe—he'd be one of them. Recently, he'd found out about the largest concrete skatepark on the globe, Black Pearl in the Grand Cayman Islands—62,000 square feet! He'd made a promise to himself to skate there someday. *Life couldn't get much better than that,* he thought.

But school . . . that was a different story. Schoolwork had never captured his attention. In primary school, his physician had diagnosed him with Attention Deficit Disorder (ADD). *No wonder I don't like school,* he remembered thinking then. But finally knowing why he couldn't focus didn't change his attitude. He still hated sitting in a classroom.

Despite these challenges, his parents had always told him he was smart. "You can do anything you want to do," they'd said. "Look at you: you're a

Manuel Fernandes/Shutterstock.com

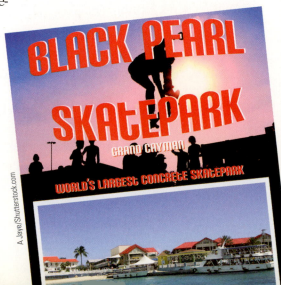

A Jaye/Shutterstock.com

good-looking kid with plenty of talents. The world is your oyster!" *What a funny phrase,* he'd always thought when they said that. By the time he finally learned what it meant, he totally believed it. His life would become whatever he chose to make of it.

The problem was there were too many choices. How could anyone decide what he wanted to be when he was only nineteen? Ethan remembered liking geometry; he was good at creative writing; he played the drums like a real jazz musician; and he was an incredible artist. *But what do you do with that combination of skills?* he'd asked himself more than once. What possible college major and career would really fit him? He'd spent plenty of time on career websites to try and figure it out.

He'd managed to pull decent grades his first term—a B average—at the college close to home. He'd taken Geography, Interpersonal Communication, Drawing 101, and Study Skills, and while he'd done well, none of the course

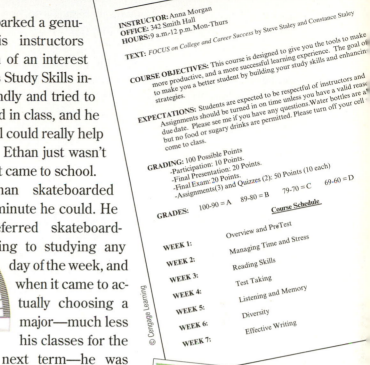

Picsfive/Shutterstock.com

material really sparked a genuine interest. His instructors didn't take much of an interest in him either. His Study Skills instructor was friendly and tried to get him interested in class, and he knew the material could really help him. But frankly, Ethan just wasn't motivated when it came to school.

Instead, Ethan skateboarded every minute he could. He preferred skateboarding to studying any day of the week, and when it came to actually choosing a major—much less his classes for the next term—he was clueless. The one thing that did interest him was a certificate in entrepreneurship. It was all about starting a business of your own. Now that sounded intriguing. Ethan didn't quite fit any molds, and doing his own thing might just be "his thing!"

But the more he thought about it, dropping out sounded like a good idea, too. He could get a job delivering pizzas, think about his life, and try to figure it all out. He'd have nobody to tell him what to do, nobody to hold him accountable, nobody to pressure him, nobody to force him into making decisions—and plenty of free time to skateboard.

Lisa F. Young/Shutterstock.com

Study Skills (ID 102)
Course Syllabus

INSTRUCTOR: Anna Morgan
OFFICE: 342 Smith Hall
HOURS: 9 a.m-12 p.m. Mon-Thurs

TEXT: *FOCUS on College and Career Success* by Steve Staley and Constance Staley

COURSE OBJECTIVES: This course is designed to give you the tools to make you more productive, and a more successful learning experience. The goal of to make you a better student by building your study skills and enhancing strategies.

EXPECTATIONS: Students are expected to be respectful of instructors and due date. Assignments should be turned in on time unless you have a valid reason but no food or sugary drinks are permitted. Please see me if you have any questions. Water bottles are a come to class. Please turn off your cell

GRADING: 100 Possible Points
-Participation: 10 Points.
-Final Presentation: 20 Points.
-Final Exam: 20 Points.
-Assignments(3) and Quizzes (2): 50 Points (10 each)

GRADES: 100-90 = A   89-80 = B   79-70 = C   69-60 = D

Course Schedule

WEEK 1:	Overview and PreTest
WEEK 2:	Managing Time and Stress
WEEK 3:	Reading Skills
WEEK 4:	Test Taking
WEEK 5:	Listening and Memory
WEEK 6:	Diversity
WEEK 7:	Effective Writing

© Cengage Learning

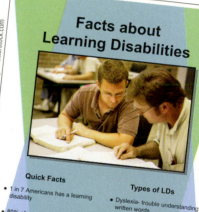

Facts about Learning Disabilities

Quick Facts

- 1 in 7 Americans has a learning disability
- 80% of students with learning disabilities have reading problems
- Learning disabilities can be genetic
- Multiple learning disabilities can occur at the same time

Types of LDs

- Dyslexia- trouble understanding written words
- Dyscalculia- trouble grasping mathematical concepts
- Dysgraphia- trouble writing letters or words
- Aural and Visual Processing Disorders

Bruce Newell/Shutterstock.com

Stephen VanHorn, 2009/Used under license from Shutterstock.com

indeed.com

1. Do you have anything in common with Ethan? If so, how are you managing the situation so that you can be successful?

2. In your view, what will become of Ethan? What are his prospects for the future? Do you think he'll decide on a career and finish college? Why or why not?

3. Why is Ethan experiencing problems? Are these problems serious? Should they hold him back? List all the problems you can identify.

4. Which majors and careers might Ethan be well suited for? If you were an academic advisor, what advice would you give him?

5. Who would you send Ethan to for help at your college? What are his options? What do you think he should do at this point?

What's the Connection?

College is about becoming an educated person—learning how to think, solve problems, and make decisions. College is much more than the "sum of its tests." It's about developing yourself as a person and becoming well educated. What does it mean to be well educated? Simply put, being well educated is about the pursuit of human excellence.[1]

Colleges help societies *preserve the past* and *create the future*. Studying the history of the U.S. Constitution in a political science course as opposed to studying potential cures for cancer in a cell biology course are concrete examples. Colleges help us look back (preserve the past) and look ahead (create the future).

College in a Box?

Have you ever thought about the fact that college courses appear to exist in discrete "boxes"? Schools tend to place courses in academic departments, and your class schedule reflects these divisions. For example, your schedule this term might look something like the one in Figure 11.1.

This organizing system helps you keep things straight in your head, and it also helps your school organize a complex institution. Instructors normally work in one department or another. And classes are categorized into particular **academic disciplines**.

But something students often wonder about is how to connect the dots. What's the big picture? Knowledge isn't quite as neat as departments and boxes;

academic discipline a branch of learning, instruction, or emphasis

VARK It!

Aural: What courses are you taking this term? How would your "College in a Box" look? As you read this section, talk through the problems with this approach.

FIGURE 11.1

Most Schools Compartmentalize Learning

	M	T	W	Th	F
9–10	ENG			COMM	
10–11		MATH			
11–12			PSYCH		PSYCH

© Cengage Learning

it's messy. It overlaps and merges. Despite the divisions and abbreviations colleges use to divide up knowledge, you might be able to take a somewhat similar course in visual art as an art course, a computer science course, or a communication course. You've probably noticed that you sometimes hear something discussed in one of your classes that's also being discussed in another one. Knowledge is interconnected. College in a Box isn't an accurate way of looking at things.

Even though each academic discipline has its own history and identity and way of asking questions and finding answers, the disciplines aren't as distinct as your class schedule might lead you to believe.

It takes courage to grow up and become who you really are.

e. e. cummings, American poet (1894–1962)

How Do the Disciplines Connect?

The Circle of Learning (see Figure 11.2) illustrates the interconnectedness of knowledge. Although this circle could be drawn in many different ways, using many different traditional academic disciplines, here is an example to get you thinking.[2]

It works like this. Let's start at the top of the circle with *math,* which is a basic "language" with rules and conventions, just like spoken language. You manipulate numbers and operations and functions, just as you manipulate sounds and words and sentences. Now, move clockwise around the circle.

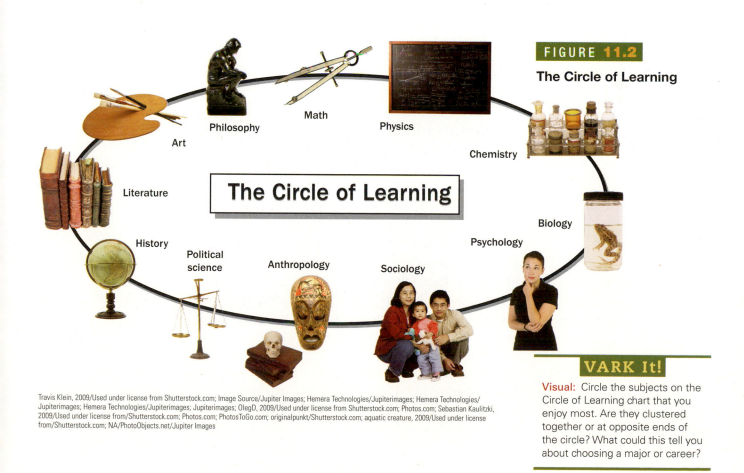

FIGURE 11.2

The Circle of Learning

The Circle of Learning

Philosophy · Art · Math · Physics · Chemistry · Literature · Biology · History · Political science · Anthropology · Sociology · Psychology

Travis Klein, 2009/Used under license from Shutterstock.com; Image Source/Jupiter Images; Hemera Technologies/Jupiterimages; Hemera Technologies/Jupiterimages; Hemera Technologies/Jupiterimages; Jupiterimages; OlegD, 2009/Used under license from Shutterstock.com; Photos.com; Sebastian Kaulitzki, 2009/Used under license from Shutterstock.com; Photos.com; PhotosToGo.com; originalpunkt/Shutterstock.com; aquatic creature, 2009/Used under license from Shutterstock.com; NA/PhotoObjects.net/Jupiter Images

VARK It!

Visual: Circle the subjects on the Circle of Learning chart that you enjoy most. Are they clustered together or at opposite ends of the circle? What could this tell you about choosing a major or career?

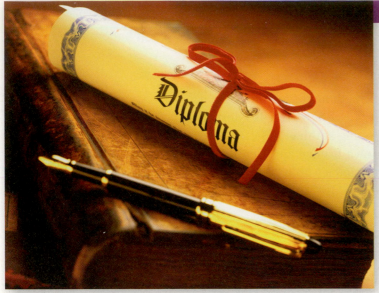

David Chasey/Photodisc/Getty Images

VARK It!

Visual: Select a quote from this chapter that is particularly memorable to you. Create a poster of the quote, using a large font and graphics, to hang on a wall in your room.

Math is the fundamental language of *physics,* one branch of which studies atomic and subatomic particles. When atoms combine into molecules, such as carbon dioxide, the academic discipline involved is called *chemistry.* Chemicals combine to create living organisms studied in *biology* courses. Living organisms don't just exist; they think and behave, leading to the study of *psychology.* They also interact in groups, families, and societies, which you study in *sociology.* You can also study units of living beings throughout time and across cultures in the discipline of *anthropology.* These units—people—who live and work together are typically governed or govern themselves, leading to *political science.* Let's keep going.

When an account of peoples and countries and their rulers is recorded, you study *history.* These written accounts, sometimes factual or sometimes fictional (for pleasure or intrigue) comprise the study of *literature.* Literature is one way to record impressions and provoke reactions—poetry is a good example—through the use of words. But images and symbols can do the same things—enter *art.* A particular question artists ask is "What is beauty?" otherwise known as aesthetics*,* which is also a particular topic of study in *philosophy.* Philosophy also includes another subspecialty called number theory*,* one of the earliest branches of pure mathematics. And now we're all the way around the Circle of Learning, arriving right back at *math.*

That's a quick rundown. Of course, many academic disciplines don't appear on this chart, but they could and should. The point isn't which disciplines are represented. Instead, the Circle of Learning demonstrates that academic disciplines are interconnected because knowledge itself is interconnected. *Anthropology* (understanding people throughout time and across cultures) can provide an important foundation for *political science* (how people are governed or govern themselves), and *history* (a record of peoples and countries and rulers) can easily be the basis for *literature.* Using what you're learning in one discipline can lead to deeper understanding in another, and although some of your instructors will help you connect the dots, putting it all together is basically your responsibility.

In your career, you'll need to use knowledge without necessarily remembering in which course you learned it. You'll be thinking critically, creatively, and connectedly, solving problems and calling upon all the skills you're developing in all the courses you're studying in college. The bottom line is that connections count. Recognize them, use them, and strengthen them to reinforce your learning.

> *If you can absolutely be relied upon; if when you say a thing is so, it is so; if when you say you will do a thing, you do it; then you carry with you a passport to universal esteem.*
>
> ~GRENVILLE KLEISER

Do what you'll say you'll do. When you're given a task, complete it on time and with real quality. When you say you'll do something, do it. In college, your professors rely on you to get assignments done on time and according to their instructions. And when working on team projects, your classmates must be able to trust not only your intentions, but your results. This character trait, reliability, is a cornerstone of professional achievement and recognition. When your colleagues and supervisors learn that they can trust you to do what you say you'll do, you become recognized—and rewarded—as a valuable member of the team.

How to Choose a Major and a Career

Like many students, you probably put value in how well college prepares you for a profession.[3] Choosing a college major and directing yourself toward a prospective career can be stressful. Many students feel pressure to make the right decision—and make it right now! You might hear conflicting advice from family members that put a high priority on financial success above other important factors, for example, and feel overwhelmed by the number of possibilities from which to choose.[4] You may know what you want to do with the rest of your life right now, but many of your classmates don't, and even if they *say* they do, they may well change their minds. Yes, these decisions are important, but there's evidence that you don't have to have it all figured out right away.[5] Where do you start? The decision-making process should involve these critical steps. If you're still deciding, or even if you think you already have, consider how they apply to you.

> **The self is not something that one finds. It's something one creates.**
>
> *Thomas Szasz, Professor Emeritus in Psychiatry, State University of New York Health Science Center, Syracuse*

PhotostoGO.com

Step 1: Follow Your Bliss

In an ideal world, which major and career would you choose? Don't think about anything except the actual content you'd be studying. Don't consider career opportunities, requirements, difficulty, or anything else that might keep you from making these choices in an ideal world. What are you passionate about? If it's skateboarding, think about which majors might apply. Majoring in physics would help you understand skateboard "flight paths," spin, and angles. Majoring in landscape architecture would allow you to design skateparks. Majoring in journalism would put you in a good position to write for a skateboarding magazine.

> ❝ The laws of science do not distinguish between the past and the future. ❞
>
> —STEVEN W. HAWKING

Reason 11: They have unrealistic expectations.

It's easy to lose your focus when you aren't realistic. You may think you can finish a paper in half an hour when it's really going to take a minimum of three hours. When you're not present and honest, you can lose your focus. You may even get discouraged and give up.

Think back on what you actually accomplished today. Did you pay attention to the things and people that are most important to you? Did you make progress toward the future you're trying to create?

TRY It!

Keep track of how realistic you were about your time this week and be prepared to be accountable to your instructor and classmates next week. Keep a journal of each day's biggest accomplishment and most distracting obstacle, and see whether you recognize patterns. Create one pointer of your own to share with your classmates.

Example:
Monday I thought I would study for an exam in the evening, but a new TV show started, and I watched it (just like I knew I would...) That was an obstacle, but on the other hand, I did finish a paper for another course later on. Pointer: Be honest about my tendencies and pat myself on the back when I finish something important!

_____

_____

> ❝ Follow your bliss and be what you want to be. Don't climb the ladder of success only to find it's leaning against the wrong wall. ❞
>
> *Dr. Bernie Siegel, physician and writer*

Bryan Allen/CORBIS

Like Ethan Cole from the "FOCUS Challenge Case," you may be wondering what to do with your life. Perhaps the *idealist* in you has one potential career in mind and the *realist* in you has another. The $300,000 salary you'd earn as a surgeon may look very compelling until you consider the years of medical school required after college, the time invested in an internship and residency, and the still further years of specialization. It takes long-term commitment, dedication, and resources—yours or borrowed ones—to make that dream come true. Do these factors lessen the appeal?

Perhaps there's conflict between your ideal career and someone else's idea of an ideal career for you. Comedian Robin Williams once said, "When I told my father I was going to be an actor, he said, 'Fine, but study welding just in case.'"

And perhaps you just don't know yet. If that's the case, don't panic. Despite the increased pressure these days to choose the right major because of rising tuition and a changeable economy, Ethan Cole is right: It's hard to have it all figured out from the start.[6]

One thing is certain: You'll be a happier, more productive person if you do what *you* want to do *and* pursue it vigorously. When it comes to success, ability (*Can* you do it?) and effort (Are you *willing* to invest what it takes?) go hand in hand. Whatever your motivation, remember this. It's unusual for people to become truly successful halfheartedly. There are undeniable emotional and psychological components involved in success. Wayne Gretzky, called the greatest player in the history of hockey, once said, "God gave me a special talent to play the game . . . maybe he didn't give me a talent, he gave me a *passion*."

Having said that, what if your "bliss" just isn't feasible? You'd give anything to play for the NBA, but you're five foot two and female. You dream of being a rock star, but you can't carry a tune. Then it may be time to set aside the dream and get real. Maybe then it's time to translate—or shift—your dreams into goals.

When the statistics are against you, achieving success isn't impossible, but it might take more than expert skill. It might also take some luck, very specific planning, and perseverance.

Step 2: Conduct Preliminary Research

Has it ever occurred to you that you may not have all the facts—accurate ones—about your ideal major? Do you know what it *really* takes? Have you gotten your information from qualified sources—or are you basing your opinion on your friend's reaction to one course he took?

Try an experiment. Choose three majors you're considering, one of which is your ideal major, and send yourself on a fact-finding mission. To find out whether you're on target, get the answers to the following ten questions for each of the three possibilities. Go to the physical location (department) where each major is housed, and interview an instructor. The experiment requires legwork; don't just let your fingers do the clicking.

1. What is the major or certificate?
2. Who is the interviewee?
3. What is the name of the academic department where this major is housed? Where are the department offices physically located on campus?
4. Which introductory courses in this major would give you information about your interests and abilities?
5. Which specialized courses in this major interest you? (List three.)
6. What courses do you have to complete before you can major in the subject?
7. How many students major in this discipline on your campus?
8. Which required course in the major do students usually find most challenging? Which is most engaging? Which is most valued? Why?

VARK It!

Kinesthetic: When you have some free time, go online and look up successful people who have achieved your dream. How did they translate their dreams into goals?

VARK It!

Read/Write: Consider a possible college major or career option and create a list of reasons why it would or wouldn't be a good choice for you.

Carsten Reisinger/Shutterstock.com; Alexander A.Trofimov/Shutterstock.com

> **The elevator to success is out of order, but the steps are always open.**
>
> *Zig Ziglar, American author, salesman, and motivational speaker*

9. How would the interviewee describe the reputation of this department on campus? What is it known for?

10. From the interviewee's perspective, why should a student major in this discipline?

After you complete your interviews, review the facts. Did you change any of your opinions based on what you learned?[7]

Step 3: Take a Good Look at Yourself

EXERCISE 11.1

What Are Your Job Preferences?

Take a good look at yourself and answer the following questions about how you prefer to work. Rank each item 1 or 2 based on your general preference. Although many careers, if not most, require both, your task is to decide which of the two you prefer.

I prefer to work at a job:

1. Alone	_____	With other people	_____
2. Indoors	_____	Outdoors	_____
3. With people	_____	With equipment or materials	_____
4. Directing/leading others	_____	Being directed/led by others	_____
5. Producing information	_____	Managing information	_____
6. In an organized, step-by-step way	_____	In a big-idea, big-picture way	_____
7. Starting things	_____	Completing things	_____
8. Involving a product	_____	Involving a service	_____
9. Solving challenging problems	_____	Generating creative ideas	_____
10. Finding information	_____	Applying information	_____
11. Teaching/training others in groups	_____	Advising/coaching others one-on-one	_____

Now look at your eleven first choices. Identify several career fields that come to mind that would allow you to achieve as many of them as possible.

Here's a bottom-line question: For you—as Dr. Bernie Siegel would say—what *is* the "right wall" to lean your ladder of success on? How do you know? Many first-year college students don't know. They don't have enough experience under their belts to plan for a lifetime. They're in college to *discover*. It all comes down to questions this book has been asking you all along: Who are you? And what do you want? If you're unsure of how to proceed in your decision making, follow these recommendations to see whether they help you bring your future into focus.

VARK It!

Aural: Discuss your personality, strengths, and weaknesses with a close friend. Use this conversation to help inform your decisions about careers and majors.

Send in the SWOT Team! A SWOT analysis is an excellent way to begin taking a good look at yourself in relation to your future. SWOT stands for Strengths, Weaknesses, Opportunities, and Threats. SWOT analyses are typically used in business, but creating one for yourself may be useful when it comes to deciding on a college major and a career. Make a chart with four sections, label each one, and fill them in as objectively as you can.

> **Strengths** are traits that give you a leg up. These are talents you can capitalize on and qualities you can develop.

> **Weaknesses** are traits that currently work against you. You can, however, work to reduce or eliminate them.

> **Opportunities** are conditions or circumstances that work in your favor, like a strong forecast for the future of your prospective career.

> **Threats** are conditions that could have bad effects. Some of these factors are beyond your control; however, sometimes you can figure out ways to make them matter less.

As you create your own chart, begin with two basic questions:

What kinds of forces will impact your potential career?

Internal—forces inside you, such as motivation and skill

External—forces outside you that may affect your success: the job market or economy, for example

What kind of influence can these forces exert?

Positive—some forces will give you a boost toward your goals.

Negative—other forces will work against you.[8]

Let's complete a SWOT analysis for Ethan and his dream of becoming a professional skateboarder. Of course, you might say that, technically, he doesn't need an academic degree for that particular career. But if he wants to pursue related, more traditional careers—design a new skatepark or write for a skateboard magazine, for example—he would need knowledge from design and writing to finance and marketing. Besides, college isn't just about jobs, it's about living a fuller life as a well-educated person.

Look back at the "FOCUS Challenge Case," and see whether you agree with the basic SWOT analysis shown in Figure 11.3.

VARK It!

Read/Write: Before you look carefully at Figure 11.3, make a list of the pros and cons of being a professional skateboarder. Compare your list with what's on the chart here in the chapter.

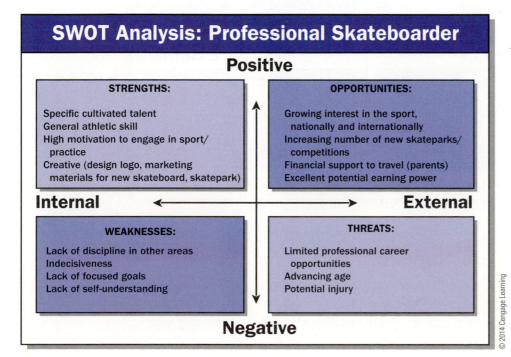

SWOT Analysis: Professional Skateboarder

Positive

STRENGTHS:
Specific cultivated talent
General athletic skill
High motivation to engage in sport/ practice
Creative (design logo, marketing materials for new skateboard, skatepark)

OPPORTUNITIES:
Growing interest in the sport, nationally and internationally
Increasing number of new skateparks/ competitions
Financial support to travel (parents)
Excellent potential earning power

Internal ← → **External**

WEAKNESSES:
Lack of discipline in other areas
Indecisiveness
Lack of focused goals
Lack of self-understanding

THREATS:
Limited professional career opportunities
Advancing age
Potential injury

Negative

© 2014 Cengage Learning

FIGURE 11.3

SWOT Analysis

Looking at his SWOT analysis, what would you conclude? Is professional skateboarding a good career for him? In your view, do the opportunities outweigh the threats? For example, does the possibility of earning big bucks outweigh the risks of possible injuries? If not, could he move toward other potential careers, perhaps some that also involve skateboarding? "Ethan remembered liking geometry, he was good at creative writing, he played the drums like a real jazz musician, and he was an incredible artist." Do you see potential majors for him in college? Sports management? Kinesiology? Architecture? Journalism? Jazz studies? Creative writing? What should Ethan do?

SWOT Analysis

Looking at the model in Figure 11.3, try doing a SWOT Analysis of a career you're considering. If you have no idea where to begin, choose the career of someone you know—a friend or family member. Carefully analyze the Strengths, Weaknesses, Opportunities, and Threats as you see them. It may help to Google the career for specifics and check information-rich, accurate sites like OOH (Occupational Outlook Handbook), compiled by the U.S. Bureau of Labor Statistics. After you're done, write your conclusions below, and share your results in class, if asked. Is the career you've analyzed worth pursuing in your view?

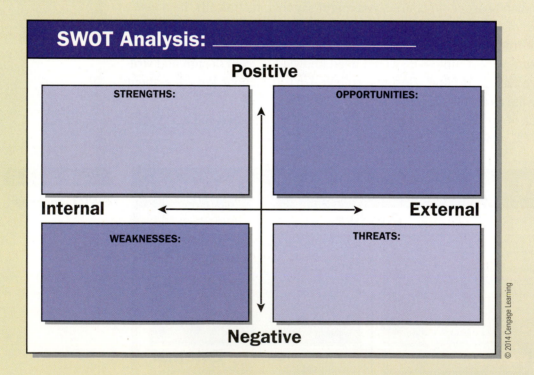

SWOT Analysis: _____

Positive

STRENGTHS:

OPPORTUNITIES:

Internal ← → External

WEAKNESSES:

THREATS:

Negative

© 2014 Cengage Learning

1. _____

2. _____

3. _____

Step 4: Consider Your Major versus Your Career

Which comes first, the chicken or the egg? The major or the career? Silly question? The obvious answer, of course, is that you must first major or earn a certificate in something in college before you can build a career on it. But the question isn't as straightforward as it seems.

Should you choose a major based on an intended career? Perhaps you know you want to be a science teacher, first and foremost. You don't know whether to get an associate's degree in physical science or an associate of arts degree in teaching. You like all sciences, but teaching is your real interest. If you major in science, which one should you emphasize (see Figure 11.4)?

Or instead, should you choose a major first, and then decide on a career? Say you made a firm decision to major in chemistry when your favorite science teacher did "mad scientist" experiments for the class in eighth grade. But at this point, you're not certain of the professional direction you'd like to pursue. Chemistry is your passion, but should you apply your chemistry degree as a forensics expert, a pharmaceutical salesperson, a chemical technician, or a teacher (see Figure 11.5)? You could enter some of these career fields with an associate's degree, but others might require transferring to a four-year school.

So which comes first—major or career? It depends.[9] The answer sounds uncertain, and it's meant to. Although some professional degree programs put you into a particular track right away (nursing, for example), generally either direction can work well. Doors will open and close for you, and as you gain more knowledge and experience, you'll narrow your focus. As you learn more about your chosen major, you'll also learn about its specific career tracks. But it's important to remember that a major doesn't have to lock you into one specific career. And you can always narrow or refocus your area of emphasis by earning your bachelor's degree and continuing your education beyond that.[10]

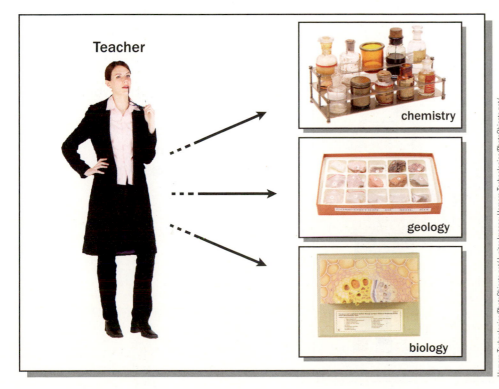

FIGURE 11.4

Which Science Should a Science Teacher Major In?

Teacher

chemistry

geology

biology

Hemera Technologies/PhotoObjects.net/Jupiter Images; Hemera Technologies/PhotoObjects.net/ Jupiter Images; Hemera Technologies/PhotoObjects.net/Jupiter Images; Hemera Technologies/ PhotoObjects.net/Jupiter Images

FIGURE 11.5

Which Career Should a Chemistry Major Choose?

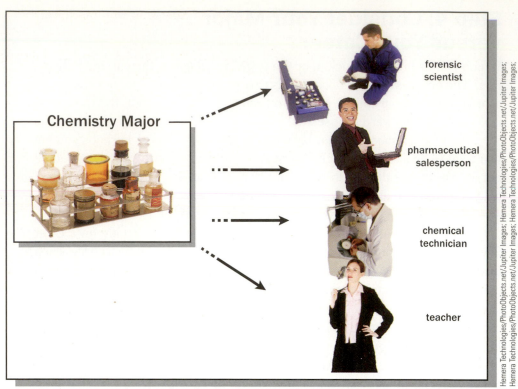

Chemistry Major

forensic scientist

pharmaceutical salesperson

chemical technician

teacher

Hemera Technologies/PhotoObjects.net/Jupiter Images; Hemera Technologies/PhotoObjects.net/Jupiter Images; Hemera Technologies/PhotoObjects.net/Jupiter Images; Hemera Technologies/PhotoObjects.net/Jupiter Images

What's Your Academic Anatomy? Thinking about your academic anatomy is a simple way to begin to get a handle on what you find fulfilling. If you had to rank order the four parts of you listed in Figure 11.6, what would you put in first place? Second, third, and last? To get yourself thinking, ask these questions:

1. Do you find fulfillment by using your *head*? Do you enjoy solving complex problems or thinking through difficult situations? Do you like to reason

FIGURE 11.6

What's Your Academic Anatomy?

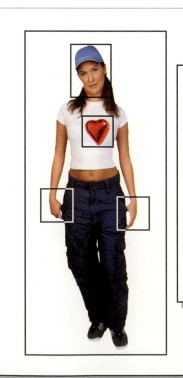

Another way of analyzing your preferences is by considering your "Academic Anatomy." What do you find most satisfying? Working with your

Head?
Heart?
Hands? or
Whole Body?

Hemera Technologies/PhotoObjects.net/Jupiter Images

things out, weigh evidence, and think critically? Someone working toward a paralegal certificate might fit this category.

2. Do you find it satisfying to work with matters of the *heart*? Are you the kind of person others come to with problems because you listen and care? Does trying to make others happy make you happy? A nursing major might be what students with this preference choose, for example.

3. Do you like to create things with your *hands*? Do you enjoy making art? Doing hands-on projects? Building things out of other things? A drafting major who designs and builds models might be what students with this preference choose, for example.

4. Do you excel at physical activities that involve your *whole body*? Are you athletic? Do you like to stay active, no matter what you're doing? A physical therapy major who goes on to work in a rehabilitation facility helping stroke victims relearn to walk might be what students with this preference choose, for example.

Now look at your academic anatomy rankings. Of course, the truth is that "all of you" is involved in everything you do. And achieving balance is important. But what are your priorities? This type of simple analysis can be one way of informing you about who you are and where you should be headed.

However, no system for choosing a major is perfect. In fact, most are imperfect at best. Here are four things to consider:

1. Sometimes students who don't select a likely major based on their "anatomical preferences" can still be successful. A whole-body person (like Ethan Cole probably is) may decide to major in art (using his hands). But he'll have to find other ways to meet his whole-body needs unless he becomes a sculptor involved in creating large constructed projects.

2. You may intentionally choose an unlikely major. Perhaps art (using your hands) comes so naturally to you that you decide to major in science (using your head). You need the challenge to stay fully involved in getting your education. Although it may sound unlikely, it's been known to happen.

3. You may choose an unlikely major because one particular course turns you on. You had no idea majoring in this subject was even possible, and you didn't know what it entailed. But you find studying it fascinating—so you shift gears to focus all your attention on it.

4. You may be equally engaged, no matter what. You love subjects that require using your head, hands, heart, and whole body. The anatomy of learning is less important to you than other factors—a teacher whose enthusiasm is contagious, for example.[11]

Are you fit company for the person you wish to become?

Anonymous

How do I find a job? Increasingly, job searches (and even applications) may take place on the Internet. Such powerful job-search sites as Monster.com, TheLadders.com, and Job.com can help in your job searches in many ways:

- Such sites help you search for jobs by category and location.
- They help you apply with features such as "Create Your Resume," "Job-Hunt Strategy," and "Plan Your Career."
- They also help you market yourself, plan for interviews, and test potential salaries using online salary calculators.

Many of the strengths you've developed while taking online courses—self-discipline, scheduling, focus, working ahead—will come in handy as you search for and start on that new job. Increasingly the skills that are useful in tomorrow's workplace are often the skills you've sharpened in your college work. And the online courses and concentrations you complete may well prepare you for work in a growing field. Perhaps you've already chosen your career field; but if not,

it may help you to know this information about some of the fastest growing occupations in the coming years:

- **Networks systems and data communications analysts** perform tasks in data communication systems like the Internet. This is one of the fastest growing occupations with a 55% increase in the number of jobs over ten years.
- **Healthcare assistants,** including physician, medical, dental, and other assistants, work with healthcare professionals to provide the best possible patient care. This area may show an increase of around 50%.
- **Physical therapist assistants** help treat victims of accidents or people with disabilities. This area may grow by 44%.[12]
- **Computer software engineers** develop, design, test, and evaluate the systems that operate our computers. This area may experience an increase of 43%.
- **Dental hygienists and assistants** support dentists in providing patient care. These fields should increase by 43%.

Improve Your Grade
Online Flashcards
Glossary

Ethan's rankings would probably go something like this: (1) whole body, (2) hands, (3) heart, and (4) head. And just because "head" is in last place for him doesn't mean he's doomed in college. A career as a financial analyst sitting behind a desk probably wouldn't be his cup of tea, for example. But it may well be yours. As you decide, you may want to consider whether your choice is "anatomically correct."

Whatever major or career you're aiming for—or still looking for—make sure you follow the four steps outlined in this chapter to create the future you want.

EXERCISE 11.3

Get a Job!

Bring an employment ad from a newspaper or Internet website to class, perhaps for a job that's related to your prospective career. After carefully considering your individual ads in small groups of three or four, create an employment ad for the "job" of college student. For example, "_____ College seeks applicants with excellent skills in oral and written communication, problem solving, time management, and technology, for positions as professional students preparing for a variety of future opportunities. . . ." Your ad should list particular job requirements, benefits, information about your institution, and so on, and be as much like a real ad as possible. When your group is finished constructing its ad, present it to the entire class.[13]

What's In **YOUR** Briefcase?

ZOOM IN, ZOOM OUT

Perhaps the most common question asked during hiring interviews is this one: "Where do you see yourself in five years?" Undoubtedly, it's a tough question. In today's uncertain economy, the most honest answer is "Are you kidding—who knows? I'm not even sure what I'll have for dinner tonight." Five years seems like forever. Although your imaginary answer may be the most truthful one, it's not necessarily smart.[14]

One thing that trips up many first-year college students is thinking that they have to have it all figured out—now. They think there should be a linear path between their major and their career.[15] For example, a student should enter college having declared a business major, earn business degree, and then land a good job in the business world. "On a clear day," as the old song goes, "you can see forever." It should be that easy.

Realistically, clarity typically unfolds as you go. Many students don't have a particular major or a career in mind. When things become increasingly foggy during their "trip" through college, they lose their way or maybe even give up. Rather than being linear, the path is often nonlinear. You work toward success by keeping two concurrent perspectives in mind: zooming out on your big-picture goals and zooming in on the "up close and personal" details of managing yourself on a daily basis. While you're in college, you must be able to zoom in on your individual courses and zoom out to your overall degree plan. The same principle definitely holds in your career.[16]

So when the time comes and the interviewer asks you the inevitable question, "Where do you see yourself in five years?" take this advice:

1. Reflect on what you will say beforehand.
2. Figure out what the interviewer is trying to learn about you. Does she expect a full-blown answer, or is she just trying to see how you think?
3. Shorten the time frame so that you can answer: "I'm not really sure how many years it will take, but I do know that I want to join an organization just like this one and work on a highly creative team to learn all I can. Challenges are important to me."

On the other hand, don't:

1. Make up something so far-fetched that even you don't believe what you're saying.
2. Identify the exact job you want in the future. ("Honestly? I'd like your job. Are you planning to retire in the next five years?")
3. Feel obliged to answer the question literally, even if you don't really know for sure. Turn the question into one you can answer, communicating what you want the interviewer to know about you.[17] Although you're being asked to zoom out, instead zoom in on who you are and what you want. It's important to keep both perspectives in mind in your journey toward success.

Think about how you would answer the question identified in this section if you were applying for a job you could get today. When you finish your degree or certificate, would you expect your answer to be different in some ways? Might it be the same in some ways?

_____

_____

_____

At the beginning of this chapter, Ethan Cole, a confused and discouraged student, faced a challenge. Now after reading this chapter, would you respond differently to any of the questions you answered about the "FOCUS Challenge Case"? Using what you learned in the chapter, write a paragraph ending to Ethan's case study. What are some of the possible outcomes for Ethan?

step
4 ACTION Your Plans for Change

1. Where are you when it comes to choosing a major or career? If you haven't decided yet, what specific information from this chapter will you use? If you've already decided, had you already taken these suggestions into account? Will you change any of your plans?

2. Do you know someone working in a career field that is disillusioned or disappointed with the choice he or she made? How will you know your decision is a wise one? What can you do to make sure?

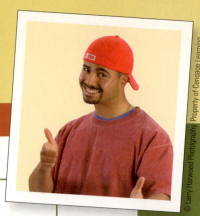

READINESS CHECK

How this chapter relates to YOU

1. When it comes to creating a future for yourself, what, if anything, do you find challenging?

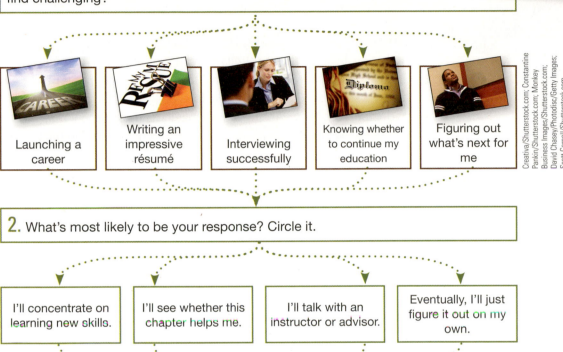

| Launching a career | Writing an impressive résumé | Interviewing successfully | Knowing whether to continue my education | Figuring out what's next for me |

2. What's most likely to be your response? Circle it.

| I'll concentrate on learning new skills. | I'll see whether this chapter helps me. | I'll talk with an instructor or advisor. | Eventually, I'll just figure it out on my own. |

3. What would you have to do to increase your likelihood of success? Will you do it this term?

Example: Find a role model to talk with about these issues. Yes!

How YOU will relate to this chapter

What are you most interested in learning about? Put check marks by those topics.

☐ How to launch a career

☐ How to write a résumé

☐ How to interview successfully

☐ What to consider if you're thinking of continuing your education

☐ How to put what you've learned in college to good use

☐ How to think about the future

● How motivated are you to learn more about getting the right start in college? (5 = high, 1 = low) ___

● How ready are you to read now? ___ (If something is in your way, take care of it if you can, zero in and focus.)

● How long do you think it will take you to complete this chapter? If you start and stop, keep track of your overall time. ____ hour(s) ____ minutes

Anthony Lopez

Anthony Lopez was average in nearly every sense of the word. He played T-ball as a kid, but not particularly well. He didn't like school much, but he went when he felt like it. He didn't have many friends except for a few kids that lived in the eight city blocks that made up his neighborhood. He was even sandwiched between two older brothers and two younger sisters. His brothers were successful—one was an attorney and the other a doctor. Somehow, deep inside himself, Anthony knew that measuring up would be hard for him. Maybe that's why he decided to make his mark in his own way.

You could say that Anthony's kid sister, Gina, was his closest friend. Even though she was four years younger, the two of them would pal around the neighborhood. They could laugh over absolutely anything, and their specialty was pulling pranks on all the other neighborhood kids. For a while, the two of them were inseparable. Whenever you saw Gina, you knew that Anthony was close by.

But as Anthony got older, things changed. The trouble started in middle school. His mom, who worked more than one job to keep the family afloat, was worried that he was getting in with the wrong crowd. But Anthony wasn't worried. His friends knew where to get cigarettes and alcohol—even drugs. When he was with them, he imagined the other kids looked up to him and his tough-guy friends. By the time high school rolled around, Anthony already had a record. Eventually, he dropped out, left home, and basically lived on the streets. When he needed money, he snatched a purse or wallet. He lost contact with his family, and there seemed to be no turning back. Drugs were a way of life for him, and he began sinking deeper and deeper into a life that most people predicted wouldn't turn out well.

Monkey Business Images/Shutterstock.com

© Larry Harwood Photography. Property of Cengage Learning

© Cengage Learning

City Youth Connect

City Youth Connect is a not-for-profit organization designed to give young people an opportunity to thrive and succeed through involvment in after-school activities, jobs, and training programs.

- After School Programs
- Jobs and Internships
- Family Support
- Reading and Writing
- Tutoring
- Intramural Sports

Contact Nicky Russo
2015 East Front St
222-556-8545

Sap/Shutterstock.com

DRUG REHABILITATION

TAKE THE FIRST STEP TO YOUR NEW LIFE

Criminal Search- County		
Name: Lopez, Anthony	**DOB:** 7-10-1989	**SSN:** XXX-XX

RESULT: RECORD FOUND	
STATE/COUNTY:	VERIFIED INFORMATION
Case #:	T3-13145
Filing Date:	8-18-08
Offense Date:	8-03-08
Disposition Date:	9-05-08
Charges:	
	(MISDEMEANOR) PETTY LARCENY – T ITEMS

But that was then, and this was now. Anthony's life probably would have been headed in the wrong direction entirely, if it hadn't been for several wakeup calls, including seeing his little sister, Gina, on the street one day. He tried to talk with her, but she was so high that she didn't even recognize him. Anthony saw that she was repeating his worst mistakes, which troubled him deeply. The stark realization that he might be ruining her life in addition to his own shocked him back into reality.

Now Anthony was part of an inner-city youth organization for kids like him. The group's leader, Nicky Russo, had once been a gang member himself. He reached out to Anthony, and Anthony responded. Anthony was on a mission to find Gina and get her into the group. Anthony's life was changing, and his life's goal was becoming clear: to help other people like him. He decided to earn his GED and enroll in the best local college he could find to earn an associate's degree in social services. And that's exactly what he did.

As he sat in his favorite class, Urban Social Issues, Anthony realized that he had made the right choice. So much of what he heard his instructor lecturing about had been a part of his own past. As he got deeper into the associate's program, Anthony learned that an associate's degree in social services was a general degree that prepared graduates for many types of jobs. But what if he

wanted to be an actual social worker? He learned that the need for social workers was very high, working with young children to older adults. He was taking classes like Racial, Ethnic, and Minority Groups and Sociology of the Family.

Even though the classes were hard, it wasn't long before Anthony was totally engrossed, and he knew he wanted to continue his education. With an associate's degree in social services, he could certainly work more knowledgeably alongside Nicky in the inner city. But what if he transferred to a four-year school for a bachelor's degree in sociology? What if he wanted to earn a master's degree in social work to specialize and become a school or hospital social worker? What if he wanted to conduct research and teach, like his college instructors? What would getting a Ph.D. require, and should he even be thinking that far ahead? A million questions were forming in his mind.

What did the future hold for Anthony? Right now, he couldn't answer that question. But he did know that his future would be different from the future he might have had without college. What had always been true about Anthony was now true in the best possible sense: Anthony would make his mark.

Scholastic Studio 10/Photolibrary/Getty Images

Sociology Program Comparison

	Bachelor's Degree
Ethnic Relations	
City in a Global Society	
Societal Change and Development	
Environmental Sociology	
Global Sociology	
Sociological Analysis	
Classical Theories of Society	
Contemporary Theories of Society	
Sociological Field Methods	
Gender and Society	
Global Sociology	
Quantitative Methods	
Regression and Multivariate Data Analysis	
Policy Issues in Education	
Economics of Educational Policy	
Public Policy	
Demographic Analysis	
Evaluation of Educational Programs	
Race and Class in American Cities	
Masters Thesis Project	
Qualitative Research	
Sociological Analysis	

© Cengage Learning

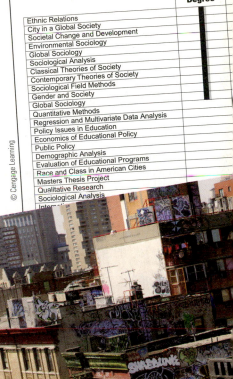
Philip Lange/Shutterstock.com

© Cengage Learning

© Cengage Learning

an sociology text
ps you understand
t, present & future
around the globe

Kleniewski • Thomas

FOURTH EDITION

Cities,
Change
& Conflict

A POLITICAL ECONOMY OF URBAN LIFE

ties for the economic, cultural and political life
s accessible text from Nancy Kleniewski and
Change and Conflict: A Political Economy of
onomy perspective to introduce you to the basic
in sociology. At the same time, the authors also

Cities, C
POLITI

SOCIAL SERVICES
ASSOCIATE OF ARTS DEGREE

The AA degree with an emphasis in Sociology is designed to provide a better understanding of how humans act and interact in social settings. The program offered provides an excellent foundation for students seeking to continue their education in Sociology, either pursuing a Bachelor's or Master's degree.

First Semester

		3
ENGL 101	English Composition I	3
SOC 101	Introduction to Sociology	3
	Science Elective	3
	Humanities Elective	12
	Total Credits	

Second Semester

		3
		3
ENGL 102	English Composition II	3

step 2 REACTION What Do *You* Think?

1. Do you have anything in common with Anthony? If so, how are you managing the situation so that you can be successful?
2. Anthony appears to be headed toward a life of service. Do you know anyone like him who has turned his or her life around? Describe the situation.
3. What are the pros and cons of continuing his education beyond an associate's degree?
4. In your view, should he continue his education beyond a two-year degree? Why or why not?

What's the Next Step?

You've done it. You've nearly finished your first term of college. Perhaps at this point, you're even jumping ahead to when you finish all of your courses. Then what? Yogi Berra, the baseball giant, is known for having a way with words. His advice was, "When you come to a fork in the road, take it." *Which one?* you ask. Precisely! (Yogi Berra is said to have been giving directions to his New Jersey home, and both streets worked equally well.)

After you achieve your college goals—whether you're taking a few targeted classes for a particular reason or earning a certificate or associate's degree—you'll come to a fork in the road. Should you take the fork leading toward pursuing a particular career right away or the fork leading toward continuing your education? This chapter won't answer the question *for* you, but it will give you some things to think about. Just as was the case with Yogi Berra's famous advice, both forks in *your* road will lead you toward the same thing: *your* future. What you decide to do and when you decide to do it will be up to you.

VARK It!

Visual: Draw a mind map that shows the various "forks" in your future. Where might you go, and why? Provide some possibilities and reasons.

ilbusca/iStockphoto.com

When you come to a fork in the road, take it.

Yogi Berra, baseball player and manager

Launching a Career: Plan Your Work and Work Your Plan

Career Auction

Assume you have $100,000 to spend on the following items. In a few minutes, your instructor will begin a real-live auction, putting one item at a time up for auction. Before the auction begins, budget your money in the first column. You may select as many items as you wish to bid on, but you may not place all your money on any single item. As the group auction proceeds, fill in the appropriate amounts that are actually spent by members of the class for each item.

	BUDGETED AMOUNT	WINNING BID
1. Becoming the CEO of a leading Fortune 500 company	_____	_____
2. Being a top earner in your career field	_____	_____
3. Being the number-one expert in your profession	_____	_____
4. Having good friends on the job	_____	_____
5. Being your own boss	_____	_____
6. Creating a good balance between productive work and a happy family life	_____	_____
7. Having opportunities for travel and adventure in your job	_____	_____
8. Doing work you find fully satisfying	_____	_____
9. Working in a beautiful setting	_____	_____
10. Being a lifelong learner so that your career can develop and change over time	_____	_____

Let's assume, for now, that you decide to go straight into your chosen career field after college. You've been focused all along, earned your degree, and now you're ready to find a job that fits your new skills, your personality—*you*! "Fit" is the key word in that last sentence. Where you choose to launch your career and who you work with will be critical factors in your job satisfaction.

The two questions posed early in this book resurface now: "Who are you?" and "What do you want?" Working your way through *FOCUS*, you have learned more about who you are (although this is a lifelong quest). In this final chapter, we'll deal with "What do you want?" The answer to that question can be just as important.

What do you really want from a career? What's important to you? Even though your views may change over time, it's important to start thinking about them now. In Exercise 12.1, item 4, "Having good friends on the job," may be a top priority now, but item 5, "Being your own boss," may be more appealing a few years down the road, after you have some additional work experience under your belt. Maybe you already prepared for a career once, but something has changed. The field you entered has transformed over time, so that you need

> **I always wanted to be somebody, but I should have been more specific.**
>
> *Lily Tomlin, comedian*

to retool. Or a career that attracted you earlier turned out to be much less engaging than you expected. Or your family has grown and you need a career that brings in more resources. Going back to college can give you exactly the help you need. You may be older than the students sitting around you, but you deserve the same educational opportunities. Interestingly, according to research, the most important factor in job satisfaction isn't any of the ten items in Exercise 12.1. The number one contributor to job satisfaction, statistically speaking, is the quality of your relationship with your boss.[1] Here are some suggestions to help you launch the career you're aiming for.

Try on a Career for Size

If all your jobs thus far have been just that—*jobs*—to help you pay the bills, how do you know what you want in a *career*? A career is different from a job. It's a profession you've chosen and prepared for. Perhaps you've had more than a string of jobs, and your career is well under way, but now you'd like to go in a

GOING PRO

BE REMARKABLE

> **You are the only one who can use your ability. It is an awesome responsibility.**
> ~ZIG ZIGLAR

Go for extra credit. In some of your courses, your instructors may give extra credit. You could be allowed to do something extra, beyond the requirements on the syllabus, to raise your grade. But what's extra credit in terms of your career? On the job, you have "extra credit" when you develop abilities that stand out. You speak German and no one else does, so when something needs translating, you're the go-to person. You know how to use Excel spreadsheets to organize complicated information and make it useful. Or you're so exceptional at PowerPoint that you're affectionately referred to as the "PowerPoint King." Think of what your special talent might be, and come up with a plan to develop and practice that ability. Find ways of showing others that your talent is helpful to the organization. Mention your special gift in interviews, and give examples of when it has been useful in the past. Volunteer to take on tasks where you can use your special skills to make a difference. In your professional career as well as in school, go for "extra credit."

different direction. Or perhaps you haven't launched your career yet. Exactly how *do* you launch a new career? You have to start somewhere, so perhaps you'd search online or through actual newspaper want ads. There are plenty of career exploration websites online. Check out these career mega websites to explore some options:

> Careerbuilder.com
> Monster.com
> The Occupational Outlook Handbook (www.bls.gov/oco/)
> Americasjobexchange.com/
> Career-Journal.com
> US.jobs/ (by the National Labor Exchange)
> USAJobs.gov
> TrueCareers.com
> AllJobSearch.com[2]

You can Google and surf to your heart's content.

But you may be likely to read something like this: "Opening in . . . (anything). Experience required." Isn't that the way it always goes? You have to *have* experience in order to get a job that will *give* you experience. This problem is one many people face. Sure, you have experience. It's just not the right kind. Perhaps you've bagged fries, mowed yards, bussed tables, and chauffeured pizzas up to this point. If that's not the kind of experience the posted opening is looking for, how do you get the right kind? Or perhaps you're in school to switch career fields. You have experience, but it won't help you go in a different direction. The process of job-hunting includes many different steps. Here are some things for you to consider doing during your time in college. One important suggestion is to try a job on for size. Take a look at the three possibilities described in Figure 12.1.

These experiences help you in three ways. First, they allow you to test a potential career field. The actual day-to-day work may be exactly what you expected, or not. They show you whether that particular career field is one you'd really be interested in. *I had no idea this field was so cutthroat, hectic, dull . . . exciting, stimulating, invigorating. . . .* A thumbs-down can be just as informative as a thumbs-up. At least you can remove one option from your list. Second, internships, co-ops, and service-learning opportunities give you experience to list on your résumé. And third, they help you make connections with others in the field, and sometimes they even lead to employment.

> It is not what we get but who we become, what we contribute . . . that gives meaning to our lives.

Anthony Robbins, motivational speaker and author

Eric Robert/SYGMA/CORBIS

	Description: What is . . . ?	What kind of experience do I get?	Why would I want to do it?	How do I get involved?
Internship	An internship is an opportunity for you to work alongside a professional in a career field of interest to you, and to learn from him or her.	Your supervisor will mentor you, and you'll get a clearer picture of what the career field is like.	Some majors will require you to complete an internship as a part of your program, for licensure or certification, for example.	Internships may be offered through your academic major department, or through a central office on campus, or sometimes you can pursue one on your own through the Internet or personal connections.
Co-op Program	Co-op programs allow you to take classes and then apply what you've learned on the job, either after or while you take classes.	You may take classes for a term and then work full-time for a term. You can test a career field.	A potential employer can get a sense of your potential, and you can gain practical experience to put on your résumé.	Your advisor will be able to tell you whether your program has co-op opportunities.
Service-Learning	Some classes contain service-learning experiences in which you volunteer your time.	A service-learning component built right into the syllabus can give you valuable, practical experience.	The emphasis is on hands-on learning and connecting what you're learning in class with what you're experiencing out of class. If you take a class on aging, for example, you may work with a senior citizen at an assisted living facility to apply what you're learning in class.	If you're particularly interested in hands-on learning, ask your advisor to recommend classes with service-learning components that will benefit you.

FIGURE 12.1

Three Ways to Try a Job on for Size

The key to successful trial experiences such as internships is the relationship between you and your sponsor in the host organization. If you're not being given enough to do, or not allowed to test your skills in a particular area, speak up. The answer may be put in terms of company policy, or you're "not quite ready for prime time." Nevertheless, you must communicate about these kinds of important issues. No one can read your mind! As you work toward launching your career, keep up with the latest information. Read up on résumé writing and interviewing, networking, hot career fields, and the latest employment trends. Use the information in this chapter to pique your interest, and search further on your own.

Group Résumé[3]

Your instructor will provide a sheet of newsprint and several markers per team of three to four students. Your job is to work on the floor, desktops, or somewhere with sufficient space to create a group résumé, highlighting all the characteristics you bring with you as a group that can help you succeed in college. Your combined group qualifications may look like this:

Qualifications:
- 27 combined years of work experience
- background in four different industries
- familiarity with Word, PowerPoint, Photoshop, and Excel
- proven research skills
- eagerness to learn
- well-developed time management skills
- interest in networking with others

After each team has completed the task, hang the newsprint sheets on the walls to create a gallery and present your group résumé to the rest of the class.

Build a Portfolio of Your Best Work

Even though it feels good to progress through your degree plan, and move on from one course to another, it's important to keep a record of each class. A potential employer may want to know exactly what you learned in Principles of Web Design, so that she can tell if what you learned matches the way her company does things. An interviewer may ask you about the course you were most successful in. You don't want to stammer and say, "Uh, let me get back to you on that. . . ." You want to sound knowledgeable. Build a portfolio of your best work. Your college may have a formal way to help you do that through a course management system like Blackboard or an online electronic portfolio requirement, for example. If not, begin compiling a portfolio of your own. Keep copies of your best papers or other assignments, and write a summary of how each assignment relates to your career goals. If a prospective employer asks you about your writing skills, you can produce a paper on the spot. Or if you bring a laptop with you to an interview, you can access your best PowerPoint presentation or show a website you designed yourself.

> **VARK It!**
>
> **Kinesthetic:** Build a portfolio of your best work from each learning style. For example, include your best essay, best recorded (video or audio) presentation, and so on.

Network, Network, Network!

The old saying is partially true: "It's not *what* you know, it's *who* you know." Who you know *is* important, but what you know is important, too. Another

Don't follow your dreams; chase them.
Richard Dumb

iStockphoto.com/Michael Svoboda

© Larry Harwood Photography. Property of Cengage Learning.

version of the saying, which is more accurate, goes like this: "It's not who you know, it's who you know, knows (and who THEY know)." If you're a Facebook addict, put these skills to work as you start to launch your career. Online sites help you "hook up" professionally with people who can help you, like LinkedIn (www.linkedin.com), where you can build an online network of contacts, contacts of your contacts, and so forth. In minutes, you can find thousands of people who know people who work in the industry you're interested in. According to the site, you can connect, stay informed about your contacts and industry, and find the people and knowledge you need to achieve your goals. And of course, instead or in addition, you can network with real people in person, too. Ask people you know about who they know that works in your career field, contact these people, meet for coffee, for example, and pursue networking the old-fashioned (but highly effective) way.[4]

Write the Right Résumé

Interestingly, today companies may receive hundreds of applications for particular positions. Some experts say that instead of simply looking at résumés, companies may request and look at your social media presence on Facebook, LinkedIn, blogs, YouTube, and so forth. This trend has already begun.[5] However, learning how to write a written résumé is still a vital skill for most of the jobs you might apply for.

In today's competitive world, when literally hundreds of people may be applying for one choice position, how should a résumé be written? Can a résumé be solid, but not stuffy? Professional, but still personal? Thorough, but brief? Actually, there's more than one way to write a résumé, depending on how much experience you have in the career field you'd like to work in.

> **Skills Approach:** If your work experience has little to do with the career field you'd like to enter, but you've learned important skills you could transfer to your new job, use a *skills* approach, as shown in Marcus Brown's résumé.

> **Chronological Approach:** If you have a work history that's relevant, use a chronological approach (that details job by job what you've done), as shown in Jennifer Ortega's résumé.

Take a look to see whether you can detect the differences between these two sample applicants' résumés. Assume they earned the same degree and are applying for the same job.

It's likely that Marcus Brown is a traditionally aged college student. Notice that he has little experience in the field he'd like to work in after getting his certificate in Web Design. Contrast his résumé with the following

chronological arranging information in time order beginning with the most recent job

MARCUS BROWN
1234 Aspen Way, Apartment 105
Great Bluffs, CO 89898
(555) 987-6543
mbrown@gbtc.edu

CAREER OBJECTIVE

To obtain a position as a web designer for a large health care organization

EDUCATION

Great Bluffs Technical College, Great Bluffs, CO
Certificate in Web Design
GPA 3.2/4.0
Personally financed 100% of college tuition by working two jobs

HONORS

Selected for City Council Outstanding Leadership Award (College Division), 2014
Awarded Technology Scholarship, GBCC Foundation

SUMMARY OF ACADEMIC COURSEWORK

Introduction to Web Graphics	Web Development Software
Introduction to Web Multimedia	Electronic Commerce
Principles of Web Design	Emerging Technologies

SKILLS

Technology
Do part-time freelance work, web-page design
Work in Word, PowerPoint, Excel, Access, Macromedia Flash, Dreamweaver, Java, HTML,
    PHP, Adobe Acrobat, and Photoshop

Graphics
Designed flyers and posters for campus events for GBCC Office of Campus Activities

Writing
Wrote columns for GBCC student online newsletter

EMPLOYMENT HISTORY

Server, Pancake Heaven, 2010–2012
Cashier, Toyland, 2010–present
Ticket Taker, Movies at the Mall, 2012–present

REFERENCES (available on request)

Annotations:

Center your name, and use a standard résumé format. Many companies now scan résumés so that they can be read conveniently from one source, so use key words from the job ad. If you submit a hard copy, skip the neon pink paper that you may think helps you stand out from other applicants. Go for a highly professional look.

Make sure your résumé is well organized and cleanly formatted. Recent research indicates that recruiters in many fields spend approximately six seconds on each résumé. Eye tracking studies show that they spend more time reading highly organized résumés with clear formatting.[6]

Provide numbers whenever you can. Text can be glossed over, but numbers stand out and make your accomplishments more "quantifiable."

Match words used in the job ad. If the add says, the company is looking for a candidate who has "outstanding leadership" skills, make sure those words appear somewhere on your résumé. Don't lie, of course, but some companies now use software that searches for particular terms.[7]

Select coursework that applies directly to the advertised position.

Even if you aren't applying for a job as a web designer, remember that technology is important in today's workplace. Don't underrate your competence. If you're a traditionally aged, younger student who's very tech-savvy, you should realize that many senior employees don't know as much as you do!

If you're able, show that you have worked all through college to demonstrate your commitment to your goal. If you don't have much experience, you may also emphasize volunteer work that you have done, if it relates.

Always obtain preapproval from your references, even if you don't list their names. You may be asked to provide them on a moment's notice.

© 2014 Cengage Learning

---

one, where Jennifer Ortega has considerable experience working in the IT field. Rather than using a skills approach, her résumé uses a chronological approach that shows everything she's done that's related to the job she's applying for.

You may automatically assume that Jennifer has the advantage over Marcus, but the health care company with the opening may be looking for fresh, new talent, and Marcus should capitalize on his web design freelance work or get an actual internship with a professional web designer. Everyone has to start somewhere. Do your best with whichever approach fits you. Finally, remember that you can hire a professional to write a résumé for you, but if you read up

JENNIFER ORTEGA
789 Breckenridge Court, Apartment C
Great Bluffs, CO 89898
(555) 333-9999
jortega@gbtc.edu

CAREER OBJECTIVE
To obtain a position as a web designer in a large health care organization

EMPLOYMENT HISTORY
2011–present   Technology Helpdesk Manager, Central College
· Developed new phone answering system that increased the unit's responsiveness by 50%
· Oversaw a staff of 10 student technology experts
· Installed software and made troubleshooting visits to approximately 15 faculty offices
   per week
2010–2011   IT Supervisor, Great Bluffs School District 1
· Coordinated software maintenance in 12 elementary school administrative offices
· Managed a team of 8 technology employees
· Installed financial software to improve budget management at the K-6 level
2004–2008   Sales staff member, Tech 4 U, Great Bluffs, Colorado
· Earned Salesperson of the Quarter Award, Jan–Mar, 2010
· Recognized with Sales and Service Award, June 2010
· Initiated store display rearrangement

EDUCATION
Great Bluffs Technical College, Great Bluffs, CO
Certificate in Web Design
GPA 3.2/4.0
Personally financed 100% of college tuition

HONORS
Selected as the student body representative to GBCC faculty government
Earned a place on the GBCC Dean's Honor Role each term

SUMMARY OF ACADEMIC COURSEWORK

Introduction to Web Graphics	Web Development Software
Introduction to Web Multimedia	Electronic Commerce
Principles of Web Design	Emerging Technologies

SKILLS
Technology
Do part-time freelance work, web-page design
Work in Word, PowerPoint, Excel, Access, Macromedia Flash, Dreamweaver, Java, HTML, PHP,
   Adobe InDesign, Acrobat, and Photoshop
Graphics
Design brochures for local health care organizations as a freelancer:
   Forest Hills Rehabilitation Center, Mercy Hospital, and Sunnydale Senior Center
Writing
Write brochure content after consulting with management at these organizations

REFERENCES (available on request)

Jennifer has had several jobs in the IT field. On her résumé, she lists what she did in each one that might be useful in the job she wants.

Numbers are important and memorable! Notice how they stand out.

Notice that Jennifer gives specific dates and has listed a variety of things to discuss with an interviewer.

Note that there are many different ways to say the same thing. Jennifer has noted that she was selected as the student representative. She has chosen particular wording to emphasize that this was an honor.

Notice that Jennifer starts each phrase with a verb to emphasize action, and that all verbs are in the same tense (past or present).

VARK It!

Read/Write: Bring a current résumé to class and trade with another Read/Write student. Read the résumé, and give your classmate written feedback.

Cover Letter Critique

When you submit a résumé, either in person, through the mail, or online, you should send a well-written cover letter along with it that briefly outlines your qualifications for the job, expresses your interest, and gives the person who reviews your résumé some idea of who you are. Take a look at the following cover letter from Marcus Brown and critique it. What has he done right, and what has he done wrong?

---

15 September

To Whom It May Concenr,

I'd like to apply for your opening at Anderson-Wallace Healthcare Industries. I have heard a lot about your company and it sounds great. A friend of mine works there, and he said his starting salary was unbelieveable. What exactly do you do at your company? He's told me a few things, but I'm eager to learn more!

As you can see from my résumé, I don't have much experience. But I have just earned my web design certificate from GBCC, and I did pretty well. I want to start my career at a great company like yours.

I hope to hear from you soon.

Warmly,

Marcus Brown

After finding the mistakes Marcus made, rewrite this letter to bring to class or submit to your instructor.

on résumé writing and follow the suggestions here, you can do just fine on your own. Hiring a professional or going through an employment agency can be helpful, but they can also be expensive propositions. And if they promise you the moon ("You'll have a new job at the starting salary of your dreams in just one week!"), be wary.

Interview at Your Best

By now, you have probably already been interviewed several times to get a job. But when you're ready to launch your career, you'll be facing interviews for the new job you really want, the one you prepared for by earning a certificate or degree. Often interviewers aren't particularly skilled at asking questions. They haven't been trained on how to interview prospective employees, so they just ask whatever questions come to them. And often, interviewees don't quite know what they're doing either. Of course, you should always be honest, but there are various ways to communicate the same information. Telling an interviewer you "like to work alone" sounds antisocial. But if you say you "like to really focus on what you're doing without distractions," you show dedication to your work ethic. You also need to be aware of real pitfalls to avoid. See what you think of these suggestions.

1. **Play up the positive, and downplay the negative.** A trap question interviewers sometimes ask is "What's your worst fault?" Although you may be tempted to say the first thing that comes to mind, that could be a big mistake. "Umm . . . sleeping too much! I really like to sleep in. Sometimes I sleep half the day away." Not good. But some faults you could identify might actually be seen as strengths: "I have a little too much nervous energy. I'm always on the go. I like to stay busy."

2. **Stay focused.** "Tell me about yourself" is a common question interviewers ask. How much time do you have? Most of us like to talk about ourselves, but it's important to stay on track. Think possible questions through in advance, and construct some hypothetical answers. Keep your answers job focused: what your long-term career goals are, how this job can help you prepare, what you liked about your last job. You don't need to go into your family background or your personal problems. And it's always a bad idea to bash a previous job or former boss. The interviewer may worry that you'll bring whatever didn't work there with you to this new job.

3. **Don't just give answers, get some.** A job interview is like a first date. Find out what you need to know. If the job is one you're interested in long term, ask questions such as these three key ones:

   > **What does this company value?** Listen to the answer. Hard work? New ideas? Communication skills? The answer will tell you about the personality of the company.

   > **What's a typical day like for you?** Ask the interviewer. An answer such as "I get up at 5:00 A.M., get here at 6:30 A.M., and go home around 7:00 P.M.—and then I do paperwork all evening" tells you something. This may—or may not—be the job or the company for you.

   > **What happened to the last person in this job?** If you find out he was promoted, that's one thing. But if you learn he was fired or quit, see whether you can find out why. Maybe he had job performance problems, or maybe this is an impossible job that no one could do well. Listen to the interviewer. She may be looking for an opportunity to tell you things she thinks are important, too.

4. **Watch for questions that seem to come out of left field.** Some companies like to get creative with their interviewing. Microsoft, for example, is known for asking problem-solving questions, such as "If you could remove any of the fifty states, which would it be? Be prepared to give specific reasons why you chose the state you did." There is no right or wrong answer, although some answers are better than others. ("We should just nuke state X. I had a bad experience there once" would probably concern some people, and naming Washington state, where Microsoft is located, might be a bad choice.) The interviewer just wants to hear how you can think critically and give reasons for your answers.[8] Remember: Today's interviewers are looking for more than technical skills; they're looking for critical thinking skills, problem-solving skills, and creativity.[9]

5. **Don't start off with salary questions.** Make sure the first question out of your mouth isn't "So tell me about the salary again? Any way to notch that up a bit?" The last thing you want to do is give the interviewer the idea

you're in it for the money. Of course, you are, but not just for that. More importantly, in every job you have, you'll gain experience and knowledge that will always better prepare you for every job that will be a part of your long-term career. Don't start negotiating a salary until you've actually been offered a job.

6. **Negotiate wisely.** If the interviewer asks you to name a salary figure, be careful. Saying "I could probably live on $30,000," when the actual figure the interviewer is authorized to start with is $38,000, has just given the employer the option to lower the salary, based on your expectations. A good rule of thumb is: Never name a number. It's always best to ask the interviewer what the salary range for the job is. It's also good to research the salaries of similar jobs, and it's even better to have another job offer you're considering, so you have choices. Otherwise, you're not negotiating; you're begging.[10]

7. **Know what you're dealing with.** One of the easiest ways to blow a job interview is by doing nothing. Candidates who don't do their homework usually don't pass an interview. If the interviewer asks, "So what do you know about the company?" and you reply, "Oh, not much, but I'm a fast learner," you'll be perceived to care very little about the outcome of the interview. Go online to read up about the place you'd like to work. Your knowledge, and therefore your interest, will show. And it goes without saying (although here it is, anyway) that you should arrive early, dress professionally, overprepare, and send a follow-up thank-you note or e-mail.[11]

Continuing Your Education

Like Anthony Lopez, perhaps you're exploring the idea of continuing your education. Typically, the more education you get, the more money you can make, the more you can do, and the more responsibility you have. Figure 12.2 summarizes both earnings and unemployment rates by educational level achieved, but the decision to continue is yours and yours alone. You know yourself and your interests best.

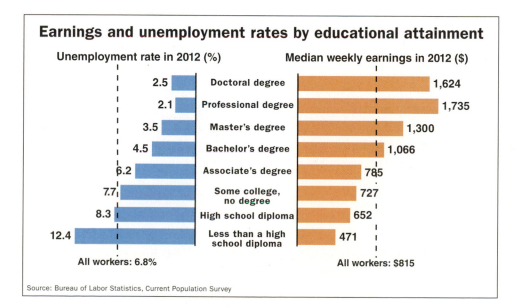

Earnings and unemployment rates by educational attainment

Unemployment rate in 2012 (%) | | Median weekly earnings in 2012 ($)
2.5	Doctoral degree	1,624
2.1	Professional degree	1,735
3.5	Master's degree	1,300
4.5	Bachelor's degree	1,066
6.2	Associate's degree	785
7.7	Some college, no degree	727
8.3	High school diploma	652
12.4	Less than a high school diploma	471

All workers: 6.8%   All workers: $815

Source: Bureau of Labor Statistics, Current Population Survey

FIGURE 12.2

Education Pays

Source: Bureau of Labor Statistics. (2013, May 22). Available at http://www.bls.gov/emp/ep_chart_001.htm.

	Associate's Degree in Social (Human) Services	Bachelor's Degree in Sociology (or a related field)	Master's of Social Work (MSW)	Ph.D. in Sociology (or Doctorate of Social Work)
Average Time to Complete:	2 years	4–5 years	2 years beyond a bachelor's degree	3–4 years beyond a master's degree
Average Number of Required Courses:	Approximately 20	Approximately 40	10 courses and 900 hours of supervised field experience or internship	10 (plus dissertation)
Type of Work:	Social Service Assistant or Aid: work with social workers, pharmacists, psychologists, etc. Varying levels of responsibility. Help people in need.	Social Worker (although an MSW is increasingly required): help clients cope with disabilities (like substance abuse or homelessness). Work in schools, public health agencies, hospitals, etc., and visit clients in their homes.	Social Worker clinical work: supervise other social workers, manage case loads. Must pass state licensure exam. May wish to go into private practice at least part-time. May specialize in such areas as • Child, family, or schools • Medical and public health • Mental health and substance abuse	Professor, High-level administrator, researcher: May teach at the college or university level, conduct research, or run a health-care or nonprofit organization, for example.
Future Demand:	Higher than average. Expected growth of 28 percent between 2010 and 2020.	Favorable (varies by type of specialization).	Favorable, much faster than average (varies by type of specialization).	Generally good for faculty positions (although varies by type of specialization and preference for full- or part-time work).
Median salary:	$28,200 (as of May 2010)	$42,480 (as of May 2010)	$48,140 and higher (as of May 2010)	$62,050 (for all full-time college professors as of May 2010)

FIGURE 12.3

An Educational Career Path[12]

> There are two mistakes one can make along the road to truth . . . not going all the way and not starting.
>
> *Buddha (c. 563–483 B.C.)*

By the end of the "FOCUS Challenge Case," Anthony was considering four alternatives: an associate's degree, a bachelor's degree, a master's degree, and a Ph.D. Each level of these four educational paths has distinct differences he needs to know about. Anthony seems to have "found his bliss," and his heart is in the work. He is convinced that being a social worker is the right career field for him. He is motivated, engaged in what he's learning, and looking forward to a career of service. But at what level? Figure 12.3 lists some basic considerations for Anthony. Can you compare his choices to ones you may be considering?

If Anthony thinks he may wish to take the first step beyond getting his associate's degree, he must begin planning now. Sometimes students who transfer to a four-year institution experience what's called "transfer shock." Courses can be taught differently, classes can be larger, and in a class with several hundred students, the atmosphere can seem more impersonal. According to research, math and science courses, in particular, may seem (and be) harder.[13] The campus itself may have a very different feel to it, and transfer students can feel lost and isolated, which can hurt their academic performance. Anthony must work closely with his college advisor and an advisor at the school where he plans to transfer, to make sure his credits are transferable. His goal should be to make the process as seamless as possible by visiting the new campus now and talking with advisors and professors there. Take control of the situation: Ask for help, if you need it, and get involved in campus life.[14]

The important thing for Anthony—and for you—is to determine what you really want. Many different educational and career paths exist. Don't feel pressure from others to continue your education if you know that decision isn't right for you—or isn't right for you *now*. Think about your goals in life, what you want to achieve, and what kind of work you would find most fulfilling, and then decide which educational level is right for you.

EXERCISE 12.4

Circling the Right Career[15]

Different people are motivated by different types of careers. Think of motivation as three overlapping circles, with one circle labeled "Service," one labeled "Power," and one labeled "Money." Anthony Lopez is choosing a career that focuses primarily on service. Power and money are not particularly important to him, it seems. Think of six different careers (several of which you may be considering), and place them on the chart wherever you think they belong. Start with careers that you think belong primarily in one circle, and then brainstorm some careers that overlap into two (money and power, for example). Can you think of any careers that contain elements of all three circles? Then compare notes with your classmates. Where would you put the career you think you would find most fulfilling?

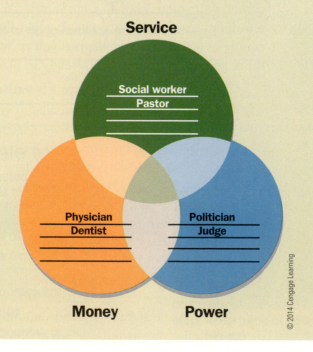

© 2014 Cengage Learning

> " Time is the quality of nature that keeps events from happening all at once. Lately it doesn't seem to be working. "
>
> —ANONYMOUS

Reason 12: They lack time management skills.

Your time management skills are something a prospective employer will be interested in. An interviewer may ask you: "How good are you at focusing when you have to juggle several different projects?" or "This is a fast-paced company. Are you willing to work overtime?" It seems that most jobs today require a significant—sometimes frantic—investment of your time and energy. When requests are coming at you from all sides on the job, how will you fare? Can you sharpen your focus and prioritize?

TRY It!

At the beginning of each day, decide on three things that must get done, no matter what. Check back at the end of the day to see how successful you've been. If you're a stay-at-home mom, it may be preparing three nutritious meals for your kids. If you're in the workforce, it may be making continual progress on a big project with a deadline. When everything seems to be happening at once, you have to decide which of those things are most important. Try it tomorrow.

Priority 1:

Priority 2:

Priority 3:

Put What You've Learned to Good Use: Ten Things Employers Hope You Will Learn in College

You must motivate yourself EVERY DAY!

Matthew Stasior, motivational speaker

© Larry Harwood Photography. Property of Cengage Learning

Regardless of which fork in the road you choose—launching a career or transferring to a four-year school—college teaches many lessons, and they're not all about the subject matter in your classes. Much of the academic professionalism you've developed in college can easily translate into career professionalism, with some thought and application on your part. Thanks to having gone to college, you can begin your career with some ready-to-go professional advantages. Here is a set of ten things employers care about, regardless of exactly which college courses you've taken or degree you've worked on. As you evaluate, think about which ones are already in place for you. Employers want you to:

1. **Exhibit a work ethic.** In college, you demonstrated your work ethic. Perhaps you labored over assignments to produce your best work. In the world of work, organizations prefer to hire winners, not slackers. Winners are motivated and reliable. They know how to kick into high gear when necessary. Not only is day-to-day performance important, but so is how you handle yourself at crunch time. Someone once said, "Every job is a self-portrait of the person who did it. Autograph your work with excellence." Your work ethic says a great deal about who you are.

2. **Study up.** In college, you were encouraged to learn deeply, not just memorize facts. Transfer this principle to the workplace. On the job, learn the ins and outs of your industry. If you are an automotive mechanic, know more than just about the nuts and bolts

and transmissions of the cars you work on. Learn about the automobile maker's history, what the company stands for, its vision and values, and the reputation it has earned from customers. It's easy to get tunnel vision and lose sight of the bigger picture.

3. **Prove you're a problem solver.** While taking your college classes, you learned problem-solving skills. Some of those problems were personal (*Who can I get to watch my kids at the last minute?*), and some were academic (*Why was Edgar Allen Poe so "dark"?*). On the job, everyone values the person who comes up with a workable solution when everyone else is stumped. And your boss will value you more if you come up with solutions yourself. Instead of, *What should I do about X?* say, *We're facing Problem X. Should I do A, B, or C?* You've proven that you've already thought about the problem and generated three possible solutions and demonstrated that you can think on your own.

4. **Speak and write well.** Your college career may have put more emphasis on these skills than any others. In today's world of abbreviated text messages (AYS = Are you serious?) and empty conversation ("And she's . . . like so . . . you know . . . whatever . . ."), you can become a super star on the job by just speaking and writing well. And in addition to speaking and writing, learn to listen to what's *really* being said and why. With practice, you can listen past the bravado or baloney and get to the *real* message. That's important!

5. **Polish your people skills.** Your college instructors may have assigned group projects in your classes to help you learn teamwork skills. Good teamwork skills are key to a successful career in anything! People can be difficult to work with, yet *people* are the way work gets done.

6. **Learn the rules of the game.** In school—and throughout your life—you have learned what's sometimes called "The Hidden Curriculum": things everyone knows, more or less, but never learned formally. For example, most people know that it's not polite to tell off-color jokes to people you've just met or smack your gum while giving a speech. In the same way, on the job, the "grapevine," or informal network, is important to understand. To be successful, you must be tuned in. Understand the culture of the organization you work for. What does it value? Who holds the power? Where do you fit in, and what can you contribute?

Goals are the fuel in the furnace of achievement.

Brian Tracy, Eat that Frog

Glowimages/Getty Images

When one door closes, another opens. But often we look so long, so regretfully, upon the closed door that we fail to see the one that has opened for us.

Helen Keller, American author, activist, and lecturer (1880–1968)

Put What You've Learned to Good Use: Ten Things Employers Hope You Will Learn in College

7. **Know how to gather information and use it.** In college, you're asked to develop your research skills. It's easy to think that each paper for a class is just another assignment to check off the list, when, actually, you're developing skills that will be critical to your success later. You don't just string together pieces of information when you do research for your college classes. You analyze research through the "eyes" of the problem you're trying to address and *your* perspective on it. You weave ideas together to make an argument.

8. **Understand that numbers count.** Unfortunately, math gets a bad rap. Many people approach math classes in college with "fear and loathing," when, actually, math is a key to success in the world of work. If you can understand spreadsheets or figure out the budget, you'll be ahead of the game. Some people de-emphasize the importance of financial skills by referring to them as "bean counting" or "number crunching," but people who know how to apply math on the job are highly sought after.

9. **Go for extra credit.** In some of your courses, your instructors may give extra credit. You could be allowed to do something extra, beyond the requirements on the syllabus, to raise your grade. But what's extra credit in terms of your career? On the job, you have "extra credit" when your abilities stand out. You speak German and no one else does, so when something needs translating, you're the go-to person. Or you're so exceptional at PowerPoint that you're affectionately referred to as the "PowerPoint King."

10. **Manage your time, your attention, and yourself.** College is about self-responsibility. You're in charge of your education; you call the shots. If you manage your time and money, you can focus as you should on your courses. If you "spend" unwisely—in either area—you lose your focus and your performance slips. In your career, the same will be true. Your ability to manage time, your attention, and yourself will affect your personal and professional future.[16]

What Ifs

Life is full of "what ifs?" isn't it? What if you had dated someone else? What if you took the other job? What if things were different?

What If College Isn't Right for You?

What if you decide, after a term or two, that college isn't right for you? Perhaps your heart just isn't in it, and neither is your head. If so, know that you aren't alone. That realization comes to many students. The important question to ask yourself is whether you're really making the right decision, not just getting discouraged if college seems too challenging. Remember that "College is a team sport," and use all of the campus resources available to you before you abandon your efforts. But something other than college may also be the right decision for you—right now at this particular point in your life. However, this kind of decision is one you shouldn't make lightly.

This course is almost over, but the online skills and practices you're developing will carry over into other courses, and even into your jobs during and after college. In almost any career field, you'll be able to use the skills and habits you've formed while taking courses online.

- **Organization and time management**
- **Working ahead**
- **General communication skills**
- **E-mail skills**
- **Information technology skills**
- **Online teamwork**

Here are some cautionary tips on using technology in the workplace—rules that extend those you'll find in your college coursework.

- **Downloading some programs may be prohibited.**

- **Understand that your company has the right to monitor your use of e-mail.** Violating company policies can have serious consequences.
- **Learn your company's policies on the use of electronic devices at work.**
- **Beware of a false sense of security in sending e-mails.** Ask yourself if you would mind if your message was sent to the world. Remember you have no control over where your message goes after you click send.
- **Certain websites can be off-limits.** Let your IT department know right away if you accidentally encounter one of these.
- **Some companies prohibit personal use of office technology.** You may have to use a personal e-mail address for such purposes.
- **You may want to limit your personal use of the Internet to breaks, lunch hours, or time at home.**[17]

Improve Your Grade
Online Flashcards
Glossary

What If You Can't Finish a Degree Now?

Even though you have dreams and goals, sometimes "life happens." A turn of events changes everything, a new job consumes all of your time and energy, or someone needs you. Don't feel like a failure if that happens. Take time off, regroup, and come back when you can. Going to college expands your thinking and gives you a whole new take on life. Beyond a certificate or diploma, the learning that takes place in college changes you forever—and it's worth the investment in your future.

My, How You've Grown! Goodbye and Good Luck!

Remember Aunt Ruth (or whatever her name was)? Every time she visited when you were a kid, she remarked about how much you'd grown. Or when you went to visit her, she'd measure you and mark a notch on

Every adversity, every failure, every heartache carries with it the seed of an equal or greater benefit.

Napoleon Hill, author, Keys to Success: The 17 Principles of Personal Achievement *(1883–1970)*

© Larry Harwood Photography. Property of Cengage Learning.

> People succeed in as many ways as there are people. Some can be completely fulfilled with destinations that are much closer to home and more comfortable. But if you long to keep going, then I hope you are able to follow my lead to the places I have gone. To within a whisper of your own personal perfection. To places that are sweeter because you worked so hard to arrive there. To places at the very edge of your dreams.

Michael Johnson, American sprinter

the wall to compare your height now to the one from last year's visit. She loved watching you grow, and the fact that she noticed made you feel special.

There's no doubt about it. In this first term of college, you have grown. You have gained new perspectives, new insights, and new ways of thinking about things. Like Aunt Ruth, others may notice. If those close to you are threatened by these changes, reassure them that your newfound knowledge hasn't made you think less of them. Remember the words of writer M. L. Boren, "You should have education enough so that you won't have to look up to people; and then more education so that you will be wise enough not to look down

What's In **YOUR** Briefcase?

KEEP YOUR BALANCE

You're a winner. You're working hard as a highly motivated, ultra-competent employee. Your boss is impressed—so much so that you get promoted. Your new position requires you to work harder, and before you know it, you're promoted again. This cycle keeps repeating itself, and over time, you have success written all over you. You're well on your way to mapping out a great future.

There's an underlying question worth exploring, however. Why are you working so hard? Is it because you're passionate about your work? Perhaps it fuels you, gives you purpose, direction, and fulfillment. You love it.

But what if your success isn't about fulfillment at all? What if it's about moving up, making more money, reveling in the prestige? What if you actually dislike your work? One work-life balance expert asks, why do people "work long hard hours at jobs they hate to enable them to buy things they don't need to impress people they don't like"?[18] Good question. The why of success is fundamentally important.

If you ever lose your professional balance, take charge of your own future. Your company is unlikely to say, "You know what? You've been working far too hard. You need to chill for a few weeks." Corporations won't fix things for you. You must take control and assume responsibility for living the type of life you want to live. For example, make a rule for yourself that evenings are for family or your romantic partner, and stick to it. Or make a pact that you'll only check your e-mail once a day on weekends so that you can let your mind "idle" for a while.

A recent study asked dying people to identify their biggest regrets. "Their most common regret? 'I wish I'd had the courage to live a life true to myself, not the life others expected of me.' Their second most common regret? 'I wish I didn't work so hard.' There are two ways to address these regrets. One, work less hard and spend your time living a life true to yourself, whatever that means. Or two, work just as hard—harder even—on things you consider to be important and meaningful. If you put those two regrets together, you realize that what people really regret isn't simply working so hard, it's working so hard on things that don't matter to them. If our work matters to us, if it represents a life true to us. . . . then we will have lived more fully."[19]

What does balance mean to you as a college student? What will it mean in your anticipated career?

_____

_____

_____

on people." If they are proud of you and your accomplishments, and have supported you along the way, thank them!

The important thing is to keep learning and never stop. Continuing to learn—whether in college or in life—is what will determine who you are and what you will become. Learn new things, update your goals, and reinvent yourself. This book, and the course for which you're reading it, have begun that process. Now the rest is up to you!

step 3 INSIGHT *Now* What Do You Think?

At the beginning of this chapter, Anthony Lopez faced a series of challenges as a new college student. Now after learning from this chapter, would you respond differently to any of the questions you answered about the "FOCUS Challenge Case"? Using what you learned in the chapter, write a paragraph ending to Anthony's case study. What are some of the possible outcomes for Anthony?

step 4 ACTION Your Plans for Change

1. Identify one new thing you learned in reading this chapter. Why did you select the one you've selected? How will it affect what you do in your college classes?

2. How will this chapter change how you approach your future, no matter which fork of the road you choose as a next step? What will be most challenging for you?

3. How do you plan to increase your skills in college so that you can be more successful in your next step?

INFORMATION ABOUT YOU

Name _____

Student Number _____   Course/Section _____

Instructor _____

Gender _____   Age _____

Although you may not have quite completed your first term as a college student, we're interested in your reactions to college so far: how you have spent your time, what challenges you've experienced, and your general views about what college has been like. Please answer thoughtfully.

NOTE: Questions 1–10 were asked on the Entrance Interview and need not be repeated here. The numbering below begins with number 11 so that the Entrance and Exit Interview results can be compared, if you or your instructor would like to do that. It may be interesting to see how your original expectations of college compare to your actual experience. Note, too, that the Exit Interview contains several added questions at the end about your future education.

YOUR COLLEGE EXPERIENCE

Your Reactions to College

11. **Which of the following reasons to finish your college degree seem important to you now? (Check all that apply.)**

_____ I want to build a better life for myself.

_____ I want to be well off financially in the future.

_____ My friends are going to college.

_____ It is expected of me.

_____ I want to continue learning.

_____ I am unsure of what I might do instead.

_____ I want to build a better life for my family.

_____ I need a college education to achieve my dreams.

_____ My family is encouraging me to continue.

_____ I want to prepare for a *new* career.

_____ The career I am pursuing requires a degree.

_____ other (please explain)

12. **How did you find you learned best in college? (Check all that apply.)**

_____ by looking at charts, maps, graphs

_____ by listening to instructors' lectures

_____ by reading books

_____ by going on field trips

_____ by looking at color-coded information

_____ by listening to other students during in-class discussions

_____ by writing papers

_____ by engaging in activities

_____ by looking at symbols and graphics

_____ by talking about course content with friends or family

_____ by taking notes

_____ by actually doing things

13. The following sets of opposite descriptive phrases are separated by five blank lines. Put an X on the line between the two that best represents your response, like this: For me, high school was easy _____:__X__:_____:_____:_____ hard

My first term of college:

challenged me academically	_____:_____:_____:_____:_____	was easy
was very different from high school	_____:_____:_____:_____:_____	was a lot like high school
was exciting	_____:_____:_____:_____:_____	was dull
was interesting	_____:_____:_____:_____:_____	was uninteresting
motivated me to continue	_____:_____:_____:_____:_____	discouraged me
was fun	_____:_____:_____:_____:_____	was boring
helped me feel a part of this school	_____:_____:_____:_____:_____	made me feel like an outsider

14. How many total hours per week did you study outside of class for your college courses?

____ 0–5   ____ 6–10   ____ 11–15   ____ 16–20   ____ 21–25
____ 26–30   ____ 31–35   ____ 36–40   ____ 40+

15. Now what do you expect your grade point average to be at the end of your first term of college?

____ A+   ____ A   ____ A−   ____ B+   ____ B
____ B−   ____ C+   ____ C   ____ C−   ____ D or lower

Your Strengths, Personality, and Interests

16. Which of these *strengths* or personal characteristics contributed to your college success? (Check all that apply.)

____ a. I am good at building relationships.

____ b. I can usually convince others to follow my plan.

____ c. I like to win.

____ d. I work toward future goals.

____ e. I like to be productive and get things done.

____ f. I have a positive outlook on life.

____ g. I'm usually the person who gets things going.

____ h. I enjoy the challenge of learning new things.

____ i. I am focused.

____ j. I can usually look at a problem and figure out a plan of action.

____ k. I work to keep everyone happy.

____ l. I'm a take-charge kind of person.

____ m. I help other people develop their talents and skills.

____ n. I'm a very responsible person.

____ o. I can analyze a situation and see various ways things might work out.

____ p. I usually give tasks my best effort.

17. How confident are you now in yourself in each of the following areas? (1 = very confident, 5 = not at all confident)

____ overall academic ability

____ mathematical skills

____ leadership ability

____ reading skills

____ public speaking skills

____ study skills

____ technology skills

____ physical well being

____ writing skills

____ social skills

____ emotional well being

____ teamwork skills

18. For each of the following pairs of descriptors, which set sounds most like you based on what you've learned about yourself this term? (Please choose between the two options on each line and place a check mark by your choice.)

_____ Extraverted and outgoing   or   _____ Introverted and quiet

_____ Detail-oriented and practical   or   _____ Big-picture and future-oriented

_____ Rational and truthful   or   _____ People-oriented and tactful

_____ Organized and self-disciplined   or   _____ Spontaneous and flexible

19. _FOCUS_ is about twelve different aspects of college life. Which did you find to be most interesting as they applied to your academic success? (Check all that apply.)

_____ Getting the right start   _____ Learning styles and studying

_____ Building dreams, setting goals   _____ Thinking critically and creatively

_____ Managing time, energy, and money   _____ Engaging, listening, and note-taking in class

_____ Learning online   _____ Developing memory, taking tests

_____ Reading, writing, and presenting   _____ Choosing a college major and career

_____ Building relationships, valuing diversity   _____ Creating a future

Your Challenges

20. Of the twelve aspects of college life identified in the previous question, which were most challenging to apply to yourself in your academic work? (Check all that apply.)

_____ Getting the right start   _____ Learning styles and studying

_____ Building dreams, setting goals   _____ Thinking critically and creatively

_____ Managing time, energy, and money   _____ Engaging, listening, and note-taking in class

_____ Learning online   _____ Developing memory, taking tests

_____ Reading, writing, and presenting   _____ Choosing a college major and career

_____ Building relationships, valuing diversity   _____ Creating a future

21. Which one of your current classes was most challenging this term and why?

Which class? (course title _or_ department and course number) _____

Why? _____

Did you succeed in this course? _____ yes _____ no _____ Somewhat (please explain): _____

22. Please mark your _top three areas of concern_ relating to your first term of college by placing 1, 2, and 3 next to the items you choose (with 1 representing your top concern).

_____ I did not fit in.   _____ My social life interfered with my studies.

_____ I did have difficulty making friends.   _____ My studies interfered with my social life.

_____ I was not academically successful.   _____ My instructors did not care about me as an individual.

_____ My performance disappointed my family.   _____ I may not finish my degree.

_____ My personal life interfered with my studies.   _____ I did not manage my time well.

_____ My studies interfered with my personal life.   _____ I was bored in my classes.

_____ I had financial difficulties.   _____ I felt intimidated by my instructors.

_____ My job(s) interfered with my studies.   _____ I was overwhelmed by all I had to do.

_____ My studies interfered with my job.   _____ other (please explain) _____

Your Future

23. How certain are you now of the following (1 = totally sure, 5 = totally unsure)?

_____ Finishing your degree or certificate

_____ Finishing your degree or certificate at this school.

_____ Sticking with the major you've chosen.

_____ Continuing on to work toward a bachelor's or advanced degree

24. What are you most looking forward to after this semester/quarter?

25. Did you achieve the outcomes you were hoping to achieve at the beginning of this first semester/quarter? Why or why not?

You may gain some personal insights if you compare the questions in this "Your College Experience" section of the Exit Interview with the matching questions from the "Your College Expectations" section in the Entrance Interview at the front of the book. Or your instructor may ask you to write about your Insights and intended Actions. Now continue on to these final questions about "Your Next Steps."

YOUR NEXT STEPS

26. Looking ahead, how satisfied do you expect to be with your decision to attend this school?

_____ very satisfied   _____ satisfied

_____ somewhat dissatisfied   _____ very dissatisfied

_____ not sure

27. Which of the following statements best reflects your educational intentions?

_____ I plan to stay at this school until I complete my degree.

_____ I plan to transfer to another institution (please identify which one _____).

_____ I plan to stop out of college for awhile (to work, for example) and then return to this school.

_____ I plan to drop out of college.

28. If you are thinking about transferring to another institution, why would you do so? Check all that apply.

_____ This school does not offer my intended major (which is _____).   _____ This school is too small.

_____ This school is too large.   _____ This school is too expensive.

_____ I don't feel I fit in.   _____ I want to go to a school in another location.

_____ I think I might like another school better.   _____ I want to be closer to my boy/girlfriend.

_____ I want to be closer to my friends.   _____ I will change job locations.

_____ I want to transfer from a two-year to a four-year institution.   _____ other (please explain)

29. What was the biggest difference between what you thought college would be like and what it was actually like for you?

30. How have you changed most over this first semester/quarter? In what ways are you different now that you've been in college? How will this introductory semester/quarter affect or change your future college experience?

CHAPTER 1

1. Knowles' Andragogy. Available at http://www.learningandteaching.info/learning/knowlesa.htm.

2. Jacobs, L. F., & Hyman, J. F. (2010). 10 reasons to go to a research university. *U.S. News*. Retrieved from http://www.usnews.com/education/blogs/professors-guide/2010/04/28/10-reasons-to-go-to-a-research-university.

3. *Community colleges. The College Board.* (2005). Retrieved from http://www.collegeboard.com/student/repository/final_cc_flyer_pdf_8_11_05__49035.pdf.

4. Koebler, J. (2012, April 21). Report: Community college attendance up, but graduation rates remain low. *U.S. News*. Retrieved from http://www.usnews.com/education/best-colleges/articles/2012/04/21/report-community-college-attendance-up-but-graduation-rates-remain-low.

5. (2012). Career and technical colleges: Careers in focus. *NACAC*. Retrieved from http://www.education.com/reference/article/Ref_Career_Technical/.

6. Spielberg finally to graduate. (2002, May 15). *BBC News*. Retrieved from http://news.bbc.co.uk/2/hi/entertainment/1988770.stm.

7. Balderrama, A. (2009, May 1). The ten best jobs requiring two-year degrees. Available at http://www.careerbuilder.com/Article/CB-1366-Job-Search-10-Best-Jobs-Requiring-Two-Year Degrees/?ArticleID=1366&cbRecursionCnt=1&cbsid=960a4ed9fa914960bc395ac1534070d9-322921368-w0-6&ns_siteid=ns_us_g_percentage_of_jobs_re_.

8. Crosby, O. (2002–2003, Winter). Associate degree: Two years to a career or jump start to a bachelor's degree. *Occupational Outlook Quarterly*, 2–13. Available at http://www.bls.gov/opub/ooq/2002/winter/art01.pdf.

9. What's the Difference between an Associate Degree and a Certificate? *Brookhaven College*. Available at http://www.brookhavencollege.edu/studentsvcs/advising/faq.aspx#q17.

10. Certificate program vs. associate's degree—What's the difference? *Top Colleges Blog*. Available at http://www.bestdegreeprograms.org/what-is-the-difference-between-associates-degree-programs-and-certificate-programs.

11. Different paths for different majors. (2007, January/February). Datanotes: *Achieving the Dream*. Available at http://eric.ed.gov/?id=ED521303.

12. Marchand, A. (2010, 29 March). 6 strategies can help entering community-college students succeed. *The Chronicle of Higher Education*. Available at http://chronicle.com/article/6-Strategies-Can-Help-Entering/64871.

13. Hart Research Associates. (2010, January 20). *Raising the bar: Employers' views on college learning in the wake of the economic downturn.* Available at http://www.aacu.org/leap/documents/2009_EmployerSurvey.pdf.

14. Shoenberg, R. (2005). *Why do I have to take this course? A student guide to making smart educational choices.* Association of American Colleges and Universities. Washington, DC: AAC&U.

15. Linda Foltz and the Student Success Center advisors at the University of Colorado at Colorado Springs; Jennifer Sengenberger and Wayne Artis, Pikes Peak Community College; Kocel, K. C., (2008, March 12). Advising first-generation college students for continued success. Kocel, K. (2008, March 12). *The Mentor: An Academic Advising Journal.* Available at http://www.psu.edu/dus/mentor/080312kk.htm; Knight, T. M. (2000, May 17). Planting the seeds of success: Advising college students with disabilities. *The Mentor: An Academic Advising Journal.* Available at http://psu.edu/dus/mentor/000517tk.htm.

16. The challenges of remedial education: Views of 3 presidents. (2006, October 27). *The Chronicle of Higher Education.* Available at http://chronicle.com/article/The-Challenges-of-Remedial/32361/.

17. Developmental education and student success. (2006, September/October). *Datanotes: Achieving the Dream.*

18. Crews, D. M., & Aragon, S. R. (2004). Influence of a community college developmental education writing course on academic performance. *Community College Review, 32*(2), 1–18.

19. Settle, J. S. (2011). Variables that encourage students to persist in community colleges. *Community College Journal of Research and Practice, 35*, 281–300.

20. Dweck, C. S. (2006). *Mindset: The new psychology of success.* New York: Random House. pp. 104–105.

21. Employment Projections—2008–2018 Summary. Available at http://www.bls.gov/news.release/ecopro.nr0.htm.

22. Rampell, C. (2009, July 13). Preparing today's workers or tomorrow's jobs. *The New York Times.* Available at http://economix.blogs.nytimes.com/2009/07/13/preparing-todays-workers-for-tomorrows-jobs/.

23. (2006, July). Fact Sheet. Community Colleges: Challenges and Benefits. *Achieving the Dream.* Available at http://www.ccp.edu/site/about/achieving_thedream/pdfs/ChallengeBenefit.pdf

24. Greenstone, M., & Looney, A. (2012, February 26). Where is the best place to invest $102,000—in stocks, bonds, or a college degree? *Brookings.* Available at http://www.brookings.edu/papers/2011/0625_education_greenstone_looney.aspx.

25. Leonhardt, D. (2011, June 25). Even for cashiers, college pays off. *The New York Times.* Available at http://www.nytimes.com/2011/06/26/sunday-review/26leonhardt.html.

26. (2006, July). Fact Sheet. Community Colleges: Challenges and Benefits. *Achieving the Dream.* Available at http://www.ccp.edu/site/about/achieving_thedream/pdfs/ChallengeBenefit.pdf

27. Omara-Otunnu, E. (2006, July 24). Conference examines transition from high school to college. University of Connecticut *Advance.* Available at http://advance.uconn.edu/2006/060724/06072407.htm.

28. Pascarella, E. T., Pierson, C. T., Wolniak, G. C., & Terenzini, P. T. (2004). First-generation college students: Additional evidence on college experiences and outcomes. *Journal of Higher Education, 75*(3), 249–284.

29. Tyler, M.D., & Johns, K. Y. (2009). From first-generation college students to first lady. *Diverse Issues in Higher Education Psychology, 25*(25). Available at http://diverseeducation.com/article/12184/.

30. Based on Lynch, M. M. (2004). *Learning online: A guide to success in the virtual classroom.* New York: Routledge Falmer, 18.

31. McCarron, G. P., & Inkelas, K. K. (2006). The gap between educational aspirations and attainment for first-generation college students and the role of parental involvement. *Journal of College Student Development, 47*(5), 534–549.

32. Martinez, J. A., Sher, K. J., Krull, J. L., & Wood, P. K. (2009). Blue-collar scholars? Mediators and moderators of university attrition in first-generation college students. *Journal of College Student Development, 50*(1), 87–103; Collier, P. J., & Morgan, D. L., (2008). Is that paper really due today? *Higher Education, 55*(4), 425–446.

33. Cox, R. D. (2009). *The college fear factor: How students and professors misunderstand one another.* Cambridge, MA: Harvard University Press.

34. http://www.counselingcenter.illinois.edu/?page_id=142.

CHAPTER 2

1. Multi-tasking adversely affects brain's learning, UCLA psychologists report. (2006, July 26). *ScienceDaily*. Available at http://www.sciencedaily.com/releases/2006/07/060726083302.htm.

2. Bregman, P. (2010, May 20). How (and why) to stop multitasking. *Harvard Business Review*. Available at http://blogs.hbr.org/bregman/2010/05/how-and-why-to-stop-multitaski.html; "Infomania" worse than marijuana. *BBC News*. Available at http://news.bbc.co.uk/2/hi/uk_news/4471607.stm.

3. Seven, R. (2004, November 28). Life interrupted. *Pacific Northwest*, seattletimes.com. Available at http://seattletimes.nwsource.com/pacificnw/2004/1128/cover.html; Richtel, M. (2010, June 6). Addicted to technology and paying a price. *The New York Times*. Available at http://www.nytimes.com/2010/06/07/technology/07brain.html?ref=yourbrainoncomputers; Richtel, M. (2010, August 24). Digital devices deprive brain of needed downtime. *The New York Times*. Available at http://www.nytimes.com/2010/08/25/technology/25brain.html?ref=yourbrainoncomputers.

4. Hamilton, J. (2008, October 9). Multitasking teens may be muddling their brains. *NPR: Your Health*. Available at http://www.npr.org/templates/story/story.php?storyId=95524385; Tierney, J. (2009, May 5). Ear plugs to lasers: The science of concentration. *The New York Times*. Available at http://www.nytimes.com/2009/05/05/science/05tier.html?scp=1&sq="ear plugs to lasers: the science of concentration"&st=cse; Tugend, A. (2008, October 25). Multitasking can make you lose . . . um . . . focus. *The New York Times*. Available at http://www.nytimes.com/2008/10/25/business/yourmoney/25shortcuts.html?pagewanted=all; Walls, C. (2006, March 19). genM: The multitasking generation. *Time*. Available at http://www.time.com/time/magazine/article/0,9171,1174696,00.html.

5. Staley, C. (2003). "Spending Time." In *50 ways to leave your lectern*. Beverly, MA: Wadsworth, p. 54.

6. Davis, J. R. (1993), *Better teaching, more learning*. Phoenix, AZ: Oryx Press.

7. French, B. F., & Oakes, W. (2003). Measuring academic intrinsic motivation in the first year of college: Reliability and validity evidence for a new instrument. *Journal of the First-Year Experience, 15*(1), 83–102; French, B. F. Executive summary of instruments utilized with systemwide first-year seminars. Policy Center on the First Year of College; French, B. F., Immerkus, J. C., & Oakes, W. C. (2005). An examination of indicators of engineering students' success and persistence. *Journal of Engineering Education, 94*(4), 419–425.

8. Based on Harrell, K. (2003). *Attitude is everything: 10 life-changing steps to turning attitude into action*. New York: Harper Business.

9. Dweck, C. S. (2000). *Self-theories: Their role in motivation, personality, and development*. New York: Psychology Press, p. 1.

10. Berglas, S., & Jones, E. E. (1978). Drug choice as a self-handicapping strategy in response to non contingent success. *Journal of Personality and Social Psychology, 36,* 405–417; Jones, E. E. & Berglas, S. (1978). Control of attributions about the self through self-handicapping strategies: The appeal of alcohol and the role of underachievement. *Personality and Social Psychology Bulletin, 4,* 200–206; Dweck, C. S. (2006). *Mindset: The new psychology of success*. New York: Random House.

11. Dweck, C. S. (2000). *Self-theories: Their role in motivation, personality, and development*. New York: Psychology Press; Dweck, *Mindset*.

12. Robins, R. W., & Pals, J. (2002). Implicit self-theories of ability in the academic domain: A test of Dweck's model. *Self and Identity, 1,* 313–336.

13. Mangels, J. A., Butterfield, B., Lamb, J., Good, C. D., & Dweck, C. S. (2006). Why do beliefs about intelligence influence learning success? A social cognitive neuroscience model. *Social Cognitive and Affective Neuroscience, 1*(2), 75–86.

14. Bauer, A. R., Grant, H., & Dweck, C. S. (2006). *Personal goals predict the level and impact of dysphoria*. Unpublished manuscript.

15. Based on DuVivier, R. (2009). *100% online student success*. Clifton Park, NY: Delmar Cengage Learning, 12.

CHAPTER 3

1. Leamnson, R. (1999). *Thinking about teaching and learning: Developing habits of learning with first year college and university students*. Sterling, VA: Stylus.

2. Shuster, W. G. (2001). *Less stress? Yes! Jewelers' Circular Keystone, 172*(2), 98.

3. Caine, R. N., & Caine, G. (1994). *Making connections: Teaching and the human brain*. Menlo Park, CA: Addison Wesley.

4. Brandt, R. (1998). *Powerful learning*. Alexandria, VA: Association for Supervision and Curriculum Development, p. 29.

5. Campbell, B. (1992). Multiple intelligences in action. *Childhood Education, 68*(4), 197–201; Gardner, H., & Hatch, T. (1989). Multiple intelligences go to school: Educational implications of the theory of multiple intelligences. *Educational Researcher, 18*(8), 4–9; Gardner, H. (1983). *Frames of Mind: The Theory of Multiple Intelligences*. New York: Basic Books.

6. Armstrong, T. (2000). *MI and cognitive skills*. Available at http://www.ascd.org/publications/books/100041/chapters/MI_and_Cognitive_Skills.aspx.

7. Davis, B. (2009). *Tools for teaching*, 2nd ed. San Francisco: Jossey-Bass, p. 273.

8. Fleming, N. D. (1995). I'm different; not dumb: Modes of presentation (VARK) in the tertiary classroom. In A. Zeimer (Ed.), *Research and development in higher education, Proceedings of the 1995 Annual Conference of the Higher Education and Research Development Society of Austral-Asia (HERDSA), HERDSA, 18,* 308–313; Fleming, N. D., & Mills, C. (1992). Not another inventory, rather a catalyst for reflection. *To Improve the Academy, 11,* 137–149. Available at http://digitalcommons.unl.edu/cgi/viewcontent.cgi?article=1245&context=podimproveacad.

9. Fleming, I'm different; not dumb.

10. Fleming, N. D. (2005). *Teaching and learning styles: VARK strategies*. Christchurch, NZ: Microfilm Limited.

11. Based on DiTiberio, J. K., & Hammer, A. L. (1993). *Introduction to type in college*. Palo Alto, CA: Consulting Psychologists Press.

12. Tessler, L. G. (1997). How college students with learning disabilities can advocate for themselves. *LD OnLine*. Available at http://www.ldonline.org/article/6136.

13. Mangrum, C. T., & Strichart, S. S. (Eds.) (1997). *Peterson's guide to colleges with programs for students with learning disabilities*. Princeton, NJ: Peterson's Guide.

14. Strichart, S. S., & Mangrum, C. T. II. (2002). *Teaching learning strategies and study skills to students with learning disabilities, attention deficit disorder, or special needs*, 3rd ed. Boston: Allyn and Bacon; *Learning Disabilities Online*. Available at http:// ldonline.org; Sousa, D. A. (2001). *How the special needs brain learns*. Thousand Oaks, CA: Corwin Press.

15. Soldner, L. B. (1997). Self-assessment and the reflective reader. *Journal of College Reading and Learning, 28*(1), 5–11.

16. Van Blerkom, M. L., & Van Blerkom, D. L. (2004). Self-monitoring strategies used by developmental and non-developmental college students. *Journal of College Reading and Learning, 34*(2), 45–60.

17. Melchenbaum, D., Burland, S., Gruson, L., & Cameron, R. (1985). Metacognitive assessment. In S. Yussen (Ed.), *The growth of reflection in children*. Orlando, FL: Academic Press. p. 5.

18. Hall, C. W. (2001). A measure of executive processing skills in college students. *College Student Journal, 35*(3), 442–450; Taylor, S. (1999). Better learning through better thinking: Developing students' metacognitive abilities. *Journal of College Reading and Learning, 30*(1), 34–45.

19. Learning to learn. *Study Guides and Strategies*. Available at http://www.studygs.net/metacognition.htm.
20. Simpson, M. L. (1994/1995). Talk throughs: A strategy for encouraging active learning across the content areas. *Journal of Reading, 38*(4), 296–304.
21. How Air Traffic Control Works. *How Stuff Works*. Available at http://science.howstuffworks.com/transport/flight/modern/air-traffic-control.htm.
22. Glenn, D. (2010, February 7). How students can improve by studying themselves. *The Chronicle of Higher Education*. Available at http://chronicle.com/article/Struggling-Students-Can/64004/?sid=pm&utm_source=m&utm_medium=en.
23. Elias, M. (2004, April 5). Frequent TV watching shortens kids' attention spans. *USA Today*. Available at http://www.usatoday.com/news/health/2004-04-05-tv-kids-attention-usat_x.htm.
24. Carey, B. (2010, September 6). Forget what you know about good study habits. *The New York Times*. Available at http://www.nytimes.com/2010/09/07/health/views/07mind.html?_r=1&pagewanted=1&ref=homepage&src=me.
25. Bol, L., Warkentin, R. W., Nunnery, J. A., & O'Connell, A. A. (1999). College students' study activities and their relationship to study context, reference course, and achievement. *College Student Journal, 33*(4), 608–622.
26. When students study makes a difference too. (2005, November). *Recruitment & Retention*.
27. Trainin, G., & Swanson, H. L. (2005). Cognition, metacognition, and achievement of college students with learning disabilities. *Learning Disability Quarterly, 28,* 261–272.
28. Guibert, S. (2012, March 23). Learning best when you rest: Sleeping after processing new info most effective. *Daily*. Available at http://www.sciencedaily.com/releases/2012/03/120323205504.htm.
29. http://dictionary.reference.com/browse/grit.
30. Halvorson, H. G. (2011, February, 25). Nine things successful people do differently. *Harvard Business Review Conversation*. Available at http://blogs.hbr.org/cs/2011/02/nine_things_successful_people.html#; Duckworth, A. L.; Peterson, C.; Matthews, M. D.; Kelly, D. R. (2007). Grit: Perseverance and passion for long-term goals. *Journal of Personality and Social Psychology, 92*(6), 1087–1101; Mangan, K. (2012, August 5). Traits of the "get it done" personality: Laser focus, resilience, and true grit. *The Chronicle of Higher Education*. Available at http://chronicle.com/article/Traits-of-the-Get-it-Done/133291/.

CHAPTER 4

1. Sakai, J. (2012, March 15). A wandering mind reveals mental processes and priorities. *Science Daily*. Available at http://www.sciencedaily.com/releases/2012/03/120315161326.htm.
2. Coleman, J. (2012, February 22). Faced with distraction, we need willpower. *HBR Blog Network*. Available at http://blogs.hbr.org/cs/2012/02/faced_with_distraction_we_need.html.
3. Saunders, F. (2009, November–December). Multitasking to distraction. *American Scientist*. Available at http://www.americanscientist.org/issues/pub/multitasking-to-distraction.
4. Khawand, P. (2009). *The accomplishing more with less workbook*. On the Go Technologies, LLC.
5. Austin, C. (2010). Go with the flow: Fresh ideas for managing time. *Prezi.com*. Available at http://prezi.com/7gypurup9uke/go-with-the-flow/.
6. Rafter, M. V. (2012, February 23). Siri says it's time to get to work. *Workforce.com*. Available at http://www.workforce.com/article/20120223/NEWS02/120229973/siri-says-its-time-to-get-to-work#.
7. Eade, D. M. (1998). Energy and success: Time management. *ClinicianNews,* July/August.
8. Loehr, J., & Schwartz, T. (2003). *The power of full engagement: Managing energy, not time, is the key to high performance and personal renewal.* New York: Free Press.
9. Bittel, L. R. (1991). *Right on time! The complete guide for time pressured managers.* New York: McGraw-Hill, p. 16.
10. DeMaio, S. (2009, March 25). The art of the self-imposed deadline. *Harvard Business Review*. Available at http://blogs.hbr.org/demaio/2009/03/the-art-of-the-selfimposed-dea.html.
11. Bittel, *Right on time!* p. 16.
12. Loehr, *The power of full engagement.*
13. Astin, A. W., Astin, H. S., Lindholm, J. A., & Bryant, A. N. (2005). *The spiritual life of college students: A national study of college students' search for meaning and purpose.* Los Angeles: Higher Education Research Institute, UCLA; http://spirituality.ucla.edu/; Crosby, J. (2010, April 4). College students struggle with religion and spirituality. *Cape Cod Times.* Available at http://www.capecodonline.com/apps/pbcs.dll/article?AID=/20100404/LIFE/4040307/-1/NEWSMAP.
14. Allen, D. (2012, March 17). When technology overwhelms, get organized. *New York Times.* Available at http://www.nytimes.com/2012/03/18/business/when-office-technology-overwhelms-get-organized.html?pagewanted=all.
15. Based on Covey, S. R., Merrill, A. R., & Merrill, R. R. (1996). *First things first: To live, to love, to learn, to leave a legacy.* New York: Free Press, 37.
16. Fortino, M. (2001). *E-mergency.* Groveland, CA: Omni Publishing. Also see The American Time Use Survey results at http://www.bls.gov/news.release/atus.nr0.htm.
17. Hobbs, C. R. (1987). *Time power.* New York: Harper & Row, pp. 9–10.
18. Based on Berglas, S. (2004, June). Chronic time abuse. *Harvard Business Review*, 90–97.
19. Solomon, L. J., & Rothblum, E. D. (1984). Academic procrastination: Frequency and cognitive-behavioral correlates. *Journal of Counseling Psychology, 31,* 503–509.
20. Hoover, E. (2005, December 9). Tomorrow I love ya! *The Chronicle of Higher Education, 52*(16), A30–32.
21. Ferrari, J. R., McCown, W. G., & Johnson, J. (2002). *Procrastination and task avoidance: Theory, research, and treatment.* New York: Springer Publishing.
22. Hoover, Tomorrow I love ya!.
23. Khawand, P. (2009). *The accomplishing more with less workbook.* On the Go Technologies, LLC.
24. Sandholtz, K., Derr, B., Buckner, K., & Carlson, D. (2002). *Beyond juggling: Rebalancing your busy life.* San Francisco: Berrett-Koehler Publishers.
25. Adapted from Sandholtz et al., *Beyond juggling.*
26. Farrell, E. F. (2005, February 4). More students plan to work to help pay for college. *The Chronicle of Higher Education, 51*(22), A1. Available online at http://chronicle.com/weekly/v51/i22/22a00101.htm.
27. McFaddon, L. (2009, August 20). 8 major benefits of new credit card law. *Bankrate.com*. Available at http://www.bankrate.com/finance/credit-cards/8-major-benefits-of-new-credit-card-law-1.aspx.
28. See FinAid at http://www.finaid.org/loans/studentloandebtclock.phtml.
29. Ludlum, M., Tilker, K., Ritter, D., Cowart, T., Xu, W., & Smith, B. C. (2012). Financial Literacy and Credit Cards: A Multi Campus Survey. *International Journal of Business and Social Science*, 3(7), 25–33. Available at http://www.ijbssnet.com/journals/Vol_3_No_7_April_2012/3.pdf; http://moneyland.time.com/2012/04/12/college-students-are-credit-card-dunces/.
30. Choosing a credit card. *The Federal Reserve Board.* Available at http://www.federalreserve.gov/pubs/shop/default.htm.
31. Muller, K. New credit card laws (2009) and students. *ezine@rticles.com.* Available at http://ezinearticles.com/?New-Credit-Card-Laws-(2009)-And-Students&id=2410035; Miranda. (2009, May 21). Credit CARD Act of 2009: How it affects you. *Personaldividends.com.* Available at http://personaldividends.com/money/miranda/credit-card-act-of-2009-how-it-affects-you.

32. Kantrowitz, M. (2007). *FAQs about financial aid*. FinAid: The Smart Student Guide to Financial Aid. Available at http://www.finaid.org/questions/faq.html; Jevita Rogers, Director of Financial Aid, University of Colorado, Colorado Springs.

33. Fried, J., & Hanson, D. (2010). *Rework*. New York: Crown Business, p. 25–26.

34. Rock, D. (2009). *Your brain at work: Strategies for overcoming distraction, regaining focus, and working smarter all day long*. New York: HarperCollins Business.

CHAPTER 5

1. Perry, J. (1995–2008). *Procrastination and perfectionism. Philosophy Talk @Stanford*. Original essay reposted at http://people.tribe.net/aecb0f57-afa4-49a6-a13f-cbc588cd0923/blog/d75959db-01a7-4121-8b6f-ce3a18ddb9a7.

2. Halx, M. D., & Reybold, E. (2005). A pedagogy of force: Faculty perspective of critical thinking capacity in undergraduate students. *The Journal of General Education, 54*(4), 293–315.

3. Walkner, P., & Finney, N. (1999). Skill development and critical thinking in higher education. *Teaching in Higher Education, 4*(4), 531–548.

4. Diestler, S. (2001). *Becoming a critical thinker: A user friendly manual*. Upper Saddle River, NJ: Prentice Hall.

5. Arum, R., & Roksa, J. (2011). *Academically adrift: Limited learning on college campuses*. Chicago: University of Chicago Press.

6. Falcione, P. A. (1998). *Critical thinking: What it is and why it counts*. Millbrae, CA: California Academic Press.

7. Paul, R. (2005). The state of critical thinking today. *New Directions for Community Colleges*, 27–38.

8. Nosich, G. M. (2005). Problems with two standard models for teaching critical thinking. *New Directions for Community Colleges*, 59–67.

9. Twale, D., & Sanders, C. S. (1999). Impact of non-classroom experiences on critical thinking ability. *NASPA Journal, 36*(2), 133–146.

10. Thomas, C., & Smoot, G. (1994, February/March). Critical thinking: A vital work skill. *Trust for Educational Leadership, 23*, 34–38.

11. Kaplan-Leiserson, E. (2004). Workforce of tomorrow: How can we prepare *all* youth for future work success? *Training & Development, 58*(4), 12–14. 13. Based in part on Brookfield, S. D. (1987). *Developing critical thinkers: Challenging adults to explore alternative ways of thinking and acting*. San Francisco: Jossey-Bass.

12. Van den Brink-Budgen, R. (2000). *Critical thinking for students*, 3rd ed. Oxford: How to Books; Ruggiero, V. R. (2001). *Becoming a critical thinker*, 4th ed. Boston: Houghton Mifflin.

13. Blakey, E., & Spence, S. (1990). Developing metacognition. *ERIC Digest*. Available at http://www.ericdigests.org/pre-9218/developing.htm.

14. Florida, R. (2002). *The rise of the creative class: And how it's transforming work, leisure, community and everyday life*. New York: Basic Books, xii.

15. Sternberg. R. J. (2004). Teaching college students that creativity is a decision. *Guidance & Counseling, 19*(4), 196–200.

16. Rowe, A. J. (2004). *Creative intelligences: discovering the innovative potential in ourselves and others*. Upper Saddle, NJ: Pearson Education, pp. 3–6, 34.

17. Michalko, M. (2001). *Cracking creativity: The secrets of creative genius*. Berkeley, CA: Ten Speed Press.

18. Adapted from Adler, R., & Proctor, R. F. II (2011). *Looking out/Looking in*. (13th ed.) New York: Holt, Rinehart, and Winston, pp. 110–116.

19. Douglas, J. H. (1977). The genius of everyman (2): Learning creativity. *Science News, 111*(8), 284–288.

20. Harris, R. (1998). Introduction to creative thinking. *VirtualSalt*. Available at http://www.virtualsalt.com/crebook1.htm.

21. Eby, D. Creativity and flow psychology. Available at http://talentdevelop.com/articles/Page8.html.

22. Schwartz, T., Gomes, J., & McCarthy, C. (2010) *The way we're working isn't working: The four forgotten needs that energize great performance*. New York: Free Press, 149.

23. Schwartz, T., Gomes, J., & McCarthy, C. (2010) *The way we're working isn't working: The four forgotten needs that energize great performance*, 147–149.

CHAPTER 6

1. Dahlstrom, E., de Boor, T., Grunwald, P., & Vockley, M. (2011). National study of undergraduate students and information technology. *Educause*. Available at http://net.educause.edu/ir/library/pdf/ERS1103/ERS1103W.pdf.

2. Jaschik, S. (2008, April 7). Distance ed continues rapid growth at community colleges. *Inside Higher Ed*. Available at http://www.insidehighered.com/news/2008/04/07/distance.

3. Bollet, R. M., & Fallon, S. (2002). Personalizing e-learning. *Educational Media International, 39*(1), 39–45; Barber, S., in Shank, P. (Ed). (2011). *The online learning idea book: Proven ways to enhance technology-based and blended learning, vol 2.* San Francisco: Pfeiffer.

4. Guess. A. (2007, September 17). Students' "evolving" use of technology. *Inside Higher Ed*. Available at http://www.insidehighered.com/news/2007/09/17/it; (2007, September). Key findings: The ECAR study of undergraduate students and information technology, 2007. *Educause*. Available at http://net.educause.edu/ir/library/pdf/ERS0706/ekf0706.pdf; Smith, S. D., Salalway, G., & Caruso, J. B. (2009, October). Key findings: The ECAR study of undergraduate students and information technology, 2009. *Educause*. Available at http://net.educause.edu/ir/library/pdf/EKF/EKF0906.pdf.

5. Roach, R. (2004). Survey unveils high-tech ownership profile of American college students. *Black Issues in Higher Education, 21*(16), 37.

6. Jones, S., & Madden, M. (2002, September 15). The Internet goes to college: How students are living in the future with today's technology. *Pew Internet*. Available at http://www.pewinternet.org/PPF/r/71/report_display.asp.

7. *Internet World Stats*. Available at http://www.internetworldstats.com/stats.htm.

8. Billout, G. (2008, July/August). Is Google making us stupid? *The Atlantic.com*. Available at http://www.theatlantic.com/magazine/print/2008/07/is-google-making-us-stupid/6868/.

9. (2010, June). Social insecurity. *Consumer Reports: Best and worst computers*, 24–27.

10. Holson, L. M. (2010, May 8). Tell-all generation learns to keep things offline. *The New York Times*. Available at http://www.nytimes.com/2010/05/09/fashion/09privacy.html.

11. (2010, June). Social insecurity. *Consumer Reports: Best and worst computers*, pp. 24–27.

12. Kelly, W. E., Kelly, K. E., & Clanton, R. C. (2001). The relationship between sleep length and grade-point average among college students. *College Student Journal, 35*(1), 84–86; Stein, R. (2005, October 9). Scientists finding out what losing sleep does to a body. *The Washington Post*. Available at http://www.washingtonpost.com/wp-dyn/content/article/2005/10/08/AR2005100801405.html; Frisinger, C. (2009, October 24). Not getting enough sleep is more serious than you think. *The News Argus*. Available at http://www.thenewsargus.com/2.5246/not-getting-enough-sleep-is-moreserious-than-you-might-think-1.799912.

13. New Media Consortium. (2012). *NMC horizon report: 2012 higher education edition*. Available at http://www.nmc.org/publications/horizon-report-2012-higher-ed-edition.

14. Dahlstrom, E., de Boor, T., Grunwald, P., & Vockley, M. (2011). National study of undergraduate students and information technology. *Educause*. Available at http://net.educause.edu/ir/library/pdf/ERS1103/ERS1103W.pdf.

15. Dahlstrom, E., de Boor, T., Grunwald, P., & Vockley, G. (2011). National study of undergraduate students and technology. *Educause*. Available at http://net.educause.edu/ir/library/pdf/ERS1103/ERS1103W.pdf.

16. http://compnetworking.about.com/od/dns_domain namesystem/a/domain-name-tld.htm; http://lists.econsultant.com/top-10-domain-name-extensions.html; http://webfoot.com/advice/email.domain.php.

17. Top 15 most popular search engines, April 2012. *eBiz/MBA: The eBusiness Knowledgebase*. Available at http://www.ebizmba.com/articles/search-engines.

18. Caruso, J. B., & Salaway, G. (2007, September). Key findings: The ECAR study of undergraduate students and information technology, 2007. *Educause*. Available at http://net.educause.edu/ir/library/pdf/ERS0706/ekf0706.pdf.

19. Trunk, P. (2008, July/August). Show me the blog. *Wild Blue Yonder*, p. 44.

20. New Media Consortium. (2012). *NMC horizon report: 2012 higher education edition*. Available at http://www.nmc.org/publications/horizon-report-2012-higher-ed-edition.

21. Adapted from Leedy, P. D. & Ormrod, J. D. (2012). *Practical Research* (10th ed.). Boston, MA: Pearson.

22. Fitzgerald, M. A. (2004). Making the leap from high school to college. *Knowledge Quest, 32*(4), 19–24; Ehrmann, S. (2004). Beyond computer literacy: Implications of technology for the content of a college education. *Liberal Education*. Available at http://www.aacu.org/liberaleducation/le-fa04/le-fa04feature1.cfm; Thacker, P. (2006, November 15). Are college students techno idiots? *Inside Higher Ed*. Available at http://www.insidehighered.com/news/2006/11/15/infolit.

23. Christina Martinez, Reference Librarian, University of Colorado, Colorado Springs.

24. Ableson, H. Ledeen, K., & Lewis, H. (2008). *Blown to bits: your life, liberty, and happiness after the digital explosion*. Boston: Pearson Education, Inc.

25. Thacker, P. (2006, November 15). Are college students techno idiots? *Inside Higher Ed*. Available at http://www.insidehighered.com/news/2006/11/15/infolit.

26. Ibid.

27. Based on Wood, G. (2004, April 9). Academic original sin: Plagiarism, the Internet, and librarians. *The Journal of Academic Librianship, 30*(3), 237–242.

28. Cassagrande, J. (2010). *It was the best of sentences, it was the worst of sentences*. Berkeley, CA: Ten Speed Press.

29. Selberg, A. (2011, March 19). Teaching to the text message. *The New York Times*. Opinion Pages. Available at http://www.nytimes.com/2011/03/20/opinion/20selsberg.html.

CHAPTER 7

1. Marchand, A. (2010, 29 March). 6 strategies can help entering community-college students succeed. *The Chronicle of Higher Education*. Available at http://chronicle.com/article/6-Strategies-Can-Help-Entering/64871.

2. Burchfield, C. M., & Sappington, J. (2000). Compliance with required reading assignments. *Teaching of Psychology, 27*(1), 58–60; Hobson, E. H. (2004). *Getting students to read: Fourteen tips*. IDEA Paper No. 40, Manhattan, KS: Kansas State University, Center for Faculty Evaluation and Development; Maleki, R. B., & Heerman, C. E. (1992). *Improving student reading*. IDEA Paper No. 26, Manhattan, KS: Kansas State University, *Center for Faculty Evaluation and Development*. Most Idea Center papers available at http://www.theideacenter.org/research-and-papers/idea-papers.

3. Marburger, D. R. (2001). Absenteeism and undergraduate exam performance. *Journal of Economic Education, (32)*, 99–109; Romer, D. 1993. Do students go to class? Should they? *Journal of Economic Perspectives 7*(Summer), 167–74.

4. Perkins, K. K., & Wieman, C. E. (2005). The surprising impact of seat location on student performance. *The Physics Teacher,* *43*(1), 30–33. Available at http://scitation.aip.org/journals/doc/PHTEAH-ft/vol_43/iss_1/30_1.html?bypassSSO=1.

5. Armbruster, B. B. (2000). Taking notes from lectures. In R. F. Flippo & D. C. Caverly (Eds.), *Handbook of college reading and study strategy research*. Mahwah, NJ: Erlbaum, pp. 175–199.

6. Hughes, C. A., & Suritsky, S. K. (1993). Notetaking skills and strategies for students with learning disabilities. *Preventing School Failure, 38*(1).

7. Staley, C., & Staley, R. (1992). *Communicating in business and the professions: The inside word*. Belmont, CA: Wadsworth.

8. Kiewra, K. A., Mayer, R. E., Christensen, M., Kim, S., & Risch, N. (1991). Effects of repetition on recall and note-taking: Strategies for learning from lectures. *Journal of Educational Psychology, 83,* 120–123.

9. Brock, R. (2005, October 28). Lectures on the go. *The Chronicle of Higher Education, 52*(10), A39–42; French, D. P. (2006). iPods: Informative or invasive? *Journal of College Science Teaching, 36*(1), 58–59; Hallett, V. (2005, October 17). Teaching with tech. *U.S. News & World Report, 139*(14), 54–58; *The Horizon Report*. (2006). Stanford, CA: The New Media Consortium.

10. Adapted from Mackie, V., & Bair, B. Tips for improving listening skills; *International Student and Scholar Services*. University of Illinois at Urbana–Champaign. Available at http://www.isss.illinois.edu/publications/english/englang.html#listen.

11. Adapted from *Effective listening skills. Elmhurst College Learning Center*. Available at http://www.elmhurst.edu/library/learningcenter/Listening/listening_behaviors_survey.htm.

12. Palmatier, R. A., & Bennett, J. M. (1974). Note-taking habits of college students. *Journal of Reading, 18,* 215–218; Dunkel, P., & Davy, S. (1989). The heuristic of lecture notetaking: Perceptions of American and international students regarding the value and practices of notetaking. *English for Specific Purposes, 8,* 33–50.

13. Armbruster, *Handbook of college reading and study strategy research*.

14. Van Meter, P., Yokoi, L., & Pressley, M. (1994). College students' theory of note-taking derived from their perceptions of note-taking. *Journal of Educational Psychology, 86,* 323–338.

15. Davis, M., & Hult, R. (1997). Effects of writing summaries as a generative learning activity during note taking. *Teaching of Psychology 24*(1), 47–49; Boyle, J. R., & Weishaar, M. (2001). The effects of strategic notetaking on the recall and comprehension of lecture information for high school students with learning disabilities. *Learning Disabilities Research & Practice 16*(3); Kiewra, K. A. (2002). How classroom teachers can help students learn and teach them how to learn. *Theory into Practice 41*(2), 71–81; Kiewra, How classroom teachers can help students learn and teach them how to learn; Aiken, E. G., Thomas, G. S., & Shennum, W. A. (1975). Memory for a lecture: Effects of notes, lecture rate and informational density. *Journal of Educational Psychology, 67,* 439–444; Hughes, C. A., & Suritsky, S. K. (1994). Note-taking skills of university students with and without learning disabilities. *Journal of Learning Disabilities, 27,* 20–24.

16. Bonner, J. M., & Holliday, W. G. (2006). How college science students engage in note-taking strategies. *Journal of Research in Science Teaching, 43*(8), 786–818.

17. Pauk, W. (2000). *How to study in college*. Boston: Houghton Mifflin.

18. Montis, K. K. (2007). Guided notes: An interactive method of success in secondary and college mathematics classrooms. *Focus on learning problems in mathematics, 29*(3), 55–68.

19. Pardini, E. A., Domizi, D. P., Forbes, D. A., & Pettis, G. V. (2005). Parallel note-taking: A strategy for effective use of Webnotes. *Journal of College Reading and Learning, 35*(2), 38–55. Available at http://www.biology.wustl.edu/pardini/Teaching Materials/JCRL_spring2005_pardini.pdf.

20. Glenn, D. (2009, May 1). Close the book. Recall. Write it down. *The Chronicle of Higher Education*. Available at http://chronicle.com/article/Close-the-Book-Recall-Write/31819.

21. De Simone, C. (2007). Applications of concept mapping. *College Teaching, 55*(1), 33–36.

22. For a list of the top ten online note-taking tools, see Ningthoujam, P. Top ten online note taking applications. Available at http://mashable.com/2008/08/19/online-note-taking-applications/.

23. Kiewra, How classroom teachers can help students learn and teach them how to learn.

24. Porte, L. K. (2001). Cut and paste 101. *Teaching Exceptional Children, 34*(2), 14–20.

25. Adapted from Staley, C. (2003). *50 ways to leave your lectern,* Belmont, CA: Wadsworth, p. 116.

26. Craik, F. I. M., & Watkins, M. J. (1973). The role of rehearsal in short-term memory. *Journal of Verbal Learning and Verbal Behavior, 12,* 599–607.

27. Ancowitz, N. (2010, June 24). How to increase your self-promotion intelligence, or SPQ. *Psychology Today.* Available at http://www.psychologytoday.com/blog/self-promotion-introverts/201006/how-increase-your-self-promotion-intelligence-or-spq.

28. Hanson, M. (2009, June 17). Is bragging good for your career? *LiveCareer.* Available at http://www.livecareer.com/news/Career/Is-Bragging-Good-for-Your-Career-_$$00858.aspx.

Chapter 8

1. Rogers, M. (2007, March–April). Is reading obsolete? *The Futurist,* 26–27; Waters, L. (2007, February 9). Time for reading. *The Chronicle of Higher Education, 53*(23), 1B6.

2. Caverly, D. C., Nicholson, S. A., & Radcliffe, R. (2004). The effectiveness of strategic reading instruction for college developmental readers. *Journal of College Reading and Learning, 35*(1), 25–49; Simpson, M. L., & Nist, S. L. (1997). Perspectives on learning history: A case study. *Journal of Literacy Research, 29*(3), 363–395.

3. Colarusso, K. (2000). Using a faculty survey of college-level reading and writing requirements to revise developmental reading and writing objectives. Kellogg Institute final report, practicum 1999 (ERIC Document Reproduction Service No. ED448823).

4. English language. *Wikipedia.* Available at http://en.wikipedia.org/wiki/English_language.

5. The sounds of English and the International Phonetic Alphabet. *Antimoon.com.* Available at http://www.antimoon.com/how/pronunc-soundsipa.htm.

6. Bean, J. C. (1996). *Engaging ideas: The professor's guide to integrating writing, critical thinking, and active learning in the classroom.* San Francisco: Jossey-Bass; Wood, N. V. (1997). College reading instruction as reflected by current reading textbooks. *Journal of College Reading and Learning, 27*(3), 79–95.

7. Saumell, L., Hughes, M. T., & Lopate, K. (1999). Underprepared college students' perceptions of reading: Are their perceptions different than other students? *Journal of College Reading and Learning, 29*(2), 123–125.

8. Smith, B. D. (2006). *Breaking through college reading.* New York: Pearson Education, Inc., p. 351.

9. Paulson, E. J. (2006). Self-selected reading for enjoyment as a college developmental reading approach. *Journal of College Reading and Learning, 36*(2), 51–58.

10. Buzan, T. (1983). *Use both sides of your brain.* New York: E. P. Dutton.

11. Ibid.

12. Sternberg, R. J. (1987). Teaching intelligence: The application of cognitive psychology to the improvement of intellectual skills. In J. B. Baron & R. J. Sternberg (Eds.), *Teaching thinking skills: Theory and practice.* New York: Freeman, pp. 182–218.

13. Based on Bean, *Engaging ideas.*

14. Glenn, D. (2009, May 1). Close the book. Recall. Write it down. *The Chronicle of Higher Education.* Available at http://chronicle.com/free/v55/i34/34a00101.htm.

15. McCarroll, C. (2001). To learn to think in college, write—a lot. *Christian Science Monitor, 93*(177), 20.

16. De Vos, I. (1988, October). Getting started: How expert writers do it. *Training & Development Journal,* 18–19.

17. Based on "10 tips to retain more of what you read online." http://vandelaydesign.com/blog/blogging/10-tips-to-retain-more-of-what-you-read-online/; Agger, M. "Lazy eyes: How we read online." http://www.slate.com/id/2193552/.

18. Bean, J. C. (1996). *Engaging ideas: The professor's guide to integrating writing, critical thinking and active learning in the classroom.* San Francisco: Jossey-Bass.

19. Portions of this section are based on Staley, C., & Staley, R. (1992). *Communicating in business and the professions: The inside word.* Belmont, CA: Wadsworth.

20. Portions based on Staley, C., & Staley, R. (1992). *Communicating in business and the professions: The inside word.* Belmont, CA: Wadsworth.

21. Smith, T. E., & Frymier, A. B. (2006). Get "real": Does practicing speeches before an audience improve performance? *Communication Quarterly, 54*(1), 111–125.

22. Engleberg, I. N. (1994). *The principles of public presentation.* New York: HarperCollins; Daley, K., & Daley-Caravella, L. (2004). *Talk your way to the top.* New York: McGraw-Hill.

23. Decker, K. (9 May, 2012). Airline-inspired analogies. *Decker Blog.* Available at http://decker.com/airline-inspired-analogies/.

24. Ibid.

25. VitalSmarts. Crucial conversations explained in 2 minutes. *Youtube.* Available at http://www.youtube.com/watch?v=qHRF8q3ltRw.

26. Patterson, K., Grenny, J., McMillan, R., & Switzler, A. (2011). *Crucial conversations: Tools for talk when stakes are high,* second edition. Excerpt available at http://www.leadershipnow.com/leadershop/0194-6excerpt.html.

Chapter 9

1. Bolla, K. I., Lindgren, K. N., Bonaccorsy, C., & Bleecker, M. L. (1991). Memory complaints in older adults: Fact or fiction? *Archives of Neurology, 48,* 61–64.

2. Higbee, K. L. (2004). What aspects of their memories do college students most want to improve? *College Student Journal, 38*(4), 552–556.

3. Higbee, K. L. (1988). *Your memory: How it works and how to improve it* (2nd ed.). New York: Prentice Hall.

4. Ibid.

5. Nairine, J. S. (2006). *Psychology: The adaptive mind.* Belmont, CA: Wadsworth/Thomson Learning.

6. Miller, G. A. (1956). The magical number seven plus or minus two: Some limits on our capacity for processing information. *Psychological Review, 63,* 81–97; Raman, M., McLaughlin, K., Violato, C., Rostom, A., Allard, J.P., & Coderre, S. (2010). Teaching in small portions dispersed over time enhances long-term knowledge retention. *Medical Teacher, 32,* 250–255.

7. Narayanan, K. The neurological scratchpad: Looking into working memory. (2013, February 26). *Brain Connection.com.* Available at http://brainconnection.positscience.com/?s=working+memory; *Human memory.* Available at http://www.threes.com/index.php?view=article&id=2973%3Ahuman-memory&option=com_content&Itemid=39; Kerry, S. (1999–2002). Memory and retention time. *Education Reform.net.* Available at http://www.education-reform.net/memory.htm; Goodhead, J. (1999). The difference between short-term and long-term memory [On-line].

8. Rozakis, L. (2003). *Test-taking strategies and study skills for the utterly confused.* New York: McGraw Hill; Meyers, J. N. (2000). *The secrets of taking any test.* New York: Learning Express; Ehren, B. J. *Mnemonic devices.* Available at http://onlineacademy.org/modules/a304/support/xpages/a304b0_20600.html; Lloyd, G. (1998–2004). Study skills: Memorize with mnemonics. *Back to College.* Available at http://www.back2college.com/memorize.htm; Raman, M., McLaughlin, K., Violato, C., Rostom, A., Allard, J. P., & Coderre, S. (2010).

Teaching in small portions dispersed over time enhances long-term knowledge retention. *Medical Teacher, 32,* 250–255.

9. Willingham, D. T. (2004). Practice makes perfect—but only if you practice beyond the point of perfection. *American Educator.* Available at http://www.aft.org/newspubs/periodicals /ae/spring2004/willingham.cfm.

10. Raman, M., et al. Teaching in small portions.

11. Tigner, R. B. (1999). Putting memory research to good use: Hints from cognitive psychology. *College Teaching, 47*(4), 149–152.

12. Murdock, B. B., Jr. (1960). The distinctiveness of stimuli. *Psychological Reports, 67,* 16–31; Neath, I. (1993). Distinctiveness and serial position effects in recognition. *Memory & Cognition, 21,* 689–698.

13. Cahill, L. (2003). Similar neural mechanisms for emotion–induced memory impairment and enhancement. *Proceedings of the National Academy of Sciences, 100*(23), 13123–13124. Available at http://www.pnas.org/cgi/content/full/100/23 /13123.

14. Higbee, *Your memory.*

15. Bean, J. (1996). *Engaging ideas.* San Francisco: Jossey-Bass.

16. Higbee, *Your memory.*

17. Berk, R. A. (2002). *Humor as an instructional defibrillator.* Sterling, VA: Stylus; Berk, R. A. (2003). *Professors are from Mars®, students are from Snickers®.* Sterling, VA: Stylus.

18. Dodeen, H. (2008). Assessing test-taking strategies of university students: developing a scale and estimating its psychometric indices. *Assessment & Evaluation in Higher Education, 33*(4), 409–419.

19. Coren, S. (1996). *Sleep thieves.* New York: Free Press; Cox, K. (2004, October 14).

20. Grant, K. B. (2003, September 4). Popping pills and taking tests. *The Ithacan Online.* Available at http://www.ithaca .edu/rhp/ithacan/articles/0309/04/news/2popping_pill.htm

21. Segerstrom, S. C., & Miller, G. E. (2004). Psychological stress and the human immune system: A meta-analytic study of 30 years of inquiry. *Psychological Bulletin, 130*(4), 601–630. Available at http://www.apa.org/pubs/journals/releases /bul-1304601.pdf; (2004, July 4). Stress affects immunity in ways related to stress type and duration, as shown by nearly 300 studies. *APA Press Release.* Available at http://www.apa .org/news/press/releases/2004/07/stress-immune.aspx.

22. Brinthaupt, T. M., & Shin, C. M. (2001). The relationship of academic cramming to flow experience. *College Student Journal, 35*(3), 457–472.

23. Tigner, R. B. (1999). Putting memory research to good use: Hints from cognitive psychology. *Journal of College Teaching, 47*(4), 149–152.

24. Small, G. (2002). *The memory bible.* New York: Hyperion.

25. (2010). Test anxiety. *University of Oregon Counseling and Testing Center.* Available at http://counseling.uoregon.edu /dnn/SelfhelpResources/StressandAnxiety/TestAnxiety /tabid/337/Default.aspx.

26. Tozoglu, D., Tozoglu, M. D., Gurses, A., & Dogar, C. (2004). The students' perceptions: Essay versus multiple-choice type exams. *Journal of Baltic Science Education, 2*(6), 52–59.

27. Schutz, P. A., & Davis, H. A. (2000). Emotions and self-regulation during test taking. *Educational Psychologist, 35*(4), 243–256.

28. Coren, *Sleep thieves.*

29. Perina, K. (2002). Sum of all fears. *Psychology Today.* Available at http://www.psychologytoday.com/articles/pto-20021108 -000001.html.

30. Perry, A. B. (2004). Decreasing math anxiety in college students. *College Student Journal, 38*(2), 321–324.

31. Perry, Decreasing math anxiety in college students.

32. Jonides, J., Lacey, S. C., & Nee, D. E. (2005). Processes of working memory in mind and brain. *Current Directions in Psychological Science, 14*(1), 2–5.

33. Ashcraft, M. H., & Kirk, E. P. (2001). The relationships among working memory, math anxiety, and performance. *Journal of Experimental Psychology: General. 130*(2), 224–237.

34. Beilock, S. L., Kulp, C. A., Holt, L. E., & Carr, T. H. (2004). More on the fragility of performance: Choking under pressure in mathematical problem solving. *Journal of Experimental Psychology: General, 133*(4), 584–600.

35. Mundell, E. J. (2005, March 9). Test pressure toughest on smartest. *Healingwell.com.* Available at http://news.healingwell.com /index.php?p=news1&id=524405.

36. Based partially on Arem, C. (2003). *Conquering math anxiety,* second edition. Belmont, CA: Brooks/Cole.

37. Glenn, D. (2010, February 7). How students can improve by studying themselves. *The Chronicle of Higher Education.* Available at http://chronicle.com/article/Struggling -Students-Can-Imp/64004/.

38. Firmin, M., Hwang, C., Copella, M., & Clark, S. (2004). Learned helplessness: The effect of failure on test-taking. *Education, 124*(4), 688–693.

39. Heidenberg, A. J., & Layne, B. H. (2000). Answer changing: A conditional argument. *College Student Journal, 34*(3), 440–451.

40. Based on Barrett, S. (2009) *Power up: A practical student's guide to online learning.* Upper Saddle River, NJ: Pearson, 82; and DuVivier, R. (2009) 100% online student success. Clifton Park, NY: Delmar Cengage Learning, 120.

41. See http://news.bbc.co.uk/2/hi/uk_news/scotland/glasgow _and_west/4755297.stm.

42. Preparing for tests and exams. (2007). *York University.* Available at http://www.yorku.ca/cds/lss/skillbuilding/exams. html#Multiple.

43. Taking exams. *Brockport High School.* Available at http:// www.frontiernet.net/~jlkeefer/takgexm.html. Adapted from Penn State University; On taking exams. *University of New Mexico.* Available at http://www.unm.edu/~quadl/college _learning/taking_exams.html; Lawrence, J. (2006). Tips for taking examinations. *Lawrence Lab Homepage.* Available at http://cobamide2.bio.pitt.edu/testtips.htm; The multiple choice exam. (2003). *Counselling Services, University of Victoria.* Available at http://www.coun.uvic.ca/learning/exams /multiple-choice.html; General strategies for taking essay tests. *GWired.* Available at http://gwired.gwu.edu/counsel /asc/index.gw/Site_ID/46/Page_ID/14565/; Test taking tips: Guidelines for answering multiple-choice questions. *Arizona State University.* Available at http://neuer101.asu.edu /additionaltestingtips.htm; Landsberger, J. (2007). True/false tests. *Study Guides and Strategies.* Available at http://www .studygs.net/tsttak2.htm; Landsberger, J. (2007). Multiple choice tests. *Study Guides and Strategies.* Available at http:// www.studygs.net/tsttak3.htm; Landsberger, J. (2007). The essay exam. *Study Guides and Strategies.* Available at http:// www.studygs.net/tsttak4.htm; Landsberger, J. (2007). Short answer tests. *Study Guides and Strategies.* Available at http:// www.studygs.net/tsttak5.htm; Landsberger, J. (2007). Open book tests. *Study Guides and Strategies.* Available at http:// www.studygs.net/tsttak7.htm; Rozakis, L. (2003). *Test-taking strategies and study skills for the utterly confused.* New York: McGraw-Hill; Meyers, J. N. (2000). *The secrets of taking any test.* New York: Learning Express; Robinson, A. (1993). *What smart students know.* New York: Crown Trade Paperbacks.

44. *Plagiarism.org.* Available at http://www.plagiarism.org/facts .html; A cheating crisis in America's schools. (2007, 29 April). *ABC News.* Available at http://abcnews.go.com/Primetime /story?id=132376&page=1.

45. Young, J. R. (2010, March 28). High tech cheating abounds, and professors bear some blame. *The Chronicle of Higher Education.* Available at http://chronicle.com/article/High-Tech-Cheating-on-Homew/64857/; Gabriel, T. (2010, August 1). Plagiarism lines blur for students in digital age. *The New York Times.* Available at http://www.nytimes.com/2010/08/02 /education/02cheat.html?_r=1&src=me&ref=homepage.

46. Caught cheating. (2004, April 29). *Primetime Live,* ABC News Transcript. Interview of college students by Charles Gibson; Zernike, K. (2002, November 2). With student cheating on the rise, more colleges are turning to honor codes. *The New York Times,* p. Q10, column 1, National Desk; Warren, R. (2003, October 20). Cheating: An easy way to cheat yourself. The Voyager via U-Wire. *University Wire (www.uwire.com);* Thomson, S. C. (2004, February 13). Heyboer, K. (2003, August 23). Nearly half of college students say Internet plagiarism isn't cheating. *The Star-Ledger Newark, New Jersey;* Kleiner, C., & Lord, M. (1999).

47. Tagg, J. (2004, March-April). Why learn? What we may really be teaching students. *About Campus,* 2–10; Marton, F., & Säljö, R. On qualitative differences in learning: I-Outcome and process. (1976). *British Journal of Educational Psychology, 46,* 4–11.

CHAPTER 10

1. Some situation topics are suggested at Hay Group Transforming Learning EI Quiz. *Haygroup.com.* Available at http://www.haygroup.com/leadershipandtalentondemand/Demos/EI_Quiz.aspx.

2. Gardner, H. (1993). *Multiple intelligences: The theory in practice.* New York: Basic Books; Checkley, K. (1997). The first seven . . . and the eighth: A conversation with Howard Gardner. Expanded Academic ASAP (online database). Original Publication: *Education,* 116.

3. Parker, J. D. A., Duffy, J. M., Wood, L. M., Bond, B. J., & Hogan, M. J. (2005). Academic achievement and emotional intelligence: Predicting the successful transition from high school to university. *Journal of the First Year Experience & Students in Transition 17*(1), 67–78; Schutte, N. S., & Malouff, J. (2002). Incorporating emotional skills content in a college transition course enhances student retention. *Journal of the First Year Experience & Students in Transition 14*(1), 7–21.

4. Berenson, R., Boyles, G., & Weaver, A. (2008). Emotional intelligence as a predictor for success in online learning. *International Review of Research in Open and Distance Learning, 9*(2), 1–16; Zeidner, M., & Roberts, R. (2010). Coping mediates the relationship between emotional intelligence (EI) and academic achievement. *Contemporary Educational Psychology,* 36 (2011) 60–70.

5. EQ-i:HEd, Multi-Health Systems, Inc. North Tonawanda, NY. Available at http://www.mhs.com. Used with permission.

6. Turning lemons into lemonade: Hardiness helps people turn stressful circumstances into opportunities. (2003, December 22). *Psychology Matters.* Available at *APA Online* at http://www.apa.org/research/action/lemon.aspx; Marano, H. E. (2003). The art of resilience. *Psychology Today.* Available at http://www.psychologytoday.com/articles/pto-20030527-000009. html; Fischman, J. (1987). Getting tough: Can people learn to have disease-resistant personalities? *Psychology Today, 21,* 26–28; Friborg, O., Barlaug, D., Martinussen, M., Rosenvinge, J. H., & Hjemdal, O. (2005). Resilience in relation to personality and intelligence. *International Journal of Methods in Psychiatric Research, 14*(1), 29–42; Schulman, P. (1995). Explanatory style and achievement in school and work. In G. M. Buchanan & M. E. P. Seligman (Eds.), *Explanatory style* (pp. 159–171). Hillsdale, NJ: Lawrence Erlbaum; American Psychological Association. (1997). Learned optimism yields health benefits. *Discovery Health.* Available at http://health.discovery.com/centers/mental/articles/optimism/optimism.html.

7. Cherniss, C. (2000). *Emotional Intelligence: What it is and why it matters.* Paper presented at the Annual Meeting of the Society for Industrial and Organizational Psychology, New Orleans, LA. Available at http://www.eiconsortium.org/reports/what_is_emotional_intelligence.html.

8. Ibid.

9. Goleman, D. (2002, June 16). Could you be a leader? *Parade Magazine,* pp. 4–6.

10. Boyatzis, R. E., Cowan, S. S., & Kolb, D. A. (1995). *Innovation in professional education: Steps on a journey from teaching to learning.* San Francisco: Jossey-Bass.

11. Saxbe, D. (2004, November/December). The socially savvy. *Psychology Today.* Available at http://www.psychologytoday.com/articles/pto-3636.html.

12. Kelly, W. E. (2003). Worry content associated with decreased sleep length among college students: Sleep deprivation leads to increased worrying. *College Student Journal, 37,* 93–95.

13. Knox, D. H. (1970). Conceptions of love at three developmental levels. *The Family Coordinator, 19*(2), 151–157; Fisher, *Why we love;* Cramer, D. (2004). Satisfaction with a romantic relationship, depression, support and conflict. *Psychology and Psychotherapy: Theory, Research and Practice, 77*(4), 449–461.

14. (2012, June 12). Boosting team productivity through emotional intelligence. *Agile Project Management Student.* Available at http://agilepmstudent.blogspot.com/2012/06/boosting-team-productivity-through.html; Barth, S. (2001). *3-D chess: Boosting team productivity through emotional intelligence.* Boston: Harvard Business Publishing; (2004). *Teams that click.* Boston: Harvard Business School Press.

15. (2012, June 12). Boosting team productivity through emotional intelligence. *Agile Project Management Student.* Retrieved from http://agilepmstudent.blogspot.com/2012/06/boosting-team-productivity-through.html; Barth, S. (2001). *3-D chess: Boosting team productivity through emotional intelligence.* Boston: Harvard Business Publishing; (2004). *Teams that click.* Boston: Harvard Business School Press.

16. Tims, A. (2011, March 4). The secret to understanding soft skills. *The Guardian.* Available at http://www.guardian.co.uk/money/2011/mar/05/secret-to-understanding-soft-skills.

17. Parker-Popel, T. (2009, April 20). What are friends for? A longer life. *The New York Times.* Available at http://www.nytimes.com/2009/04/21/health/21well.html?_r=1; Ybarra, O., Burnstein, E., Winkielman, P., Keller, M. C., Manis, M. Chan, E., & Rodriguez, J. (2008). Mental exercising through simple socializing: Social interaction promotes general cognitive functioning. *Personality and Social Psychology Bulletin, 34.*

18. Knox, D., Schacht, C., & Zusman, M. E. (1999, March). Love relationships among college students. *College Student Journal, 33*(1), 149–154. Available at http://findarticles.com/p/articles/mi_m0FCR/is_1_33/ai_62894068/.

19. Schwartz, P. (2003, May–June). Love is not all you need. *Psychology Today.* Available at http://www.psychologytoday.com/articles/200302/love-is-not-all-you-need.

20. Bach, G. R., & Goldberg, H. (1974). *Creative aggression: The art of assertive living.* Garden City, NJ: Doubleday; Bach, G. R, & Wyden, P. (1972). *The intimate enemy: How to fight fair in love and marriage.* New York: Avon; Bach, G. R., & Deutsch, R. M. (1985). *Stop! You're driving me crazy.* New York: Berkley Publishing Group; Tucker-Ladd, C. E. (1996–2006); *Driving each other crazy. Psychological self-help.* Available at http://psychologicalselfhelp.org/Chapter9/chap9_90.html.

21. Fisher, *Why we love.*

22. Fisher, R., & Brown, S. (1988). *Getting together: Building a relationship that gets to yes.* Boston: Houghton Mifflin, p. xi.

23. Wilmot, W. W., & Hocker, J. L. (2010). *Interpersonal conflict* (8th ed.). New York: McGraw Hill.

24. Based in part on Marano, H. (2002). Relationship rules. *Psychology Today.* Available at http://www.psychologytoday.com/articles/200410/relationship-rules.

25. Dakss, B. (2006, March 3). Study: Bad relationships bad for heart. *CBS News.* Available at http://www.cbsnews.com/2100-500194_162-1364889.html. (2005, December 5) Unhappy marriage: Bad for your health. *WebMD.* Available at http://www.webmd.com/sex-relationships/news/20051205/unhappy-marriage-bad-for-your-health. Based on Keicolt-Glaser, J. (2005). *Archives of general psychiatry, 62,* 1377–1384.

26. Dusselier, L., Dunn, B., Wang, Y., Shelley, M. C., & Whalen, D. F. (2005). Personal, health, academic, and environmental predictors of stress for residence hall students. *Journal of American College Health, 54*(1), 15–24; Hardigg, V., & Nobile, C. (1995). Living with a stranger. *U.S. News & World Report, 119*(12), 90–91. Available at http://www.usnews.com/usnews/edu/articles/950925/archive_032964_print.htm; Nankin, J. (2005). Rules for roomies. *Careers & Colleges, 25*(4), 29.

27. Thomas, K. (1977). Conflict and conflict management. In M. D. Dunnette (Ed.), *Handbook of industrial and organizational psychology*, 889–935 Chicago: Rand McNally; Kilmann, R., & Thomas, K. W. (1975). Interpersonal conflict handling behavior as reflections of Jungian personality dimensions. *Psychological Reports, 37*, 971–980; Rahim, M., & Magner, N. R. (1995). Confirmatory factor analysis of the styles of handling interpersonal conflict: First-order factor model and its invariance across groups. *Journal of Applied Psychology, 80*, 122–132; Wilmot, W. W., & Hocker, J. L. (2001). *Interpersonal conflict* (6th ed.). New York: McGraw Hill. Kilmann, R. H., and K. W. Thomas. (1977). Developing a Forced Choice Measure of Conflict-Handling Behavior: The MODE Instrument, *Educational and psychological measurement, 37*(2), 309–325.

28. Miller, G. R., & Steinberg, M. (1975). *Between people: A new analysis of interpersonal communication.* Chicago: Science Research Associates.

29. Staley, C. (2003). *50 ways to leave your lectern*, Belmont, CA: Wadsworth, p. 32.

30. Staley, C. (2003). *50 ways to leave your lectern.* Belmont, CA: Wadsworth, p. 67. Based on Defining "Diversity." (1995). In B. Pike & C. Busse, *101 games for trainers* (p. 11). Minneapolis: Lakewood Books.

31. Fulbeck, K. (2010). *Mixed: Portraits of multiracial kids.* San Francisco: Chronicle Books.

32. *Race, the power of an illusion. PBS.* California Newsreel. Available at http://www.pbs.org/race/000_General/000_00-Home.htm.

33. Based on "Sorting People" activity at http://www.pbs.org/race/002_SortingPeople/002_00-home.htm.

34. Wyer, K. (2007). Today's college freshmen have family income 60% above national average, UCLA survey reveals. *UCLA News.* Available at http://www.heri.ucla.edu/PDFs/PR_TRENDS_40YR.pdf.

35. Humphrey, D., & Davenport, A. (2004, Summer/Fall). What really matters in college: How students view and value liberal education. *Liberal Education.* Excerpt: Diversity and civic engagement outcomes ranked among least important. Available at http://www.diversityweb.org/Digest/vol9no1/humphreys.cfm.

36. Laird, T. F. (2005). College students' experiences with diversity and their effects on academic self-confidence, social agency, and disposition toward critical thinking. *Research in Higher Education, 46*(4), 365–387.

37. Bucher, R. D. (2004). *Diversity consciousness: Opening our minds to people, cultures, and opportunities* (2nd ed.). Upper Saddle River, NJ: Pearson Education.

38. Based on Nilsen, L. B. (1998). The circles of awareness. *Teaching at Its Best.* Bolton, MA: Anker Publishing; Bucher, R. D. (2008). *Building cultural intelligence: Nine megaskills.* Upper Saddle River, NJ: Pearson.

39. Carnes, M. C. (2005). Inciting speech. *Change, 37*(2), 6–11.

40. Lyons, P. (2005, April 15). The truth about teaching about racism. *The Chronicle of Higher Education, 51*(32), B5.

41. Epstein, G. (2005, June 5) More women advance, but sexism persists. *College Journal from the Wall Street Journal*; Leahey, C. (2012, July 18). Update: Fortune 500 women CEOs hits a record 20. *CNN Money.* Available at http://postcards.blogs.fortune.cnn.com/2012/07/18/fortune-500-women-ceos-2/.

42. Wessel, D. (2003, September 9). Race still a factor in hiring decisions. *College Journal from the Wall Street Journal.* Available at http://www.iseek.org/news/fw/fw4522FutureWork.html.

43. Beilke, J. R., & Yssel, N. (1999). The chilly climate for students with disabilities in higher education. *College Student Journal, 33*(3), 364–372.

44. Parker, P. N. (2006, March–April). Sustained dialogue: How students are changing their own racial climate. *About Campus, 11*(1), 17–23.

45. Gortmaker, V. J., & Brown, R. D. (2006). Out of the college closet: Differences in perceptions and experiences among out and closeted lesbian and gay students. *College Student Journal, 40*(3), 606–619.

46. FBI releases 2010 hate crime statistics. (2010, November 14). *FBI, Department of Justice.* Available at http://www.fbi.gov/news/pressrel/press-releases/fbi-releases-2010-hate-crime-statistics.

47. Based on Earley, P. C., & Mosakowski, E. (2004, October). Cultural intelligence. *Harvard Business Review,* p. 143.

48. Earley, P. C., & Mosakowski, E. (2004, October). Cultural intelligence. *Harvard Business Review,* 139–146; Early, C. P., Ang, S., & Tan, J. (2006) CQ: *Developing cultural intelligence at work.* Stanford, CA: Stanford University Press; Osborn, T. N. (2006). *"CQ": Another aspect of emotional intelligence.* Available at http://www.teaminternational.net/resources/docs/ cultural%20intelligence.pdf.

49. Earley, P. C., & Mosakowski, E. Cultural intelligence.

50. Based on Barrett, S. (2009) *Power up: A practical student's guide to online learning.* Upper Saddle River, NJ: Pearson, 34.

51. Ten things we know to be true. *Google Company.* Available at http://www.google.com/about/company/philosophy/.

52. Advertising, Marketing, & Communications. (2010). *Quicksilver Translate.* Available at http://www.quicksilver translate.com/customers/industry-solutions/advertising-branding-and-marketing.

53. Farrell, E.F. (2005, August 5). Student volunteers are worth billions. *The Chronicle of Higher Education,* 51(48), A33; 2011 annual survey executive summary: Deepening the roots of civic engagement. *Campus Compact.* Available at http://www.compact.org/wp-content/uploads/2008/11/2011-Annual-Survey-Executive-Summary.pdf.

54. Zlotkowski, E. (1999). Pedagogy and engagement. In R. G. Bringle, R. Games, & E. A. Malloy (Eds.). (1999). *Colleges and Universities as Citizens* (pp. 96–120). Needham Heights, MA: Allyn & Bacon.

55. Honnet, E. P., & Poulsen, S. J. (1989). *Principles of good practice for combining service and learning: A Wingspread special report.* Racine, WI: The Johnson Foundation. Available at http://servicelearning.org/filemanager/download/Principles_of_Good_Practice_for_Combining_Service_and_Learning.pdf/.

56. Eyler, J., Giles, Jr., D. E., & Schmiede, A. (1996). *A practitioner's guide to refection in service learning: Student voices and reflections.* Nashville, TN: Vanderbilt University Press.

57. Bregman, P. (2010, July 21). How to avoid (and quickly recover from) misunderstandings. *Harvard Business Review Blog.* Available at http://blogs.hbr.org/bregman/2010/07/how-to-avoid-and-quickly-recov.html; Bregman, P. (2011, January 3). The best way to use the last five minutes of the day. *Harvard Business Review Blog.* Available at http://blogs.hbr.org/bregman/2011/01/the-best-way-to-use-the-last-f.html.

58. Ibid.

Chapter 11

1. Gregory, M. (2003, September 12). A liberal education is not a luxury. *The Chronicle of Higher Education, 50*(3), B16.

2. Staley, R. S., II. (2003). In C. Staley, *50 ways to leave your lectern* (pp. 70–74). Belmont, CA: Wadsworth.

3. Farrell, E. F. (2006, December 12). Freshmen put high value on how well college prepares them for a profession, survey finds. *The Chronicle of Higher Education.* Farrell, E. F. (2007, January 5). Report says freshmen put career prep first. *The Chronicle of Higher Education, 53*(18), A32. Available at http://chronicle.com/article/Report-Says-Freshmen-Put-Ca/19260/; Bok, D. (2010, January 31). College and the

well-lived life. *The Chronicle of Higher Education*. Available at http://chronicle.com/article/Collegethe-Well-Lived-/63789/.

4. Associated Press (2007, January 22). Polls say wealth important to youth. *NewsOK*. Available at http://newsok.com/ article/3002446; Schwartz, B. (2004, January 23). The tyranny of choice. *The Chronicle of Higher Education, 50*(20), B6.

5. Berrett, D. (2012, June 3). Changing majors is no big deal if the timing is right, studies find. *The Chronicle of Higher Education*. Available at http://chronicle.com/article/Changing-Majors-Is-No-Big-Deal/132105/.

6. Koeppel, D. (2004, December 5). Choosing a college major: For love or for the money? *The New York Times,* section 10, p. 1, column 4. Available at http://www.nytimes.com/2004/12/05/jobs/05jmar.html?ex=1259989200&en=51dcc14fa52a65e7&ei=5090&partner=rssuserland; Dunham, K. J. (2004, March 2). No ivory tower: College students focus on career. *Wall Street Journal* (Eastern Edition), pp. B1, B8. Available at http://online.wsj.com/article/SB107818521697943524.html.

7. Based in part on Gordon, V. N., & Sears, S. J. (2004). *Selecting a college major: Exploration and decision making,* 5th ed. Upper Saddle River, NJ: Pearson Education.

8. Based on Hansen, R. S., & Hansen, K. Using a SWOT analysis in your career planning. *Quintessential Careers*. Available at http://www.quintcareers.com/SWOT_Analysis.html.

9. Rowh, M. (2003, February–March). Choosing a major. *Career World, 31*(5), 21–23.

10. Ezarik, M. M. (2007, April–May). A major decision. *Career World, 35*(6), 20–22.

11. Rask, K. N., & Bailey, E. M. (2002). Are faculty role models? Evidence from major choice in an undergraduate institution. *The Journal of Economic Education, 33*(2), 99–124.

12. To read more about these and other fast-growing occupations, go to http://education.yahoo.net/articles/careers_built_to_last.htm; http://jobsearch.about.com/od/cooljobs/a/topjobs_2.htm; http://www.careerexplorer.net/ten-hottest-careers.asp?affiliateid=4085&type=&adgroup=&kw=&acctid=&ovkey=&SearchEngine=&Keyword=&AffiliateSite=&SubAffiliateID=&TrackingCode=;http://careerplanning.about.com/od/exploringoccupations/tp/hi_growth_bach.htm; and http://www.newsday.com/classifieds/jobs/the-fastest-growing-jobs-1.229#16.

13. Based on Staley, *50 ways to leave your lectern,* p. 82.

14. Gallo, A. (2011, March 18). Where will you be in five years? *HBR Blog Network.* Available at http://blogs.hbr.org/hmu/2011/03/where-will-you-be-in-five-year.html.

15. Brooks, K. (2009). *You majored in what?* New York: Viking.

16. Kanter, R. M. (2011, March). Managing yourself: zoom in, zoom out. *Harvard Business Review Magazine*. Available at http://hbr.org/2011/03/managing-yourself-zoom-in-zoom-out/ar/1.

17. Gallo, A. (2011, March 18). Where will you be in five years? *HBR Blog Network.* Available at http://blogs.hbr.org/hmu/2011/03/where-will-you-be-in-five-year.html.

6. Giang, V. (2012, April 9). What recruiters look at during the 6 seconds they spend on your resume. *Business Insider*. Available at http://www.businessinsider.com/heres-what-recruiters-look-at-during-the-6-seconds-they-spend-on-your-resume-2012-4.

7. Why sneaky resume tactics may no longer aid job hunters. (2009, March 10). *Vault Blogs.com*. Available at http://blogs.vault.com/blog/resumes-cover-letters/why-sneaky-resume-tactics-may-no-longer-aid-job-hunters/.

8. *Job interviews get creative.* (2003, August 22). *NPR.* Available at http://www.npr.org/templates/story/story.php?storyId =1405340.

9. Vance, E. (2007, February 2). College graduates lack key skills, report says. *The Chronicle of Higher Education, 53*(22), A30.

10. Ashler, D. (2004). *How to get any job with any major.* Berkeley, CA: Ten Speed Press.

11. Pollak, L. (2007). *Getting from college to career.* New York: HarperCollins.

12. *Occupational Outlook Handbook 2012–2013.* Available at http://www.bls.gov/ooh/Community-and-Social-Service/Social-and-human-service-assistants.htm and http://www.bls.gov/ooh/Community-and-Social-Service/Social-workers.htm.

13. Cedja, B. D., Kaylor, A. J., & Rewey, K. L. (1998). Transfer shock in an academic discipline: The relationship between students' majors and their academic performance. *Community College Review, 26*(3), 1–13.

14. Thurmond, K. (2007). Transfer shock: Why is a term forty years old still relevant? *National Academic Advising Association (NACADA)*. Available at http://www.nacada.ksu.edu/clearinghouse/AdvisingIssues/Transfer-Shock.htm; Rhine, T. J., Milligan, D. M., & Nelson, L. R. (2000). Alleviating transfer shock: Creating an environment for more successful transfer students. *Community College Journal of Research and Practice, 24,* 443–452.

15. Idea from Wallace, P. C. (2005). *Life 101.* New York: iUniverse, p. 3.

16. Coplin, B. (2003). *10 things employers want you to learn in college.* Berkeley, CA: Ten Speed Press.

17. Adapted from Jobweb's "General Rules for Using Technology in the Workplace" at http://www.jobweb.org/studentarticles.aspx?id=2353.

18. Marsh, N. (2011, February). How to make work-life balance work. *TedTalks*. Available at http://www.ted.com/talks/nigel_marsh_how_to_make_work_life_balance_work.html.

19. Bregman, P. (2010, July 30). Don't regret working too hard. *HBR Blog Network.* Available at http://blogs.hbr.org/bregman/2010/07/dont-regret-working-too-hard.html.

CHAPTER 12

1. Goldhaber, G. M. (1986). *Organizational communication* (4th ed.). Dubuque, IA: Wm. C. Brown, p. 236. In Staley, R. S., II, & Staley, C. C. (1992). *Communicating in business and the professions: The inside word.* Belmont, CA: Wadsworth.

2. See *Top Job Search Websites* at http://www.quintcareers.com/top_10_sites.html.

3. Staley, *50 ways to leave your lectern,* p. 33. Based on "Group Resume." (1995). In M. Silberman, *101 ways to make training active* (pp. 49–50). Johannesburg: Pfeiffer.

4. McConnon, A. (2007, August 30). Social networking is graduating—and hitting the job market. *BusinessWeek.* pp. IN 4, IN 6.

5. Stewart, J. (2012, March 23). Working: No resume needed. *GPB News.* Available at http://www.gpb.org/news/2012/03/23/working-no-resume-needed.

Index

Note: pages followed by a "b" indicate boxes; followed by an "e" indicate exercises; followed by a "f" indicate figures.

A

Abbreviations, 179–180
A-B-C method, 96
Ability, 41–42, 310
Absolutes, 244
Academic advisor, 12e, 13, 50, 100e
Academic anatomy, 300–301
Academic disciplines, 290–292
Academic Intrinsic Motivation Scale
 (AIMS), 36e–37
Academic professionalism, 8–11
Academic responsibility. *See*
 Responsibility
Academic Search Premier, 155
Accountability, defined, 232
Accuracy, in information literacy, 158
Acronyms, defined, 231f
ACT, 16, 246e–247e
Action
 in CRIA system, 33, 35
 plan of, 128
Active-learning lecturer, 174
Active voice, 200
Adams, Franklin P., 154
Adaptability skills, 262
Addison, Joseph, 206
Adequacy, 119
ADHD. *See* Attention-Deficit/Hyperactivity
 Disorder (ADHD), 69b
Adobe technology, 150, 315, 316
Affordability, on Internet, 244
Age diversity, 276
"aha" moments, 243
AIMS. *See* Academic Intrinsic Motivation
 Scale (AIMS)
"All of the above" options, 247
Allen, David, 103
Alexander, Katie, 194–195
AllJobSearch.com, 311
All-nighters, 87–88, 234, 239
All-over-the-map lecturer, 174
Alternating strategy, 102–103
Altshuler, Michael, 98
American Psychological Association
 (APA), 162
Americasjobexchange.com, 311
Analogy, 218f
Analytical decision-making style, 127
Analyze, defined, 248
Answers, 242, 247, 249

Anthropology, defined, 292
Antivirus program, 140
Anxiety
 blocking, brain and, 33
 concentration and, 236
 contributing factors, 238–239
 cramming and, 235–236
 math, 239–241
 memory and, 240
 perfectionists and, 238
 procrastination and, 99
 reduction, 239–241
 sleep and, 236
 speaking, 216b
 survey, 237e
 test, 237e–239, 239–241
 usefulness of, 236
APA. *See* American Psychological
 Association (APA)
Assessment tool, 264
Appearance, learning and, 43, 56, 216b
Application letter, 317e
Aptitude, 39
Arguments, 117–121
Aristotle, Greek philosopher, 119
Ask, 53, 187–189
Assertions, defined, 248
Aspen Commons apartment complex, case
 study, 124e–125e
Assignments, 73–74, 159e, 169–170,
 208–209, 213e
Assumptions, 119–120
Attendance, 78, 169
Attention, focused thinking and, 13, 114
Attention-Deficit/Hyperactivity Disorder
 (ADHD), 69b
Attention management, 84
Attention span, 73–74
Attitude
 ability versus, 41
 adjustments, 39–40
 aptitude versus, 39
 defined, 39
 goals and, 43
 learning and, 41b, 56
 negative, 234, 238
 reading and, 203
 statements and, 41b
 tests and, adjusting, 232
Auditory learner, 206
Aural learner, 63, 66. *See also* VARK

Author, reading and, 204
Authority, in information literacy, 158
Availability, on Internet, 143–144

B

Bach, Richard, 44
Balance, 102–103, 129, 326
Bard, Carl, 25
Barrett, Colleen, C., 160
BDNF (brain-derived neurotrophic
 factor), 54
Bean, John C., 214
Behavioral aspects, 238, 254
Behavioral decision-making style, 127
Behaviors, learning and, 61
Benedict Arnolds, 269
Berle, Milton, 228
Bernard, Claude, 57
Berra, Yogi, 11
Bias, 115, 275–276
Bibliography, 162, 191, 215e, 220b
Bing, 149e
Biology, defined, 292
Blamers, 269
Blended, defined, 138
Blessings, acknowledgment of, 40
Bloch, Robert, 140
Blogs, 149e
Bloom, Harold, 204
Bly, David, 71
Bodily-kinesthetic intelligence, 59e
Body
 academic anatomy and, 300, 301
 CQ and, 282, 283
 energy and, 87
 physical quotient and, 283
 in problem-solving, 59e
 test anxiety and, 238
Bookmark, defined, 158
Books, buying, 19–20
Boorstin, Daniel J., 78
Brain. *See also* Mind map
 bias and, 278
 binge drinking and, 125
 conversations and, 221
 creativity and, 130
 CRIA system and, 34
 exercise and, 53, 54
 fatigue, 33, 147
 focus and, 84